BERLIT

DISCOVER
SCANDINAVIA

Typeset and designed by
D & N Publishing,
Ramsbury, Wiltshire.

Cartography by
Visual Image, Street, Somerset.

Although we have made every effort to ensure the accuracy of all the information in this book, changes do occur. We cannot therefore take responsibility for facts, addresses and circumstances in general which are constantly subject to alteration.

If you have any new information, suggestions or corrections to contribute to this guide, we would like to hear from you. Please write to Berlitz Publishing at one of the above addresses.

Photographic Acknowledgements

All photographs by Jon Davison and © Berlitz Publishing Company Ltd. except for the following: Bobby Andström 14, 16, 18/19, 40, 44, 47 (lower), 51, 132, 257, 271, 274, 280, 280 (inset), 284, 286, 288, 291, 292, 294, 295, 296, 298, 300/301, 302, 305, 307, 310/311, 312, 317, 319, 321, 324, 326, 328, 331 (lower), 332; Mick Barnard 6, 47 (upper), 53, 88, 146/147, 148, 160 (upper), 163 (inset), 165, 174, 178/179, 184, 188, 192, 197, 199, 200, 205, 208, 209, 214, 215, 220, 222, 227, 229, 233, 238, 242, 244, 245; Hilary Hughes 75, 82, 85, 89 (upper), 93, 97 (upper and lower), 98.

Front cover: A view of Aurlandsfjord, Flåm, Norway (Mick Barnard).

Back cover: Stadshuset (Town Hall), Stockholm (Jon Davison/Berlitz).

Photograph previous page: Windmill near Søby, Denmark.

The Berlitz tick is used to indicate places or events of particular interest.

Phototypeset, originated and printed by C.S. Graphics, Singapore.

BERLITZ®

DISCOVER
SCANDINAVIA

Doreen Taylor-Wilkie

SCANDINAVIA

0   300 miles

0   400 km

1. N. SJÆLLAND
2. S. SJÆLLAND
3. FYN & ITS ARCHIPELAGO
4. GOTHENBURG, THE WEST
    & THE GREAT LAKES
5. OSLO & SURROUNDINGS

FINNMARK

ARCTIC OCEAN

NORRLAND & TROMS

NORRLAND & THE ARCTIC

TRONDHEIM & CENTRAL NORWAY

Trondheim●

RUSSIA

GULF OF BOTHNIA

FINLAND

BERGEN & THE FJORDS

Bergen●

DALARNA & CENTRAL SWEDEN

⑤

Oslo■

SOUTHLAND & TELEMARK

④

Stockholm■

STOCKHOLM & SURROUNDINGS

ESTONIA

N

Gothenburg●

JYLLAND
Arhus●

SOUTHLAND & THE BALTIC ISLANDS

① ■Copenhagen

③
②

LATVIA

LITHUANIA

NORTH SEA

BALTIC SEA

GERMANY

POLAND

Contents

Planning Your Trip to Scandinavia

Scandinavians are fortunate to live in one of the most beautiful areas in Europe. Dramatic scenery varies from mountain to sea, fjord to forest. The three capitals, Copenhagen, Oslo and Stockholm, are cities of sea and lake, with wide open green spaces, and both Stockholm and Oslo have archipelagos with hundreds of islands, which are particularly wonderful in summer. All three countries have this close contact between water and land with islands galore, and share a common history and culture, but they are also different in many aspects.

Denmark is wide sandy beaches, islands, neat farms, apple orchards and gentle hills. Here, there are no mountains. The grandiose name Himmelbjerget (Sky Mountain) which graces Denmark's highest hill at 137m (some 450ft), merely indicates the Danish sense of humour. Norway's scenery is dramatic: long fjords cut deep into the land, where the mountains plunge into tranquil water, reflecting the beauty all around. Sweden has swathes of forest that seem to go on for ever with thousands of lakes, some as big as seas, others small gems huddled into trees and moor.

Both Sweden and Norway stretch endlessly north. From Norway's southernmost lighthouse at Lindesnes, it is 2,318km (1,765 miles), as the crow flies, north along the beautiful coast to Nordkapp (North Cape). The Swedish coast on the Gulf of Bothnia is not as long, but when it bumps into Finland at Haparanda, the cross-country road northwest to the Norwegian border still means another 400km (280 miles), far beyond the Arctic Circle. Mountains lie along this lonely northern border, with great rivers running from the northwest down to the cliffs and beaches of the Gulf of Bothnia. These northern territories, on both sides of the boundary are the traditional home of Scandinavia's second race, the Samis or Lapps, and their

One of the most famous landmarks in the world – Nordkapp (North Cape) reached by Hurtigruten, *Norway's coastal steamer, and by road or small boat.*

SCANDINAVIA

ARCTIC OCEAN

0 — 200 miles
0 — 300 km

N

Arctic Circle

Hammerfest • • Vardø
Tromsø • • Alta • Kirkenes
• Murmansk

R U S S I A

Narvik • • Riksgränsen
Nordfold • Kiruna
Bodø • Sodankylä
• Gällivare
Mo-i-Rana • Jokkmokk • • Rovaniemi
Arjeplog • Haparanda • Tornio
• Luleå

Namsos • Skellefteå • Raahe • Oulu

N O R W A Y

S W E D E N

GULF OF BOTHNIA

Trondheim • Hoting • Umeå
Kristiansund • Östersund • Iisalmi
Ålesund • Andalsnes
Dombas • Idre Sundsvall

F I N L A N D

Lillehammer • Mora • Tampere
Bergen • Hamar • Gävle
Telemark • Oslo ■ Turku • Helsinki
Stavanger • Västerås • Uppsala
Örebro • Mälaren ■ Stockholm • Tallinn
Arendal • Vänern

E S T O N I A

Kristiansand
Skagerrak • Gothenburg • Jönköping • Pskov

SEA

Limfjorden • Ålborg • Riga • LATVIA
• Kalmar

D E N M A R K ■ Copenhagen • BALTIC • Daugavpils
N O R T H • Malmö • Klaipėda • LITHUANIA
S E A • Odense • Bornholm
Gdynia • Vilnius
GERMANY • Rostock Kaliningrad • Minsk ■
■ Hamburg • POLAND

huge reindeer herds. It is also the Land of the Midnight sun, where in summer people play golf or go fishing at midnight.

Further south, there are the forests and uplands and, in Norway, great mountain *vidda* (massifs) such as Jotunheimen and Hardanger. In contrast, in the south of Sweden, the province of Skåne has all the richness of Denmark's farms and orchards.

For centuries the sea has been the other constant in all three countries, carrying the early Vikings, in their purposefully designed longboats – the spacecraft of their day – all over Europe, as far as North America, and southeast through Russia to Constantinople. Sea travel, of a more peaceful style, is still an important part of life here. Ferries and cargo ships link the coastal communities but air networks also cut down the distances, as do good railway systems and roads which are rarely crowded. Marvellous long bridges cross fjords and sounds (Denmark's

Great Belt between Sjælland and Fyn will soon have its own bridge system), tunnels cut through the mountains and even under the sea to reach some islands.

Scandinavians are outdoor people and make the most of the seemingly limitless space for walking, skiing, touring and just breathing the clean air. Many sports and leisure activities are based on sea, lake and river, from sailing, canoeing, rafting and waterskiing to fishing, swimming and more. The Swedes have taken to golf with all the zest that they earlier applied to tennis. The

*E*ast *of the great Jotunheim massif, Oppland is a place for winter skiing, summer walking and climbing – home of the legendary Peer Gynt of Ibsen's play and Grieg's music.*

Copenhagen's pubs, clubs, cellars, outdoor bars and cafés are very much part of city life. This is the well-known 'English Pub'.

other nations are fast catching up and there is no shortage of golf courses. Riding, bird-watching, climbing and driving husky dog sledges all feed Scandinavia's love of the outdoors and are a delight to visitors.

Denmark may not have skiing facilities on any scale but it is an easy journey across the Kattegat, and travellers move freely between the three countries. Perhaps in compensation, Copenhagen can claim to be Scandinavia's liveliest capital. It had the wit to close many streets to traffic long before anyone else thought of it, which makes Copenhagen a marvellous place to stroll or sit at an outside café for coffee or a Danish beer. At night, music floating from the open doors of music pubs, bars and particularly jazz clubs makes for a vibrant mood. But, today, all three capitals are sophisticated centres, where people stay up late and dine on the cuisine of many lands, as well as local specialities.

Most visitors come to Scandinavia in the summer months of June, July and August, to a climate often considerably hotter than they expect, which may be the reason that summer Stockholm, to mention just one city, seems to be full of tall, slim people in shorts with long tanned legs.

But spring, coming suddenly in early May, is wonderful, especially in the orchards of Fyn in Denmark and Norway's fjords where the slopes are a haze of blossom reflected in the water. The light nights also start early and by late May and early June, darkness lasts but an hour or two, even less the further north you go. Here, at its height, the Midnight Sun will never set. Autumn too can be very fine, with blazing colours – red, yellow, orange – in town and countryside and a bright clarity to the air.

Come winter in the far north, the snow lies deep and long. Throughout Norway and in many parts of Sweden, every community has its own ski hill and every Norwegian child will ski jump any hillock.

In the north, Sweden and Norway seem to be endless, with beautiful quiet roads wending their way through the autumn colour.

In practical terms, summer has one main advantage for city visits. During the holiday period many hotels and guesthouses normally aimed at business travellers cut their prices dramatically. Against that, theatres, opera houses, concert halls and other cultural venues are often shut for the summer period. But who can really say which is the best season? With all its great variety, Scandinavia can be a delight at any time of the year.

In many cases, details given below apply to all three countries. Where there are differences, each country is listed separately. Brochures, leaflets and lists with detailed information on most subjects are available from national tourist offices (see p.32–35).

M̈älardrottningen was once owned by American millionairess, Barbara Hutton. Today, it is a beautiful floating hotel, beside the quay of Riddarholmen.

ACCESS LAW IN SCANDINAVIA

Allemansrätt (Everyone's Right) gives freedom to camp for a night anywhere, without seeking permission (even on private property) but campers must not intrude close to dwelling houses, damage ground, leave litter or light a fire if there is a danger of damage and never on rocks. You may also swim, sail a boat and go ashore, fish with hand tackle on the coast (a local licence may be needed on lake or stream), pick wild berries and mushrooms, always with care not to do damage and with the proviso given above that you are not too close to a dwelling house or likely to damage gardens or crops. There are a few military areas to which access does not apply and these are always well marked.

Accommodation

Hotels

Hotels are usually of a high standard – clean, comfortable, warm in winter and well-run. More expensive hotels often have saunas and plunge pools and many

have swimming pools as well. Various hotels cooperate in offering 'go as you please' passes, such as the Scandinavian Bonus Pass which offers a choice of some 250 hotels in the three countries. There are other similar three-country schemes, as well as each country's individual hotel passes and hotel group schemes. Norway makes a speciality of the *fjellhotell* (mountain hotel) in more remote areas, aimed at skiers and walkers, with good indoor facilities, often including a swimming pool.

Self-catering

Self-catering is a good option. Many Scandinavians rent out their own wooden holiday houses – *hytter* (Norwegian), *stugor* (Swedish). Many more are purpose-built, often as holiday villages in beautiful rural and mountain areas, or by sea or lake, with boats, bicycles and fishing gear for hire. Local tourist offices and many tour operators can also arrange self-catering packages.

Inns

All three countries have *gästgiverie, vertshus, wärdhus* or *kro* and Denmark in particular makes a feature of *kro* holidays. You buy a book of inn-cheques and can book ahead at 80 different inns, among them some lovely old stagecoach inns.

Farmhouses

Farmhouse holidays are good for families and, again, Denmark has made them a special feature.

Camping

Campsites are of high standard, often in beautiful areas, close to sea or lake, with canoes and cycles, some with horseriding, tennis and mini-golf, others conveniently close to towns. Except in wintersports areas where many are year-round, they are open fully from early June to the end of September. Instead of caravans or tents, sites may have log cabins, with two to six beds and cooking facilities. It is usually necessary to take your own sleeping bags.

Hostels

Hostels are open to any age and are of a high standard, from the simplest wooden building to an imposing house or city building. In summer, it best to book ahead as Scandinavians favour this sort of holiday. You are expected to provide sheets or sheet-sleeping bags but they can be hired for a small charge. Except in very remote areas, and even then sometimes, the hostels have many amenities. Scandinavian hostel organizations are affiliated to the International Youth Hostel Federation.

Denmark You will need a valid membership card issued by your home youth hostel association, or you can buy one in Denmark at Landsforeningen Danmarks Vandrerhjem, Vesterbrogade 39, DK-1620; tel. (0)31-31-36-12; fax (0)31-33-36-26.

Norway Some of the 90 hostels have two-, four- and six-bedded family rooms, and living rooms. All have self-catering facilities, some also have cafeterias. They are run by Norske Vandrehjem, Dronningsgt 25, N-0154 Oslo; tel. (0)22-42-14-10; fax (0)22-42-44-76. More remote accommodation (for long-distance walking, for example) is run by DNT, Den Norske Turistforeningen, Postboks 1963, Vika, N-0125 Oslo; tel. (0)22-83-25-50; fax (0)22-83-24-78. There is an information desk at Stortingsgt 28, Oslo.

Sweden There are some 280 hostels (over 100 are open year-round) with two- and four-bedded, and family rooms. All have self-catering facilities, some also have cafeterias. Members of other youth hostel associations qualify for cheaper rates on presentation of a membership card. Hostels are run by STF, Svenska Turist-föreningen, Drottnnggt 31, Box 25, 101-20 Stockholm; tel. (0)8-790-32-00; fax (0)8-720-80-16.

Brochures and Information

For brochures and information, unless specified otherwise, contact either the tourist boards' overseas office in your own country (see pp.33–35), or any of the national tourist information offices given below:

Denmark Copenhagen Tourist Office (which covers the whole country), Vesterbrogade 6D, 1620-Copenhagen; tel. (0)33-11-14-15.

Norway Norway Information Centre, Vestbaneplassen 1, N-0250, Oslo; tel. (0)22-83-00-50; fax (0)22-83-81-50.

Sweden Stockholm Information Office (for the whole of Sweden), Sverigehuset, Kungsträdgården, Box 7542, S-103-93 Stockholm; tel. (0)8-789-20-00; fax (0)8-789-24-50.

T racery in the snow in the Lake District of Sweden (Östergötland), at Kolmmården Zoo and Safari Park, which is one of Scandinavia's wildlife parks par excellence.

Climate and Clothing

Summer Scandinavia can be a surprise. In the south, it is often much warmer, much earlier than visitors anticipate, with days above 20°C not unusual in high summer. But Scandinavian summer weather also varies and it can be unpredictable, particularly in the west. The further east, the more continental the climate becomes: hotter and drier in summer, much colder in winter. In the west, the useful Gulf Stream keeps up winter temperatures and, as far north as North Cape in Norway, the west coast ports are open and ice free throughout the winter.

Particularly in Norway and Sweden, winter is certainly cold, calling for warm outdoor clothing, but it is usually the sort of dry cold that is exhilarating and keeps the air feeling warmer than it really is. Denmark, which does not reach as far north, misses winter extremes.

At most times of the year, especially winter, dressing in layers is a good principle. In summer try layering a tee shirt with shorts or a skirt, under a sweater and light trousers, and a light jacket. Well-dressed travellers always have a waterproof and a swimsuit in their luggage, and, even in summer, tuck in a pair of gloves, just in case.

Winter essentials are wool or fur headgear, two pairs of gloves or mitts (thick and thin), and good strong footwear for slushy streets. If you are spending a long time outside or taking part in active sports, a thermal layer is useful and in the north essential. At any time of the year, boots are necessary for hill and upland walking, plus a woolly hat and a water- and windproof anorak, and gloves. At lower levels, use walking shoes, comfortable sandals and, unless you have an invitation to an official function, or a restaurant specifies otherwise, evening informality is the general rule. Midge-repellent and soother can be a relief from May to early August.

Complaints

In an area which gave the world the word *ombudsman* you can expect to find a sense of fair play and honesty. This means that complaints will almost always be dealt with swiftly and courteously. A quiet word in a hotel, shop or restaurant is usually sufficient. More serious complaints about major services, which you cannot resolve, should be made to the appropriate tourist board, airline, railway, shipping line or other service. Scandinavians are accustomed to providing receipts for anything and everything, and attempts to overcharge or cheat, for example, are virtually unknown.

Communications

Post Offices

Hours may be shorter in July, and post offices are often closed on Saturdays in July. Stamps are also on sale at newspaper stands, kiosks and gift shops.

Denmark Danish postboxes, and postmen, are colourful in red. Post offices have a red sign with a crown, bugle and crossed arrows. Usual opening times for larger offices are 9am-5.30pm weekdays, 10am-1pm Saturday. Most of the stamp machines take 1Dkr pieces. Post offices handle faxes, telegrams (by phone dial 122), telegrams (by phone dial 122).

Norway Postboxes are also red. The post office sign is a yellow horn on a red background and offices are generally open from 8 or 8.30am-4 or 5pm weekdays, 8am-1pm Saturday.

Sweden Postboxes are yellow. Post offices have a yellow sign with a blue post horn and are open 9am-6pm weekdays, 10am-1pm Saturday.

Telephone, Faxes, Telegrams

Scandinavian post offices do not have telephones but all have high-technology systems with very efficient overseas links. There are plenty of public pay phones in streets, stations and hotels. An automatic pay phone is always cheaper than using the phone in a hotel room. Many hotels will send faxes.

A telephone box in Sweden's Dalarna, known as the 'folklore country' because so many old customs still survive.

Denmark From overseas the national code is 45. There are no area codes for long-distance calls within Denmark, just dial 8-digit numbers. Post offices handle telegrams, also faxes.

Norway From overseas the national code is 47. Norway is introducing green payphones which take special payment cards available at Narvesen kiosks (street kiosks). Main Televerket offices provide telegram, telephone and fax services during working hours.

Sweden From overseas the national code is 46. In addition to the normal payphones, credit card telephones are also plentiful (marked CCC), and special telegraph offices, Telia, also send faxes.

Crime

Scandinavia has a deserved reputation as a law-abiding, low-crime area, and these three countries are among the safest societies in the world. Possibly because the working day starts early, Scandinavians tend to keep major social occasions for the weekend, the favourite time for having a night out and a drink. But seemingly noisy crowds are almost always rowdy rather than dangerous, and the well-lit city centres are safe to walk in. At weekends, nevertheless, some women may prefer to take a taxi, but for ease rather than fear. Theft of, and from, cars has increased marginally, though the rate is much lower than it is in most countries. Nevertheless, make sure valuables are out of sight, lock the car, use the alarm if you have one, and take any other reasonable precautions.

In the unlikely event of your spotting serious criminal behaviour, always contact the police immediately. **Emergency police** numbers are all free from payphones:

Denmark 112 (specify whether Police, Fire or Ambulance required)

Norway 112

Sweden 90-000

Customs and Entry Formalities

Europeans and North Americans need only a valid passport to enter Scandinavia.

16

Others should check with local embassies or consulates whether a visa is necessary.

There are usually no limits on the amount of currency you can bring into or take out of Scandinavia as a non-resident, though each country has its own limits.

Denmark As above, with the proviso that anything over 50,000Dkr can be exported only if it does not exceed the amount originally imported.

Norway As above, with the proviso that anything brought in over 25,000Nkr must be declared. You can take out local currency up to 5,000Nkr, and foreign monies up to the amount imported.

Sweden As above, with no restriction on the amount though it must be declared.

Disabled Travellers

Scandinavia's attitude to its disabled citizens could be summed up as 'integration and equality'. This also applies to disabled visitors, with facilities that cover access ramps, lifts and hotel rooms specially adapted for people with mobility problems or allergies. Public transport usually offers good access and many activities such as swimming and horseriding have been adapted for disabled people. Wheelchairs are often available. When booking, always mention any disability. Useful booklets and organizations are:

Denmark Dansk Handicap Forbund (DHF), Hans Knudsens Plads 1A, DK-2100, Copenhagen O; tel. (0)31-29-35-55. *Access in Denmark: Travel Guide for the Disabled* from the Danish Tourist Board (see p.33).

Norway Norwegian Association for the Disabled, PO Box 9217 Grønland, N-0134 Oslo; tel. (0)22-17-02-55; fax (0)22-17-61-77.

Sweden National Council for the Disabled, Regeringsgatan 67, S-103-96 Stockholm; tel. (0)8-787-73-20; fax (0)8-723-03-12.

Driving

The number of motorways is not high compared with most of Europe, but roads are well maintained and uncrowded. Driving is not difficult, and becomes a pleasure in rural areas on the smaller roads, their verges often full of flowers and trees.

Mountain roads can be slow, twisting and turning, but are always attractive. In winter, however, high mountain roads in Norway, in particular, and in Sweden may be closed until well into spring, the date dictated by the speed of the thaw. Check before setting off. Some passes are kept clear all winter or are bypassed by tunnels. Norwegians are among the world's best tunnel builders, with some 530 tunnels on the road network, many linking islands to the mainland or saving a lengthy detour around a mountain.

Though city traffic is often busy, it is strictly controlled, with well-marked pedestrian crossings. Oslo, for example, now routes virtually all through traffic under the city centre!

Driving Rules

Scandinavians drive on the right, overtake on the left and, unless roadsigns indicate otherwise, give way to traffic approaching from the right. Traffic already on a roundabout usually has right of way. On two-

*J*ämtland, well north of Gothenburg, lies on the border with
Norway – a land of forests, lakes, elks and other animals. There are few
people, but all have a liking for hunting and a dialect near Norwegian.

lane roads, it is usual to drive in the right-hand lane except when overtaking or turning left. Cars must use dipped headlights at all times. Right-hand drive cars need to have headlights adjusted with masking triangles. Seatbelts are obligatory and, when fitted, must be worn by everyone in the car. Drink-and-drive laws are very strict and are diligently enforced. Drinking when in charge of a car attracts very high fines and could even lead to a prison sentence. Police are efficient in using their spot-check

19

rights to examine licences and vehicles, and to detect drivers over the very low alcohol limit. The best advice is never to drink if you are driving.

Bringing Your Own Car

In addition to your driving licence, bring the car's registration documents and certificate of insurance. Car insurance is compulsory and for Europeans, though not mandatory, the green card system is recommended. If you are in any doubt, contact the tourist office or embassy before you leave home.

Accidents and Breakdowns

Procedures are similar but vary a little between each country. By law, you must carry a red warning triangle in case of a breakdown. Serious accidents, certainly with injuries, warrant the use of the emergency numbers given below. It is not mandatory to call the police to an accident but, even if damage is slight, drivers must give their name and address to others involved and may not leave the scene until this has been done. Drivers who do not stop after an accident may be fined.

Denmark The emergency service for breakdowns is Falck, available night and day in all areas, tel. (0)44-92-22-22 (local number in phone books) or ask a passerby to phone. If trouble cannot be remedied on the spot, Falck will tow the car to the nearest garage. A fee is charged.

Danish Motoring Organization, affiliated to AIT (Alliance Internationale de Tourisme), Forended Danske Motorejere (FDM), Firskovvej 32, (Box 500), 2800-Lyngby; tel. (0)45-93-08-00; fax (0)45-93-08-00.

Police emergency number for serious accidents: 112

Norway Many home motoring organizations are affiliated to AIT and their members can get help from NAF (Norges Automobilforbund) with journey planning as well as breakdown or accident assistance. NAF patrols main roads and mountain passes have emergency phones. More comprehensive repairs can be carried out at NAF-contracted garages. NAF, Storgt 2, N-01550 Oslo; tel. (0)22-34-14-00; fax (0)22-22-13-73. Alternatively look in the phone book under *Redningsteneste* for nearest Falken Redningskorps (rescue corps).

Police emergency number for serious accidents: 112

Ambulance: 113

Sweden Contact either local police or Larmtjänst run by Swedish insurance companies, which operates a 24-hour towing service. The name is in local phone books.

Police emergency number for serious accidents: 90-000

Parking

There are differences from place to place and it is a good idea to enquire at a tourist office. Generally, cities have good off-street parking, and meters. Parking on street is often on the right-hand side only. Keep an eye open for signs indicating which night of the week the street will be cleaned and do not park on those nights. In winter particularly, places to park may vary with weather conditions.

Electricity

Scandinavian electricity is 220 volts AC, and standard two-pin round continental plugs are used. Adaptors are necessary for visitors from countries with different plugs and sockets.

Embassies and Consulates

Denmark

UK: Embassy of Great Britain, Kastelvej 36-40, 2100-Copenhagen O; tel. (0)35-26-46-00

Holland: Netherlands Embassy, Toldbodgade 33, 1253-Copenhagen K; tel. (0)33-15-62-93

France: French Embassy, Kongens Nytorv 4, 1050-Copenhagen; tel. (0)33-15-51-22

Italy: Italian Embassy, Gl. Vartovvej 7, 2900 Hellerup; tel. (0)31-62-68-77

USA: Embassy of the United States of America, Dag Hammerskjolds Alle 24, 2100 Copenhagen O; tel. (0)31-42-31-44

Japan: Embassy of Japan, Pilestræde 61, 1113-Copenhagen; tel.(0)33-11-33-44

Norway

UK: British Embassy, Ths Heftyes gate 8, Oslo; tel. (0)22-55-24-00

Holland: Nederlands Embassy, Oscars gate 29, Oslo; tel. (0)22-60-21-93

France: French Embassy, Drammensveien 88E, Oslo; tel. (0)22-44-18-20

Italy: Italian Embassy, Inkognito gaten 7, Oslo; tel. (0)22-55-22-29 or (0)22-44-31-94

USA: Embassy of the United States of America, Drammensveien 18, Oslo; tel. (0)22-44-85-50

Japan: Japanese Embassy, Parkveien 33B, Oslo; tel. (0)22-55-10-11

Sweden

UK: Britiske ambassade, Skarpögata 6-8, Stockholm; tel. (0)8-667-01-40

Holland: De Nederlandse Ambassade, Götgatan 16A, Stockholm; tel. (0)8-624-71-80

France: Ambassade de France, Box 10241, Stockholm; tel. (0)8-663-02-70

Ireland: Irländske Ambassade, Östermalmsgatan 97, Stockholm; tel. (0)8-661-80-05 or (0)8-661-74-09

Italy: Amassade d'Italia, Oakhill, Djurgården, Stockholm; tel. (0)8-24-38-05

USA: Amerikanske ambassade, Strandvägen 101, Stockholm; tel. (0)8-783-53-00

Japan: Japans ambassade, Gändesgatan 10, Stockholm; tel. (0)8-663-04-40

Emergencies and Police

For police, fire brigade or ambulance dial the following numbers in each country, from anywhere in the country. No money is needed from a payphone:

Denmark 112 and specify Fire, Police or Ambulance

Norway Fire 110; Police 112; Ambulance 113

Sweden 90-000 and specify Fire, Police or Ambulance

Radio Denmark, Radio Sweden and NRK Radio (Norwegian Broadcasting) will broadcast vital messages (death or critical illness) to visitors in Scandinavia. For Denmark, relatives should contact their own national police who will liaise with police in Denmark for a broadcasting service. For Norway and Sweden, contact the broadcasting organization in your own country, or the appropriate embassy in Scandinavia.

Scandinavian police are always co-operative and ready to help. The word for police is *politi* (*polis* in Sweden), shown on stations and cars, and given in the telephone book. Police wear black uniforms and drive marked cars which may be stopped for assistance. The police are courteous, speak good English and will always stop to give advice or help to visitors.

Food and Cuisine

Scandinavian food in hotels and restaurants has in some ways come full circle. Earlier this century, hotels served largely the traditional range and styles of food, only slowly incorporating European cuisine. Gradually things changed and it became possible to sample many dishes from dozens of different countries, particularly in the capitals and larger communities. For a time, it was easier to find French, Italian, Chinese or Indian food than to eat Scandinavian. The paradox today is that the old traditions are coming back and it is now much easier to find truly Scandinavian cooking as restaurateurs regain the confidence to present their own distinctive menus.

Though food is rarely cheap, and drink even more expensive, a few hints will keep costs manageable. Top restaurants, often attached to luxury hotels, tend to be aimed at expense-account diners and they serve substantial meals. But, especially at lunchtime, good but cheaper alternatives can be found and, as with hotel prices, many restaurants have special, cheaper menus in summer.

The more modest cold tables, notably in hotels at breakfast time, included in the room price, are among the best Scandinavian bargains, and anyone with a good early morning stomach could eat enough to last the day. Many cafés, smaller city restaurants and outdoor eating places have a *dagens ret* or *dagens rätt* (daily menu),

Gamla Stan is Stockholm's Old Town where the city began. With narrow lanes, and little traffic, it is a place for locals and visitors alike to stroll and shop.

which includes a special dish of the day, usually with a salad to start and coffee to follow. Open sandwiches make an interesting and filling meal. In cities, small lunch restaurants, often in cellars, are good value and it is not necessary to go far outside the city for prices to drop considerably if you chose an inn (*kro, wärdhus, vertshus* or *gästjeveri*).

As a rule, Scandinavians eat earlier than many. Breakfast allows for a working day that may start at 8 or 8.30am. Lunch, often a *matpakke* (food brought from home), begins around 11.30am, and the traditional time for the evening meal at home is 5.30 or 6pm, even though it is called *middag*. Despite that, most hotels, motels and restaurants begin serving dinner much later, and many cafés, dance restaurants and clubs serve food well into the night.

Scandinavia has not escaped the international fast-food chains. McDonald's signs and the like are visible everywhere. Yet, in a sense, fast food is not something new to Scandinavia. Try a *pølsevogn* or *korvkiosk* along Scandinavian city streets. A bit like the British chip shop, these covered stalls or wagons, at one time dedicated to many forms of sausage, now also sell grilled chicken, hamburgers and so on, well cooked and scrupulously clean. The appetising smell greets you at a corner and, for a cheap and cheerful meal, there is nothing to beat it.

When to Go

Scandinavia comes to a halt during July when everyone who can takes to a *hytte* or *stuga* (wooden holiday house) on lake, mountain, forest or coast, to devote themselves to sailing, swimming, fishing, canoeing, walking, berry-picking and generally getting back to nature. July and early August can be a good time to find the sort of entertainment and sightseeing aimed at visitors, plus cheaper lodgings (see p.12) but theatres, concert halls and other arts venues often close for July or longer.

May, with the sudden rush of summer, and June are usually beautiful months for weather, with long, light nights, and the Scandinavian summer can stretch into a mellow late August and a September of rich colours, but there can also be rain. The months after the turn of the year are best for skiing, dog-sledging, snow-mobiling, and other wintersports in Norway and Sweden and the beauty is that almost every town and city will have cross-country skiing close by. In the north, year-round skiing is possible.

Getting to Scandinavia

By Air
Scandinavia's flag carrier, SAS, several smaller national airlines, most main European and several North American airlines, some 40 in all, fly into Scandinavian airports. Many come direct, some via Copenhagen which is the hub airport for the region, and for incoming and onward flights for Eastern Europe and the Far East. The size and terrain of both Norway and Sweden calls for a great deal of internal air traffic, through Oslo and Stockholm, either via SAS or smaller national airlines such as Transwede or Norway's Braathens SAFE.

Main international airports in each country are:

Denmark–Kastrup, Copenhagen. Some 12km (8 miles) from the city centre. Frequent SAS buses take 20 minutes to Hovedbanegården (main railway station). There are also taxis and a (slower) bus service. Banking, restaurant, duty-free and car hire facilities are available.

There are a few international services to three smaller airports in Jylland and plenty of domestic flights: **Esbjerg** on the west coast; **Århus** (Denmark's second city) in the north, **Billund**, home town of Lego and Legoland in Central Jylland.

Norway – Fornebu, Oslo, is some 10 km (6 miles) from the town centre and has full airport facilities. Buses leave the airport every 30 minutes for Sentral Stasjon (central station) via SAS city terminal, with various stops on the way in.

Flesland, Bergen, is 19km (12 miles) from the centre, with an airport bus to the city terminal (at the SAS Royal Hotel) via the Hotel Norge and other stops. Flesland has good modern airport facilities.

Norway's long distances demand several airports which can bring international as well as domestic flights to more distant areas. Oil has dramatically increased the size of **Stavanger** airport on the west coast, and there are also international flights to **Trondheim**, in Central Norway, and **Trømso**, on the far northwest coast.

Sweden – Arlanda serves Stockholm and Uppsala as Sweden's main airport, with one international and three domestic terminals. It has all the usual facilities. By SAS bus it is 42km (26 miles) to the centre of Stockholm, stopping in the suburbs before reaching the central station. There are also taxis, with special (lower) airport rates and an SAS limousine which is costly for a single person.

Landvetter, Gothenburg, though smaller, has some international flights and facilities, and is 24km (17miles) from the centre. The airport bus takes around 30 minutes. **Malmö-Sturup** in the south is mainly for internal use but takes a few international flights. It takes around 30 minutes to travel the 30km (21 miles) to or from the city centre.

By Sea

For people with cars, travelling by sea can be ideal, cutting down the time of long overland journeys. Ferries arrive from various parts of northern Europe, and all three Scandinavian countries are extensively linked by ferry, both internally and cross-border. The main ferry routes into Scandinavia are:

Denmark From **Britain**, Scandinavian Seaways sails year-round Harwich–Esbjerg; end-March to end-October, Newcastle–Esbjerg. From **continental Europe** main routes are from **Germany**: Puttgarden–Rødby, Rostock–Gedser, Travemünde–Gedser, Mukran–Rønne, Sassnitz–Rønne, Kiel–Bagenkop, Kiel–Halsskov, Gelting–Faaborg, Sylt– Rømø, Travemünde–Lübeck–Malmö–Copenhagen by Silja-Euroway. There is also a ferry from Swinoujscie in **Poland** to Copenhagen, and from the **Faroe Islands–Iceland**–Hantshals.

Norway From **Britain**, Color Line sails year-round Newcastle–Stavanger–Bergen. From June to August, P&O sails Aberdeen–Shetland–Bergen. Main routes from **continental Europe** are: from **Germany**, Color Line, Kiel–Oslo; from the **Netherlands**, Scandinavian Seaways, Amsterdam–Kristiansund. There are also sailings between Murmansk in **Russia** and Kirkenes, and the Smiryl Line runs between **Iceland** and the **Faroe Islands** and Bergen.

Sweden From **Britain**, Scandinavian Seaways sails Harwich–Gothenburg year-round, and Newcastle–Gothenburg in the summer. From **continental Europe**, main routes are from **Germany**, Kiel–Gothenburg by Stena Line and Trave-münde–Trelleborg and Sassnitz-Trelleborg by Silja-Euroway. From the **Netherlands**, Scandinavian Seaways sails Amster-dam–Gothenburg; both Viking and Silja Lines sail from **Finland**, Helsinki–Stock-holm, Turku–Stockholm via Åland Islands; also Vaasa and Jakobstad, to Sundsvall, Umeå and Skellefteå across the Gulf of Bothnia. There are services between St Petersburg in **Russia** and Stockholm (Nynäshamn), from Tallinn in **Estonia**, and from Gdansk in **Poland** to Karlskrona.

By Rail

Most Scandinavian cities and bigger towns are easily reached by rail from the Continent though, except in the case of Denmark, this usually also necessitates a

Since before Viking times, Scandinavians have been good sailors and boatbuilders. Here, a modern Scandinavian Seaways ferry meets a much earlier vessel.

ferry. Britain is also connected by rail: from London (Victoria) via Dover and Os-tend; from London (Liverpool Street) via Harwich and Hook of Holland; and from London via the Channel Tunnel.

By Coach

Many countries are connected to Scandi-navia by coach and the three countries also operate networks of scheduled coaches throughout Europe. Coaches also leave from London, via the Continent, best suited to fit travellers on tight budgets as journeys last around 26 hours to Århus, Denmark, and over 40 hours to Stockholm, Sweden.

Guides

As English is a second language to most Scandinavians, it is easy to get an English-speaking guide. German-speaking guides are almost as plentiful, and tours are also guided in French, Italian and more. Tours by bus or boat are often multilingual, as is guiding in some museums and other places of interest. Personal guides for individuals are not cheap. Local tourist offices can advise, make bookings and tell you where to book tours with guides and how to arrange individually tailoured tours.

Health and Medical Care

No special vaccinations or health precautions are required for Scandinavia. The three countries have reciprocal agreements with Britain and most other western European countries. It is best to enquire before you leave home about details of individual agreements which may vary, and also if and what treatment costs may be reclaimed after you return home. Medical insurance as part of travel insurance is a necessary precaution on which tour operators may insist. Show your passport when asking for medical attention.

Denmark In normal circumstances (ie visitors have not come to Denmark for the purpose of getting treatment) reciprocal arrangements with many countries, particularly members of the European Union, mean that visitors are entitled to free treatment in hospitals and casualty wards in the event of an illness or accident. In the event of a patient having to be transported to his or her own country, the visitor is responsible for the journey.

Some categories may be due a refund of dentists' and chemists' bills; always ask. If cash payment is required, a refund may be obtained in the health insurance office of the municipality where a visitor is staying. Most hotels and other lodgings have contacts with doctors and hospitals. Copenhagen has a special Doctor-on-Duty service (tel. 33-93-63-00). Patients pay doctors' fees, Dkr300-400, in cash.

Norway Norway is an EEA member (European Economic Agreement) and European Union visitors (and others with whom Norway has reciprocal agreements) have the same rights as Norwegians, on production of a valid passport, and own country's appropriate medical form. Ambulance travel and hospital treatment are free. Doctors, however, are paid in cash at a cost of around Nkr70-100 for a routine visit. If you need treatment outside surgery hours, go to the nearest casualty ward (*akuttmottak*). *Legevakt* means a doctor who is open evenings and at night. Prescriptions are dealt with by *apotek* (chemist).

Dental treatment is also paid for by the patient. Some charges may be partially refunded by Norway's special insurance scheme. Enquire and, if applicable, obtain a receipt and claim at the district social insurance office, called *Trygdekontor*. Medical services are listed in *gule sider* (yellow pages in phone books).

Sweden If you are able, go to a hospital casualty department (*akutmottagning*), or health centre (*vårdcentral*) in rural areas. If impossible, ask your hotel to call a doctor. Make sure the doctor is affiliated to the Swedish National Health Service (*Försäkringkassan.*). A doctor's prescription is necessary for medicines from an *apotek* (chemist), open during shopping hours. Most cities have all-night chemists which are shown on health or blue pages of *gula sidorna* (yellow pages), with other health emergency services.

Hospital visits cost Skr90-200 for casualty department treatment. Visitors pay 70 percent of dental treatment up to Skr3000, 50 percent between Skr3-7000, and 25 percent of charge for metal used in treatment.

Language

Scandinavia has three main languages, all so similar that, for example, crews of SAS aircraft usually use their own language. Written Danish and Norwegian are very similar, though manner and accent are very different and, in general, there are many dialects within each country. West Norway also has a special version of Norwegian, Nynorsk, which is in essence an amalgamation of many different old dialects. Swedish is the least like the other two, and Danes and Swedes make something of a virtue of being unable to understand one another! For a foreigner, spelling can be confusing. You might see a simple word, for example, church, with variations ranging through *kirke*, *kirka*, *kyrke*, *kyrka* and one or two more, all correct in their area. Scandinavian languages also have three extra vowels å, æ, ø (å, ä, ö in Swedish), which are the last three letters of the alphabet.

Scandinavians learn English early and most speak it well, sometimes with a slight American accent from watching a lot of television, for which they frequently apologize! German is often the next most frequently spoken language and there is also some French. City menus often have an English translation. In Sweden, you may hear Finnish, one of the results of the long historic connection between Swedes and Finns. In the north of Norway and Sweden (and into Finland and even Russia) the Sami language is the old tongue, no longer discouraged.

Lost Property

In general, first try the hotel, inn or campsite where you have been staying, and the main police station, airport, railway or bus station. Some bigger cities may also have special lost property offices.

Denmark Politets Hittegodskontor, Slotsherrensvej 113, DK-2720, Vanløse, Copenhagen; tel. 31-74-88-22

Norway Grønlandsleiret 44, Oslo; tel. (0)22-66-98-65). For losses on trolleys and trams, Nationaltheatret Stasjon, Oslo; tel. (0)22-66-49-27). For losses on trains, Sentral Stasjon, Oslo; tel. (0)22-326-80-47

Sweden Main Lost Property, Stockholm; tel. (0)8-769-30-75). For losses on buses, Tunnelbana (underground) and local trains, Local Traffic Office, Stockholm; tel. (0)8-600-10-00). Lost Property Office, Gothenburg; tel. (0)31-61-8-00). Lost Property Office, Malmö; tel. (0)40-20-10-00.

Maps

Tourist information centres in all three countries hold stocks of good, simple maps for cities and countryside. Except in Norway, these are usually free of charge. Hire cars usually come with good road maps, and the Falck road organization can be a good source. A few examples of good maps to buy are Cappelen, Terrac (Berlin) Kümmerly and Frey (Switzerland) and Danish Kraks Vejviser. There are many more and in Britain, Stanfords in London (12-14 Long Acre, London WC2E 9LP; tel. 0171-836-1321, fax 0171-836-0189) has a good range of Scandinavian maps.

Media

Newspapers, Magazines and Books

Scandinavian countries have a comprehensive spread of national and provincial daily and Sunday papers, both broadsheet and tabloid, in their own languages, and some magazine-style publications in English. Capital and larger cities, airports and main stations have kiosks and shops selling British and American newspapers, as well as German, French and other European language publications.

Scandinavia's excellent bookshops also stock English-language books and guidebooks. There is a particularly good selection at the Swedish Institute's centre at Sverigehuset, above the Tourist Information Centre, Hamngatan, Stockholm.

Radio and Television

All three countries have public service broadcasting channels in radio and television. Danmarks Radio, Norskringskasting (NRK), Sveriges Radio and Sveriges Televison are the main companies, though the number of local and commercial channels is growing. Most hotels offer satellite channels with at least one in English. Danmarks Radio (Channel 3) broadcasts news programmes on weekends at 8.30am in English, German and French. NRK broadcasts a 30-minute

radio programme on the week's events, Norway Now, on Channel P1 (Oslo FM 93MHz, elsewhere shortwave) in English only, and also news in English, German and French.

There are no special television programmes for visitors but, as Scandinavia uses a large number of foreign programmes and films in their original language with sub-titles, visitors are well served.

Money Matters

Currency

The basic currency of all three Scandinavian countries is the krone (krona in Sweden), 1 krone equals 100 øre (öre in Sweden) with minor differences in the notes and coins in circulation.

Danish krone: abbreviated kr, Dkr or banker's DKK (not usually shown on prices). Bank notes in circulation are: 1,000, 100, 50 krone. Coins are 20, 10, 5 and 1 krone, and 50 and 25 øre.

Norwegian krone: abbreviated kr, Nkr or banker's NOK. Bank notes in circulation are 1000, 500, 1000, 100, 50 krone. Coins are 10, 5, 1krone, and 50 øre.

Swedish krona: abbreviated kr, Skr or banker's SEK. Bank notes in circulation are: 10,000, 1,000, 100, 50, 20 krona. Coins are 10, 5, 1 krona, and 50 öre.

Exchange Facilities

You can change money at airports, central stations in many bigger cities, almost all commercial and savings banks, at post offices, hotels and exchange bureaux such as Forex in many towns in Sweden and ApS in Denmark. There are also the No 1 Exchange bureaux at Rådhuspladsen and Østergade 16 in Stockholm. Denmark has currency exchange automats at branches of Unibank at Axeltorv, Vimmelsaftet 35, and Rådhuspladsen, in Copenhagen, operating with bank notes of several European currencies and US dollars.

General banking hours are given below but banks at airports and stations usually open longer and some are also open at weekends. General banking hours, from Monday to Friday are:

Denmark 9.30am-4pm. Exchange bureaux at Kastrup airport, Copenhagen, are only open to arriving passengers.

Norway 9.30am-3.30pm, and to 5 or 6pm on Thursdays and Fridays, except from June to the end of August.

Sweden 9.30am-3pm. In larger cities banks may open later, especially on Thursdays.

Credit Cards

Most international credit cards, for example Barclaycard/Visa, Access/Mastercard/Eurocard, Diners Club and American Express, are widely accepted in Scandinavia. Shops and restaurants usually display signs showing which cards they accept.

City Cards (Kort)

Most major Scandinavian cities, such as the capitals and towns the size of Bergen or Gothenburg, sell a concessionary card, *kort*, of one, two or three days' duration, which gives big savings on sightseeing tours, free entry to many museums and main places of interest, free public transport and concessions in some restaurants. In a similar way, bigger cities offer packages, generally available mid-June to mid-August and at weekends year-round. These include accommodation at selected hotels and a *kort* if available.

For all these concessions, enquire at area or national tourist boards either in Scandinavia or in your home country. Sweden

All three capitals and the bigger cities have a 'Kort' system. Cards last for 1, 2, or 3 days. Once bought, city transport is usually free and museums and the like are much cheaper.

is currently converting its *Stockholmkort* into a smart card.

Banks

Scandinavian cities and towns all have banks, as do many larger villages. Banks close Saturdays except for airport and main station banks. Different banks have links to different credit cards and allow withdrawals of cash against linked credit cards. Banks at major airports and railway stations stay open longer than normal banking hours, and may also have *bureaux de change* (see p.28).

Opening Hours

Banks
Bank opening hours are given on page 29.

Shops
It was not long ago that Scandinavian shops closed early, but hours have stretched remarkably. Shopping varies slightly between countries, and between cities and smaller communities. Many shopping complexes and supermarkets now stay open until 8pm. Shops will close early on the day before a holiday. General rules for each country are:

Denmark Weekdays 9 or 10am-5.30 or 6pm; on Thursdays some stay open to 7pm; on Fridays some stay open to 7 or 8pm; Saturdays 9 or 10am-12 noon or 2pm. In summer, all shops may be open to 5pm on the first Saturday of the month, and in Copenhagen on all Saturdays throughout June, July and August. Some florists, petrol station shops and news kiosks are open Sundays. The latter two and some holiday area shops may be open in the evenings as well.

Norway Normal shopping hours are Monday-Friday 9am-4 or 5pm; Thursdays 9am-6 or 8pm; Saturdays 9am-1 or 3pm. Kiosks rarely close until 10 or 11pm. Petrol stations may also sell groceries and stay open until 11pm.

Sweden Shops weekday opening 9am-6pm, weekends until 1 or 4pm. Some big stores and shopping centres in larger towns may stay open as late as 10pm. In rural areas, closing time for shops and petrol stations is usually 5 or 6pm.

Rådhuspladsen, Copenhagen's central square, houses the Town Hall and is a hub for transport. It is also the start of the west end of the walking street, Strøget, which Copenhagen claims was Europe's first pedestrianized area.

Police

Cities, towns and most large rural communities have police stations. Main stations open 24 hours and have a public desk for incidents, thefts or other problems, and usually house the local lost property office. The police tour the streets on foot or in cars. Random car checks for documents and drinking drivers are more frequent than in many other countries. Scandinavian police are courteous, speak reasonable or good English, and can be stopped if necessary. Emergency numbers are on page 16.

PUBLIC HOLIDAYS

Banks, shops and offices are closed on public holidays and may close earlier the day before. Museums, cinemas and restaurants will open on some public holidays, perhaps with reduced hours. Everything shuts down at least from noon on Christmas Eve, and throughout Christmas and Boxing Day.

Denmark

New Year's Day	1 January	*Whit Sunday*	May
Maundy Thursday	late March/early April	*Constitution Day*	5 June (from noon)
Good Friday	late March/early April	*Christmas Eve*	24 December (from noon)
Easter Sunday/Monday	late March/ early April	*Christmas, Boxing Days*	25, 26 December
Great Prayer Day	late April/May	*New Year's Eve*	31 December (from noon)
Ascension Day	May		

Norway

New Year's Day	1 January	*May Day (Labour Day)*	1 May
Maundy Thursday	late March/early April	*Ascension Day*	May
		National Day	17 May
Good Friday	late March/early April	*Whit Sunday*	May
		Christmas Eve	24 December (from noon)
Easter Sunday, Monday	late March/early April	*Christmas, Boxing Days*	25, 26 December

Sweden

New Year's Day	1 January	*Whit Monday*	May
Twelfth Night	6 January	*Midsummer Day*	Saturday between 21 and 26 June
Good Friday	late March/early April		
Easter Sunday, Monday	late March/early April	*All Saints' Day*	Saturday between 31 Oct and 6 Nov
May Day (Labour Day)	1 May	*Christmas Eve*	24 December
Ascension Day	May	*Christmas, Boxing Days*	25, 26 December

Religion

Around 95 percent of native-born Scandinavians are of the Lutheran faith, the established church in all three countries. There are also Roman Catholics, Jews and representatives of other faiths. The number of Muslims has grown with immigration but they are still a small minority. Religious services and other meetings are listed in daily papers and church names appear in telephone directories and in tourist literature. Tourist offices also have information. One or two churches in the capitals hold services in English.

Time Differences

Scandinavia adheres to Central European Time, which suits continental Europeans, but is one hour ahead of Greenwich Mean Time. Clocks go forward by one hour during the summer (late March to late September). This period may differ in duration from British Summer Time and can cause some confusion with airline schedules. As a rough guide, when it is noon in Scandinavia, it is 6am in New York, 11am in London, noon in Johannesburg, 8pm in Sydney and 10pm in Auckland.

Tipping

On the whole, egalitarian Scandinavia does not go in much for tipping. Service charges are almost always included in restaurant and hotel bills, as is sales tax. It is usual, however, to round up restaurant bills to the nearest 10kr. It is not necessary to leave a tip for chambermaids, only for extra service. Taxi drivers do not normally expect a tip either but appreciate rounding up to

nearest 10kr. Add 10 percent if the driver, for example, carries a case up a flight of stairs. When you leave a coat in a cloakroom (and you are always expected to do so, perhaps because winter means changing boots and heavy outdoor clothing), the charge is usually posted; if not, give 8-10kr.

Toilets

You will find public lavatories in railway and underground stations, parks, squares, busier streets and some department stores. Some are identified by the standard symbols for men and women. You may also see *WC-Damer* (or *D*) for women, and *WC-Herrer* or *Herrar* (or *H*) for men. Most are free, but some have coin locks; a few have an attendant to provide soap and a towel, in which case there is a small charge.

Tourist Information

Each Scandinavian country is divided into regional tourist organizations, with tourist offices (*turist byrer*) around the country. They have a good selection of brochures, leaflets and maps of their own areas (as well as of the rest of the country) and are a fund of information. Many can also arrange to book tours in the area. The offices are marked with the international tourist sign (white 'I' on a green background) and, in season, are very busy.

Many European and other countries have Scandinavian tourist offices which are usually the best first contact point when planning a trip. Start with the country's general information brochure which gives a taste and has many holiday ideas and contacts. Similar information is also available from each country's national tourist office.

Denmark

Denmark is divided into nine regional tourist areas, and has over 100 tourist information offices around the country. They are open year-round Monday to Saturday. Some also open on Sundays. Contact addresses for tourist information in the main cities and for the Danish Tourist Board information office are:

Copenhagen Tourist Information (Copenhagen and whole of Denmark), Bernstorffsgade 1, D-1577l, Copenhagen; tel. (0)33-11-13-25, fax (0)33-93-49-69

Odense Tourist Office: Rådhuset, DK-5000 Odense C; tel. (0)66-12-75-20, fax (0)66-12-75-86

Aalborg Tourist Office: Østeraa 8, DK-9000 Aalborg; tel. (0)98-12-60-22, fax (0)98-16-69-22

Århus Tourist Office: Rådhuset, DK-8000 Århus C; tel. (0)86-12-16-00, fax (0)86-12-08-07

Overseas offices of Danish Tourist Board include:

Norway: Danmarks Turistkontor, Tollubgaten 27, (Postboks: 406-Sentrum), N-0103, Oslo; tel. (0)22-41-17-76, fax (0)22-41-38-02

Sweden: Danska Turistbyrån, Riddargatan 7A (Box 5524), S-114 Stockholm; tel. (0)8-662-05-80, fax (0)8-661-17-36

Finland: Danska Turistbyrå, Bensowgränd 6, (PO Box 48) FIN-2700 Grankulla; tel. (9)0-505-00-15, fax (9)0-505-00-04

UK: Danish Tourist Board, 55 Sloane Street, London SW1X 9SR; tel. (0)171-259-5958, fax (0)171-259-5955

Germany and Switzerland: Dänisches Fremdenverkehsamt, Glockengiesserwall 2, (Postfach 10-13-29) D-20095 Hamburg; tel. (0)40-32-78-03, fax (0)40-33-70-83

Netherlands: Deens Verkeersburo, Schipolweg 96a (Postbus 266) NL-2316 Leiden; tel. (0)71-233-283, fax (0)71-211-794

France: Le Conseil du Tourisme du Danemark, 4 Rue Henry Monnier, F-750009 Paris; tel. (0)1-45-96-02-72, fax (0)1-49-95-03-63

Italy: Ente Danese per il Turismo, Via Capopuccio 11, I-20 123 Milano; tel (0)2 87-48-03, fax (0)2-86-07-12

USA and Canada: Scandinavian National Tourist Office (Denmark), 655 Third Avenue, 18th floor, New York, NY 10017; tel. (0)212-949-2333, fax (0)212-286-0896

Japan: Scandinavian Tourist Board (Denmark), Sanno Grand Building, Room 912-913, 14-2 Nagata-cho, 2-chome, Chiyoda-ku, Tokyo 100; tel. (0)3-3580-5030, fax (0)3-3503-4457

Norway

Norway is divided into 18 different regional tourist areas, and has over 300 tourist information offices around the country, three-quarters of which are open year-round, giving advice on travel and accommodation, but they do not sell tickets.

Norway Information Centre (Information on Oslo, and rest of Norway), Vestbaneplassen 1, Oslo (opposite Rådhuset); tel. (0)22-83-00-50, fax (0)22-83-05-50

Bergen Information Centre, Bryggen 7, N-5003 Bergen; tel. (0)55-32-14-80, fax (0)55-32-14-64

Oslo Promotion (HQ), Grev Wedels plass 4, N-0151 Oslo; tel. (0)22-33-43-86, fax (0)22-33-43-89. No counter service

Overseas offices of the Norwegian Tourist Board include:

Denmark: Norges Turistkontor, Trondhjems Plads 4, DK-2100 Copenhagen O; tel. (0)31-38-41-17, fax (0)31-38-96-96

Sweden: Norska Turistbyrån, Sven Rydellsgata 3, 3 tr. S-412-51 Gothenburg; tel. (0)31 18-80-80, fax (0)31 778-09-86

Finland: Norges Turistbyrå, Georgsgatan 23, FIN-00101 Helsinki; tel: 0-605-245, fax 0-603-558

UK: Norwegian Tourist Board, Charles House, 5-11 Lower Regent Street, London SW1Y 4LR; tel. (0)171-839-6255; fax (0)171-839-6014

Germany, Austria and Switzerland: Norwegisches Fremdenverkehrsamt, Mundsburger Damm 45, D-22087 Hamburg; tel. (0)40-22-71-08-0, fax (0)40-22-71-08-88

Netherlands and Belgium: Noors Nationaal Verkeersbureau, Saxen Weimarlaan 58, NL-1075 CE Amsterdam; tel. (0)20-671-00-61, fax (0)20-679-88-8

France: Office National du Tourisme de Norvège, 88 avenue Charles de Gaulle, F-92523 Neuilly-sur-Seine Cedex; tel. (0)1-4641-49-00, fax (0)1-4641-49-05

Italy: Ufficio Nazionale Norvegese per il Turismo, Corso XXII Marzo 4, 1-20125 Milano; tel. (0)2-5519-3588, fax (0)2-5519-3584

USA and Canada: Scandinavian Tourist Board (Norway), 655 Third Avenue, 18th Floor, New York NY10017; tel. (0)212-949-2333, fax (0)212-983-5260

Japan: Scandinavian Tourist Board (Norway), Sanno Grand Building, Room 401, 14-2 Nagata-cho, 2-chome, Chiyoda-ku, Tokyo 100; tel. (0)3-3580-5030, fax (0)3-3503-4457

Sweden

Sweden has 24 regional tourist organizations and there are some 300 tourist information offices around the country. The Sweden Travel Shop, which occupies the same building as the Stockholm Information Centre also has information on regions other than Stockholm, and can advise and book both travel and accommodation. Higher up in Sweden House are the Swedish Institute's library and a fine book shop on all things Swedish.

Stockholm Information Service: Sverigehuset, Kungsträdgården, Box 7542, S-103-93 Stockholm; tel. (0)8 789-20-00, fax (0)8-789-24-50

Gothenburg Tourist Office: Kungsportplatsen 2, S-411 Gothenburg; tel. (0)31-10-07-40, fax (0)31-13-21-84

Malmö Tourist Office, Skeppsbron 2, S-211 Malmö; tel. (0)40-30-01-50, fax (0)40-34-34-47

The following are overseas offices of the Swedish Travel and Tourism Council:

Norway: Sveriges Reise-og Turistråd, Inkognitogate 17, N-0256 Oslo; tel. (0)22-241-21-67, fax (0)22-255-23-08

Denmark: Sveriges Reise-og Turistråd, Ny Østegade 20, Dk-1101 Copenhagen K; tel. (0)33-939-90-49, fax (0)33-93-90-47

Finland: Roustin Matkalluneuvostod, Norra Järnvägsgatan 19, SF-00100 Helsinki; tel. 0-443-900, fax 0-499-790

UK: Swedish Travel and Tourism Council, 11 Montagu Place, London W1H 2AL; tel. (0)171-724-5868, fax (0)171-724-5872

Germany: Schwede-Webung für Reisen under Touristik, Lilienstrasse 19, D-2000 Hamburg 1; tel. (0)40-33-79-50, fax (0)40-33-05-99

Netherlands: Zweeds Bureau Voor Toerisme en Verkeerd, Zeestraat 71, 25118-AA Den Haag; tel. (0)70-345-52-83, fax (0)70-363-27-22

Italy: Ene Svedese Viaggi e Turismo, Via Mauritzio Gonzaga 7, I-20123 Milan; tel. (0)2-8646-4869, fax (0)2-8745-44

Switzerland: Schweden-Werbung für Reisen und Touristik, Wienenstrasse 9,

CH-8008 Zurich; tel. (0)1-383-41-30, fax (0)1-383-45-32

France: Office Suédois du Tourisme et des Voyages, 146-150 avenue des Champs Elysées, F-75008 Paris; tel. (0)1-422-565-52, fax (0)1-456-364-93

USA: Scandinavian Tourist Board (Sweden), 655 Third Avenue, 18th floor, New York, NY 10017; tel. (0)212-949-2333, fax (0)212-697-0835

Japan: Scandinavian Tourist Board (Sweden), Sanno Grand Building, Room 401, 14-2 Nagato-cho, 2-chome, Chiyoda-ku, Tokyo 100; tel. (0)3-3580-8360, fax (0)3-3503-4457

Travelling around Scandinavia

It is possible to reach most places in Scandinavia by public transport, though huge distances sometimes mean long journeys. All three countries are well linked both internally and cross-border by air, rail and road, and there is a good network of domestic airports. Norway and Sweden are well served by rail despite the distances involved and, when the tracks at last run out, buses take over, reaching some surprisingly remote places.

Norway's long west coast in particular is studded with small airports and it is simple to make short hops which avoid very long detours around fjords and mountains, which may, in any case, be closed in the winter. On the same coast, Hurtigruten (the coastal route) runs from Bergen to Kirkenes on the Russian border, around 1200km (800 miles) each way. Once the lifeline of the small coastal communities, the shipping line is still used to transport cargoes of every sort and is useful to local Norwegians who treat it like a bus,

hopping on and off at any of the 35-or-so stops (see p.208). The big, coastal steamers are now also popular for cruising holidays. In general, Scandinavians use boats and ferries more than many countries, to link different areas in and between their three countries.

By Air

There are around 100 airports and airfields in Scandinavia. Always ask about special offers, which may be within one country or cross-border. SAS, for example, has 'Visit Scandinavia' flights in conjunction with an international flight. Priced on a sliding scale from approximately 500kr for one flight, they range up to around 2400kr (depending on exchange rates) for six domestic flights in Denmark, Norway and Sweden.

Denmark Copenhagen is the hub airport of a surprisingly large network for a small country, with some 10 domestic airports, usually placed so that they can serve several towns. Flight times are short, from 30-50 minutes. If the domestic flight has connected with an overseas flight, the fare to the domestic airport may be the same as that to Copenhagen. Always ask about discounted fares. In addition to SAS, the domestic airlines include Maersk Air, Sun Air and DanAir.

Norway Some 50 airports and airfields bring even the north of Norway relatively close. Oslo is the major airport but Bergen and Trondheim are both important hubs. Apart from SAS, the main domestic airlines are Braathens SAFE and Widerøe. Braathens' 'Visit Norway' pass is good value with discount-rate flight coupons; Widerøe also offers summer fares. Check before you book.

Sweden Again, long distances make domestic flights an important alternative to ground travel. Cities and bigger towns are linked by an efficient network of flights by SAS and Transwede, plus a few smaller airlines. Stockholm has flights to more than 35 destinations within Sweden, most leaving from Arlanda airport; there are also some from Bromma airport, within Stockholm's city boundaries. Other main domestic airports are Gothenburg and Malmö. There are a number of discounted fares, including weekend and family fares.

By Train

Each country has its own railway service, all of high standard, and interlinked. On virtually all long-distance trains there is a restaurant car and buffet, with excellent meals, drinks and snacks. For longer, overnight journeys, trains have sleeping cars and couchettes. There are many offers and discount travel tickets for visitors. Particularly good value is the ScanRail pass which gives go-as-you-please travel throughout Denmark, Norway, Sweden and Finland priced according to duration. There is also a good value InterRail pass for younger travellers, covering the same area.

Denmark You can reach Denmark by rail from Germany and the country has a dense network of domestic routes, all run by Danish State Railways (DSB). Trains are modern, fast, comfortable and punctual, and have historically used a ferry between Sjælland and the island of Fyn. This, however, will soon be superseded by a new superbridge across the Great Belt, expected

to open in 1996. Fare reductions include cheap day tickets with special conditions, group travel for three adults or more travelling together, and child fares.

Norway Norwegian State Railways (Norges Statsbaner, NSB) run trains from the southern tip of Norway right up to Bodø on the northwest coast, and many places in between. The focal points of the network are Oslo, Bergen, Stavanger and Trondheim. Trains are modern, efficient and usually punctual, even in heavy winter weather, with comfortable carriages and provision for disabled people on medium and long-distance routes. There are various discount rates, which include ferry and bus routes when necessary, and 'EuroDomino Norway' is a flexible rail pass for Norway only, on the lines of the ScanRail Pass. Norwegian State Railways have an overseas office in Britain: NSR Travel, 21-24 Cockspur Street, London SW1Y 5DA; tel. (0)171-930-6666, fax (0)171-321-0624.

Sweden Swedish Railways (SJ) is an efficient network which covers the whole country, with the new X2000 high-speed trains cutting times between Stockholm and Gothenburg, and Stockholm and Karlstad. On some trains marked 'R' or 'IC' you must reserve a seat, which can be done up to the time of departure. Sweden's

*D*rivstua is well-known to walkers and climbers making for the heights of Dovrefjell, south of Trondheim. All year the trains are full of people with boots, and in winter skis, rucksacks and brown faces, ready for the mountains.

northernmost line continues on to Narvik in Norway, leaving Sweden at Riksgränsen on the border, north of Kiruna.

For visitors to Sweden, the *Reslustkort* (*wanderlust* card) offers half-price, second-class travel on certain trains, and other cost-cutting benefits such as first-class travel on Saturdays year-round, and summer (mid-June to mid-August) for an extra 50Skr. The card lasts a year and is excellent value. A good tip is that full-fare rail tickets can be bought outside Sweden free of VAT, which is charged on tickets bought in Sweden. Ask travel agents.

By Bus or Coach

Where the Scandinavian rail lines stop, buses take over and it is possible to get to small and remote villages this way. There is also a good network of long-distance buses that eat up the miles. These may require advance booking.

Denmark Shorter distances make Denmark ideal for bus travel, with many cross-country routes. They stretch from Hantsholm in northern Jylland to Copenhagen, linking the island of Fyn with Jylland, and also north and south Sjælland, not just to Copenhagen but to and from many bigger communities.

Norway Southern Norway as far as Trondheim has an excellent network of buses, which then stretch north as far as Nordkapp (North Cape), Kirkenes on the Russian border, and the extreme north coast. Norway Bussekspress guarantees a seat for every passenger.

Sweden Southern and central Sweden has an excellent network of express bus services between large towns and cities, and between Stockholm and the northern coastal towns. The biggest operator is Swebus, plus several weekend-only services on main routes. A postal bus network carries passengers in the far north.

In Cities and Towns

Getting around Scandinavian cities and bigger towns by public transport is a gift. Buses are frequent, comprehensive and well integrated with other transport such as underground systems, trams and local rail networks. Special city discount cards (*kort*) such as the Copenhagen Card, which offer many free admissions and reductions, include free travel within the area. Ordinary bus tickets last for a specific time within which you can change buses freely to reach a particular place.

Denmark Copenhagen has buses and underground trains (S-tog), which start early and leave plenty of time for late evening entertainment before the last service. Other towns and cities are also well served by local buses.

Norway Oslo has a well-integrated system of buses, trams and an underground railway which emerges on the surface to become the suburban network. Buses run through the centre of town. Oslo's terminus for underground lines is Stortinget Stasjon in Karl Johans Gate. There is a 24-hour tourist ticket giving unlimited travel. Bergen has buses and trolley buses, and offers a special 48-hour tourist ticket which offers unlimited travel at a fixed price and is available from the tourist information office (see p.33). Other towns are well-served by public transport though not all have special discounts for visitors.

Sweden In Stockholm, the underground Tunnelbana (T-banan) has 60 miles of track with some 100 stations. Stations are very clean and are nicknamed the 'world's largest art exhibition' because the specially commissioned artwork, from murals to sculpture, alone would make a journey worthwhile. Stockholm also runs a good system of local trains, and both train and underground fit into a comprehensive bus network. These are all run by Stockholm Transit Authority. Gothenburg and Norrköping have ecologically friendly tram networks to back up the buses.

By Taxi

Most Scandinavian cities have a plentiful supply of taxis which, as they do everywhere, disappear when it is wet. You can either find a taxi at a rank, order one by phone or hail one in the street. In Norway, taxis rarely cruise for passengers. In fact, they are not allowed to pick up passengers within 100 metres (110 yards) of a taxi rank where customers have priority. In Denmark and Sweden, you can flag down a taxi when the sign *Taxi* (in Denmark) or *Ledig* (meaning 'free' in Sweden) is illuminated. Norwegian taxis also show the sign *Taxi* when vacant. Hotels and restaurants will call a taxi for you. All taxis have meters, tips included, but it is customary to round up the fare to the nearest 10kr if you are happy with the service.

By Boat or Ferry

Scandinavia has so many islands that travel by boat is inevitable, to many more than just the largest and best-known islands and island groups, such as Bornholm (Denmark), Lofoten and Vesterålen or the bird island of Runde (Norway), and Öland and Gotland (Sweden).

Especially in Norway, the geography may mean that boat and ferry are the quickest way of getting around some mainland areas, more like a bus than a pleasure cruise. In the fjords, ferries are a necessity and they operate across the water from early until late. There is no need to book and it is rarely possible. From Bergen, there is a regular fast hydrofoil service to Stavanger, well used by business people who have their own working lounge. It is much quicker than by road.

Though Sweden also has many waterways and large lakes, ferries mostly connect the mainland with other countries, for example across the Gulf of Bothnia. Many islands have regular boat connections, among the busiest being the Stockholm archipelago, which has regular services as well as pleasure boats. The same applies to the big lakes such as Vänern, Vättern, Mälaren and Siljan.

Special Tours

Many Scandinavian cities, such as the three capitals and others, offer sightseeing by boat, right in the centre. Examples are the harbours and canals of Copenhagen and Gothenburg, the island boats of Oslofjord, and the huge waterway area of Stockholm, through Lake Mälaren to inland Sweden.

Sweden's Göta Canal is a classic pleasure route for both Swedes and overseas visitors. It links Gothenburg, through the Great Lakes to Mälaren and the Stockholm coast to Stockholm itself, and sails between mid-May and early September. The voyage, which is run by the Göta Canal Steamship Company, takes four days and uses beautiful vintage steamers. Details: Rederi AB Göta Canal, Hotellplatsen 2, Box 272, S-401-24 Göteborg; tel. (0)31-80-63-15.

The *Inlandsbanen* (Inland Railway) is a special scenic line in Sweden which runs from Mora in Dalarna to Gällivare beyond the Arctic Circle. The *Wildmarksexpressen* (Wilderness Express) has 1930s coaches with a gourmet restaurant and runs on the northern route between Östersund and Gällivare, with stops and excursions (see p.322). Details can be obtained from Inlandståget AV, Kyrkagatan 56, S-831-34 Östersund; tel. (0)63-12-76-92.

'Norway in a Nutshell' is a journey through mountain, plateau and fjord, using road, rail and boat, which can start at Bergen or Voss in western Norway. The mountain railway down from Myrdal to the fjord at Flåm is extremely dramatic. Details from the Bergen Tourist Board (see p.33).

Water

Scandinavian water is among the world's best, very pure and safe to drink straight from the tap or stream. But, like everyone else, Scandinavians have also gone in for bottling their own good water and Sweden's *Ramlösa* is a favourite; so too are *Farris* and *Imsdal* in Norway, and *Blå Special* and *Hvid Special* in Denmark. This is all really unnecessary; just scoop up a cupful from a hillside burn.

Weights and Measures

Scandinavia uses the metric system of measurement for distance, weight and fluid quantity. Temperatures are given in degrees Celsius (named after the Swedish inventor of the system, Anders Celsius). Beware the Swedish *mil*, often called 'mile'. This old Swedish name for 10,000 metres (six miles) can mean a long walk for an unwary American or British visitor!

The Pleasures of the Table

Danes, Norwegians and Swedes argue about which country has the best food. Usually, the Danes put forward the loudest claims which makes it all the stranger that *smörgåsbord*, the Swedish name for the famous Scandinavian cold table, is the one that has become known in the outside world. In Danish or Norwegian, the equivalent in its grandest form is called *det store koldtbord*, just *koldtbord* for everyday.

In its grandest form, it is a substantial, celebratory meal served on special occasions, with a slightly smaller version on Sundays in some homes and many hotels. It starts with herring, marinated in different ways, and goes on to fish, caviar, paté, eggs, cold meats and a garden of salads. Even though this is a 'cold' table, hot dishes steam contentedly in warming bowls, along with puddings – often a creamy mixture of some sort – pastries, fruit and coffee. You use a separate plate for fish, meat, egg and salad dishes, taking only small portions each time and coming back to this loaded table again and again.

There are many slightly more modest cold tables, served sometimes on a family Sunday as the early dark closes in at the end of a winter's day out on skis in the forest. Many hotels also make a speciality of a Sunday cold table. *Akvavit*

The Swedish Smörgåsbord has become known as the name for the Scandinavian Cold Table, served in all three countries and, at its most lavish, is a sumptuous feast.

and beer will be served with the meal and you could say that these two drinks go better with Scandinavian food than wine. In Denmark, *en platte*, usually eaten at lunchtime, is a smaller version: a plate with half a dozen cold table dishes. Notable cold tables are the hotel breakfast variety. Usually included in the price of the room, they are one of the best eating bargains, and anyone with an active early-morning stomach could eat enough to last the day.

Smørbrød or *smørrebrød*, not to be confused with *smörgåsbord*, means literally buttered bread, but that is far too modest a title for the glorious open sandwiches that come under this heading. They may be covered with meat, paté, smoked eel or fish, cheeses of many sorts or salad. The beauty comes in the decoration, designed to complement the main layers, on many different types of bread. Two or three are enough for a good meal that will not break the bank.

Scandinavians are great ones for natural foods, from river, lake, sea or forest, and also for fruit, particularly the beautiful tangy apples that wreathe Hardangerfjorden and other fjords with clouds of spring blossom, and weigh down the trees in the orchards of Fyn – the Garden of Denmark – every autumn. Salmon is popular and good, either fresh or as *gravlaks* (*gravad lax* in Swedish), deliciously marinated and served with dill. Many are surprised to find that they prefer it to smoked salmon, though that is tasty too. Trout from lake or river is good, halibut rates as a delicacy and Norwegians have a taste for a combination of boiled cod with liver (*kokt torsk med lever*), an acquired taste perhaps for a visitor.

Shrimps are superb and the start of the *kräftor* (crayfish) season is the cue for a big festive meal, especially in Sweden, with coloured lanterns and decorations strung over the (preferably) outdoor table. These small lobster-like creatures are eaten with a caraway cheese, and lots of *akvavit*, followed by fresh, hand-picked berries. Danish oysters, especially from the Limfjord are as good as, or better than, oysters from anywhere else.

In addition to the usual selection of meat – lamb, pork and veal – Scandinavia has both venison and, from the north of Sweden and Norway, reindeer on the menu. Lamb is a comparative newcomer to Denmark, otherwise famous for bacon and pork. Beef too is now becoming much more popular in all three countries as Scandinavian farmers take on cattle, with the ubiquitous doorstep of steak offered in many restaurants. Game, such as woodcock and ptarmigan, are also a feature on many hotel menus.

Berries, preferably picked wild in the forest, do a lot to fulfill the Scandinavian need for natural things. The forests also provide a selection of mushrooms of different varieties. But the most ubiquitous vegetable is the boiled potato, which Scandinavians usually eat very simply with butter and a sprinkling of dill – with almost everything.

Countries everywhere have their own homely specialities and in Scandinavia they are often reminders of the days when the choice of food was limited by climate and distance, and a peasant way of life. The Danish variety of meat balls, which many countries cook, is *frikadeller*, minced pork and veal. The Danish hamburger is *hakkebøf*, which has long pre-empted the modern fast food and far surpasses it. *Bikesmad* is a typical way of using up leftovers: fried chopped meat, onion and potatoes, served with a fried egg.

As befits a northern land, Norway has some special soups, such as *gul ertesuppe* (yellow pea and ham) and *betasuppe* (vegetable and meat soup) thick enough to be a meal in itself. Norwegians also go in for cured meat, *spekemat*, which may be ham, mutton or sausage served with *flatbrod*, which looks like a big dry pancake and is crisply delicious.

One of the most famous Norwegian dishes is a pudding, *rømmegrøt*, a sour cream porridge which bears little relation to its Scottish counterpart. In the past, this was a celebration dish, used often at weddings. As guests had to travel so far for the ceremony, weddings lasted for several days and everyone made a contribution to the feast. This meant that a dish that could be brought in a bowl or bucket with a handle was much easier to carry.

Both Norway and Sweden produce a version of *fiskebullar* (fish balls) and also popular in Sweden are *kötbullar*, meat balls. Even more typical of the peasant economy of the past, when nothing was left to waste, are *Jannsons frestelse* (Jansson's temptation), a deliciously sharp mixture of potatoes, onions and anchovies, and *pyttipana* ('put in the pan'), a tasty hotchpotch of leftovers, all fried up together. In some rural areas you can still enjoy these traditional dishes, known as *husmanskost*, and you will certainly find them in family homes. A modern use for *pyttipana* is as the last meal in the family *stuga* (summerhouse) before the journey home. In addition to being valued at home, many old dishes have become national specialities, served with pride in top restaurants.

The SAS Royal Hotel in Copenhagen not only serves a fine cold table, but provides a wonderful view of the city.

Unlike the countries in which bread means a white sliced loaf, Scandinavia has not lost the taste for colours and crispness both in its bread and sweet buns, often spiced. When they are baking, the smell of Swedish *bullar* and similar buns is enough to attract passers-by off the street and into the shop. Pastries are good too. Among the best are *vaffler* or *våfflor* (waffles), often claimed by North Americans as their contribution to world cuisine. In fact, waffles were probably taken the other way across the Atlantic by the hundreds of thousands of Scandinavian (and German) emigrants. In Scandinavia, waffles are delicious served with jam and whipped cream, or perhaps ice cream, and Denmark can claim with justification to make the quintessence of ice cream. Pancakes of all sorts are eaten in all three countries, many special to their own area, and *lefsa* from Hardangerfjorden are amongst the best.

There are curiosities. The Norwegian port of Kristiansand, not far south of Trondheim, is the biggest exporter worldwide of dried cod, *klippfisk*. The trade started with Spain and Portugal and in return, the Norwegians acquired their method of cooking it, *bacalao,* served in Kristiansand restaurants and a favourite for parties. A test for the tongue and stomach is the odiferous *surströmming*, very old herring that has been buried in the earth. Now often sold in cans, as the tin is opened, the sour smell can clear a Swedish household, and the host may have to go out into the garden to expose this elderly herring. *Lutefisk*, a favourite in Norway, is also a test for the foreigner: dried fish is marinated which gives it a peculiarly thick, jelly-like consistency, that can only be washed down with copious *akvavit* (aquavit). In Sweden's 'Glass Country', in Småland in the southeast, the old tradition of Hytsill Evenings has been revived. Held in the glassblowing workshops and once part of the social as well as the working life of the glassworkers, the meal starts with herring cooked on the furnace, and finishes with the most delicious curd cake, with sour cherry or strawberry jam.

Keeping what is arguably the best until last, come Danish pastries, curiously called *Vienerbrød* or *Vienerbröd* (Vienna bread). It is tempting to think that the name must have been devised by a Norwegian or Swede, reluctant to give the Danes the accolade. But it cannot be true: Danes also use *Vienerbrød*. Whether it is the Scandinavian water or some other local ingredient, whatever

their shape or size *Vienerbrød* are all of equal succulence. Outside Scandinavia, the so-called Danish pastry can somehow never match it.

All over Scandinavia, the favourite 'firewater' is *akvavit* – the water of life – sometimes called *snaps*. Among Denmark's best brands is Aalborg, Norway has Linje, and Sweden favours Skäne. It is served in tiny glasses and drunk ice-cold – many people cool it in the freezer rather than the fridge – at the beginning of the meal, usually as an accompaniment to fish, preferably the herring that starts off a good *smörgåsbord* or *koldt bord*.

Skol or *skål* and its customs are an essential part of drinking *akvavit*. A guest should wait until the host or hostess proposes the first toast and, particularly in Sweden, there is a regular pecking order of toasts among the guests at the table. It is also polite, having raised your glass, to take a look around the table, catching as many eyes as possible, before and after you take a sip.

Akvavit is distilled from potatoes or barley. The trick that makes each brand different is what goes into it afterwards: juniper or coriander, perhaps myrtle or whatever distinctive flavour the distiller can devise. Many people flavour their own, putting a leaf or a sprig of herb into a half bottle and leaving it to mature, a bit like sloe gin. With alcohol priced high in Scandinavia, there are always stories about people making their own *akvavit* and, in a private house, should you be offered a selection in rather anonymous bottles, it would be courteous not to enquire too closely about the different brands. Home distilling is an open secret and all sorts of stories persist about it. In Norway, so they say, when the police are ready to make checks for home distillation in a particular district, somehow or other the news gets out about three or four days in advance. True or false? Nobody can, or rather will, say.

Three Nations with Family Ties

Scandinavia is three countries with a common history; centuries old sea-faring traditions go right back to the days of the Vikings. Yet there are differences too. Sweden and Norway have huge empty spaces, stretching far north, with mountains, great rivers and lakes, they have been nick-named Europe's last green lung. Denmark is smaller, its highest mountain, Himmelberget (Sky Mountain) no more than a hill. Yet it too has the wonderful coastline, beaches, lakes and greenery of its bigger cousins. All are monarchies, and democratic societies, based on compromise and concensus. Yet there are differences too in the language and character of all three nations, a fascinating study that could keep the visitor occupied for a lifetime.

All over the world nations are labelled with stereotypes and so it is with Scandinavia and the Scandinavians. The Danes, they say, are easy-going and light-hearted; Norwegians have the longest life expectancy and are strong, shy and silent; while the Swedes are reported to be formal, with no sense of humour. The reality is that the best jokes about Swedes are told by Swedes; anyone who pops into a Norwegian bar or disco on Friday or Saturday night will be quickly disabused of ideas about shyness

*N*o-one is quite sure how the Dalahest (Dalarna horse) came into being, but it has long been the area's emblem. The most famous carvers are in Nusnäs.

or silence, though the rumour about life expectancy is true; and the Danes may be 'the Italians of Scandinavia', but they can be very managing when the occasion demands, a reminder perhaps that Denmark once ruled all Scandinavia.

What undoubtedly is true is that, like most of us, Scandinavians are moulded by geography, climate and history. In all three countries, there is a long tradition of warm hospitality. Where else do they light a candle when a visitor arrives, as well as offer food and warmth? It may be because in the past, as today, the winter was harsh and dark, travel was hard, distances long, villages and small towns were far apart, and visitors needed immediate light, warmth and comfort.

Scandinavia had a late industrial revolution, with most people still earning their living on the land until late in the 19th century and, today, even in the cities, Scandinavian attitudes often owe more to farm than firm, factory and profession. Belated industrialization has had two main benefits: Scandinavians were able to make swift use of experience already gained by other countries, and a longer-lasting agricultural tradition has left a wonderful inheritance of small rural buildings, now much used as summer, and sometimes winter, retreats.

Since then, the inherent skills and inventiveness that once produced the longboat, led to swift advances that have transformed Scandinavia. Last century, this was one of Europe's poorest areas,

A late industrial revolution left Scandinavia with a variety of old rural buildings, that have been brought together in outdoor museums such as Skansen, in Stockholm.

with some two million people, particularly Norwegians and Swedes, forced to emigrate. By the middle of this century, Denmark, Norway and Sweden had become three of the richest nations with a standard of living that is rarely equalled.

Denmark, Norway and Sweden each has a strong sense of its individual nationhood. Scandinavians are not embarrassed to show national pride and national cynicism has not yet become as popular as it has in many European countries. But there is also a feeling of family between the three, even if families sometimes squabble.

Long but Little-Known Past

In the same way, the history of Scandinavia is both separate and interwoven. It is almost a surprise to realize how early on people came to these northern climes, venturing north along the coasts as the Ice Age drew to a close and the thaw began, revealing the

While crossing the lake to Nigardsbreen, an arm of the mighty Jostedalsbreen glacier can be seen.

The best time to visit the Bronze Age rock carvings at Tanum on Sweden's west coast is the evening, when the late sun seems to bring them to life.

newborn peninsulas which became Scandinavia. Glaciers became torrents and whole areas tilted and rose, the earth grumbling below. These were hunters and fishermen, and their traces have been found in rock carvings such as the 4,000-year-old figure of a skier found at Rødøy in Nordland, and four large rock carving sites at Hjemmeluft at Alta, further north, only discovered in 1973. Archaeologists estimate their age to be between 2,500 and 6,000 years.

Jumping ahead to the Bronze Age (1,500-500BC), two corpses have emerged in Denmark, well enough preserved in the bogs for archaeologists to realize they were victims of execution. They are Tollund Man and Grauballe Man, now in Silkeborg and Århus museums in Jylland; like hard, black leather but recognizable as human beings (see p.39). Collections of jewellery, pottery, domestic tools and the like have also come to light in many burial mounds. They are now displayed in several Scandinavian museums, and the collection at Nordiska Museet in Stockholm is particularly good.

By this time, people had come to terms with the sea and their routes extended far, bringing back with them the technology to create bronze and also the skill to work it.

*D*enmark's Grauballe Man was one of two human figures, probably executed around 300BC, which somehow survived in the marshes of Jylland, near Århus. He now graces the Århus Prehistoric Museum.

One of the first to refer to Scandinavia, which he called Outer Thule, was the Roman historian, Tacitus, who visited northern Europe in the first century AD, and wrote of people whom he called *fenni*, later referred to as skiing-hunters.

The Vikings

One reason why Scandinavia's early history is not well-known is that, even in the early centuries AD, very little was documented. Scandinavia came late to Christianity which was not established until the 11th and 12th centuries, and had none of the early scholarship and writings of the monastery and monk. What the Scandinavians did have were the good ships and excellent seamanship which added up to the Viking era. Even this period left few contemporary records to reveal the Viking mind. The Icelandic saga writer, Snorri Sturleson, fine scholar though he was, in recording the

The Viking Ship Museum on Bygdøy (Oslo) has three longships, from around AD 800–900 (above). Viking metalwork at Moesgaard (Århus Prehistoric Museum; right).

The Kalmar Union

sagas and oral histories wrote of the Vikings some 200 years after their era closed.

The first recorded Viking attack was in the 8th century on Lindisfarne Abbey, a treasure house of early Christianity on England's northeast coast. It was plundered and burned 'by vicious barbarians from Outer Thule. So primitive were they, they spared not the library from the torch nor the timid monks from the sword.' That was only a beginning. From then on, for over two centuries, the Vikings rampaged over, traded with, and settled much of the known world.

If the reason for the Viking's sudden outpouring from Scandinavia was a problem of over-population or a curious system of inheritance which drove out all but the eldest son, any danger of too many people was overcome for the next 500 years by the arrival of the Black Death around 1350. Its horrors are immortalized in Sigrid Undset's novel, *Kristin Lavransdatter* and, in Norway alone, estimates vary from the death of one third to one half of the population from the dread disease.

By this time, German merchants, mostly from Hamburg and Lübeck, had created the

Hanseatic League, a model of a monopoly trading group, and had moved into ports and islands all around Scandinavia. From its northernmost port in Bergen, the League controlled Norway's west coast trade as far as Trondheim, and their old wharf is now on the UN World Heritage Site list. Gotland, one of Sweden's east coast islands, owes its fine medieval walls to the League but, at the time, they prospered out of all proportion to the benefits to countries where they traded.

By 1389, there had long been conflict between these emerging nations when Denmark, closest to Europe and the most developed, made the first serious attempt to unite the three countries under the remarkable Queen Margrethe. As wife of King Håkon of Norway and daughter of Denmark's Valdemar Atterdag, with a strong, determined will, she was the person to conclude the Kalmar Union, and ruled as regent for her son, Olav.

The Union lasted some 150 years though with increasing disruption and strife, especially between Denmark and Sweden. Then in 1520, the authoritarian Danish king, Christian II, invited the Swedish nobles to a banquet in Stockholm's Stortorget (Great Square). Christian's men attacked and overcame their unsuspecting guests and chopped off 80 heads, from nobles and bystanders alike. This raised a whirlwind of protest and Gustav Vasa, a young noble fortunate enough to have been in exile in Denmark when his relatives were slaughtered, roused his countrymen. His army drove Christian II out of all but the extreme south of the country, and Sweden proclaimed him king. The Norwegian part of the Union remained under Danish rule for almost another 300 years, a time the Norwegians refer to with resigned cynicism as 'The Four Hundred Year Sleep'.

Some 3km (2 miles) of Visby's medieval walls are still intact today. They are reminders of the times when this old port on the island of Gotland was an important trading post of the German Hanseatic League.

Sweden's Age of Greatness

Gustav Vasa was a formidable ruler who ran Sweden like a family estate and made good use of the Reformation to close monasteries and churches, passing their wealth to the Swedish state. He built castles and fortresses, formed a standing army, initiated political reforms to modernize Sweden and ensured her growing importance as a Baltic power.

His illustrious military descendant, Gustav Adolf, coincided with Denmark's builder-king Christian IV, who kept firm control on all shipping passing through the Kattegat, rebuilt Oslo, renaming it Christiania, and gave his name to several new Norwegian towns, as well as many fine buildings in his Danish kingdom. Christian then determined to regain Danish control over Sweden, but he was no match for Gustav Adolf who defeated the Danes, driving them out of most of southern Sweden. By 1658, Gustav's successors had completed that task.

Known as the Lion of the North, Gustav Adolf also annexed parts of Norway, including the west coast north and south of Gothenburg, and expanded his realm around the Baltic, where Denmark had once held territory as far east as Estonia, and which now gained the nickname 'The

Swedish Pond'. In the Thirty Years War, Gustav Adolf ranged as far as Austria. Who knows where he might have gone, had he not met an early death at Lutzen in 1632.

It is an irony of history that the man who lost most of Gustav Adolf's territory is also hailed as a military genius, and even more of an irony that in the short term he was. Karl XII, Sweden's romantic soldier-king, had courage and military skill but little judgement, rather like Scotland's celebrated Bonnie Prince Charlie. In 1700, Denmark, Poland and Russia all declared war on Sweden. Karl defeated the Russians and broke the alliance, but his subsequent attempts to crush Tsar Peter I met the fate that befell later attacks on Russia by Napoleon and Nazi Germany. Outside the Polish fort of Poltava, in 1709, Karl XII was injured in the foot two days before the Battle of Poltava, which he then directed from a sling between two horses. The Swedes suffered a heavy defeat and Karl retreated to Turkey. He continued to rule Sweden from exile, making a dramatic, swift return across Europe in 1718. In the

THE REGION, ITS HISTORY AND ITS PEOPLE

RISE OF THE ARTS

Sweden remained Scandinavia's dominant 18th-century power in a period of political and democratic development and, later, in a flourish of the arts and sciences. The man responsible for the last two was Gustav III, who encouraged science, theatre, music and opera, and founded the Swedish Academy, based on the French model.

His life ended tragically when he was assassinated at a masked ball by opponents of his gradual return towards autocracy, an episode on which Verdi based his opera *Un Ballo in Maschera*. The Gustavian era struggled on into the 19th century, from 1810 under a new and more democratic constitution.

---

campaign that followed, Karl XII was killed in battle by a mysterious bullet at Fredriksten on the Norwegian border, some say by his own side, eager for home. By 1721, the great Swedish empire had mostly dissolved and her days as a great military power were over.

Napoleon and All Change

Even if it had wanted to, Scandinavia could not escape the next major European upheaval, the Napoleonic wars. In 1801, the British Admiral, Lord Nelson, bombarded Copenhagen, to make sure Napoleon did not get control of the Danish navy. The Duke of Wellington made certain of it in 1807 by again attacking the city and taking over the fleet.

The Swedes, who had opted for the British side, were in turn attacked by Russia, and the result of these wars was a complete change in the Swedish structure. Backed by younger elements in the army who saw it as a means of getting

Napoleon's assistance against Russia, the Swedes picked an unlikely candidate to inherit the Swedish throne, the French Marshall Jean Charles Bernadotte. In 1818, he became King Karl Johan XVI.

The Long Road to Independence

For a long time Norway had been eager to wake up from the 'Four Hundred Year Sleep' and when the Peace of Kiel, which ended the Napoleonic wars, moved Norway from Danish to Swedish overlordship, the fever for independence mounted. In 1814, a constitutional convention of 37 farmers, 16 businessmen and 59 politicians gathered at Eidsvoll, near Lake Mjøsa, and hammered out a constitution.

It was signed on 17 May, now celebrated as National (Constitution) Day. They selected the Danish Prince, Christian Frederik as future king but, as Swedish troops moved over the border, the Norwegians had no chance against superior numbers. Independence had to wait almost a 100 years. Later that year, Karl Johan became king of both countries in an agreement that left the Eidsvoll Constitution in place.

It was never an easy alliance, with constant disputes as the two countries pulled in different directions: over the powers of the king, the Norwegian aim to abolish titles, the use of the Norwegian flag on ships at sea, and the powers of Norway's new-built parliament, the Storting.

Nevertheless, the 19th century saw great expansion in Norway, and a flurry of building in the growing capital, now returned to its old name of Oslo. It also brought about a widening concern for democracy and political representation and a great upsurge in the Norwegian arts. This

*N*orway's Independence *day falls on the 17th of May. Oslo is always a centre of attention.*

Nineteenth-century Scandinavia

The upheavals prior to the 19th century and its first decade did not herald a good time for Scandinavia. All three countries were late in going through an industrial revolution. Even by the 1890s in most areas, some 90 percent of the people still gained their living from the land. Yet farming itself was not prospering, and poverty and lack of opportunity led to massive emigration, most often to North America. Close ties still remain with the many descendants who visit their ancestors' homelands.

Gradually, Scandinavia began to realise her natural assets of sea, for fishing and shipping, waterpower for the start of industry, mines which had operated for centuries, forests and, in Denmark particularly, the potential for modernizing farming, with an emphasis on dairying and the start of the cooperative movement. There was also an inventiveness, from Swedes

was exemplified by the playwright Henrik Ibsen, politician-writer Bjørnstjerne Bjørnson who, among other works, wrote the words for the national anthem, musicians such as Edvard Grieg and the world-famous violinist Ole Bull, a National Romantic movement in art, leading on to Norway's most famous painter Edvard Munch, and sculptor Gustav Vigeland.

The union between Sweden and Norway ended with a whimper in 1905, on the apparently modest issue of Norway's having its own consuls overseas. But that was a cover for a great many more ambitious aims when prime minister Christian Michelsen, led his country to independence, with King Haakon VII (a Danish prince) as monarch.

53

such as Alfred Nobel, whose invention of dynamite was constructive in mining, if the opposite in war, and G.E. Pasch, who invented the safety match. Industrialization also began to bring unrest and the start of both Scandinavia's powerful trade unions and a movement towards general education. The first murmurings of what became social democracy also extended into the areas of land reform, feminism and modern democracy.

Denmark was the only one to experience war in the later 19th century. There had long been a restlessness in the duchies of Schleswig and Holstein, on the neck of land connected to Germany, which encouraged a move to integration with Germany. In mid-century, a small uprising was put down by the Danes but Germany, led by Prussia, used the opportunity in 1864 to overrun not just Schleswig-Holstein but much of Jylland, with support for and against both points of view throughout Europe. The Swedes and Norwegians at first showed Nordic solidarity but the matter dragged to and fro in European diplomatic channels. In the end, Denmark lost both Schleswig and Holstein, and only regained her last remaining Jylland territory in 1920.

World Wars and After

In World War I, the Scandinavian countries were successful in standing clear of the fighting. Though 2,000 Norwegian merchant seamen lost their lives, the three countries continued peacefully, nursing their neutrality, and turning into democratic,

Despite some strident protests, Sweden has made good use of her great rivers. Here, on Dalälven (river), Älvkarleby Power Station has not spoilt the beauty or the salmon fishing.

welfare states. The rise of the Nazis in the 1930s brought some unease and a few Scandinavian supporters, but the countries assumed their neutrality would stand. Denmark and Norway were wrong and Germany invaded both in 1940.

Norway in particular put up a heroic but doomed resistance. Until 1943, Denmark was permitted to retain its own government but, as the war began to turn against Germany, a resistance movement started to bring success by sabotage and the like, and the government resigned. Norway's resistance movement had many successes, such as the sabotage of the Rjukan heavy water plant in Telemark. Young Norwegians used their knowledge of the sea and the inshore islands to escape to Britain, trained in Scotland and then returned on the famous 'Shetland Bus', a perilous boat service between Shetland and Norway, to fight and sabotage again.

As the only one to maintain its neutrality, even today many Swedes feel a sense of guilt, particularly over their government allowing a right of passage to German troops on their way to attack Norway. But it is fair to say that neutral Sweden, as somewhere to escape to, saved many Norwegian and Danish lives. The most celebrated escape was that of over 7,000 Danish Jews, spirited away to Sweden by resistance workers on the eve of their deportation to concentration camps.

After World War II, the Scandinavians continued to follow their aim of becoming comprehensive welfare states and Sweden, in particular, continued the path of social democracy. For only two periods of three years each has Sweden had other than a Social Democrat government in more than half a century. Governments in both Norway and Denmark have been more mixed but the social democratic tradition continues.

The mixture of capitalism and control of industry has proved very successful; the greatest triumph coming to Norway with its discovery of oil in the late 1960s and early 1970s, which made Stavanger Norway's oil capital. As exploration has revealed more and more oil fields, the industry has expanded steadily north, and now, with its ancillary industries, stretches as far as Trondheim. With the additional discovery of huge fields of natural gas, Norway should not only be self-sufficient but should continue as a huge exporter of gas and oil well into the next century.

Denmark has turned her comparative lack of large oil resources to the good, by becoming one of the leaders in developing wind and other forms of alternative energy, and is a strong advocate of environmental protection, with advanced systems of water purification and pollution control.

All three countries have played a big part in the United Nations, providing many troops and medical facilities for peace-keeping forces around the world. Both Norway and Denmark were early members of NATO, but Sweden, strong in the pursuit of its policy of neutrality, did not join. With Iceland and Finland, Scandinavia is also part of the Nordic Council, a cooperative venture in inter-Nordic affairs.

Denmark has been a member of the European Union since 1972, joining at the same time as Britain. During 1994, Sweden and Finland also voted to join, but Norway again voted 'no' to membership. In 1972, Norway voted against joining the Common Market but many expected 1994 to be different. Its energy riches may well have influenced the Norwegian decision, but so too did the importance of the Norwegian fishing and fish-farming industries, the impressive farming lobby, and a strong sense of national identity.

Just the Essentials

There are so many places of interest and delight in Scandinavia's wide open spaces, old cities and small rural communities, often far apart. In one journey, it is better to decide on a main base or bases and cover what is within reasonable distance.

Copenhagen and North-west Sjælland
Copenhagen from harbour and canals
Stroll through Strøget
Tivoli Gardens: entertainment and fun
Roskilde: Viking Ship Museum

South Sjælland and the Islands
Castles and mansions: Gisselfeld, Gavnø Slott
Møns Klint (cliffs) and Elmelunde Kirke
Aalholm Slott and Motor Museum

Fyn and its Archipelago
Odense: Hans Christian Andersen's House and
Den Fynske Landsby (Funen Village)
Tåsinge: Troense and Valdemar Slott

Jylland
Skagen: the artists' village
Århus: Musikhuset, Scandinavian Centre,
Gamle Byen
Legoland: a world in miniature
Ribe: Denmark's oldest town
Wide, white beaches of the west

Oslo and its Surroundings
Karl Johans Gate: Storting (Parliament)
Christiania (old Oslo) and Akershus Slott
Vigeland Park and Munch Museum
Bygdøy and its Museums
Holemnkollen and Tryvannstårnet

The Southland and Telemark
Kristiansund: Dyrepark, Posebyen,
Kardemonne By
Setesdalen: traditional buildings, folk traditions
Lake Mjøsa and Gudbrandsdalen, Maihaugen

Bergen and the Fjords
Vågen, Torget, Bryggen's Hanseatic Museum
Fløyen mountain
Troldhaugen: Grieg's summer home
Gamle Stavanger (Old Stavanger)
Prekestolen: Pulpit Rock in Lysefjorden
'Norway in a Nutshell' tour
Hardanger, Geiranger etc. fjords by boat
Ålesund: Art Nouveau town
Trollstigen (mountain route, near Åndalsnes)

Trondheim and Central Norway
Nidaros Cathedral, Ringve Music Museum,
Tyholt Tårnet
Røros: old mining community
Stiklestad battle site

Towards the Far North
Svartisen Glacier in Nordland
Arctic centre on Arctic Circle
Narvik: mountain railway, war cemeteries
Tromsø: Ishavskatedral(Cathedral), top of
Storsteinen, Northern Lights Planetarium

Finnmark and the Far North
Hjemmeluft, Alta: ancient rock carvings
Hammerfest: Polar Bear Club
Kautokeino Sami Parliament
Nord Kapp (North Cape)
Sami Greek Orthodox Church, Neiden
Kirkenes and Russian border

Stockholm and Old Sweden
Gamla Stan and Riddarholmen
Drottningholm Palace grounds and Theatre
Lake Målaren and its Castles
Uppsala Slott and University
Uppsala: Linneaus Gardens and Museum

The Southland and the Baltic Islands
Malmö: Stortorget, Kulturen etc.
Karlskrona: naval town
Kalmar Slott and Kronan Museum
'Kingdom of Glass': glass workshops
Växjö Utvandranas Hus (emigrants)
Öland island and its bridge
Visby's medieval walls, Gotland

Gothenburg, the West and the Great Lakes
Gothenburg from sea and canals
Gustav Adolfs Torg, and statue
Packhuskajen: vintage ships
Kungsportavenyn and Götaplatsen
Feske Körka: fish market church
Tanum: Bronze Age rock carvings
Smögen or other fishing villages
Trollhättan (Waterfall)
At least a glimpse of the Great Lakes

Dalarna and Central Sweden
Lake Siljan: villages, church boats, folk
traditions and costumes
Anders Zorn and Carl Larsson Museums
Storakopparberget (historic copper mine)
Sonfjället National Park for bears or Grönklitt
Bear Park
Östersund with Frösön on Lake Storsjön

Norrland and the Arctic
Umeå: Gamlia Open Air Museum
Jokkmokk: Áttje Sami Museum
Arjeplog: Silvermuseet and church
At least one Church village (Kirkbyn)
Jukkasjärvi village and church (1609)
Kiruna: Hjalmar Lundbohmsgården (house)
and mine
Lake Torneträsk and Lapporten
Kebnekaise mountain (2,111m; 6,926ft):
Sweden's highest
Abisko Turiststation and National Parks

Going Places with Something Special in Mind

Instead of just coming across places by chance, many people like to travel with intent, following a route that focuses on a particular subject or selecting places of similar interest in different areas. From castles and parks, to sunswept islands and industrial archaeology, these suggestions feature routes and areas, and also reveal fine scenery and additional points of interest along the way. Always remember, particularly in Norway and Sweden, that communities can be far apart and the miles can seem long.

Viking Reminders

Of all things Scandinavian, the Vikings are probably the best-known element. Their sudden explosion out of Scandinavia in the eighth and ninth centuries was one of the most remarkable events in history. This is not so much a route as an indication of where to find the best Danish Viking remains.

*A*t 16th-century *Gisselfeld Slot in South Sjælland, Hans Christian Andersen is supposed to have written* The Ugly Duckling. *The art to be seen there in its grounds today is somewhat more modern.*

1 NATIONAL MUSEUM, COPENHAGEN
The museum has information and finds from all over Denmark (see p.83).

2 VIKINGESKIBSHALLEN (VIKING SHIP MUSEUM), ROSKILDE
The museum has five ships, brought up from Roskilde Fjord and pieced together from thousands of fragments (see p.99).

3 LEJRE
Lejre was a royal seat and archaeologists have revealed Viking and Iron Age settlements (see p.99).
Tingstenene (Thing Stones), between Lejre and Kornerup, are arched stones set in the shape of a ship some 80m (266ft) long.
Lejre Prehistoric Settlement is a reconstructed village used for research.

59

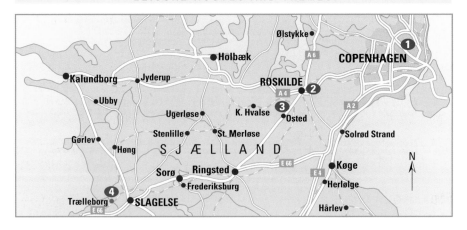

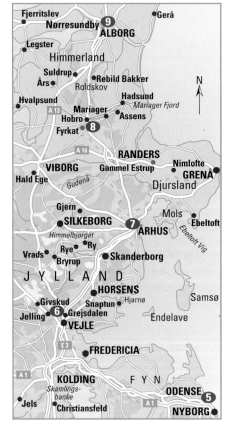

*T*he most feared of men,
The Vikings conquered all before
them, leaving behind many
important relics, which have been
excavated over the years.

5 THE LADBY SHIP, KERTEMINDE, FYN

A Viking chief was buried here in his ship with horses, hunting dogs, jewellery and weapons (see p.119).

6 JELLING, JYLLAND

Jelling is one of the most important Danish sites, a royal seat and the burial place of Viking kings (see p.141).

7 VIKING MUSEUM, ÅRHUS AND PREHISTORIC MUSEUM, MOESGÅRD, JYLLAND

A small **Viking Museum** lies under the Unibank building in central Århus, showing remains unearthed by builders during work on the bank.

The **Prehistoric Museum** at Moesgård has three reconstructed Viking houses and a collection of runic stones (see p.49).

4 TRELLEBORG, SJÆLLAND

Trelleborg was one of a string of strategic Viking ringed forts (see p.107).

8 FYRKAT, HOBRO, JYLLAND

Fyrkat was a fortress camp like Trelleborg, possibly both part of a network built by early Danish kings.

9 LINDHOLM HØJE, LIMFJORDEN, JYLLAND

Europe's largest Viking burial ground, with around 150 ship-shaped stone settings.

Herregård and Slot

There must be more manor houses per square mile in Denmark than almost anywhere else, and more than a few castles as well, some imposing, some comfortable. All the ones listed are open to the public, at least in part, together with their grounds.

These buildings are an important part of Danish history for this democratic modern society was once feudal. Not until the late 18th century were agricultural reforms supported by some estate owners, notably the Reventlow brothers. Their estate, Brahetrolleborg, under Johan Ludvig Reventlow gave its peasants freedom in 1788.

This section is a selection of manor houses and castles in Jylland and South Sjælland. Fyn's manor houses are largely covered in the main Fyn chapter (see p.117). The date given is when the house or castle was first built. Most have been rebuilt.

South Sjælland

South of Copenhagen, the area below a line from Køge to Korsor is particularly rich in castles and manor houses, and the first group are all south of Køge, to the east.

1 VALLØ SLOT (16th-CENTURY)

Destroyed by fire in 1893, but rebuilt soon after. Beautiful gardens and marked trails pass through forest, cliffs and beaches.

Valløby Kirke holds many tombs of the nobility.

2 BREGENTVED (16th to 17th-CENTURY)

Has great copper spires and five impressive avenues leading to the house.

3 GJORSLEV (15th-CENTURY)

Built by the Bishop of Roskilde, it has a unique cruciform shape. The central tower has a fine Gothic hall, occasionally used for concerts.

4 GISSELFELD (16th-CENTURY)

It has a moat and English-style gardens laid out in the 1870s by H.E. Milner. Hans Christian Andersen is said to have written *The Ugly Duckling* here.

5 VEMMETOFTE (18th-CENTURY)

Exhibits baroque and Renaissance styling. It became a home for unmarried gentlewomen, but now also houses married couples. There is an abbey garden, walks and a church.

6 SPARRESHOLM (17th-CENTURY)

Houses a great carriage collection.

Toksværd Kirke has carved tombstones from the 16th century and family pews from 1629.

7 NYSØ (17th-CENTURY)

This building was for 30 years from 1838, a centre for artists and the intelligentsia including Hans Christian Andersen, and Bertel Thorvaldsen who worked in a garden studio here.

8 VORDINGBORG SLOT

Situated in the town of the same name. It is now in ruins (see p.108).

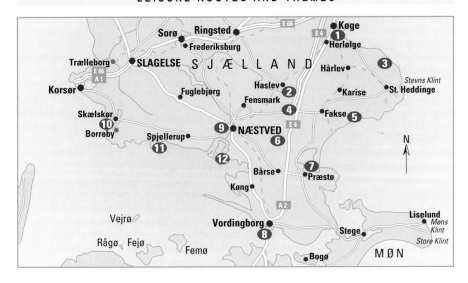

The Danish have always prided themselves on their beautiful manor houses. These selected few are some of the more imposing and have strong historical relevance.

9 HERLUFSHOLM (12th-CENTURY)

This building was for a short time a royal castle but was traded by Frederik II for Frederiksborg. It has been a school since 1565.

10 BORREBY (16th-CENTURY)

Almost unchanged since it was built by Chancellor Johan Fris some 450 years ago.

11 HOLSTEINBORG (16th-CENTURY)

Another castle visited by Hans Christian Andersen. The parkland has avenues of lime trees leading down to the beach.

12 GAVNØ SLOT (15th-CENTURY)

Houses a large private art collection and garden sculptures in wood and stone. The Great Hall has a superb ceiling, and carved door frames (c. 1590).

Queen Margrethe's Kirke is magnificent and reflects Gavnø's early days as a convent.

Jylland

Another good selection of manor houses and castles lies in the north central area of Jylland, largely between Limfjorden and the Lake District.

1 DUEHOLMKLOSTER (15th-CENTURY)

Once an abbey, but has been a manor house since the Reformation.

The Mors Museum has displays featuring the interiors of local churches.

2 VITSKØLKLOSTER

An abbey taken over after the Reformation. There is an interesting garden with medicinal herbs, arranged by diseases.

3 SPOTTRUP (15th-CENTURY)

Built by the See of Viborg but looks baronial with its red brick ramparts surrounded by a double moat.

4 NØRRE-VOSBORG (16th-CENTURY)

This house has been owned by the same family since 1786. The white-painted house with red pantile roofs won a Europa Nostra award in 1982. The 1790 gate is an unusual Dutch model.

5 HERNINGSHOLM (18th-CENTURY)

Well restored and is now used as a museum to the poet Steen Steensen Blicher.

6 TJELE (16th-CENTURY)

A ghost, a Scottish noblewoman of the Montrose family, who married unhappily into the Løvenbalk family wanders here. There is a good carriage collection.

More superbly decorated manor houses. This time illuminating the north central area of Jylland.

7 STOVRINGGÅRD (17th-CENTURY)

Became a home for unmarried gentlewomen in 1747 and there is a graveyard for the ladies to the south of the mansion.

8 HALD (14th-CENTURY)

This place has been rebuilt many times and the estate has many ruins and traces of earlier buildings.

9 FUSSINGØ (18th-CENTURY)

A simple neo-classical style. Its predecessor was built c.1555 on a headland nearby where there are remains of a baroque garden with lime tree avenues and a pond. There are marked trails in the forests.

Ålum Kirke, some 3km (2 miles) away has marble family sarcophagi from 1750, a 1650 sandstone tablet and two carved tombstones from 1568-95.

10 CLAUSHOLM (LATE 17th-CENTURY).

In 1712 King Frederik IV eloped from here with Chancellor Reventlow's daughter, Anna Sophie. She became the only Danish queen of non-royal birth. When he died, she was banished back to Clausholm. The Garden Room has superb

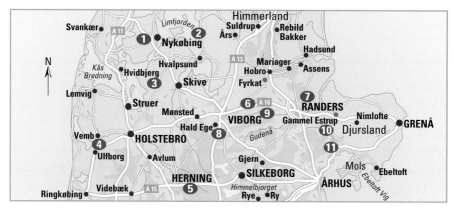

plasterwork, and Queen Anne Sophie's chapel has Denmark's oldest organ, still occasionally used for concerts.

11 ROSENHOLM (16th-CENTURY)

Owned by the Rosenkrantz family for over four centuries. The Great Hall has a well-known painting of Frederik V by Pilo and the Winter Room is decorated with Spanish gilt leather tapestries. There is a chapel and the park has a Renaissance pavilion.

Hornslet Kirke (3 km, 2 miles) away has coats of arms, tombs and paintings of the Rosenkrantz family.

Jylland's Wonderful West Coast

Denmark's beautiful west coast has miles of long white beaches and sand dunes with clumps of marram grass. On many maps this coast is outlined with the thick blue line used to indicate safe, clean bathing beaches – the choice is limitless. The dunes here are thick with summerhouses and campsites. In many places the dunes have shifted and changed the shape of the coast, sometimes turning a fjord into a lake. On some stretches, dykes have been built to stop the sea flooding in, and small communities that were once on the coast have moved inland. One side benefit of these dykes is that they provide lakes and marshes, an ideal habitat for waders and sea birds, and there are nature reserves all the way up coast. Large clumps of planted forest, called *plantage* by the Danes, are also home to wildlife. In many reserves ranger services arrange walks and tours covering birds, mushrooms, flora and fauna, and beaches (ask at tourist offices).

1 HØJER

This place been working to tame the sea since the first floodgate and dykes were built in 1556. **Vidå floodgates** built in 1982 have formed a saltwater lake and there is an exhibition here about Vade-havet and its fauna.

2 RØMØ AND SKÆRBÆK

(See p.145 & 148.)

3 RIBE

(See p.145.)

4 ESBJERG

(See p.143.)

5 VEJERS STRAND, HENNE STRAND TO NYMINDEGAB

Aal Kirke in Oksbøl was built around 1150 with grand murals, including the Knights' Frieze which shows Danish warriors from around 1200.

Varde is a pretty 15th-century town with an amusement park.

Sommerland has 40 activities in a lovely riverside setting.

Varde Miniby is a walk-around scale model of the town as it was around 1800.

Blåberg Plantage is a National Forest (public ground) beside the road from Henne Strand to Nymindegab.

Tipperne is a famed bird sanctuary with geese, swans and duck. It is open on Sundays only.

Skjern Å is a salmon river and has a nature trail known as the Odderstein (otter path).

6 RINGKØBING FJORD TO AGGER

Ringkøbing Fjord

Once open to the sea but the shifting sands reduced the entrance to a narrow channel halfway along the sandhills.

*L*ittered with stunning beaches and breath-taking scenery, the choice of what to do and see on Jylland's west coast is limitless.

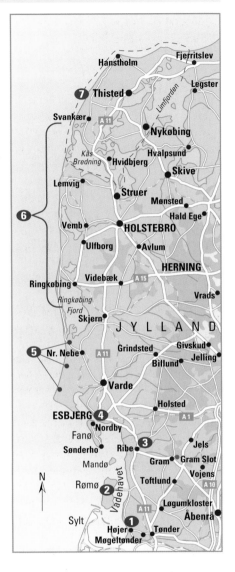

Ringkøbing Port goes back to 1250 and still has much of the feel of the days when it was one of the coast's busiest ports. **Abeline's Farm**, near Håvring, was built in 1871 and is a memory of the life of the people here before it became popular for holidays.

Fiskeriets Hus, near the channel at Hvide Sande, illustrates the history of west coast fishing.

St George **Museum** has finds brought up by divers from the wreck of the *St George* which ran aground in 1811.

Crafts Many of the small communities along this stretch have attracted craft-workers, who have opened workshops and galleries.

Stadil Kirke is one of only two churches which still have 'golden altars' from the 13th century. **Sommerland Amusement Park** is a little further west and has an animal park.

Jens Søndergaards Museum at Ferring was once the summer dwelling of the painter Jens Søndergaard; it is now a museum with 70 of his works.

Lemvig has a beautiful position on a small inlet and offers a strange trail, **Planetstiern** (path of the planets), a tour on foot or bike of the solar system along the edge of the fjord.

Klosterheden, to the south, is the largest planted forest in Denmark.

Thyborøn sees the sand dunes narrow to a ribbon of land from where a ferry takes

around 10 minutes to reach the narrow northern peninsula of Agger Tange.

Agger. Behind the dunes is another area of water which is home to wading birds.

Vestervig Kirke, west of Agger, was an abbey in 1150. It has a rich interior decorated with granite sculpture, and looks across the water to Nissum Bredning, the western entrance to Limfjorden.

7 LIMFJORDEN TO HANSTHOLM

Limfjorden is a fascinating jigsaw with dozens of peninsulas and islands, linked by bridges and ferries. Mors is the largest island with its main town of Nykøbing, but there are also Fur, Livø and Venø all creating a mecca for sailors, and sailing is undoubtedly the best way to explore this area. Struer and Skive are two of the other towns around the fjord, each on its own individual inlet. There is also Thisted and other small settlements and camping sites in this marvellous fjord with its limpid views. The north coast is a long strip of shore, sand dune, marram grass and *plantage* as far as Hirtshals, 133km (100 miles) northeast. The road then continues to Skagen.

Thy

Vorupør is a fishing village on the west coast where the fishermen still drag their boats up onto the beach.

Tvorup Klit Plantage is one of the areas of *plantage* that lie beside the coast road running north to Hantsholm.

Hansted Nature Reserve, north from Vorupør, is a wide heath with birds and other wildlife. It is not open during the birds' breeding season.

Hanstholm is one of Denmark's largest fishing ports with a fleet of modern North Sea trawlers and a ferry to the Faroes.

Vigsø Bugt is a wonderful wide sweep of sea for swimming and surfing.

Vigsø Batteriet (battery) with its huge gun emplacement was one of the fortifications which turned Hanstholm into a fortress during World War II. A bunker is now a museum.

The Viking burial site has around 100 mounds plus several burial stones in the classic ship design.

Hanstholm Lighthouse, built in 1843,

was then the most powerful beacon in the world; it has a panoramic view from the top of its 65m (21ft) tower.

The Lighthouse Museum gives details of the harbour construction, the fishing industry, and the geology and natural history of the area.

Ydby Hede, near Hurup, is a prehistoric burial ground with some 200 barrows and 30 burial mounds on a heather-clad moor, now a conservation area.

Thisted has a core of delightful squares and old houses and is a centre for trade and education.

Thisted Church names the area's earliest known citizen: for those who cannot read the runes he was 'Thor Amdissøn'. There is also a regional museum.

Bygholm Vejlerne, 5km (3 miles) inland from Øsløk, has small lakes and dykes and is a breeding ground for waders and sea birds, with many others resting here on migration.

Mors

Nykøbing is home to the **Morsland Historic Museum** which is situated in Dueholmkloster.

Hansklit is a remarkable cliff 61m (200ft) high, of white clay with layers of black ash from ancient volcanoes.

Jesperhus Blomsterpark, south of Nykøbing, is Scandinavia's largest flower park with some 500,000 plants, bird and butterfly parks.

Venø

Venø can be reached by ferry from Struer and has a tiny church.

South of Limfjorden

Struer is a largely industrial town beside Venø Bugt, looking out to the island of Venø. It has the largest marina on the fjord.

Hjerl Hede, east of Struer, has some of Denmark's finest natural countryside, including a bogland conservation area.

Den Gamle By (Old Village) has a large collection of historical buildings and **Skovbrugsmuseet** (Forestry Museum). **Krabbesholm Manor** (16th-century), at Skive on the Salling peninsula, lies between Krabbesholm Skov (forest) and the fjord, and has long been a Folk High School.

Spottrup Slot has a large collection of amber in the **Skive Museum** and a fine collection of Danish painting and sculpture from 1920 to today.

1 NORWEGIAN FOLK MUSEUM, OSLO (off map)

Bygdøy has an early stave church, built around 1200 at Gol in Hallingdal. It was re-erected on Bygdøy in 1885 and has been extensively restored. There are carved heads on top of the staves and painted choir decorations from 1652.

2 UNIVERSITY MUSEUM OF NATIONAL ANTIQUITIES, OSLO (off map)

The craftsmanship of the early woodcarvers is best seen on doors and doorways. The doorway from Ål Church, pulled down in

Norway's Unique Stave Churches

No other country can claim a church like the Norwegian stave church (*stavkirke*). First built at a time when Norway was moving from Viking paganism to Christianity, many of the 30-or-so still standing go back to the 11th and 12th centuries.

Building involves a system of thick wooden pillars (staves) standing on solid foundations which support the roof. The walls are thick upright wooden planks, and the sloping roofs of the towers and turrets are made of wood shingles. There are Viking dragon heads and other decorations on the roof which have a close affinity with longship decoration. Stave churches have no windows; the dim light filters in through small openings under the roof.

Most stave churches began as simple buildings, with a short nave and narrow shingles. As congregations grew, many became too small and, not appreciating their unique quality, many parishes demolished or extended them.

This section is a guide to finding stave churches. Most lie south of Trondheim.

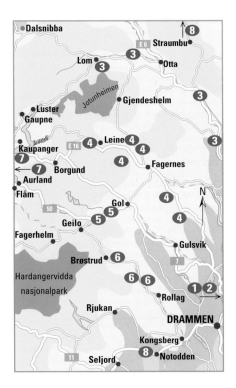

*A*rchitecturally distinct, Norway's stave churches are like no others in form.

1880, has dragons intertwined with foliage and flowers, with lions above.

3 GUBRANDSDAL

The long narrow valleys sweeping north-west from Oslo were the heartland of the stave church.

Garmo Church is now in the Maihaugen Open Air Museum at Lillehammer. It dates from 1021-1030. Pulled down in 1830, its remnants were rediscovered by Anders Sandvig who built the Maihaugen collections.

Ringebu Church from around 1200 is an interesting cruciform shape. It is still a parish church and a venue for summer concerts.

Lom Church has a nave and chancel that date from around 1200. A large church with a fine roof of layers and turrets, with many coloured carvings inside, Lom is a working church.

Vågå Church, at Vågåmo, claims to be the second oldest. Certainly its font comes from 1050.

4 VALDRES

Each of Valdres' six stave churches has some distinctive feature:

Reinli Church started off small but an 11th-century apse was added to the east gable and galleries were built. The 12 consecration crosses on the walls have all survived.

Hedalen Church has a spectacular dragon-shaped porch.

Hegge has a memory of the Norse god Odin: each of the carved heads atop the columns has only one eye.

Lomen Church has a beautiful altarpiece and carved christening font in Romanesque style.

Høre Church, from around 1180, was built by the brothers Eiling and Audun of Kvien, who also built Lomen.

Oye Church, on the eastern bank of Lake Vangmjøsi, was badly damaged in the 18th century and was replaced. In 1935, the materials were found under the floor of the present church and reconstruction was suggested. It was reconsecrated in 1956.

Vang Church was dismantled and sold, and today it stands at Riesengebirge in Silesia, Poland.

5 HALLINGDAL

Hallingdal originally had seven stave churches, but the only one to remain is Torpo.

Torpo Church, not far from Gol, is first mentioned in 1150, and is known for roof decorations more than 700 years old and based on the legend of St. Margaret.

Ål Church, was built when the old stave church was torn down in 1880. It was re-stored in 1959 and the stave tradition was revived using the original altarpiece and parts of the 18th-century chancel. The roof is a faithful copy of the original.

6 NUMEDALEN

Rollar Stave Church is a short way from the main road in an area which also has some *stabbur* (farm storehouses) from the Middle Ages.

Nore and Uvdal churches are of a design once common in Hallingdal incorporating a huge central wooden mast which holds up the structure. In 1655, both churches received ornate decoration in Renaissance and baroque styles, but Uvdal's series of drawings titled *Gunnar in the Den of Vipers* has survived from the 1100s.

7 SOGNEFJORD

Borgund Church, at Lærdal, is wonder-fully ornate, rising in three stages to a tur-reted roof, with crosses and dragons.

Hopperstad Church at Vik, from 1130, is one of the most lavish.

Kaupanger (12th-century), the biggest stave church in Sogn, was painted white in 1862 but has now been restored to its original style.

Urnes Church dates from 1130-1150, but one carved door is at least 100 years older. On the jambs, a four-legged animal is beset by dragons and more dragons battle above.

8 SOUTHERNMOST AND NORTHERNMOST

Heddal Church is one of Norway's most southerly, in Telemark. It is also one of the best-preserved early small stave churches with a beautiful altar and painted walls.

Haltedalen Church is the northernmost, but it has been moved from its original site to the Trøndelag Folk Museum at Sverresborg, on the outskirts of Trondheim.

Castles and Great Houses of Lake Mälaren and Uppland

Sweden had its birth around Stockholm's great waterway, Lake Mälaren, and the ancient town of Uppsala in Uppland, an hour north. The happy result is the most concentrated collection of old castles, palaces and great houses anywhere in Sweden.

1 KUNGLIGA SLOTTET

The Royal Palace has 608 rooms with many suites open to the public including Oskar II's writing room. The Crown Jewels are in the Royal Treasury, there is the Royal Armoury and a daily Changing of the Guard.

2 GUSTAV III'S PAVILION

The pavilion was built in Haga Park as a retreat by Gustav III who founded the Swedish arts. It has marvellous interiors and the park has the Copper Tents and a butterfly house.

3 ROSENDALS SLOTT

This castle was built by King Karl XIV Johan for his queen. The ornate Empire interiors have been virtually untouched since his early 19th-century reign.

4 ULRIKSDAL

This 350-year-old building was last used by King Gustav VI Adolf and Queen Louise (the present king's parents) between 1923 and 1973. It has fine antiques in beautiful apartments and the grounds overlook the bay.

Confidencen, Sweden's oldest theatre, holds concerts, plays and opera performances here.

5 WALDERMARSUDDE

This was home to the painter-prince Eugen, and has some of his paintings and a wide collection of Nordic art. Set in a fine park, it also has flower gardens with sculpture.

Uppsala and Uppland

6 UPPSALA SLOTT

Gustav Vasa began this castle in the 16th century. King Gustav Adolf was crowned here and his daughter, Queen Kristina, abdicated from here.

The **National Archives** are held at the castle along with the Vasa Vignettes and a historical wax museum.

7 VIKS SLOTT

This is one of Sweden's best-preserved

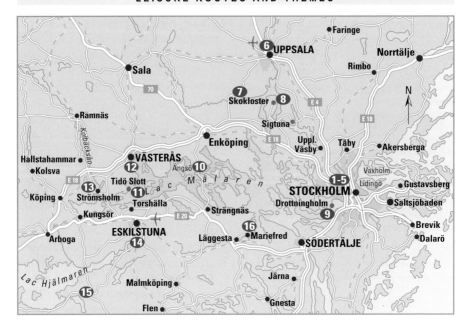

medieval castles, later modernized inside with a sculpted main entrance added.

8 SKOKLOSTER

Set among lakes, this imposing white baroque house was the family seat of the Wrangles who once ruled much of Scandinavia.

There is a collection of 17th-century weapons and a motor museum.

Around the Lake

9 DROTTNINGHOLM SLOTT

On Lövon, Drottningholm was the royal family's summer palace and is now their permanent home.

The **gardens'** superb formality gives them the nickname of 'Versailles-in-miniature', with the smaller Chinese Palace as Grand Trianon.

Drottningholm Court Theatre is a perfectly preserved 18th-century theatre, made famous by Gustav III and still in use.

*L*ake Mälaren is the focal point for many of the castles and large houses around Stockholm. Further north the Uppland region also provides a great selection of old castles and palaces.

10 ÄNGSÖ SLOTT

This island castle is first mentioned in 1185 and was built in Swedish rococo style.

There is a **Rural Life Centre** with tours of old farms and meadows. There is also a campsite, fishing and good swimming.

11 TIDÖ SLOTT

Tidö was the 17th-century home of Gustav II Adolf's great chancellor, Axel Oxenstierna (later Regent to Gustav's daughter Kristina), with magnificent state apartments.

A **toy museum** has 35,000 exhibits; there is a large deer park and a nature reserve.

70

12 VÄSTERÅS SLOTT

The original 13th-century building was a sheriff's mansion and a county prison. The 18th-century interior now holds a governor's residence and the **Västmanland's Museum**.

13 STRÖMSHOLM SLOTT

Strömsholm was a 17th-century royal residence. Open in summer only, it has royal furniture and a portrait gallery which holds a famous series of horse paintings by David Klöcker Ehrenstrahl.

In the grounds is a **riding centre** and a **carriage museum**.

14 SUNDBYHOLM SLOTT

This 17th-century castle is now a restaurant and hotel. It is a short walk through beautiful beech woods to fine prehistoric carving at Sigurdsristningen.

15 JULITA HERREGÅRD

Julita was a monastery in the early Middle Ages, a private home until 1941 and is now a **Museum of Cultural History** with parks and gardens, and estate houses.

16 GRIPSHOLM SLOTT

This is another great Gustav Vasa castle, famed for its royal portraits and with a theatre that goes back to Gustav III.

The Kingdom of Glass

The best of Sweden's world-famous glass comes from Småland, in the southeast of the country. Gustav Vasa introduced Bohemian glassblowers to Sweden but it was 200 years later, in 1742, when Anders Koskull and Georg Bogislaus Stael von Holstein, who became governors of Småland, set up the first glassworks. The site was ideal with deep forests to feed the furnaces and a need for the local people to supplement their crofting income.

Today, 16 of Sweden's most famous glassworks lie in the area between Kalmar on the coast and Växjö to the west, led by Orrefors and Kosta Boda. Starting and returning to Kalmar, this route covers them all. Several have museums and exhibitions; most have shops, often with bargains. There are also two or three smaller glass studios, plus engraving and glass-painting workshops.

1 NYBRO

Nybro was founded in 1935 and makes largely ornamental and household glass, specializing in pressed, cast and centrifugal techniques.

2 PUKEBERG

This is a typical old glassworks, dating from 1871, where 25 enthusiasts make glass by hand. Pukeberg glass is prized for its finely forged surface, using a special method – a big secret!

*S*weden is famed for it's glass-making, here you can find a list of the most prodigious and significant glasswork factories.

71

3 BODA

Founded in 1864, Boda is now part of Kosta. There are 73 workers in a traditional environment with a number of craft shops. Specialities are bowls and vases by Monika Backström and Kjell Engman. Boda pressed-glass vases are prized.

4 JOHANSFORS

This glassworks is also part of Kosta Boda, with 60 workers largely making stemware. A **Crystal Museum** has fine early 20th-century pieces.

5 ÅFORS

Åfors is also now part of Kosta Boda. The 75 workers here cast glass in sand and are famous for glassware designed by Bertil Vallien and Ulrika Hudman-Vallien with exciting designs and colours.

6 SEA

Formed in 1956, Sea is part of Orrefors. The 50 workers mainly blow ornamental and gift glassware in a 'frosted' form. Sea's speciality, nevertheless, is a clear glass oil lamp.

7 KOSTA

This is Småland's oldest glassworks, founded in 1742. Its name is a combination of the first syllables of the surnames of its governor-founders. The main Kosta Boda glassworks, it has 325 workers making a range of crystal glass, stemware and ornamental glass.

The **Old Kosta Museum** features 18th- and 19th-century glass as well as contemporary work.

8 ORREFORS

Orrefors was founded in 1883 and has 383 workers. Their hallmark is heavy cut crystal, best known through the work of two world-famous designers, Simon Gate and Edward Hald.

A big, bright **museum** shows three eras of Orrefors design.

9 MÅLERÅS

Designer Mats Jonasson has left his mark on this glassworks, founded in 1888, which now has 70 employees. Collaboration with the Worldwide Fund for Nature has led to beautiful crystal reliefs showing threatened species.

10 ÄLGHULT

Part of Orrefors, the 1876 glassworks mainly produces stemware and restaurant glass such as popular wine-tasting glasses. The unique glass elk (*älg* means elk) is only produced by a masterblower.

11 ROSDALA

The 45 workers make lighting glass both for ceiling and wall lamps. The Strindberg lamp is named after the distinguished playwright.

There is a **glass museum** here.

12 LINDSHAMMAR

Lindshammar was founded in 1905 and is nicknamed the 'coloured glassworks' because of its unusual coloured glass.

Recently, Lindshammar has turned to making lamps and its **museum** traces these changes.

13 ENERYDA

Another 1956 glassworks, with 12 employees, Eneryda is best known for handmade glass figures, usually of animals, and for ornamental and cut glass in general.

14 SANDVIK

Part of Orrefors, Sandvik's 156 workers have been producing its renowned and beautiful stemware since 1917.

15 BERGDALA

Bergdala has 15 workers who blow glass in a true glassworks atmosphere with a fine little inn next door. Bergdala specializes in stemware and ornamental glass, and is best known for its 'buttermilk bowl' which has a characteristic blue rim.

16 SKRUF

Skruf glassworks is known for its unusual water barometer, based on an 18th-century model, and one of the items made by its 17 glassworkers.

Founded in 1897, it also has an appealing **Crystal Museum**.

Industrial Archaeology from Bergslagen to Dalarna

Wherever Swedish place names end in suffixes such as *gruva* or *berg*, you can be sure that this is, or was, a mining area. *Hytta* usually denotes the workshops where ore was processed. Many lie in the mountainous Bergslagen district, covering parts of Västmanland, Dalarna and Värmland. Iron was the main ore but miners also sought copper and silver.

With forests for fuel, fast rivers for power and lakes to the south for transport, from the 16th century, Bergslagen's mines and forges laid the foundations of Sweden's prosperity. Yet so vast and spread out is Bergslagen that mining has not damaged its beauty. A tour gives a chance to see this, as well as the way of life of this hard-working area. The route starts at Örebro, at the western end of Lake Hjälmaren, just west of Mälaren, on the edge of the Bergslagen district and ends in Dalarna, where folk traditions and customs continue.

1 ÖREBRO

Örebro is a commercial centre on the Närke plateau with a fine 13th-century castle where Jean Bernadotte was elected King of Sweden.

The Wadköping area has preserved old Örebro with a number of craft workshops and an old shop, as well as a restored railway and station.

2 PERSHYTTAN

There is an iron foundry here and roots going back to the Middle Ages, with an enormous waterwheel ceaselessly turning.

3 NORA

Nora has some well-preserved wooden houses where 19th-century steelworkers lived; it is now an idyllic small town on Lake Nora.

4 SIGGEBOHYTTAN

On Lake Usken, Siggebohyttan was once the home of a wealthy mining family.

*I*ndustrial archaeology is widespread throughout Sweden. This tour shows the various types of industry that were prevalent many years ago.

5 STÅSSA GRUVOR

Visitors to this old mine can go 182m (600ft) underground in an original mine train.

6 LÖA

The ironworks show how iron was melted down and processed in the old days. Post-industrial Löa is a typical Bergslagen village of wooden houses painted rust-red.

7 KOPPARBERG

Visitors can join fascinating mineral-hunts led by an expert mineralogist with visits to quarries, mineral deposits and a mine.

West of Kopparberg, the road to Filipstad also offers interesting sites.

8 FINNSTIGEN

The Finns' Trail shows what life was like for Bergslagen's rough and tough 16th-century settlers, many of them Finns, on a trail taking in six historic sites.

*D*alarna and it's surrounding area provides anyone with an interest in trade an insight into both latter and modern day industry.

9 GRYHYTTAN

The 17th-century inn, Gästgivarigården, is an architectural gem, famed for its food and historic wine cellars, and with an unusual herb garden; it offers another chance to see how the mining magnates lived. There is also a beautiful red-shingled church with fine old paintings.

10 FILIPSTAD

This was once a major centre for processing iron ore in the area. Storbrohyttan is an old forge, restored and on display.

11 LUDVIKA AND SMEDJEBACKEN

These two towns in Dalarna now have modern hi-tech industries but have long been closely associated with iron. **Flogberget Gruva** from the 17th century,

has deep open-cast mines open to visitors, who can also tackle underground shafts. **Luddvika Gammelgård and Mining Museum** is a 16th-century master miner's house on its original site with a good collection of mining artefacts and buildings. **Flatenborg Foundry Museum** at Smedjebacken is on the site of a 400-year-old iron foundry.

12 FALUN

The great copper mine of Storakopparberg has operated for a thousand years, peaking in the 17th century. In boots, overalls and a helmet, the guided walk gives an insight into the hard life of the early miners.

Stora Museum tells the history of the mine with mineral displays and models, and an important collection of Swedish coins.

*D*enmark is a beautiful, fertile and gently rolling country with neat farms and superb white beaches, particularly on the west coast where marram grass covers the dunes with a delicate green. Copenhagen and Denmark's other main cities, Odense, Århus and Aarlborg, are full of elegant buildings, old and new, their interiors alive with examples of Danish skill in design. In these cities the motor car has largely been banished and walking is again a pleasure. This small country has infinite variety, but nowhere calls for a long journey and the new bridge across Store Bjælt will link Copenhagen to the island of Fyn, and thus on to the Jylland peninsula, bringing the country even closer together. Yet, with a population of only five million, Denmark is not crowded. Whether it be in the great orchards of Fyn, the wonderful light and the lakes of Jylland, the inns above small harbours, or the lively squares and streets of Copenhagen, Denmark is a place where people enjoy themselves.

Nyhavn, Copenhagen

DENMARK

Home of the Little Mermaid

'Wonderful, wonderful Copenhagen …' so goes the song, and there is something very special about Copenhagen that is not always easy to define. Perhaps it is the buzz of people going about their lives with an air of almost light-heartedness, or the green shade of its summer trees in the squares and streets where people congregate. There is the attraction of the waterways through the city, and the interest of a busy harbour too. To the north, Copenhagen seems to spread naturally into the countryside and the lovely northern coast. Here are castles and great houses, and, in contrast, little harbours and small villages. Some come south to here by ferry from Malmö, in Sweden. This is the main ferry from Sweden, and soon there will be a bridge here also.

Copenhagen

There is nothing that Copenhageners like more than sitting at a well-prepared dining table, unless it be sitting at a table outside. All over the summer city, the squares and lanes are full of people at pavement restaurants and cafés, enjoying a meal, drinking coffee, beer, or *aquavit* if it is a celebration. There they can relax, in good company, watching the world go by.

Denmark has a selection of fine old Royal castles, many built by, and named after Christian IV. Christiansborg Slot in Copenhagen now seats the Danish Parliament.

Copenhagen is both the most laid-back and the liveliest of the three Scandinavian capitals. Like Denmark itself, it is a neat, tidy, well-ordered city, yet one that buzzes with work and play.

At night, there are dozens of restaurants where the food is excellent. Danes claim the best Scandinavian food and few who have supped at a lavish cold table would disagree. It is also a city which loves music, especially jazz and bands, but also pop and folk, so music clubs and cafés proliferate.

In common with the other Scandinavian capitals, Copenhagen is never far from water. Be it sea, canal or lake, water is always close to the jumble of cobbled streets, modern thoroughfares and quiet courtyards, made beautiful with plants and garden furniture.

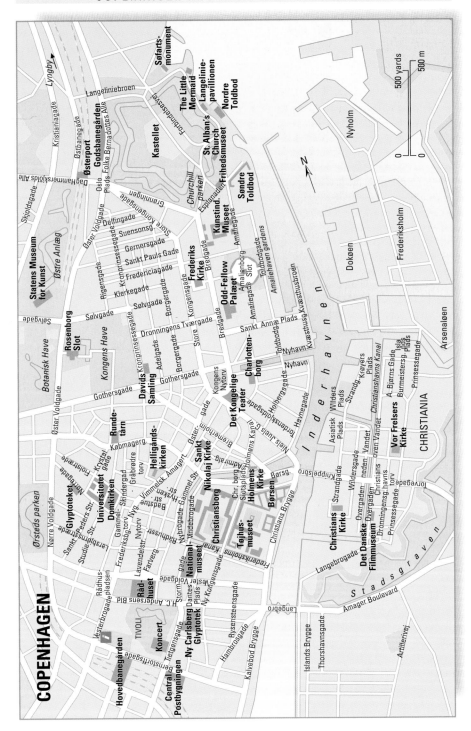

Copenhagen's widespread streets and narrow byways, along with its harbours, parks, and lakes, give a fine view from a convenient rooftop. This is the view from the SAS Royal Hotel, also a good place for a nightcap!

The first thing that most visitors notice is that Copenhagen has made friends with its traffic. It has a judicious mixture of vehicle-free streets, an addiction to the bicycle and excellent public transport system that has largely restored Copenhagen to a city where it is a pleasure to walk. A local train, the S-tog, which sometimes runs underground in the city and serves outside Copenhagen, also helps.

Copenhagen was not Denmark's first capital. That was Roskilde, some 35km (25 miles) to the west. Before the 12th century, what became Copenhagen was no more than a fishing hamlet, named Havn, a link between Sjælland and Scania (now Sweden's Skåne) across the Øresund, at the time part of Denmark. This made Havn a good choice when in 1167AD King Valdemar I ordered Bishop Absalon to found the city as a protection against Wendel pirates. Absalon built his first bastion where Christiansborg Slot, now the Danish Parliament, stands today, on Slotsholmen, an island by the harbour. In Højbro Plads, Absalon's statue looks down to where his city began. Copenhagen became the capital in 1416 but it was Christian IV, Denmark's *roi soleil* and a great royal builder, who was responsible for many of its most notable buildings.

Copenhagen has not had a quiet history. Crossing the ice from Skåne, the Swedes besieged the city in the 17th century (see p.50). Though they did not capture the city, in the treaty that followed, Denmark handed Skåne, Blekinge and Halland back to Sweden, and Copenhagen became a capital on the far eastern side of its territory.

The 18th century brought two devastating fires which blazed through the wooden medieval houses and, during the Napoleonic Wars in the early 1800s, the city was twice bombarded by the British under Admiral Lord Nelson. It was occupied by Germany during World War II. Yet curiously little of these tempestuous times is obvious in today's relaxed city.

The open-topped waterboats, which leave from Gammel Strand, just opposite Slotsholmen's fine buildings, or from Nyhavn to the northeast, are the best way to get an impression of Copenhagen past and

One of the sightseeing boats that tours the city's canals and harbours is a fine way to get the feel of Copenhagen, a city based on the sea.

TOURS IN AND AROUND COPENHAGEN

By boat: Boat tours of Copenhagen's canals, harbour and waterside leave from Gammel Strand and Nyhavn every half hour in July and August, with or without a guide. Netto boats leave from Holmens Kirke between 10am and 5pm from May to mid-September.

On foot: Guides lead Walking Tours all year in Danish and in English during July and August. Details from the Tourist Information Office.

Brewery tours: Both Tuborg and Carlsberg breweries conduct tours Monday to Friday (closed holidays, Christmas and New Year). **Tuborg**: 10am and 12.30, groups of minimum 10 only, with pre-booking. **Carlsberg**: 11am and 2pm individuals. Groups require pre-booking.

By coach: In and around Copenhagen, and as far as Odense and Legoland in summer. Starting from Lur Blowers' Statue, Rådhuspladsen. Details from the Tourist Information Office.

By train: DBS train tours 'On Your Own By Train' to Louisiana, Legoland and Round-the-Sound. Enquire at the station and at Copenhagen hotels.

present. The boats move gently along the canals, under the bridges and out into the harbour, with the city all around; wharves, warehouses, some now converted to hotels, cruise ships and Danish naval vessels. At the quays, ferries load and unload for Malmö in Sweden, and Oslo. Amalienborg, the royal palace, is set in a beautiful square not far from the water, as are the head-quarters of the Royal Danish Navy. Vor Frelsers Kirke (Our Saviour's Church) with its curious outside spiral staircase is a fea-ture of the waterfront, and, of course, there is the Little Mermaid, an enduring symbol of Copenhagen.

Strolling in Central Copenhagen

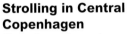

Copenhagen's main artery is **Strøget**, made up of five pedestrian ways, with shops of all sizes, cellar galleries and restaurants, craft workshops, buskers and street vendors by the dozen.

Starting at Rådhuspladsen, Copen-hagen's central square, Strøget heads east along a series of pedestrian streets to Kon-gens Nytorv, at the inner end of Nyhavn.

The square is dominated by the **Rådhuset** (Town Hall) in traditional red brick, re-flecting the national romantic style of the early 20th century, and leaning heavily on Nordic mythology. It has a tower and a relief of the city's founder, Bishop Absa-lon, official function rooms and council chambers. The World Clock is to be found

*R*ådhuset *(the Town Hall), built in redbrick, reflects the National Romantic style of the early 20th century. It is famous for its World Clock, and Bishop Absalon's statue.*

81

here too. The brainchild of Jens Olsen, it gives such details as the position of the planets and times around the world. A guided tour of the 105m (350ft) tower gives a panoramic view right across to Sweden.

In front of Rådhuset is a statue of Denmark's best-loved writer **Hans Christian Andersen** and, at Vester Voldgade to the northeast, is the **Lur Blowers Column** (showing musicians playing these ancient instruments), the starting point for sightseeing coaches. On the opposite side, a statue of a Danish soldier commemorates Denmark's 19th-century wars in which it lost not only Slesvig-Holstein but much of Jylland to Germany.

Frederiksberggade is the first of Strøget's pedestrian streets; the first double square of Gammeltorv and Nytorv has a fine fountain, popular with youngsters on the Queen's birthday on 16th April, when it spouts golden apples. Nytorv was the site of the old City Hall, and this area was the centre of the medieval town. All along Strøget, with its shady green trees, the side roads are full of old and interesting buildings, many with courtyards and quiet squares.

Amagertorv is the widest part of the street, with the 1730 **Helligaandskirken** (Church of the Holy Ghost), part of which dates from the 14th century, in its own garden behind a wrought iron railing. In addition to the department store, Illums Bolighus, which makes a feature of good design, specialist shops include Royal Copenhagen porcelain, Holmegaard glass, Georg Jensen silver, and some good clothes shops. The next stop is the **Stork Fountain**, a popular gathering place, particularly with musicians and young people. To the south, the statue of Bishop Absalon on horseback looks down Højbro Plads, where his city began (see p.79).

Following **Østergade** it would be hard to miss the towering spire of **Skt Nikolai Kirke**. It is now a venue for changing exhibitions and has a restaurant.

Strøget ends in the magnificence of Kongens Nytorv. Here is **Det Kongelige Teater** (Royal Theatre), the home of Danish opera and ballet, as well as drama. The Danish Royal Ballet is one of the world's great companies with a vast repertoire from classical to modern. Close by is **Charlottenborg**, the Danish Academy of Fine Arts, with **Charlottenborg Kunstudstilling** showing changing exhibitions by Danish artists. The figure on horseback in the centre is Charles V. To the south is the start of Nyhavn Canal with its old-time sailing ships and busy outdoor life.

In front of Rådhuset is the statue of Denmark's famous, Hans Christian Andersen. Born and brought up in Århus, he also worked and lived in Copenhagen.

*S*trøget, Copenhagen's great pedestrian street, was one of the first to become a walking-only street in Europe. It is lined with an assortment of cafés and shops.

Slotsholmen and Christianshavn

Slotsholmen is an island for walking, with a cluster of interesting buildings in one small area. **Folketinget** (Parliament) in Christiansborg Slot, is an impressive building on the site of Absalon's 12th-century fortress. These remains, and those of a medieval castle, have been excavated and are now open to visitors, as are Parliament and the Royal Reception Chambers. Near the castle, **Thorvaldsen's Museum** is devoted to works by the sculptor Bertel Thorvaldsen, who worked in Rome for most of his life. The outside frieze shows his triumphant return to Denmark.

Close together are the **Theatre History Museum** in the Royal Court Theatre of 1766 and, next door, the **Royal Stables** has a marvellous display of old vehicles used by the Danish monarchy from 1776. Across the street **Tøjhus Museet** (Royal Armoury) displays old weapons in a unique 230m (600ft) hall. The Marble Bridge over Frederiksholms Canal leads to the **National Museum** which has a particularly fine display of Viking finds. There are illustrations, diagrams and models, demonstrating that the Vikings were more than mere killers and conquerors: they were also successful shipbuilders, sailors, traders and settlers (see p.48).

King Christian IV was the inspiration behind the beautiful Renaissance **Børsen** (Stock Exchange), at the east end of the island, with gables, steep roofs and tiny windows, and four dragons forming the spire. Unfortunately it is not open to the public. Overlooking Christians Brygge is **Det Kongelige Bibliotek** (Royal Library) the country's largest collection of books, manuscripts and newspapers. The quays look across to the old district of **Christianshavn**, originally built by Christian IV.

Not so long ago, Christianshavn was a rundown district, but it has now become fashionable, with the restoration of old merchant houses, warehouses and other buildings, such as Gammel Dok, which is now the **Danish Centre for Architecture**. The dockside itself is popular in summer for an outdoor beer or coffee. Here too is Christiania, Copenhagen's 'free suburb', set up in the 1970s. The green, copper spire and the red brick of **Vor Frelsers Kirke** with its outside spiral stair, dominates Christianshavn. The view from the top and from the staircase is worth the climb.

Cathedral, University and the Latin Quarter

The easiest starting point from Strøget is to take Norregade from Gammeltorv. The first building is the 19th-century **Vor Frue Kirke**, Copenhagen's cathedral. This has been a holy place since the 12th century when it is said Bishop Absalon built a chapel here. Inside, particularly interesting are Thorvaldsen's marble sculptures of Christ and the Apostles. Close by, on the corner of Norregade, Bispegården (Bishop's Residence) from 1500 is now part of the university, and on Bispetorvet stands the 1943 monument marking the 400th anniversary of the Reformation.

Today, many university departments have moved away from the centre but, a little further north on Norregade, there is the main building of Københavns Universitet from the 15th century. On the right, in Krystalgade, is the **Synagogue**, consecrated in 1883, which holds a daily service. Opposite, the **Central Library** is, among many other things, a source of foreign newspapers and books.

To the right in Købmagergade, Christian IV built **Rundetårn** as an observatory. To reach the top is a test of fitness; a steep circling cobbled ramp inside the building climbs some 180m (600ft). It is said that the Russian Tsar, Peter the Great, once rode his horse up here, followed by the Tsarina in a horse-drawn carriage. As the architect of much of this city and of many others in his extensive territories, Christian IV was so meticulous about good workmanship that it is said he carried a ruler to check the masons' measurements. Rundetårn serves as the tower of **Trinitatis Kirke** next door, which also merits a visit. Further south on the same street, is **Museum Erotica**, a newish museum tracing the history of eroticism in words, pictures, film and tableaux.

The area of small streets between the Cathedral, Krystalgade, Rundetårnet and Strøget, once much used by students, is Copenhagen's so-called Latin quarter. It centres on the idyllic Gråbrødretorv, lined with beautiful 18th-century houses, all with different coloured façades. There are still some student houses here among the lovely old buildings, together with many second-hand bookshops and antique dealers, particularly along Fiolstræde and the surrounding streets. Not far from Heligaandskirke, north of Amagertorv in Valkendorffsgade, are the **Legetøjs-museet** (Toy Museum), which shows how children played between 1840 and 1930, and the **P og T Museum** which describes the history of Denmark's post and telegraph services when they depended on horse and man.

Kongens Nytorv to the Little Mermaid

On a lovely summer afternoon, the sides of Nyhavn are packed with people watching others working on their boats, eating one of Denmark's superb ice creams, sitting under

*H*otel Nyhavn 71, close
to the harbour, was once a
warehouse. Like the Hotel Admiral
nearby, it was converted into a fine
hotel, with some intriguing rooms
close to the roof where the porters
of old hauled up the cargoes.

big umbrellas at outdoor tables and enjoying the sun. The large anchor at the start of
the canal commemorates Danish seamen
who died in World War II, and there is also
a canal boat tour terminus here. Nearer the
sea, there is a good view of Christianshavn
and Vor Frelsers Kirke across the water.

Though the south side was always more
respectable, Nyhavn was once something
of a red-light district for seamen from faraway lands, with many sailors' bars and
a rowdy nightlife. One amusing leftover
from that time is the gaudy decoration outside Nyhavn's best-known tattooing
shop; Tato-Bob still offers the service. Today, everything is much more sedate
though the bars and restaurants built into
the well-preserved 18th-century houses do
a hectic trade. Hans Christian Andersen
once lived in Nyhavn and it is once again
a fashionable place to have an apartment.

Near the harbour is **71 Nyhavn**, one of
a couple of city hotels (the other is the **Admiral** not far away) beautifully converted
from old warehouses. Behind the hotel is
the dock for ferries sailing for Malmö and
Rønne. Further along, on the seaward side
 of Amalienborg Palace, are the beautiful
Amalie Gardens, designed by the Belgian
architect Jean Delogne; an inviting place
in which to wander and relax.

From the harbour, Skt Annæ Plads leads
into Fredriksstaden, northeast of Kongens

Nytorv. This area developed in the 18th
century when Copenhagen's nobility and
the well-to-do decided to forsake the jumble of narrow medieval lanes and build elegant houses along wide streets. On to
Amaliegade, where an archway leads into
the square of **Amalienborg Palace**. Since
1794, this has been the principal royal residence, with four identical rococo buildings
arranged harmoniously around a statue of
King Frederik V on horseback. The interior
is not open to the public but when the royal

*T*his statue of Frederick V of Denmark is the centrepiece of the square around which the Royal Amalienborg Palace stands. When the Royal Family are in residence, a popular spectacle is the changing of the Royal Guard, (inset) who first march through the streets, led by the Royal Band. In their immaculate uniforms and bearskins, they make a fine sight.

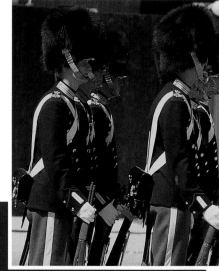

family is in residence, the Royal Guard and Band march from their barracks near Rosenborg Slot through the city for the Changing of the Guard ceremony at noon; a spectacular occasion with up to 70 guardsmen in black bearskins and dress uniforms.

Leaving the palace square by Frederiksgade, into Bredgade, opposite is **Marmorkirken** (Marble Church), with a dome that seems almost too big for the walls. Nearby are the exotic onion domes of the **Alexander Nevski Russian Orthodox Church**, with some interesting icons, and the **Museum of Decorative and Applied Arts**. A detour west from Marmorkirken, to Store Kongensgade, leads to a unique naval area. Built as long ago as 1638, the long rows of neat, yellow houses were designed

86

HERRENS·ORD·BLIVER·EVINDELIG

*M*armorkirken *(Marble Church – originally called Frederik-skirke) was meant to be the centrepiece of the 18th-century suburb, Frederikstad, but the King ran out of money, and the church was only completed in 1870. Inside, the huge dome is some 30m (90ft) in diameter.*

for naval personnel and are still used by naval staff and retired officers. With trees and shrubs between the rows of houses, it makes a calm oasis in the middle of the city.

To the north, Bredgade leads on to **Churchill Parken**, named after Britain's wartime prime minister, and thick with daffodils each spring. Here too is the 19th-century **St Alban's Anglican Church**, which has a very Church-of-England atmosphere. Before going into **Danmarks Frihedsmuseet**, (Danish Resistance Museum), have a look at **Kastellet**, one of Christian IV's defensive forts, with two rings of moats and set in parkland just north of Churchill Parken. Some of the old fort is still in use by the army, including the church, prison and guardhouse. There is also an old windmill.

The **Resistance Museum** has gathered in many mementoes and remembrances of one of Denmark's most difficult periods, between 1940 and 1945. It has researched records of passive resistance, sabotage, parachute drops, cooperation with the Allies, the rescue of Danish Jews, protests and more, to give an evocative picture of the achievements and the sorrows of the time.

From here, there are signposts to *Langelinie*, down by the waterside walk which on Sundays is thronged with promenading Danes, and here at last is Copenhagen's most famous statue, the **Little Mermaid,** who always seems smaller than one expects. Ignoring the crowds and the sightseeing boats, she gazes out steadily over the water.

*T*he *Little Mermaid, one of the many creations by Hans Andersen, must be Copenhagen's most famous statue. The best view you will get is from a boat.*

88

Tivoli and Other Parks

To many visitors, Copenhagen and Tivoli are synonymous, and the gardens must be the city's best known asset worldwide. **Tivoli Gardens** were laid out in 1843 by Georg Carstensen, a Danish architect, who persuaded King Christian VIII that if his people were well entertained, they were less likely to be interested in politics and sedition! In a comparatively short season from May to September, over four million people come through the gates on Vesterbrogade. In recent years Tivoli has been opening for a short season before and over Christmas.

There are beautiful flowers, shrubs and tree-lined walks which complement the rides, stalls, restaurants, inns and entertainments, making Tivoli a place of beauty. For many people it is the young musicians of the Tivoli Guard, a junior version of the Royal Guard, marching and playing through the park, who make the evenings special. Tivoli is at its best when the sky darkens and the fairy lights illuminate the trees and make dazzling reflections in the lakes. On weekends, the festivities end with fireworks sparkling over the water.

Tivoli is much more than just an amusement park. It attracts international artistes of all sorts, with classical concerts as well as jazz and light music. By the Tivoli entrance on Vesterbrogade is the **Museum of Holography**, the biggest collection of

*T*ivoli Gardens are high on the list for visitors and the people of Copenhagen (below). The Pantomime Theatre, is Tivoli's oldest from 1874. Tivoli is just as beautiful by night with hundreds of lights showering the lake (right).

holograms in Europe. On the northeastern side of the park (H.C. Andersens Boulevard) opposite Rådhuspladsen, is the **Tivoli Museum** telling its 150-year history and, just outside the southern end of the park, **Ny Carlsberg Glyptotek** is an elaborate building with a fine collection of French sculpture, works by Degas, Gaugin and other Impressionists, Egyptian sculpture (with a famous hippopotamus),

*T*ivoli has so much more than any amusement park. There is a
wonderful funfair, with exciting rides and stalls; a theatre and music for
everyone's taste, from classical to jazz and rock; beautiful gardens, and
the Tivoli Guard.

91

and Greek and Roman statuary. Glyptotek was given to the city of Copenhagen by the founder of Carlsberg, Carl Jacobsen.

From Tivoli, a short way north on H.C. Andersens Boulevard and right into Norrevoldgade, the next park of the five that lie in a rough semi-circle to the west of the city centre is **Ørstedsparken**. Hans Christian Ørsted is best known for the discovery of electro-magnetism, and this rectangular park satisfies the city-dwellers' need for space and water, with a lake, grass and large trees. Just north of the park, **Israels Plads** has a large vegetable and fruit market during the week, and a Sunday antiques flea market, and is close to the S-tog Nørreport station.

Between Ørstedsparken and **Botanisk Have** (Botanic Garden), further east on Øster Voldgade, is **Arbejdermuseet** (Workers' Museum), giving an account of the good and often hard times of Danish working life from 1850 to the present day. Botanisk Have has 25 acres of plants, Danish and worldwide, plus a palm house, observatory and the **Geological Museum**.

On the other side of the street stands Christian IV's **Rosenborg Slot**, a Renaissance castle. The cellar is the home of the magnificent crown jewels. Some 20 rooms are open to the public, including his favourite tower room, with costumes and many things personal to Christian himself, such as his pearl-studded saddle. The palace is also surrounded by beautiful gardens, **Kongens Have**, laid out as a country retreat, which was then outside the city walls. Taken with Botanisk Have, Rosenborg could easily fill a whole morning or afternoon. To the south of the castle grounds is the **Royal Guards Museum** and, close by, the **Musical History Museum** with some intriguing old musical instruments.

Dedicated sightseers, who take the northern exit from the gardens will find **Statens Museum for Kunst** (the National Gallery) where the commissionaire greets visitors in livery with buckled shoes and a cocked hat. There is a welcome cafeteria before you tackle the contemporary collection and some fine works by Matisse. The **Hirschsprung Collection** in a separate building is of 19th-century Danish art, with the quality of light characteristic of the period. **Østre Anlæg**, all around the galleries, has lovely shaded lawns, three lakes and a children's playground which is always busy. From here, it is not far along Dag Hammarskjolds Allé to Oslo Plads and the S-tog Østerport station.

The alternative is to turn left on Dag Hammerskjolds Allé and return along **Øster Søgade**, beside the artificial lakes which were once part of the outer defences and a source of fresh water. The first is Sortedams Sø, the biggest, followed by Peblinge Sø, and finally Skt Jørgens Sø which ends at Gammel Kongevej.

Lined with fine houses, the regular shape of the lakes makes them look like a river crossed by bridges. It is a 2km (1 mile) peaceful walk, sometimes under trees, with both indigenous waterbirds and others attracted to the habitat. At the southern end is the **Tycho Brahe Planetarium**, with an omnimax screen and exhibitions dedicated to the great astronomer.

Enthusiastic gardeners love the Palm House in the Botanic Gardens, with cacti as well as palms. The greenhouses here were inspired by those of Kew Gardens in England. Discover plants from all over the world here.

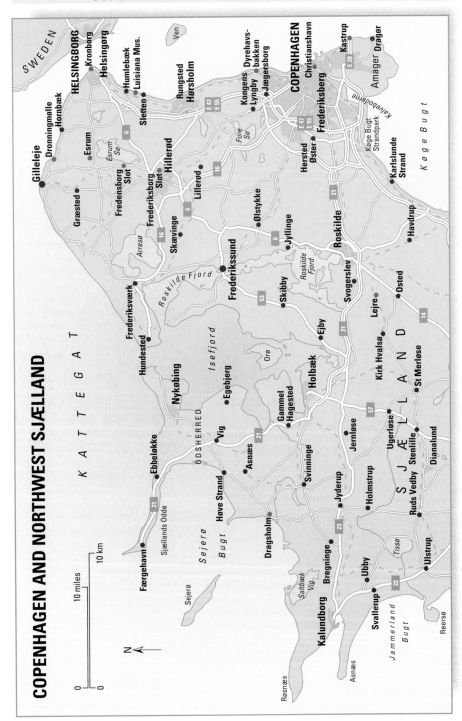

COPENHAGEN AND NORTHWEST SJÆLLAND

Excursions from Copenhagen

There are many places of interest around the city, very few more than 40km (30 miles) away, and many connected by S-tog (suburban train). On the northern outskirts, **Lyngby Open-Air Museum** has 50 old buildings from different regions to illustrate the simpler lives of days gone by.

Nearer the coast is **Dyrehaven** (Deer Park) a wonderful tree-filled park in the Klampenborg district, with some 2,000 deer. The best way to get around is by horse-drawn carriage, which is unlikely to frighten the deer. In the park are **Eremitage Slottet**, a baroque-style royal hunting lodge, and **Bakken**, at 400 the world's oldest amusement park, with more than 100 rides including a fascinating but frightening water ride.

The Helsingør motorway is the main route heading north, but there are other smaller and more interesting byways, as well as the S-tog. At Rungsted, close to the coast is the **Karen Blixen Museum**, dedicated to the writer. She was born at Rungstedlund and came back here, after returning from Kenya, to write books, run the estate and renovate the house in her own style. The north wing rooms remain as they were in Karen Blixen's day, with many mementoes of her time in Africa, and a small gallery of her paintings in oil, pastel and charcoal. The lovely grounds are also open to the public.

To the northwest at Hillerød, **Frederiksborg Slot** is another of Christian IV's castles, built between 1600 and 1620. The great redstone fortress stands on three small islands in the castle lake and has a magnificent chapel with a Compenius organ. Frederiksborg also houses **Danmarks Nationalhistoriske Museum** with a portrait gallery, furniture and industrial art. From here, it is only a short drive to **Kronborg Slot** at Helsingør, Hamlet's castle. Few would miss this echoing, gloomy castle where you expect at every turn to meet the ghost of the melancholy prince's father. Helsingør also has **Handels og Sjøfarts Museet**, a history of Danish shipping since the Middle Ages, with many beautiful model ships, and **Danmarks Teknikske Museum** which illustrates the history of science and technology, with some 2,000 exhibits. Particularly popular are the special traffic section with veteran cars and model trains, the **Hellebæk Hammer Mill** and a veteran railway.

A few miles west of Helsingør, along the north coast, **Hornbæk** is a delightful coastal village of white sand and pure water – tested every week – with the coveted Blue Flag flying proudly; and Gilleleje, Sjælland's northernmost town, further west still. At Hornbæk guided walking tours pass the house where Sweden's famous writer, August Strindberg, came on holiday. The town attracted artists from the Northern Light School, such as P.S. Krøyer, and still brings in modern painters. **Gilleleje Museet**, in the old school house from 1867, tells of the late Stone Age settlers of this long inhabited land. **Gilleleje Museums Skibshal** (Fishing Museum) is in a seamen's church, with a model boat at the doorway, and tells of the hard, everyday life of the North Sjælland fishing communities from the Middle Ages to the present day. The old **Gilleleje Kirke**, with the red and white Danish flag, is believed to date back to the 16th century and makes a revealing visit. Gilbjerg Hoved (headland) offers superb seabird watching.

A few miles inland **Tegners Museum**, close to Dronningmølle, features some 200

*F*rederiksborg Slot was another castle erected by that compulsive builder, Christian IV. It is an impressive, red sandstone fortress at Hillerød, north of Copenhagen.

*K*ronberg Slot is Hamlet's Castle at Helsingør, in the north of Sjælland, which Shakespeare anglicized to Elsinore. Inside, it is grim enough to be home for the ghost of Hamlet's father.

*L*ouisiana is easily combined on a tour with Kronberg Slot, and has a comprehensive collection of modern Danish and international art (right).

impressive works, both inside and outside the museum, of the sculptor Rudolf Tegner. It is surrounded by a unique landscape known as Rusland, where black sheep graze and, early in the season, the ground is carpeted with small violet flowers among the low shrubs; there are several rarities, all protected.

South of Helsingør, **Louisiana** is a magnificent museum of international modern painting and sculpture, from around 1945 to the present day, with works by Giacometti, Moore, Calder and more. Several stand in the park but are close enough to be seen from the gallery. There is a theatre and concert hall, in a lovely setting near the fishing village of Humlebæk.

South of Copenhagen, on the coast starting at Vallenbæk Strand, the city has a special beach park; a combination of beautiful sands, hotels, apartments, camping facilities, bed and breakfast guesthouses, shops, cycle hire agencies, river and lake fishing. Vallenbæk Strand is ideal for a holiday on and beside the sea.

Roskilde was the old capital of Denmark, and Roskilde Domkirke is a mecca for thousands of visitors, not least because all of Denmark's monarchs since the Middle Ages are buried here. This is one of the 38 Royal Tombs and five Royal Chapels.

Northwest Sjælland

Roskilde, Denmark's old capital, lies some 35km (25 miles) west of its successor and still has many links. Bishop Absalon, founder of Copenhagen, started the building of Roskilde **Domkirke**, which brings in over 175,000 visitors every year. Since the medieval period, all Denmark's monarchs have been laid to rest here, and there are 38 royal tombs. The four royal chapels are all in different architectural styles and a fifth, completed in 1985, has been added in the northwest corner.

Roskilde was founded by Harald Bluetooth, who erected the runestone in Jelling. **Stændertorvet**, the central square, has a statue of the Viking king, Roar, and his brother Helge. The square has been a meeting place since the 10th century. Legend tells that Roskilde was named after King Roar and a local spring, *kilde* in Danish. Roskilde is still famous for its springs, caused by the combination of aquiferous layers and impermeable layers of earth. It

has always been a holy place and, before the Reformation, there were as many as 13 churches and five convents and monasteries here.

Today, the town has 50,000 inhabitants and stands in a lovely position on the edge of Roskilde fjord. Many of the sacred buildings were torn down after the Reformation but one survivor is **Skt Jørgensbjerg Kirke**, on top of the hill of the same name, with an outlook over the water. The choir and nave date from the 11th century, when it was the church of the small fishing hamlet beside the port. An interesting item is the model of a medieval merchant vessel, the so-called *kogge*, engraved on the walled-up door which used to be the entrance for women.

Vor Frue Kirke (Church of Our Lady) also dates from the 11th century and was a big and important church favoured by Queen Margrethe I and Bishop Absalon. Towards the end of the 12th century, a mausoleum in honour of the local saint, Skt Margrethe of Højelse was built here. Have a look at the beautiful pews, carved by Casper Luebbeke, Master of Roskilde. There was a bishop's residence here from around 1100 linked some hundred years later by the Absalon Arch to the cathedral. The arch remains today, though the present palace was built in 1776.

Down by the fjord, the great attraction is **Vikingeskibshallen** (Viking Ship Museum) which has on display five Viking ships raised from the bottom of Roskilde Fjord in 1962. They are all different. There are commercial ships, warships and a longship, the only specimen of this most famous of the Viking boats. They had originally been sunk as a blockade, some time between 1000-1500AD, when Roskilde was an important commercial and trading centre and needed good defences. The ships came to the surface in thousands of pieces during a four-month diving exercise. The museum opened in 1969, when the first restoration was not yet complete and, at that time, visitors could watch the marine archaeologists patiently piecing them together. Now the light, modern building shows them to great effect. There is also a display on the excavation of the five ships, and the prospects of bringing a new Viking ship from Gislinge in Lammefjord which is still being restored, for permanent exhibition.

LEJRE

The Historical-Archaeological Research Centre at Lejre, to give it its full title, just west of Roskilde, uses practical techniques to test theories about the past of this very archaeologically rich area, and is keen to involve visitors and volunteers.

To do so, the Centre has recreated an Iron Age village, and a landscape to match. The underlying theory is that, by imitating primitive methods of farming and living, Lejre could discover what effects different forms of cultivation had on the land and people.

Adventurous Danish families queue up for a week's holiday in an Iron Age house, cooking and eating Iron Age food, tackling Iron Age implements, and generally getting a glimpse of Iron Age life. The Centre uses the families' time there as an interesting and quick check on various theories. It could take archaeologists many thousands of hours to trace patterns of Iron Age life in a hut from the erosion on a clay floor, but the Centre needs only to leave a family to fend for itself for a short time to find it lives to a totally different pattern.

Day visitors can also be involved, taking part in various activities, from sailing a dugout canoe to grinding corn and logging with an Iron Age axe, or just watching this interesting revelation of the past.

Roskilde has several art museums. There is also **Brøder Lützhøpfts Købmandsgaard**, a merchant house from early this century, and **Håndværksmuseet** (Old Working Tools Museum), both along Ringestedgade, giving an insight into earlier life in the area. In summer, a veteran steamship takes cruises on the fjord.

Isefjord is a wide semi-circle of water which flows into Roskilde Fjord, in the extreme northwest of Sjælland, making it a marvellous centre for every sort of watersport, and a paradise for sailing. The biggest town on the southern inner edge is **Holbæk**, a green town with many parks touching the fjordside. It has an old church **Tveje Merløse Kirke**, an authentic though smaller copy of Roskilde's first cathedral, from 1084AD, the only church with its original twin towers still standing. Holbæk also has a local history museum and an unusual **Zone-Redningkorpsets Museum**, an authentic copy of a sea rescue station from 1930. **Andelslandsbyen Nyvang** is a reconstruction of the old villages of the agricultural cooperative movement, many from different areas.

On the eastern side, **Frederikssund** snuggles into the narrowest part of Roskilde Fjord where Crown Prince Frederik's Bridge links Hornsherred peninsula to Frederikssund. A notable building is **Jægerspris Slot**, a small palace that once belonged to Countess Danner, the morganatic wife of King Frederik VII. It has lovely parkland. Not far south at Skibby, **Selsø Slot** is a 400-year-old manor house with a museum and magnificent windows, and **Willumsens Museum** displays the paintings, drawings, graphic work, sculpture, pottery and photographs of the prolific artist J.F. Willumsen.

To the west, **Nykøbing** is the main town of Odsherred, the most northwesterly peninsula, which sticks into the sound like an ancient axehead. Once it was an island, but the draining of the Lammefjord joined Odsherred to the mainland in a wide strip that became Denmark's 'vegetable garden'. Odsherred has some of Denmark's best beaches with white sand that attracts the artists who exhibit in galleries such as Nykøping's **Kulturhus** or **Huset** in Asnæs. **Sommerland Sjælland** is an aquapark, with about 50 water activities that are adored by children.

All over Odsherred are reminders of ancient times with burial mounds and four museums which show other interesting relics of the past. One of the saddest is in the dungeons of **Dragsholm Slot**, Denmark's oldest secular building, now a hotel which runs guided tours. The Earl of Bothwell, husband of Mary Queen of Scots, was imprisoned here following a shipwreck after Mary rode to her own death in England. He hoped for sanctuary but found only madness and death after years in this cell.

In this whole fjord area, doing something is as important as looking, and doing something out of doors, preferably on this magnificent sailing water, is best. People sail in their own yachts, or you can hire boats of all descriptions, including canoes. There are innumerable safe inlets and inner fjords and dozens of friendly harbours.

Kalundborg, further south on the west coast has a ferry for Jylland, via Samsø, an island famous for its cheese. The town has a splendid church with five towers, built by the brother of Bishop Absalon. **Kalundborg Museet** is in another fine building at Lindegaarden. **Lerchenfeld Herregærd**, open in summer, stands near the town on the Røsnæs (peninsula), and from here a road leads to the westernmost point which has a windmill and a lighthouse looking far over the sea to Jylland.

Every Second Person Owns a Bicycle

There are five million people in Denmark and two-and-half million bicycles. Sometimes, in the Copenhagen rush hour, it can seem that at least half that number are out on the streets. From smart young office workers to business-suited executives, students, tradesmen and schoolchildren, they are peddling steadily and, above all, safely through the city.

For if Denmark has more bicycles per head than any other country, it also has more cycle lanes, over 5,000km (3,500 miles) of them, and road rules to protect cyclists. This applies particularly in the cities and towns. Cyclists speed along the special cycle tracks, dismount carefully at cycle crossings, and push their bikes across. Motor traffic must respect this right. The cyclists do not hold up the traffic and, because they reduce the number of cars, may actually make journey times shorter. Certainly, after a short time in Copenhagen, which also has many pedestrian streets, a visitor may suddenly notice that the city is quieter and much less smelly than most.

Another interesting statistic is that Denmark, although it is a rich country, has fewer cars per head than its western European neighbours. Although before World War II, a bicycle might have been all that many could afford, cost is no longer the motive. Nor is cycling a duty, or undertaken for mere exercise, though both of those motives come into the choice. It is a way of life that Danish people have adopted, using bicycles for pleasure at the weekends and holidays, as well as for work all year round, whatever the weather. When it is not so good, in their long cycle capes, they look a bit like shiny, waterproof pyramids that have learned to balance on a bike!

Denmark has a strong Federation of Cyclists which looks after cyclists' interests with great care. This is the voice that makes sure that the cities have adequate bicycle racks, where bikes can be left without fear of damage or theft. Stations too have rows of bicycles secured to special racks while their owners take the local train or bus on to work.

Bicycles, bicycles, bicycles!

The Federation's annual cyclists' day attracts thousands to Copenhagen. It is a jolly celebration in Rådhuset where friends meet and talk about their cycling experiences and everyone has a good time. There is always a serious side to it too, with speakers from different organizations demanding more cycling facilities and even better discipline from motorists. Telling points in a speech are applauded by the shrilling of bicycle bells.

There are cycle tracks outside the urban areas as well, leading down to beaches and other public spaces. Foreign visitors driving a car should treat these with great respect or they may find themselves surrounded by an indignant crowd of Danes, determined to put them right.

Out in the countryside, Denmark has some 46,000km (32,000 miles) of country roads, often colourful and pretty, and used mostly by local people from the farms and villages nearby. These too make for safe cycling, and Danish city families often take off at the weekend, the youngest child safely attached to a baby seat, all ready to get closer to nature, something the Scandinavians prize more than most.

But Denmark's greatest asset to cyclists is perhaps that it is a level, undulating country, rising nowhere more than 179m (some 650ft) though this does not mean that cycling cannot be energetic. Like the fields, the roads rise and fall gently but much more than one realises when driving a car. A cycling holiday can at first be a test on the leg muscles, well compensated for by the sense of self-satisfaction and well-being after a shower and a pre-dinner drink in the overnight hotel or inn.

The Danes are eager to encourage all visitors to cycle. Stations hire out bicycles and both trains and ferries carry them cheaply. Some country buses will transport bicycles if they have the space, and there are many companies providing bikes and arranging routes and accommodation. Some carry luggage between night stops but, more often, the cycles have good-sized panniers and the advice is to travel light. Some of the best routes are in the islands off South Sjælland, Fyn and its islands (see p.124), and the long west coast of Jylland. The view from a bicycle is one of the best ways to get a slow, clear impression of a country.

The Wider Environmental Movement

Cycling is all part of a much wider movement to protect the environment which Denmark has very much at heart. It is the only European country that forbids the use of cans for drinks and everything from lager to cola is sold in recyclable bottles. The Danes even have a special dispensation from the European Union to keep their own ruling.

In most areas of a town or city, and at central points in the villages, are inconspicuous containers, like huge stumpy bottles, each a different colour, for the collection of waste. Danes are among the most conscientious of recyclers anywhere, and the bins accept glass, paper, tins and various other categories for recycling. Denmark seems to have had few of the difficulties in organizing this method of dealing with rubbish that have beset, for example, Germany and many other countries. More than that, it is a pleasure to look at the scrupulous cleanliness around the bins, none of the odd scraps of litter and broken glass that too often mar this sort of attempt to work for a better environment.

Beaches and Blue Flags

Denmark is eager to have its beaches as clean as possible, and some 15,000 water tests are carried out each year. In common with every other country, Denmark has been unable to escape a degree of pollution in lakes, rivers and the surrounding sea. But in typical Scandinavian fashion, instead of pretending it is not happening and keeping the matter quiet, hoping nobody will notice, Denmark issues leaflets to visitors explaining any problems and how the country is tackling them, with a five-year plan.

Local communities, for example, are in charge of the quality of their own beaches and put a great deal of effort into clearing oil, rubbish and anything else that gets washed up. On Jylland's west coast with its prevailing westerly wind, they are more often than not removing another country's rubbish. The success of the campaign is measured by the large number of Blue Flags everywhere, the European indication that a beach measures up to the 'cleanest' standard.

Alternatives
Spurred on to a degree by the oil crises of the 1970s, and further energy scares, Denmark was early in the field of looking for alternative methods of producing energy. In a country where, in the past, windpower had long been an important source of energy, Denmark was not slow to realize the possibilities of again using windmills, this time as a source of electricity.

Once again, windmills became part of the countryside, not the old picturesque windmills of the past which still stand in some places, but the soaring, slim, silver metal pillars with short shiny blades on top. Though at first they aroused a lot of controversy, today many have come to realize that they have their own beauty. The biggest marine windmill park is at Ebeltoft on the Djursland peninsula, in eastern Jylland, but there are many more smaller parks. This one has become an attraction for visitors.

Various projects are investigating the possibilities of developing an environmentally friendly town or city. The largest and most advanced is at Horsens in Jylland (see p.141). The town has built

Energy-conscious Danes make the most of windmills like this one on Fyn.

an area, Torsted Vest, which attempts to use new energy-saving methods of heating, such as solar energy, and other experimental schemes which avoid damaging the environment. This is part of the World Health Organization's project 'Healthy Towns for the Year 2000', involving the cooperation of 25 European cities.

In all these ways, Denmark has made good progress in looking for means to benefit the environment and improve people's lives. But important though they are, skimming along through the gentle Danish countryside on a bicycle, on a warm sunny day, these benefits may not be uppermost in one's mind. Cycling then is just pure, selfish pleasure.

White Cliffs, Rich Farms, Viking Remains, and Islands

In contrast to the north of Sjælland, where Copenhagen's influence extends further and further north, and the summer beach traffic is heavy, South Sjælland is a quiet place of manor houses, agriculture, peaceful small towns and villages, and the sea. The main islands, Falster, Møn and Lolland, south of the mainland, edge close to Fyn's archipelago. Though the main road from the north continues to Lolland's south coast, it can be more pleasant to take the smaller roads. The main trains from Copenhagen to the Continent pass south through the area, connecting with ferries to the rest of Europe.

South Sjælland

The 700-year-old market town of **Køge** lies some 38km (26 miles) south of Copenhagen on the great sweep of Køge Bugt (Bay), famous for two great sea battles against the Swedes. The Danes' national anthem recounts that 'King Christian stood by the lofty mast' during the first (1677) battle, but cynics claim that he was actually tucked away more safely

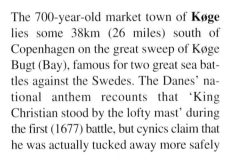

The main roadbridge linking South Sjælland and the island of Falster, crosses Størstrommen and the island of Farø. With so many islands, Denmark is a land of bridges.

in the tower of Køge's Skt Nikolai Kirke, the tower from which they hanged pirates.

This unspoilt old town has an array of well-preserved and beautiful half-timbered houses, including Denmark's oldest from 1527. Køge received its first town charter in 1288 and its long reign as a trading town is indicated by the large market square. Nowadays, Saturday is the high day; crowds of people come for fresh fruit, vegetables, cheese and smoked fish as well as handcrafts and secondhand goods. Only a kilometre (half a mile) away are woods and beaches, and the harbour is not just a resort but a busy working harbour with ships from many lands. The S-tog runs to Køge.

On the headland to the south that divides Køge Bugt from Fakse Bugt, the tall white cliffs of **Stevns Klint** whet the appetite for the bigger version at Mons Klint

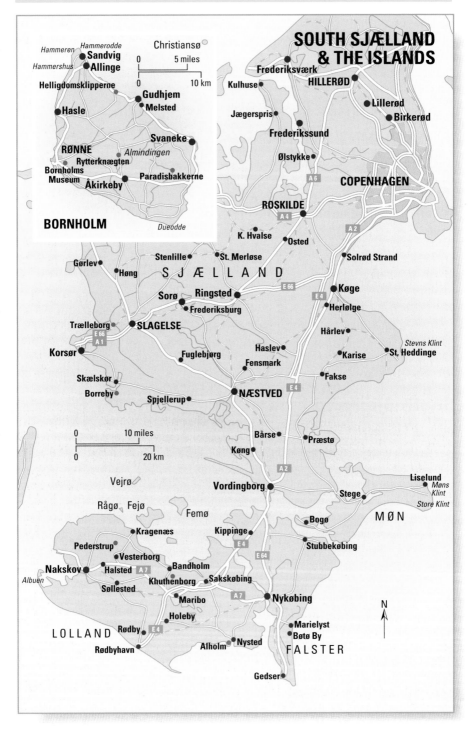

Hammeren Hammerodde Christiansø
Hammershus Sandvig 0   5 miles
          Allinge
Helligdomsklipperne   0   10 km
          Gudhjem
Hasle   Melsted
          Svaneke
RØNNE Almindingen
  Rytterknægten
Bornholms
Museum Åkirkeby   Paradisbakkerne

BORNHOLM Dueodde

**SOUTH SJÆLLAND
& THE ISLANDS**

Frederiksværk
Kulhuse **HILLERØD**
            Lillerød
Jægerspris Birkerød
  Frederikssund
Ølstykke
            A6 **COPENHAGEN**
ROSKILDE
  A4
K. Hvalse Osted A2
Stenlille St. Merløse Solrød Strand
Gørlev **S J Æ L L A N D**
  Høng E66 Køge
Sorø Ringsted E4
  Frederiksburg Herløge
Trælleborg **SLAGELSE**
  E66 Hårlev
  A1 Stevns Klint
Korsør Haslev Karise St. Heddinge
  Fuglebjørg Fensmark Fakse
Skælskør
Borreby Spjellerup **NÆSTVED** E4

0   10 miles
0   20 km
  Bårse Præstø
  Køng
Vejrø A2 Liselund
Rågø Fejø **Vordingborg** Stege Møns Klint
  Femø Bøgø Store Klint
  Kragenæs Kippinge **MØN**
Pederstrup E4
  Vesterborg Stubbekøbing
Nakskov Halsted A7 Bandholm
Albuen Khuthenborg Sakskøbing
  Søllested A7 **Nykøbing**
    Maribo
    Holeby Marielyst
LOLLAND Rødby E4 Bøtø By
  Nysted **FALSTER**
Rødbyhavn Alholm
      Gedser

N

106

further south. Højerup Kirke on the top is slowly losing a fight with the greedy sea. Earlier this century, first cemetery, then choir tumbled over the cliff. Though cliff and church foundations have since been strengthened, how much longer a church which has lasted for over 700 years will survive is not certain. Fakse Bugt, south of the headland, has a good beach and the town is the home of Fakse beer. The brewery is open to visitors.

Inland from Køge, on the E20 west, **Ringsted** was an important medieval town and has Denmark's first brick church, **Skt Bendts Kirke**. It was built in the 12th century by King Valdemar I as a memorial to his father, Knud Lavard, who had been murdered. Later canonized, he is the only Danish saint.

Today, the town also has **Fantasy World**, a children's favourite, with hundreds of mechanical figures ranging from Santa Claus to polar bears, pixies and trolls to jungle animals, in a fairytale world.

On the road to Korsør, on the west coast, a short way out of Slagelse is **Trelleborg**, one of a line of Viking ringed forts running from Jylland to Sjælland. It is around a thousand years old and was a large camp with a main stone defence circle surrounding wooden buildings. There were also ramparts, a moat and outer stone ramps. The stone circles are still clear, there are many graves, and one barrack building has been reconstructed giving an idea of life inside the fort for the thousand men stationed here. A model of the fort in its heyday is by the entrance.

Korsør, familiar to millions as the terminal for the ferry across Storebælt, will

*K*orsør has long been familiar as the Sjælland end of the ferry to the middle island of Fyn. Now it will play a similar role for the bridge.

fulfil a similar role as the eastern end of the great bridge linking the town to Nyborg on Fyn. **Storebælt Udstillingscenter** traces the story of the bridge's hi-tech construction, through video screens, models, diagrams and drawings, a record of progress. The best view of bridge and harbour is from the ramparts of the naval barracks.

Snug at the head of a fjord, **Skælskør**, south of Korsør, lies along a lagoon coastline, screened from the sea by small islands. This is one of Europe's cleanest coasts, with no less than seven Blue Flags. The 500-year-old market town grew up around the harbour, and the area's main building is nearby **Borreby**, characteristically Renaissance, with its own art gallery in the old courthouse and stable. **Borreby Moor** is a breeding ground for wading birds, with many godwit, ruff and avocet, plus some rarities. On the autumn and spring migrations, as many as 3,000 grey geese come down here.

Næstved is the capital of South Sjælland, with 45,000 inhabitants and some fine buildings from the Middle Ages. Both Gothic churches (Skt Peders and Skt Mortens) repay a visit, the latter with a famous fresco of Valdemar Atterdag and his queen. Skt Jørgens is interestingly modern. There is also a group of castles and manor houses.

Horsemanship is a tradition in Næstved. Since the 18th century, **Grønnegade Kaserne** (barracks) has served as a riding and training school for the Gardehusarerne (Royal Guards Hussars) who still ride through the old streets every Wednesday.

Northeast of Næstved is **Bon-Bon Land**, a sweet factory with play areas and, nearby in Fensmark, is **Holmegaards Glasværk**, where they make fine glassware. Visitors can watch glassblowers and follow the process to finished glass. Enquire in advance

and you might be able to see Holmegaard's famous band playing on instruments made of glass – a remarkable sight.

Vordingborg has a splendid view out over Storstrommen, which separates Sjælland from the island of Falster and the ruins of King Valdemar the Great's 1170 castle. Part of the heavy wall and the town's best known monument, **Gåsetårnet** (Goose Tower), is all that remains. Built by Valdemar Atterdag in 1366 as an addition to the castle, the tower gets its name from the golden goose he placed above it. There is a fantastic view from here of the countryside and the sound over to Falster.

Danmarks Vejmuseum (Highway Museum), which lies on the little island of Fanø close to the impressive bridge, tells the history of Danish roads and highways. But before going to Falster, detour east to the small island of Møn, either by going east via Kalvehave and the bridge over Ulvsund, or by bearing left off the main Farø bridge (junction 42).

Møn

The prime target for most visitors to Møn is **Møns Klint** on the east coast. These mighty white cliffs, 75 million years old, are brilliant even when the sun is not shining and are even finer when it is. They run 7km (nearly 5 miles) from **Lille Klint** (small cliff) in the north, south to **Store Klint** (big cliff), 128m (over 400ft) above the sea which washes in far below. Pinnacles, peaks and ledges add to the excitement, with shrubs and small flowering plants growing in the crevices, and many fossils lying in the rock. Follow a marked path down to the beach.

But Møn is more than Klint. From earliest times, this little island has been invaded and settled. It has Bronze Age

*M*øns Klint (cliffs) on the island of Møn, off the south-east coast of Sjælland, are Denmark's most famous cliffs, chalk white and over 128m (400ft) high.

tombs, medieval churches and the small town of Stege, just beyond the Ulvsund bridge, is circled by medieval walls. **Elmelunde Kirke**, from the early 12th century, is Møn's oldest church and, though all Møn's churches are famous for their frescoes, Elmelunde's are perhaps the most prized. The originator of these simple, realistic works had worked in several Møn churches and on Lolland and Falster, and was known as the *Elmelunde-mester*

*E*lmelunde Kirke on Møn, the most famous of several churches for the religious frescoes, all painted by the 12th-century Elmelunde-mester (master).

(master) in recognition of his masterwork in this church. **Kelby Kirke** has an earlier fresco from 1275 in the choir, and another with the characteristic touch of the Elmelunde master. But the largest work is in **Fanefjord Kirke**, set on a hill overlooking the narrows of Grønsund.

Liselund Slot on Møns has a Swiss cottage where Hans Christian Andersen is said to have written two of his best-known stories when visiting his family. (Inset) A modern visitor looks in!

Just north of Møns Klint, **Liselund Slot** was built in 1792 by Antoine de Calmette, a French diplomat, for his wife. It is a romantic, chateau-style building with a thatched roof, standing on the cliffs. Hans Christian Andersen is said to have written *The Little Match Girl* and *The Tinder Box* in the estate's Swiss cottage. Other buildings include the Norwegian House and the Chinese Pavilion.

Falster

Back to the bridge, and on to Falster through a landscape of woods, farms and fields, where the rich soil nurtures Denmark's sugar beet, to the main town of Nykøbing Falster, which is usually known as Nykøbing-F, to distinguish it from other Nykøbings. The name means 'new market'.

Nykøbing stands in a fine position on both sides of Guldborg Sund. The yellow tower of **Vandtårn** gives a bird's-eye view of this old trading town, and the waters of the narrow sound with a bridge to the southernmost island of Lolland. There is much evidence of the past. **Klosterkirken** (abbey church) has an old herbarium, and the Middle Ages are also remembered in **Middelaldercentret**, a 'science experience' centre where you can see the weapons of the Middle Ages in action. Tsar Peter the Great stayed at **Czarens Hus** (Tsar's House) in

Nykøbing on Falster has retained much of its early significance as a centre of trade, and still holds much of its past in interesting buildings.

1716; it now houses a museum, **Falsters Minder** (Memories of Falster).

On the north coast of the island, **Stubbekøbing** is the biggest town, with the **Stubbekøbing Motorcykel og Radiomuseum**, the world's largest collection of vintage motorcycles and radios. North Falster offers one of Denmark's most beautifully situated golf courses, near Virket Sø. **Corslitze Herregård** has lovely gardens with tours by horse-drawn vehicles. There is also horseriding, and a favourite Scandinavian spectator sport, trotting.

All the coastal towns have long seafaring traditions, and for leisure, watersports such as swimming, windsurfing, rowing, sailing and canoeing are popular. Bicycles are fine for exploring. **Marielyst** is a 20km (13-mile) stretch of especially fine beach with summer cottages looking out to the Baltic on an east coast known for its fine sandy strands. In Bøtø there is a nudist beach and **Sommerland Falster and Marielyst Aqua Park**, a family amusement park, with an aquascape with chutes and the rest.

Falster's southernmost town, **Gedser**, is a busy port, with a ferry service across to Warnemünde-Rostock, connecting with north–south trains. The town also has a **Tropical Aqualand.**

Lolland

Of the three bridges to Lolland, the most interesting is probably the Guldborg bridge, which overlooks the mouth of the sound. This is a beautiful flat, green, fertile island, with field upon field of sugar beet and waving corn. There are excellent bathing beaches, chances for cruises and fishing expeditions, and a fistful of lovely manor houses, castles, churches and old windmills. Graceful, new, shiny windmills also soar and whirl, making electricity for the island.

The island has an unexpected number of tracks where you can walk or cycle, the most intriguing being the **Baltic Way**, on the dyke along the south coast. This was one good result of several 19th-century tragedies, when the Baltic stormed into the southern towns and villages. The flood marker in the port of Rødby shows how high the water came in the worst storm in 1872 which cost 82 lives. The Lollanders built a dyke, 60km (45 miles) long, across the southern coast from Nakskov in the west, east to Nysted, draining what had been Rødby Fjord.

The dyke is 4m (14ft) high and has cycleways and footpaths on the embankment. At one stretch a trail turns inland along a disused length of railway track in what was once the fjord. A **Memorial Park** with monuments marks the draining.

Rødby itself is no longer on the coast and Rødbyhavn is further south. Near the harbour is **Lalandia**, Denmark's largest subtropical swimscape. The beaches around

Rødby are hunting grounds for amber and the town has an **Amber Museum** with a workshop which polishes the gems and makes lovely jewellery. Close to Rødby, Lolland Falster airport offers round-Lolland flights, gliding and parachuting. Other brave souls can try the **Go-Kart Racing Track**.

Almost every settlement in this long-time farming area is an old market town with a cobbled square, traditional church and houses, and winding streets. Using the Guldborg bridge, the first such town is Saks-Købing. Down by the sound, the granary of the beautifully-restored **Majbølle Mølle** (mill), is now a gallery with exhibitions in summer. The town is a fine place for hiring a canoe or kayak and setting off down the Saks-Købingfjord, though experience is required. The fjord is full of visiting yachts.

It is a fair claim that Lolland's most popular castle is **Aalholm Slot** in the gentle hilly countryside close to the port of

---

THE LOLLAND ALPS

A certain sense of irony has given Ravnsby Bakker (Ravnsby Hills) the nickname of the Lolland Alps, since hills and valleys are not usual on the north coast of Lolland. Formed during the Ice Age 15,000 years ago, though they may not be mountains, Ravnsby Bakker make fine walking country with a superb view over Smålandshavet and the little islands off the northern coast. The hills are also a good place for botany, for the Ice Age left plants here that are seldom seen in other parts of Lolland.

History is all around, particularly in the old castle ruins from 1335, built by Count Johan Pløn, to give himself control of Lolland and the islands of Smålandshavet. It was a good strategic choice with a perfect view in all directions across the fertile Lolland fields and out over the sea.

Nysted in the southeast. This 12th-century building is one of the world's oldest inhabited castles. Its most spectacular exhibit is **Automobilmuseet**, the personal collection of the owner, Baron Raben-Levetzau. The Baron has amassed one of Europe's largest assemblies of veteran and vintage cars from 1896 to 1930. Rare models include a 1911 Rolls Royce and a Ford T from 1909. The Baron still takes an enormous interest in the collection and is often found talking enthusiastically to visitors. The museum's railway section houses a marvellous model railway and, during the summer, a replica steam train from 1850 runs in the park. Also on view is the special train used by the Baron's father when he was Foreign Secretary.

On the way north towards Søndersø (lake) and Maribo, Holeby has a big international agricultural research and experimental centre, and there are demonstrations of skills, long overtaken, by retired craftsmen at an old workshop. At Tågerup, **Polakkasernen** (Polish Barracks) shows vividly the life of the Polish immigrants who came to work in the beet fields. One fascination of Lolland is that it constantly reveals these unexpected details of the past. Another delight is **Lungholm Hestesportscenter** (equestrian centre) where you can explore the estate on horseback or in a carriage.

The market town of Maribo, set beside lakes Søndersø and Maribo, grew around a nunnery, next to the **Maribo Domkirke**. The town is full of beautifully restored houses, once workshops and dwellings, and Maribo claims that its **Kunstmuseum** has one of the finest collections of Danish art outside Copenhagen.

Towards Søndersø are the wonderful **Bangs Have** gardens, with **Frilands-museet**, a typical Scandinavian open-air museum of old rural buildings, furniture and tools, showing life two centuries ago. On the lake, m/v *Anemone* gives round trips, sailing serenely past little islands full of unusual birds. The lake is also ideal for fishing. A museum railway runs through lovely country from Maribo to Bandholm on the northern coast which has a fine old station. This was Denmark's first privately owned steam railway when the trains first began pulling carriages some 30 years ago.

Near Bandholm, **Knuthenborg** is a manor house with a safari park, where visitors drive around 16km (12 miles) of road passing giraffes and other exotic species roaming freely.

The west, and particularly the southwest, is farmland and has no less than eight typical churches. Its only manor house, the half-timbered **Rudbjerggård**, is not open to the public but one of its many woods, Vindeholme Skov, has a large collection of the lovely scented, small-leafed lime trees that once covered most of Denmark.

In 1920, a rich Iron Age find of two decorated vessels was made at Hoby, probably from a chief's grave. Their inscriptions are from the *Iliad* indicating how long ago and how far this area has been trading. Down on the coast at Kappel are the great arms of one of the oldest mills, **Kappel Mølle** from 1723, while clusters of its modern descendants stand silver-tall and futuristic in many places in this environment-conscious country.

The south coast ends in the west in a long spit of land, with the appropriately named **Albuen** (elbow) which forms an excellent yacht harbour at the southern end of Nakskov Fjord. Reached on foot or by boat, the point of the spit is a fine spot to watch birds and boats, and unbelievable sunsets.

Nakskov, Lolland's capital, in the inner fjord, was 'Town of the Year' in 1991.

The small islands of the fjord make this a wonderful sailing area, which visitors can enjoy even without their own boat by taking the small mail boat that calls at islands such as Slotø which has the ruins of Denmark's first naval dockyard.

In the town itself, **Den Gamle Smedie** (old smithy) in Tilegade is a working museum with horseshoes still beaten out by hand. **Skt Nicolai Kirke** is one of the biggest in Lolland with a 72m (250ft) spire. During a Swedish siege in 1659, a cannonball crashed through the vaulted roof during a service. It still lies there. At Axeltorv **Theisens Købmandsgård** is an old merchant house from 1785, next to **Det Gamle Apotek** (Old Apothecary), over a century older. Market days are busy and colourful. One of Nakskov's most interesting exhibition spaces is **Toggalleriet** (Train Gallery) which uses old railway carriages. In summer, the carriages stand beside the harbour but during the rest of the year they tour the small Lolland station towns.

Inland, and heading east, at Søllested, the old manor of **Søllestedgård** has been known since the 15th century. Not far away is one of Lolland's two folk high schools; a peculiarly Danish form of adult education, popular with students from both Denmark and abroad. The house where the Danish writer Kaj Munk was born is open to the public.

The town of Halsted has **Halsted Kloster** with the original church from 1500 and beautiful English gardens. To the north is another reminder of the long-gone past, **Kong Svends Høj**, a passage grave with a burial chamber 12m (40ft) long and 2m (some 7ft) high. Built around 5,000 years ago, the grave has recently been restored to its original form. Leading to it, a traditional country road some 7km (5 miles) long runs through **Teofiliskoven** (wood) near Vesterborg, with the distance markers still in place. The old road is lined with rare trees, parks and the gardens of the estates. Also in this area is **Pederstrup**, the centrepiece of the great Reventlow estates, with its own museum.

On the northern coast, **Kragenes** is the jumping off point for the islands of Smålandshavet, Fejø, Femø, Vejrø and Rågo, favourite holiday islands but also examples of how small communities can survive. Kragenæs Havn (harbour) has a wonderful setting, looking out to these delightful sailing waters, and set between Torrig Skov (wood) to the west and **Ravnsby Bakker** to the south. This hill and valley area, unusual for Lolland, is called semi-mockingly the 'Lolland Alps'. Still clear are the ruins of a fortified castle, built around 1335, to control Lolland, the islands and the sea.

Bornholm

Far out in the Baltic, Bornholm is closer to Sweden and Poland than to Denmark, but it is the Danes' holiday island *par excellence*. The contrasts on an island of only 588 sq km (227 sq miles) are astonishing, varying from the lush, gentle green of woods full of wonderful wild flowers, especially orchids, to great rocky cliffs where the sea thunders in, and long stretches of gentle sand. The almost iridescent light has a quality all its own.

Bornholm has some 48,000 permanent inhabitants but, though the population increases by leaps and bounds in summer, when the fishers, golfers, sailors, swimmers, windsurfers, birdwatchers, botanists and more flock in, there are somehow never too many people.

The Scandinavian pastime of berry- and mushroom-picking is very popular. For

THE BORNHOLM CLOCK

One of the most attractive mementoes of Bornholm's seafaring past is the Bornholm grandfather clock. In 1744, on its way from Helsingør on mainland Denmark to Reval (now Tallinn) in Estonia, a Dutch vessel went aground on Bornholm. When the Bornholmers turned out in the time-honoured way to see what good things the shipwreck had brought, they found 'five clocks and a cask with weights for them'.

Sensing a challenge, Bornholm craftsmen began to make their own version of the finds. The result was tall, impressive clocks in dark wood, with metal faces and elegant decoration, the start of a Bornholm tradition.

Later, as the craze for modern techniques took over, the art of making these lovely old clocks almost disappeared. But, after World War II, as it has everywhere, the feeling for the skills and beauty of craftwork began to revive. Bornholm craftworkers set themselves to relearn the old ways of making the grandfather clocks once more and, today, the island's biggest clock-workshop is in Rønne.

birdwatchers, the island is a paradise with many migrants and seabirds. The waters of the neighbouring island of Christiansø are full of seabirds, and on the land goshawk and Tengmalm's owl are among the inhabitants. With 200km (140 miles) of cycle tracks, this is a place to forget the car.

Many nations have visited and settled in Bornholm in the past, some, such as the Wendel pirates who came to kill and plunder, not so welcome. There are grave mounds and passage graves from the Stone Age. Later, between the 13th and 15th centuries, the German Hanseatic League took over during the herring season. Four fine churches remain from the Middle Ages: 11th-century Østerlars, Bornholm's oldest round church, and Nylars, Nykirke and Olsker in the same form.

The white-painted and half-timbered farmhouses have stood for centuries.

In the north, **Hammershus** is a huge ruined fortress-castle, high on the cliffs above the sea. Nearby, distinctive rocks have special names such as the Lions' or the Camels' Heads. Offshore, a massive granite boulder **Hammeren** rises up 81m (225ft) above the Baltic, not far from **Hammerodde Fyr** (lighthouse).

On this northern tip at Allinge is **Bornholms Dyre og Naturpark**, an animal park built into an interesting old quarry, with deep clefts and small lakes. Further south on the west coast **Hasle Røgeri** is a well-kept little market town. Above five of the houses are the typical tall chimneys of the old herring smokehouses. One is now a museum.

On the northeast coast **Bornholms Kunstmuseum** has a fine collection of Bornholm art and decorative art. Nearby is the island's most famous cliff formation, **Helligdomsklipperne** (Sanctuary Cliffs), where the sea has scooped out fascinating caves and deep ravines.

Paradisbakkerne (Paradise Cliffs) are situated close to a vast area of woodland, **Almindingen**, planted in the early 19th century. **Rytterknægten** is Bornholm's highest point at 162m (over 200ft) and one of Almindingen's best known sights is an extraordinary tree with seven, linked trunks.

The south coast has miles of sandy beach, from Rønne, the main town, to **Duerodde** (lighthouse) at the tip. At the island's easternmost corner **Svaneke** is a beautifully preserved market town. Around the little town of **Gudhjem** (literally 'good home') on the northeast coast, the hills are too steep for comfortable cycling. Here the former railway station is a museum, and **Melstedgård**, to the southeast, was an important trading centre in the Middle Ages. From this north coast, only one hour's sailing distance away is **Ertholmen**, a picturesque group of islands. After that, there is only sea.

*A**ll around Denmark, the beautiful coastline is endlessly varied and part of a way of life that includes fishing, swimming and sailing.*

The Garden of Denmark with its Gentle Archipelago

Hans Christian Andersen, Denmark's famed writer of children's fairy-tales, called Fyn the 'Garden of Denmark', a title so appropriate it has lasted. Nowhere else in Denmark can you find anything more garden-like than this central island. There are small fields, cattle and sheep, winding roads with well-tended hedges, and orchards thick with spring blossom, fruit-laden in autumn. The roadside is bright with flowers of every colour, sharing the verges with wild red roses that even try to creep onto the beaches.

Fyn is a comfortable size, some 3,500sq km (1,335sq miles). No hill is bigger than 130m (450ft), and the villages have lovely white-walled houses, criss-crossed with timber, and thatched roofs. There may well be a simple white church and even a duck pond. Fyn is also the best place to find some of the most beautiful manor houses, which Denmark has aplenty. This agricultural past made Fyn the scene of one of the most important events in Danish history

*E*geskov *Slot seems to stand on the water in the surrounding lake! However, it is supported by sturdy oak piles that came from the wood that gave Egeskov its name.*

when, in 1788, men such as Johan Ludvig Reventlow of Brahetrolleborg brought about the abolition of villeinage, the feudal system that tied peasants to one landlord. It was the first step on the road to present-day Denmark's liberal social rights.

The two main towns are, in the northeast, **Odense**, best known as the hometown of Hans Christian Andersen, but also a university city with a fine cathedral, and **Svendborg** in the south, the main gateway to the southern islands of the archipelago. Odense is the only big town inland, with a ship canal to the sea. The other towns are all coastal: **Fåborg**, also on the south coast and another jumping off point for the islands, **Nyborg** and **Kerteminde** on the east coast, **Assens** on the west and **Bogense** and **Middelfart** to the north, the latter leading west to the peninsula of **Jylland**.

FYN AND ITS ARCHIPELAGO

0   10 miles

0   20 km

- Egeskov
- Nordskov
- FREDERICIA
- Vr. Egense
- Krogshulle
- Bogense
Hindsholm
- Skovby
- Særslev
- Otterup
- Middelfart
- Søndersø
Odense Fjord
- Morud
- Munkebo
- Kerteminde
- Ejby E20
- Ladbyskibet
- Ladby
Kerteminde Bugt
- Gelsted
ODENSE
- H-G-Andersen Hus
- Årup
- Frilandsmus
- Ullerslev
- Sandager
- Tommerup Stby
- Højby
- Vindinge
- Nyborg
Bagø
- Nørre Lyndelse
- Assens
- Hørrested
Arø
- Ebberup
- Nr. Broby
F Y N
- Ørbæk
Torø Huse
- Ringe
- Hårby
Nyborg Fjord
N
- Egeskov
- Kværndrup
- Hesselager
Helnæs
Helnæs Bugt
- Stensgård
- Brahetrolleborg
- Gudbjerg
Lohals
- Svanninge Bakker
- Bøjden
- Fåborg
- Skårup
- Nordborg
- Ollerup
SVENDBORG
- Havnbjørg
Lyø
- Troense
- ALS
Avernakø
- Valdemarsslot Orlogsmuseum
- Fynshav
Tåsinge
Drejø
- Mommark
- Søby
- Rudkøbing
SØNDERBORG
- Ærøskøbing
Kegnæs
Ærø
LANGELAND
- Marstal
- Humble

Northeast Fyn

Coming from Copenhagen and the east, whether by boat or by the new bridge over **Storebælt** (Great Belt), the chances are you will arrive in **Nyborg**, with its fortress gate that is a relic of the fierce wars between Sweden and Denmark. Then it was

the only way into the town from the landward side and, even today, at 9.45pm, the bells of the Church of Our Lady ring out the warning that once told travellers the gates were about to close.

Nyborg also has a fine castle, **Nyborg Slot**, built as long ago as 1170, to keep out the Wends from north Germany. Once it was the scene of meetings of the three strands of power – king, nobles and clergy. The great empty meeting rooms are still here today, and there is a wonderful view from the ramparts. The **Exhibition Centre** of the Great Belt Link, close to the car ferry terminal, reflects modern times and

Twelfth-century Nyborg Slot, part of the fortress town of Nyborg in the north of Fyn, was once a seat of power, and today the empty rooms still seem to echo with the past.

the progress of the new bridge across the sea to Sjælland. Nyborg has a fine beach.

North of Nyborg, to the south of the Hindsholm peninsula, **Kerteminde** is Fyn's main fishing village, continuing a way of life that echoes the past. Most of today's bigger towns started as trading or fishing centres, when ships from Fyn sailed the world. Today, leisure sailing is the passion, drawing boats from all over northern Europe, in a reverse of the old tradition. Kerteminde has many of the typical old half-timbered houses of Fyn and, as is usual on the island, many craft shops. Kerteminde's pottery and stoneware are particularly fine. The dramatic landscape of the Hindsholm peninsula has some ancient excavated barrows, indicating very early habitation.

On the inland route southwest to Odense, the underground remains of a Viking ship have been found at **Ladby**. It was used for a chieftain's burial around a thousand years ago. Here he lies with his weapons, eleven horses, his hunting dogs and jewellery, ready for the afterlife. Originally covered by a large mound, the ship now has a grass-covered concrete roof which looks like the original. It contains the ship and replicas of the finds. The originals are in the National Museum in Copenhagen (see p.83). **Ulriksholm**, one of the most beautiful manor houses is nearby. It is now an atmospheric hotel, a role adopted by many.

Odense

Odense became a city in 988AD, and commemorated its 1,000th anniversary in 1988 with much celebration. But the city's origins go back further. The name Odense comes from the King of the Gods, Odin, a word also meaning shrine or sanctuary. In those times, Odense stood to the north of the river with three Viking strongholds to the south, of which little remains. Its early history was turbulent and Odense has its own martyr: Knud the Holy was murdered, rather like Thomas a Becket, in front of the altar in Skt Albani Kirke (St. Alban's Church) in 1086. He was later canonized and pilgrims began to take the long road to the cathedral which bears his name and which still holds his coffin. Odense once had six monasteries and many churches, giving it all the importance of a medieval cathedral city.

Most people today think of Odense as the home of that universal children's writer Hans Christian Andersen and many make the pilgrimage to **Barndomshjem**, his childhood home, the humble rooms of the cottage where Andersen lived with his shoemaker father and family, before going on to **Hans Christian Andersen's House**. This main museum, in which tradition claims Andersen was in fact born, now has a large hall. The museum is also the place to see his personal possessions, confidential letters and the bric-a-brac of his daily life. The Dome Hall has famous frescoes by the painter Niels Larsen Stevns.

Less well known than he should be, in other than classical music circles, is another son of Odense, the composer Carl Nielsen. The **Nielsen Museum** is devoted jointly to the lives of the composer and his wife, the sculptor Anne-Marie Nielsen. It offers a chance to hear some of his music on tape, such as *Springtime in Fyn*. He too has a childhood home, a white house on Odensevej, though he was born in the village of **Nørre Lyndelse**, some 10km (7 miles) to the south.

Den Fynske Landsby (Funen Village) is one of the best Scandinavian open-air museums; in addition to the farmhouse buildings, it has a school, almshouse, smithy, wind and water mills, and traditional breeds of cattle.

Odense has **Fyns Kunstmuseum** (Art Museum) with a collection ranging from traditional to modern art. Other museums cover photography, printing and archaeology. **Kunsthallen Brands Klædefabrik**, an old spinning and weaving mill, now has changing displays of contemporary visual art. For a glimpse of Danish modern architecture, try the **Blangstedgård** area to the southeast. Architects and builders have combined to produce a post-modern style, using traditional Danish craftsmanship in modern architecture. Once an exhibition site, it is now residential.

Møntergården is a collection of town houses from the 16th and 17th centuries, which has one of the country's best exhibitions of coins and medals. There are also four interesting churches, including **Skt Hans Kirke** in **Norregade**, with its outside pulpit. In Odense is **Fyns Tivoli**, a smaller version of the Copenhagen Tivoli, a garden city with cycleways and paths. There is a boat trip along the river to the zoo, and opportunities for swimming, horseriding, tennis and golf, with cycling and fitness races.

Southwest of Odense, in what is called the 'green heart' of Fyn, **Fugleparken Frydenlund** is a bird and flower park, with some 700 species of birds from around the world, and 2,000 varieties of flowers.

South Fyn

Svendborg, south of Odense, is a market town with seafaring traditions and, with **Fåborg** to the west, it is the gateway to the archipelago. The veteran steamship *Helge* makes round trips to **Svendborgsund**, calling at the islands, including **Valdemars Slot** in summer. **Legetøjsmuseet**, the town's Mechanical Toy Museum is not only for children.

A few miles north of Svendborg, near **Kværndrup**, is **Egeskov Slot**, Fyn's most famous building, set in a lake on a foundation of oak piles (*egeskov* means oak wood). It is a wonderfully preserved castle, with gardens of every sort, including a maze restored in 1990. The **Motor Museum** includes veteran cars, aircraft and horse-drawn carriages.

The rolling country between Svendborg and Fåborg is a result of the last Ice Age, some 12,000 years ago, and many claim this to be the most beautiful part of Fyn. Heather-covered **Svanninge Bakker**, some 10 km (6 miles) north of Fåborg, is a national park. Between Fåborg and Kværndrup, the road passes **Brahetrolleborg Slot**, once a Cistercian monastery but best known as the place where, in 1788, Johan Ludvig Reventlow allowed his peasants to burn a wooden horse as a symbol of their freedom from serfdom.

Egeskov Slot has fine gardens with an ancient maze and this excellent Motor Museum, with aircraft as well as vintage cars and horse-drawn vehicles on display.

Four times a day Fåborg's **Klokketårnet** (Belfry) sends a hymn tune out over this pretty little town. **Den Gamle Gård**, once a merchant's house from 1725 and now a museum, is typical of those days. The town has one of the best collections of the work of Fyn painters, held in the **Museum for Fynsk Malerkunst**. From around 1880 to 1920, their distinctive style, particularly their depiction of light, was similar to the Nordic Light School in North Jylland. **Ymerbrønden** (Ymer Well) in Fåborg shows the work of the sculptor Kai Nielsen, which is also included in the museum.

122

*F*åarborg in the south, is surrounded by rolling countryside, with the Svanninge Bakker (hills) to the north. Fåarborg has an old clocktower set among white, half-painted-timbered houses. Nearby is Steensgård Herregård (manor), now an excellent hotel.

West Fyn

Just northwest of Fåborg, **Steensgård Herregård** is a wonderful place to stay. The manor hotel has three wings, the oldest from the 16th century, with period bedrooms (and modern facilities). It is close to Lillebælt. En route to Assens on the west coast overlooking Lillebælt, take the road closest to **Frøbjerg Bavnehøj** (hill) which has a wonderful view. Not far away Gummerup has **Vestfyns Hjemstavnsgård**, an insight into the area's unique agricultural history and handcraft traditions.

Assens was the hometown of the Danish naval hero Peter Willemoes who commanded a floating battery against the British fleet who were bombarding Copenhagen in 1801 during the course of the Napoleonic Wars. So great was his courage that even his enemy, Admiral Lord Nelson, congratulated him.

Today, his birthplace, **Willemoesgaarden** is open to the public and **Mindestuerne** (the memorial rooms) concentrate on all things connected with seafaring. This old maritime community has some lovely buildings with red pantile roofs. **Mads Lerches Gård** is a perfect example of an old merchant house and **Mands Samling** has workshops showing the skills of glassblower, silversmith, cooper and cobbler.

South of Assens, **Helnæs** (peninsula) is traversed by a remarkable road along the narrow string of land that connects it to the mainland. This haven has long been inhabited, as indicated by numerous cairns and runic stones. The peninsula also has **Helnæs Fyr** (lighthouse), a windmill, a church from 1617, a well-known inn, a hut camping site, and the bathing area of **Helnæs Sommerland**, near the old harbour. All around the views of islands and Lillebælt seem to go on for ever.

Between Assens and Helnæs, the road runs through the attractive village of **Torø Huse**, its street of small houses called Jacob Gades Vej, after the man who wrote the famous tango *Jealousy*. Nearby, **De Syv Haver** (the Seven Gardens) are a wonderful exposition of garden design in the styles of seven European traditions.

The coast between Assens and the northwestern town of Middelfart has some interesting sites for marine archaeologists in what has always been a heavy shipping lane. **Middelfart** is the 'Town of the Bridges', with a great arching suspension bridge to Jylland. Long a seafaring town, the church is dedicated to Skt Nicolai, the patron saint of sailors. It also has unusual decoration: the jaw bones of a whale hang over the tower door. Another memorial to men who have risked their lives is **Galsklint**, a park dedicated to British pilots shot down during World War II.

The area not only offers wonderful sailing but there are cruises round the Lillebælt and to places popular with divers and windsurfers. Here, as with almost all coastal spots in Fyn, most of the beaches have the coveted European Blue Flag for cleanliness and pure water.

Inland at Årup, **Fyns Sommerland** has amusements for the whole family with three swimming pools and a marvellous watershute, each lane painted a different colour. Sea fishing is very popular and people on Fyn claim to have the best fighting sea trout in Europe. Spring, autumn and winter are the best seasons. Fyn stocks its own fishing waters, releasing more than a million healthy one-year-old sea trout into the surrounding waters over a three-year period.

The further northwest you are, the flatter Fyn becomes. Just north of Middelfart at **Røjleklint**, the island ends in steep cliffs which plunge into the sea. To the east, the old town of **Bogense**, Fyn's smallest market town, looks across to Jylland. It claims to have the lowest prices anywhere in Fyn and, just to be different, the longest runic inscription in Denmark, on the **Glavendrup Stone**, near Skamby. This was raised by Ragnhild in memory of her husband, the chieftain Allee. Bogense also claims Fyn's largest marina, next to the old harbour.

There are other tales. The reef jutting out from Bogense is said to be the cobbled road out to a merman's castle in the deep waters north of the island of Æbelø. True or not, nobody knows, but from Bogense, at low tide you can walk to the island which has an untouched landscape full of wildlife. Sadly, it is not open to the public. Looking out towards Æbelø is the late-Renaissance manor house of **Gyldensteen**. During the German occupation of World War II, Karen Blixen, who as Isak Dinesen wrote *Out of Africa* and much more, chose seclusion here to continue her writing. **Dallund Herregård**, the early estate of the Blixen-Finecke family, not far away, is now a convalescent home.

The usual routes from Fyn to the archipelago is either via Svendborg, which is connected by bridge to two of the islands and by boat to the remainder, or from Fåborg, which has a direct boat link to Ærø.

The Fyn Archipelago

South of Fyn, the archipelago is a glorious stretch of islands, large and small. The biggest are Ærø, Langeland and Tåsinge, the last two joined to Svendborg by bridge. Both Fåborg to the west and Svendborg are linked by boat to Ærø. The islands' country roads are ideal cycling territory, though it would be a mistake to consider this undulating land as flat. On the islands, a cyclist is part of the countryside, with a rush of air against the skin and, all around, a delicate fragrance of wild roses.

Lyø, Avernakø and Bjørnø

Three small islands can be reached by boat from Fåborg: Lyø, Avernakø and Bjørnø. The main occupation is farming and the villages have half-timbered farmhouses, a church and sometimes a school and inn. Treasure in the shape of six gold Bronze Age bowls was found at **Guldagre** (gold acre) on Avernakø. On Whitsunday this island brings out its maypoles, an ancient custom. **Bjørnø** (Bear Isle) has a rich bird life which is protected during the breeding season. The ferry to Søby in north Ærø takes around an hour.

Ærø

Cycling is beautiful on island roads with flower-studded verges, past small fields, velvet grass and farmhouses often shaded by ancient trees in pretty villages. Vivid light brings out the subtle moor colours of longer grass near the sea, against a constant cry of gulls.

Søby harbour is always busy, and there is a thatched white church from 1745, a typical old windmill and Skoldnæs lighthouse to the north. The road down to the main town of Ærøskøbing passes **Tranderup Vindeballe**, a double village with a church and inn on each side. **Olde Møllebakke** has a fine view and a memorial stone to Ærø's inclusion under the rule of the Danish crown in 1750.

Ærøskøbing has a harbour, a church from 1758 with beautiful votive ships (given by seafarers to hang in the church), and the tiny thatched cottages of the old sea captains. In one, **Bottle Peter's** is a fascinating collection of ships-in-bottles. From the time he went to sea at age 16, Peter Jacobsen built 1700 ships-in-bottles and 50 model ships. Opposite, in what was once the Poor House, the collection of stonemason **Hans Sculptor** has furniture, copper, clocks, pewter and paintings.

Ærøskøbing's old manor house is now a first-class hotel, Hotell Ærøhus, and there is also an old Dutch windmill.

The way to the skippers' town of **Marstal** in the south runs close to the sea on an embankment, all that remains of the island defences against Wendel pirates. In the 17th and 18th centuries, its golden age,

*Æ*_røskøbing is the main town of Ærø island, long a seafaring and market town, with many interesting old doors on the seaman's houses._

Marstal was home port to more ships than Copenhagen. **Jens Hansen's Maritime Museum** tells that history and has a collection of model ships. The church's votive ships are lovingly modelled and there is a special gallery for the sea captains. The boat from Marstal takes an hour to Rudkøbing on Langeland.

Several of the old houses where the seamen lived in Ærøskøbing have become workshops and museums, with collections of copper, pewter, hand-made bottles, clocks and paintings.

Langeland

Fifty years ago, a bicycle was Langeland's main means of transport, which makes this island a natural for cycling holidays. This is interesting terrain, studded with strange little hat-shaped hills called *hattebakker*. In some cases, farmers have laid out gardens on them, sometimes topped with a copper beech or a hawthorn. Langeland was the first place in Fyn to organize cycle paths with a map to match. These can be obtained from the tourist office in Rudkøbing.

The offshore island of **Strynø**, a short ferry ride from Rudkøbing, makes a fine day out. Sport fishing is a favourite here, with the mixture of the salty Kattegat to the north and the near-freshwater of the Baltic providing a wide variety of species. Fishing expeditions are run from the harbour.

Road 305 runs from north to south, but there are even smaller roads and cycle paths.

In Skrobelev, just outside Rudkøbing, is **Aquarium Langeland**, showing 250 salt and freshwater fish species and a coral reef exhibit. Further south, Skovsgaard, on the east coast, is in the care of Denmark's Nature Conservation Society. Many restored rooms are open to the public, and the former stable and garden house hold **Langelands Museum** with marvellous old horse-drawn carriages and forestry exhibits. The park offers lovely walks and picnic spots.

Skovsgaard Mølle (mill) is set on a *hattebakke* south of the manor. The mill yard has a garden with varieties of old roses rarely seen today. All these islands were a safe haven for primitive people and Langeland has some 230 prehistoric monuments. One of the best, south of Bagenkop near the land's end, is the island's best-preserved passage grave, high up on a hill near Søgård. It is very dark and calls for a torch. At the point are **Dovnsklint** (cliffs) where birdwatchers come to see the migrations twice-yearly. **Bagenkop** is the ferry terminal for Kiel in Germany, and the island's main fishing port, with a harbour full of white painted fishing boats.

Some 5km (3 miles) north of Rudkøbing, is another barrow, **Bjerrebygård Holmen**, covered with oak trees. Langeland has a climate that encourages gardens and cycling along, particularly through villages, you see some marvellous examples. The old churches are also lovely, usually painted white.

On this north end, from its hill top, **Trannekær Slot** has watched over the village below and most of the island for 700 years. Built as a fort the original walls are 3m (10ft) thick. The Ahlefeldt-Laurvig family still own the castle they have owned since 1535. A museum tells about the family, the life of the castle and the village.

There are many good safe beaches. **Stengade**, south of Trannekær, is well sheltered by woodlands down to the shore. The island's northern tip is a swimmer's delight, with nature areas behind the dunes.

Before peddling over the bridge to Tåsinge, walk through Rudkøbing's narrow streets, with merchants' town houses. A statue of H.C. Ørsted, who discovered electro-magnetism, stands in Gåsetorvet. He was born here.

Tåsinge

It would be hard to find a prettier island than Tåsinge, with its clipped hedges, lovely orchards, old village ponds alongside immaculate small houses and neat farms, many from the 18th century.

On the road north **Valdemars Slot**, down by the sound, is one of the largest privately owned manors. Christian IV built the castle in 1644, but its present-day appearance, including the small tea pavilion and the interiors, dates from the 1750s. The castle museum illustrates the history of a large manor over 350 years. Close by is the Ambrosius Oak, a giant tree named after the poet Ambrosius Stub.

Further north on this east side is the little town of **Troense**, one of Denmark's loveliest. Though founded by fruit-growers, it soon turned to the sea and was the home port for many sailing ships. Now, on a warm evening its harbour is a forest of masts, their owners taking a sundowner outside the old harbour inn. **Troense Museum**, in an old riding-school, shows models of many local craft, including one of the schooner *Copenhagen*, and an exhibition on the China Route which played a part of the port's past.

On a bicycle, it may be a hard pull up to the top of Breginge in the northeast, but it is worth it for the view from **Breginge Kirke**, across the sound and the south Fyn archipelago. Opposite the church is the old **Skippershjem**, with memorabilia of the drama that gave Tåsinge modern fame. It is the romantic story of the two lovers Elvira Madigan and Sixten Sparre, who chose to die together in Nørreskov (wood). The film was made on location here. In real life, Elvira was Hedvig Jensen, and the lovers lie buried together in Landet churchyard in the centre of Tåsinge.

The Svendborg bridge, also built in 1962, gives more fine views. From Svendborg, the circle to Fåborg is a pleasant run along the south of Fyn (see p.120).

From Fyn, the choice is either east along the north coast, with beaches such as Torresø Strand, yacht harbours and nature reserves, then back to Sjælland and Copenhagen, or west via the bridge into Jylland, the biggest region of this small but varied country.

Nordic Light – between North Sea and Kattegat

The peninsula of Jylland is Denmark's largest land mass, the only part of the country connected to the rest of Europe. There are some 500km (350 miles) between Tønder, close to the southern border with Germany, and Skagen in the very north. Much of Jylland is field, moorland and sand dune. The dunes are at their most magnificent down the celebrated west coast which draws visitors from all parts of Europe. The farmers of this countryside pioneered the farm-holiday where visitors stay, *en famille*, in a farmhouse, giving a helping hand if they want to. This idea has now spread far outside the borders of Denmark.

North Jylland

The northernmost tip of the peninsula of Jylland ends in a curved finger pointing into the Kattegat and to Sweden. The area has great stretches of silver-white sand, spikes of marram grass, gleaming blue seas that can turn rapidly to raging cream-white waves in a wind and clouds of every imaginable sort scudding or dawdling across the open sky.

Den Gamle By: the Old Town in Århus has a fine collection of over 65 traditional buildings brought together as an old community. It is a popular place for visitors and locals alike, with concerts and other entertainment.

No wonder that the Skagen painters came here in the late 19th century, taking their name and their inspiration from this 'Nordic light' at is most magical. The first were Anna and Michael Ancher, followed by P.S. Krøyer and Christian Krogh among others. Rejecting the European Impressionist tradition that was still in fashion, they developed a more realistic style.

Today, artists are joined by holiday-makers galore, both Danish and from abroad, in this dazzling northern land of **Vendsyssel**, where holiday cottages and campsites shelter behind dunes and tree plantations. Vendsyssel is in fact almost an island cut off from Jylland by Limfjorden.

To see the power of this wind, travel just west of Skagen, to **Den Tilsandede Kirke** (sand-covered church) with only its steeple still pointing up out of the ground.

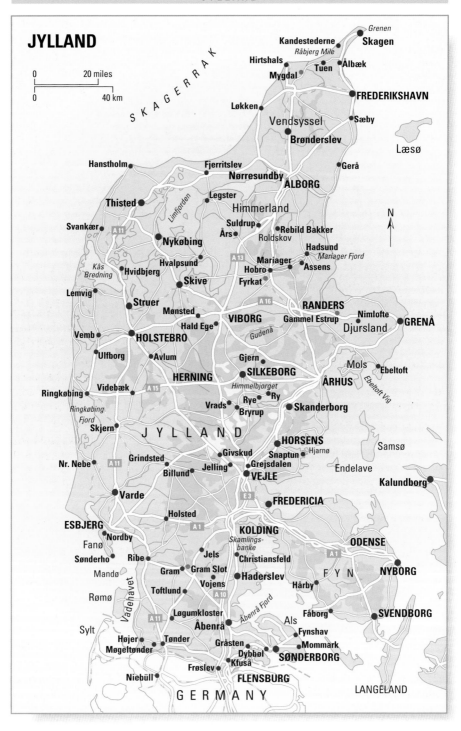

JYLLAND

0   20 miles

0   40 km

S K A G E R R A K

Grenen
Kandestederne   Skagen
Råbjerg Mile
Hirtshals   Ålbæk
Mygdal   Tuen

FREDERIKSHAVN

Løkken
Vendsyssel   Sæby

Brønderslev

Læsø

Hanstholm   Fjerritslev   Gerå
Nørresundby
ÅLBORG

Thisted   Legster
Himmerland   N

Svankær   A 11   Suldrup
Års   Rebild Bakker
Nykøbing   Roldskov
Hadsund
Hvalpsund   Mariager Fjord
Kås   Hvidbjerg   A 13 Mariager
Bredning   Hobro   Assens
Skive   Fyrkat
Lemvig   Hald Ege
Struer
Mønsted   A 16   **RANDERS**
VIBORG   Gammel Estrup   Nimlofte
Vemb   Hald Ege   Djursland   **GRENÅ**
HOLSTEBRO   Gudenå

Ulfborg   Avlum
Gjern   Mols   Ebeltoft
HERNING   **SILKEBORG**
Ringkøbing Videbæk A 15   Himmelbjerget   **ÅRHUS**
Vrads   Rye Ry
Ringkøbing   Bryrup Skanderborg
Fjord
Skjern   J Y L L A N D

HORSENS   Samsø

Nr. Nebe   A 11 Grindsted   Givskud Snaptun Hjarnø
Jelling   Grejsdalen   Endelave
Billund   **VEJLE**
Kalundborg
Varde

E 3   **FREDERICIA**

ESBJERG   Holsted
Nordby   A 1
Fanø   **KOLDING**   **ODENSE**
Sønderho Ribe   Jels Skamlings-
banke
Mandø   Gram Gram Slot Christiansfeld A 1
Haderslev   **NYBORG**
Toftlund Vojens   F Y N
Rømø   A 10   Hårby
Løgumkloster   Fåborg   **SVENDBORG**
Åbenrå Fjord
Sylt   **Åbenrå**   Als
Fynshav
Højer   Tønder Gråsten   Mommark
Møgeltønder   Dybbøl   **SØNDERBORG**
Frøslev Kfuså
Niebüll   **FLENSBURG**   LANGELAND

G E R M A N Y

*T*hanks to strong winds, this tower is all that is visible of Skt Lawrence Kirke, near Skagen, better known as the 'sand-covered church'.

It has stood like that since 1795, yet only a century earlier it had been the biggest church in Vendsyssel. Then the dunes began to drift and, dig and clear and fight as they would, the parishioners could not save it. The process continues and Råberg Mile, on the west of the northern finger, is the current best – or worst – example of migrating sand dunes. Each year, wind and sand move them a little further east. This Danish desert is fascinating and can only be entered on foot, most easily from **Kanstederne**, which has a surviving church with unique baroque wood carvings. Some 5km (3 miles) north of Skagen, the finger of land slims to nothing at **Grenen**, where every visitor feels obliged to stand with one leg in the Kattegat, the other in the Skagerrak.

The Nordic Light painters are remembered in **Skagens Museum** which has a unique collection from the 1850-1930 period. **Anchers Hus** is preserved as it was when Anna and Michael Ancher lived there. **Drachman Hus** was once the home of the marine artist and poet Holger Drachmann, another of the group. **Hjørring Museum of Art** has more examples of a style that few can resist.

Skagen has not lost its characteristic yellow fishermen's houses depicted by the painters and is still a fishing port with some 12,000 inhabitants. Apart from art galleries, it has **Skagens Fortidsminder** an open-air museum of rural buildings, fishing tackle and rescue gear.

Hirtshals on the northwest point of Jylland is a busy port with ferries to Kristiansand in Norway. **Nordsømuseet** is a saltwater aquarium with North Sea fish and seals. Inland, at Tuen, the **Ørnereservatet** is an eagle sanctuary where white-tailed and golden eagles fly freely. Inside is a photographic exhibition and the reserve has had many breeding successes. To protect the birds, opening hours are limited.

The east coast is less crowded, but old fishing ports such as **Ålbædk** are pleasantly full of summer people, as is **Frederikshavn**, Vendsyssel's largest town and port. It is a Viking city with three interesting museums: **Bangsbomuseet**, in an old manor house, holds a Viking trading ship; **Krudttårnsmuseet** is in the old powder-magazine, all that survives of the 17th-century fortifications, and holds weapons and uniforms from that period; the **Bunkermuseet** describes Frederikshavn's defences

during World War II and the exploits of the Danish resistance movement of that time.

Frederikshavn has ferries to Norway, Sweden and the offshore island of **Læsø**, just an hour-and-a-half away, a pleasant place for an excursion or holiday. It has a natural landscape of heath and small pools, with fine bird and plant life. Some houses are still thatched with the traditional seaweed, and welcoming beaches line the north coast. All round Jylland you will see the coveted Blue Flags that indicate clean sand and seawater.

The 16th-century town of **Sæby**, some 17 km (10 miles) south of Frederikshavn, was founded around its 15th-century church, Skt Maria Klosterkirke which has a treasure trove of murals. The town is full of interesting old houses, including **Sæbygård**, in woodland to the north. **Voergaard Slot**, a Renaissance castle, has a unique collection of porcelain and art, with works by Rubens, Raphael and Goya.

At the turn of the century artists from many lands discovered Skagen, delighting in its Nordic light. They built their homes here, turning it into an artists' colony. Today artists are still painting.

North Jylland has long been well known for its amber and the tradition continues with stonecutters and jewellers specializing in working the stone. There are amber workshops at **Gerå**, also on the east coast, and **Mygdal**, further northwest and the biggest in Jylland. You will also find amber in Aalborg, the north's largest town.

People all over the world know **Aalborg** for its *aquavit* alone, but this town on Limfjorden, with its twin **Nørresundby** on the north side of the fjord, has much more. First a Viking city and then a rich trading centre, by the 18th century Aalborg was Denmark's second largest city. The magnificent six-storey **Stenhus** of the rich merchant, Jens Bang, recalls the in-fighting of this period. In 1624, as he built his new house, he took revenge on his enemies by including caricature carvings of them on the front, and on one side a picture of himself sticking his tongue out at the city's great and good. Today, Stenhus has a restaurant and wine cellar. **Jørgen Olufsenshus** is a typical working merchant's house from a slightly earlier date. Both are on Østerå, once the harbour. Despite its leanings towards the sea, Aalborg lies in the middle of farming country and, each week, the old cattle market at Nyhavnsgade is still busy.

The 16th-century **Budolfi Kirke** is dedicated to the English patron saint of seamen, St Botolph, and **Helligåndsklosteret** (Monastery of the Holy Ghost) was built in 1431. **Aalborghus**, the town's castle, has just one wing left of the original four.

Jomfru Ane Gade is a little cobbled street with cafés, restaurants and bars. Aalborg can claim over 200 restaurants, bars, nightclubs and cafés, which make for a sparkling nightlife.

Today, still active in commerce, the city is a well-stirred mixture of old and new. **Aalborghallen**, a huge modern hall, was built to house exhibitions and concerts, and **Nordjyllands Kunstmuseum** was designed by the distinguished Finnish architect Alvar Aalto in the 1970s. It now specializes in Danish painting, sculpture since 1800 and modern international works.

Jom Fru Ane Gade in Aalborg is very much more than a bustling picturesque shopping street. At night more than 200 restaurants, cafés and pubs continue to keep it busy.

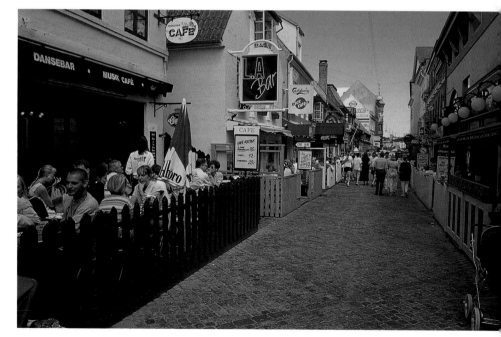

The sailing ship Danmark *at Aalborg. After the Viking's, Aalborg became a famous port and trading centre on the route between northern Scandinavia and Europe.*

ground with some 700 graves, the oldest from the seventh and eighth centuries, and some 150 ship-shaped stone settings, like those at Lejre-Kornerup, a small fleet of the dead.

Every 4th July, thousands of Danish-Americans and their Danish kin come to **Rebild Bakker**, south of Aalborg, to celebrate Independence Day in this National Park. On the open expanse of heather-clad hills there is much singing, and 'Old Glory' and the 'Dannebrog' fly high. In keeping with the mood, there is the **Lincoln Log Cabin**, a replica of his childhood home, and a Danish-American **Emigrant Museum**.

To the west, **Limfjorden** is a landscape of contrasts. Unlike the narrow, slab-sided Norwegian fjords, this fjord is largely cut off from the sea by many arms of land forming an almost circular expanse of water with many offshoots and islands.

Mariager Fjord on the east coast is very different: a long narrow ribbon leading inland to the towns of Mariager and Hobro with steep slopes, and trees and meadows reaching down to the water's edge. The hills of **Bramslev Bakker** on the north side have a unique flora among the junipers, a magnet for botanists. **Mariager** itself, on the south side, is known as 'The Town of Roses'. Many of these little North Jylland towns have remained in a remarkable state of preservation but few can match Mariager, with its perfect half-timbered

Aalborg Zoo is the largest in northern Europe with more than a thousand species in a reconstructed African savanna where animals roam freely. **Tivoliland** is North Jylland's main amusement park with 80 rides and a variety of amusements. **Søfarts og Marinemuseet** traces civil and naval shipping in Denmark over the last 200 years and there is a Danish-built submarine on display.

Across Limfjord, north of Nørresundby, **Lindholm Høje Museet** has traces of much earlier seafarers, with finds from a barrow grave dating back to the Iron and Viking ages, including Arabian coins. **Lindholm Høje** itself is Europe's largest Viking burial buildings, cobbled streets and old steam train. A cycle tour around the fjord is a good way to see the country, past manor houses, ruins and the fjord towns of Assens and Hadsund, with Hobro at the inner end.

Himmerland, between Limfjord and Mariager, and the area to the south have long been inhabited as shown by various ancient graves and Viking relics. **Borremose**, near Aars, is protected by earthworks and well preserved by the bog. It was originally built in the Bronze Age and was restored by Iron Age people. At **Suldrup** near Støvring, there is a Stone Age passage grave, with Bronze Age remains at **Frendrup Nihøje**.

Very exciting is the fortress of **Fyrkat** 3.5km (2 miles) southwest of Hobro, one of only four left by the Danish Vikings. Four earth fortifications enclose 16 buildings, designed to house 800 men, and possibly their wives and children. Just after it was built, Fyrkat burnt down and it was not until modern times that a longhouse was reconstructed. There is also a large burial site outside the fortress. Hobro Museum houses the finds from Fyrkat.

These heather-clad heaths are fine country for natural history. **Lille Vildmose** is the largest raised bog in Denmark with deer and wild boar. Though the moss is not open to the public, binoculars give a good view from Mulbjergene. Also near Hobro, **Lille Mølle Bird Sanctuary** has a huge collection of birds and **Rold Skov** is Denmark's largest wooded area, a lovely mixture of beech and conifer.

Right in the heart of Jylland, Viborg is surrounded by lakes, rivers, oak trees, heaths and farmland, most notable at **Hald**, a forest area that is managed by the State Forest Authority. It offers marvellous natural pathways and tours around **Haldsø** (lake) and the forest, which also contains

Hald Hovegård and an old inn, **Niels Bygge Kro**.

Viborg is one of Denmark's oldest towns, going back to ancient times. It is now a crossroads for six different routes. At the centre, **Viborg Domkirke** was founded in 1130 and built in granite. The present building was completed only in 1876 and has beautiful murals by Joakim Skovgaard, whose work can also be seen in **Skovgaard Museet**. **Søndersogn Kirke** has pews decorated with some 200 paintings.

Interesting documents at **Landarkivets Samlinger** contain local archives going back to around 1200AD with information about many of Jylland's people. This might not be easy for non-Danish readers were there not helpful guided tours. **Viborg Museum** has craftspeople making and selling local craftwork.

West of Viborg used to be a centre for limestone mining and two *kalk gruber* (mines) are still open to the public. **Mønsted** has 35km (25 miles) of galleries, making it Denmark's largest mine, a **Limeworks Museum** and an intriguing **Bat Museum**. **Daugbjerg** is deeper, going down 70m (230ft), but is not as big. It too has a bat museum.

Randers, east of Viborg, stands at the inner end of Randers Fjord, and is ideal for sunbathing and watersports. The town is found at the southern end of Mariager's vintage railway which runs in July. All around the town, and towards the eastern peninsula of **Djursland**, is an area of manor houses and castles. Most interesting of all is **Gammel Estrup**, built in 1620, which houses **Dansk Landbrugsmuseum** and **Jyllands Herregårdsmuseum** (farming and manor house museums). The first traces the development of agriculture, the second has opulent decorated interiors from many manor houses.

On Djursland peninsula, the forests are home to deer and other animals, and the northern coast has lovely beaches, good walking, cycling, sailing and horseriding. **Mols Bjerge** (hills), which stand on a small peninsula further south, give Djursland the profile of a misshapen beast's head, on a map. The biggest town is the port of **Grenå** with ferries to Anholt on the Kattegat island of Ørkenen, to Sweden and to Hundested on Isefjorden. It also has a good beach at **Grenå Strand**, and **Kattegatcentret** with pools and aquaria showing the Kattegat's marine life and a large display of tropical sharks. Inland from Grenå, close to Nimtofte, **Djurs Sommerland** provides a host of activities for young and old, including an aquascape.

Mols Bjerge was formed as the icecap retreated at the end of the last Ice Age, leaving great crevasses, such as **Tinghulen**. Until the 16th century this was used as the local parliament. There are many more traces of habitation going back much further. A most impressive cairn, **Porsekær Stenhus**, is the largest in Denmark. Pathways are rough and can be steep so that cycling is a challenge in this unique corner, full of deer, badgers, foxes, grass snakes and birds.

Right in the open mouth of the peninsula's 'beast-head' is **Ebeltoft**, a delightful small market town with a lovely centre. **Det Gamle Rådhus** is Denmark's smallest town hall, now converted to a museum. Its garden is bright with old-fashioned cottage flowers and the narrow cobbled ways go back centuries, taking you far from the present day. **Glassmuseet** has permanent and changing exhibitions of Danish and international glass.

From the oldest to the newest, Ebeltoft harbour has a **Wind Power Mill Park**, with 16 elegant silver-coloured generators which produce enough electricity for around 600 families. It is the biggest marine-based windmill park in the world, and is in keeping with Denmark's preoccupation with the protection of the environment.

In **Ebeltoft Vig** (bay) the old resurfaces with the *Fregatten Jylland* (*Frigate Jylland*). Built in 1862, *Jylland* is the world's longest wooden ship, the last of a long line of battleships. She has been fully restored and provides interesting tours that evoke what must have been a hard life. And, when the late summer night begins to fall, Ebeltoft goes to bed, happy in the knowledge that the town's **Vægtere**, the old brigade of night watchmen in their long dark coats, are patrolling the streets!

Mid-Jylland

Like most of Jylland, the centre of the peninsula is made up of undulating fields and water, though it does have one of Denmark's highest hills, Himmelbjerget in the beautiful Lake District. Mid-Jylland also has a number of smallish towns on the coast and inland, with the flat white sandhills of the west providing a contrast to the greater drama of the east.

Århus

People have lived in this beautiful spot at the centre of a great bay since the 10th century when the Vikings settled at Århus. Denmark's second city, it has a population of 250,000 with expanding commerce especially around the port. There is a ferry from here to Kalundborg in Sjælland.

Århus has a vigorous arts scene culminating in the September **Århus Festival**, which makes full use of **Musikhuset**, the modern concert hall, all light glass and indoor plants, as well as every other possible venue. It brings in Danish and international

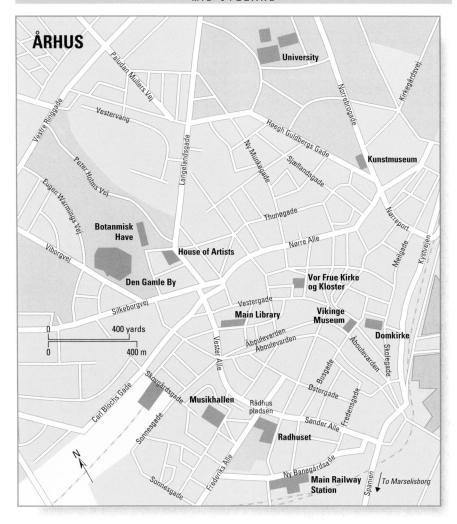

artists, from famous classical musicians to pop groups and jazz. Musikhuset is also home to the Århus Symphony Orchestra and the Danish National Opera. The greatest recent addition to Århus's amenities – Fine for the festival too – is **Scandinavian Center** with a huge glass-covered 'street' in the middle, full of shops and businesses, a great congress centre, and Kadisson/ SAS's newest hotel, all opened for the 1995 Festival.

The striking redstone cathedral, **Århus Domkirke**, is Denmark's longest church at 96m (315ft). Founded in 1201, its Gothic style and fine murals were added in the 15th century, with a wonderful three-panelled altarscreen by the famous Norwegian woodcarver, Bernt Notke.

Even older is **Vor Frue Kirke og Kloster** (Church of Our Lady and Abbey). In 1955, a small church was found under the choir, a vaulted room that dated from

137

*F*_{olk} *in Århus were delighted in the 1960s when Viking ruins were found during building work. All over Jylland, Viking remains continue to be discovered.*

around 1060. It is now a church under the choir. Dominican monks built the present church, with fine murals and an altarpiece by another famous woodcarver, Claus Berg. The monks' old chapterhouse has now also been consecrated, making Vor Frue Kirke three churches in one.

Opposite the cathedral is the **Viking Museum**, unexpectedly in a branch of Unibank. When the bank was being built in the 1960s, excavations revealed part of a semi-circular Viking rampart, six Viking houses and various middens. Now in the cellar, there is a section of the wall, a reconstructed house, belongings and tools.

God and Mammon meet on the cathedral square, in the lively and colourful market held here on Wednesdays and Saturdays. **Rådhuset** (Town Hall), not far away to the south, is unmistakable with its Norwegian marble cladding and high tower, standing among tall lime trees. Take a tour for a good view. In the square is the Pig's Well, a delightful carving of a sow with piglets.

A favourite place for visitors is **Den Gamle By**, an open-air museum with more than 65 half-timbered houses that have the atmosphere of a real community, a town rather than just farmhouses. Perhaps it is the effect of the original Mayor's House of Århus, built in 1597 and brought here from Lille Torv. There is always something going on in Den Gamle By: workshops are working, shops are selling, and there is music and entertainment.

Århus has been a university town since the late 1920s, and from the first modest buildings it has grown into the **University Park**. The fine modern yellow buildings were designed by Danish architect C.F. Møller. The university has natural history and classical archaeology museums.

Århus is not short of museums. The **Medical History Museum** is close by the university, and the **Århus Kunstmuseum** has the oldest and best collection of Danish art outside of Copenhagen from the 18th to 20th centuries. The greenhouses of **Botanisk Have** hold a remarkable collection of both tropical and sub-tropical plants. The 20 hectares

(50 acres) of garden are also home to an open-air theatre.

The university and several colleges of higher education give the city a youthful feel, with students and their bicycles in the streets and young people at the pavement cafés and in the bars. There is a good nightlife with ever-changing clubs and live music. **Tivoli Friheden** amusement park is popular with the younger age group.

Tivoli is close to the beautiful **Marselisborgskovene** (woods), at **Marselisborg**, which also has a royal residence, a 60-acre **Memorial Park** to Danes who died in World War I, a sports park, and **Marselisborghallen**, where the Århus Symphony Orchestra plays in summer. There are woods and open land all around Århus, as well as beaches, but this forest stretching along the fjord is among the most beautiful, and includes a deer park with roe and sika deer, and wild boar.

In the heart of Marselisborgskovene (reached by bus from the centre) is **Moesgård**. This beautiful manor house, at the end of an avenue of rowan trees, holds the **Forhistorisk Museum** (Prehistoric Museum). Its most famous exhibit, **Graaballe Manden**, is one of two well-preserved Iron Age men, miraculously preserved in the Jylland bogs. With skin tanned to dark leather he still has hair, nails, teeth and a cut on his throat over which archaeologists argue. Was he executed? Or sacrificed in some religious ceremony? There is also a collection of runic stones. But this is not just an indoor exhibition. Afterwards, follow the **Prehistoric Path** through fields and woods, past layouts from the Stone and Bronze ages, and reconstructed buildings from Iron Age and Viking times. En route there is also a 200-year-old mill, **Skovmølle** (mill in the woods) with a small restaurant.

MEET THE DANES

One of the most difficult things on a foreign holiday is to get to know any locals well enough to ask all the questions you are dying to ask. Danes are friendly, polite people and may well exchange a word at a pavement café, on a boat tour or at a bus stop and readily answer a query about a place or direction. But it will be a brief comment and very much on a courteous rather than an intimate level.

Now, Århus and Odense have schemes to make it easier, thanks to a 'Meet the Danes' programme, set up by a group of local people who, in turn, are interested in exchanging views and polishing their foreign languages.

As a visitor, you need do no more than enquire at the tourist bureau when you arrive. The staff will ask a few questions about interests and hobbies and will try to match you to a host family. An invitation follows for an evening of coffee, cakes and conversation in their home and, who knows, you could make a friend for life. There is no charge.

The Lake District

Jylland's Lake District is made up of the Gudenå, Denmark's longest river, and the lakes it winds through – Mossø, Knudsø, Julsø, Brassø and various smaller stretches – on its way north to Randersfjord and the sea. Around the lakes is some beautiful forest scenery. **Silkeborg** at the northwestern end of the Lake District is a newish town in a long-inhabited area, illustrated by **Tollund Manden,** the second Iron Age man, some 2,000 years old, found in a bog in 1950 by two local farmers. His preserved corpse is in **Silkeborg Museum**, just as it was found.

Modern Silkeborg was founded in the 1840s to manufacture paper, by Michael Drewesen, whose statue stands in **Torvet**, a colourful place to be on market day. **Silkeborg Kunstmuseum** is devoted both to the works of Asger Jorn, who was born in the town, and the 20th-century COBRA (Copenhagen, Brussels, Amsterdam) group of artists. Silkeborg also has an animal park and **Ferskvands Akvarium og Museum** with otters, frogs, newts, aquatic plants and fish, the last arranged so that you look at them through large windows, as though you too were underwater.

You can tour the lakes on foot, by motor boat, canoe or rowing boat, but one of the gentlest ways of getting around is on an old paddle steamer, s/s *Hjejlen*, that plies between Silkeborg and Ry, below **Himmelbjerget**, which slopes down into Julsø. The 1875 tower adds another 24m (80ft) to the hill's 147m (400ft). Himmelbjerget makes a pleasant and not-too-energetic walk.

Not far from Ry are the few remains of **Øm Kloster**, once one of the richest monasteries in the area. After the Reformation, Frederik II had it demolished and used the stone to build a new castle in Skanderborg, further south. In the Middle Ages **Gammel Rye** was a religious centre, indicated by several churches and holy springs, the best known being **Skt Sørens Kilde**. All over the Lake District there is an astonishing number of old churches and church ruins. **Gammel Rye Mølle Museum** includes the unusual **Træsko (Clog) Museum** (clogs were once worn here), and **Gudenå Museet** tells about the river and its life over the last 8,000 years.

All around are walking and cycle tracks and the small town of **Them**, which stands high on the Jylland ridge, has some of the best unspoilt forest and lake country. **Byrup**, a little further south, has a veteran railway running over bridges and dams to **Vrads**, which has a good restaurant.

The Gudenå river winds through the **Gjern Bakker** (hills). There is an old royal road along one bank, and on the other a towpath once used by boatmen to pull their barges back to Silkeborg from the port of Randers, no mean task. Today it is a nature trail. In Gjern itself, the **Jysk Automobilmuseum** (car museum) brings in big crowds. This is an area rich in history, with old monasteries in **Tvilum**, which still has an abbey church, and **Alling**, where the conspicuous ruins stand beside Allingsø (lake).

Skanderborg in the southwest dates back some 400 years and has an old town district which deserves a visit. There is also a museum with relics going back 6,000 years; **Skanderup Kirke** has interesting frescoes; and **Dyreparken**, once a royal hunting ground, is today a public park with some attractive sculpture. Skanderborg is also famed for waterskiing and **Stilling Sø** has produced many medal-winners. The annual rock music festival is very lively.

Across the rugged heathland to the west of Silkeborg, and linked by train, is **Herning**. As an education and training centre for young people, it has excellent facilities for active pursuits from fishing to horseriding and golf. There is a strong tradition of art here too, with work by Danish and international artists such as Richard Mortensen and Piero Mazoni, exhibited in **Herning Kunstmuseum** in the circular **Skulpturparken**. The **Geometrical Gardens** next door were created by Professor C. Th. Sørensen, the garden architect who also designed both the museum and the sculpture park.

The **Carl-Henning Pedersen and Else Alfelts Museum** shows the work which the two COBRA artists donated to the town. Pedersen was responsible for both the ceramic façade of this museum and the unusual yard with its 220m (370ft) ceramic frieze at Herning Kunstmuseum.

VITUS BERING

The adventurous life of Vitus Bering, seafarer and explorer, began in the Jylland town of Horsens in 1681. Like many others then, Bering left his home to serve under Peter the Great, the Russian Tsar.

Peter the Great fired Bering with his own enthusiasm to shed light on one of the great unknowns of the time: were Asia and America joined or separated by sea? In 1725, Bering set off on the *St Peter* to make the perilous journey along the north of Canada. He established that there was a sea between the two continents and, eight years later, he departed again for the same treacherous waters.

This time, disaster struck the expedition and Bering drowned when the *St Peter* was wrecked on an island in the Commander Group, which now bears his name.

Horsens already had two of Vitus Bering's cannon in the Vitus Bering Memorial Park but in 1991 came a momentous find. A group left Horsens to follow Bering's last journey and, to their great joy, discovered the explorer's island grave containing his skeleton. From a cast of the skull, Horsens Museum has been able to reconstruct his face so that, today, any visitor can look at Vitus Bering, from more than 250 years away.

Nygård Gammel Skole is a typical moorland school, with a schoolroom dating from 1878; children love to feed and play with the tame rare animals of Jylland's **Mini-Zoo**.

Southeast of the Lake District, the fjord town of **Horsens** is linked to the lakes not only by road but by a 60km (45-mile) nature path from Silkeborg, which is wonderful to walk or cycle. At the head of a broad and beautiful fjord, Horsens attracts sailors to its excellent 400-berth marina. Non-sailors can also enjoy being on the water, on regular ferries from the fishing

hamlet of **Snaptun**, at the approach to the fjord, to the islands of **Endelave** and **Hjarnø**, which has one of the smallest churches in Denmark and Viking tumuli.

Horsens dates back to the 12th century. It has a delightful pedestrian centre and the **Glud Museum** which has old village houses with their original furniture and domestic utensils. Several of Horsens' grand buildings are still in use today. **Lichtenberg Palæ**, an elegant baroque palace, is now a fine hotel in Søndergade, and **Bygholm Herregård** which has a long and turbulent history is now a conference centre. The **Klosterkirken** (Abbey Church) from 1201 has kept its original purpose and has rich, glowing decoration. The unusual, gleaming white tower of **Sønderbro Kirke** is a shining example of modern skills.

During 1991-2 Horsens town centre saw a lot of building work and this revealed a history that goes back to the year 900AD. Horsens is also prominent in the environmental movement and has several districts designed to be environmentally friendly. The town is involved in the WHO project 'Healthy Town for the Year 2000' which has brought people from around the world to watch progress.

Further south, **Velje**, a town of some 50,000, lies in a beautiful area of forest. It also has its own fjord, with a road bridge crossing north–south. Both Velje and Horsens were early pioneers of farm holidays and this is a favourite way to visit the area. The town itself is the starting point for trips by vintage steam train through the mysterious valley of **Gresdalen** to the north and on to Jelling.

Jelling is one of the most important and celebrated Viking sites in Denmark. A thousand years ago, it was the Danish royal seat and is the burial place of the Viking kings, Gorm den Gamle (the Old)

and his son Harald Blåtend (Bluetooth) who ruled from here. Beside the present church are two large burial mounds. The first is of King Gorm and his wife Queen Thyra. The smaller runic stone was raised by Gorm to his wife. The big stone was raised by Harald who wrote: 'King Harald made these memorials to Gorm, his father, and Thyra, his mother, the Harald who won for himself all Denmark and Norway and made the Danes Christians'.

Below the Romanesque church in Jelling are traces of three earlier wooden churches. In the oldest are skeletal remains which may be those of Gorm and Thyra, moved there by Harald after his baptism. Gorm's importance to Denmark is that the Danish royal line started with him and has continued, tortuous but unbroken, to the present Queen Margrethe, making Denmark Europe's oldest monarchy.

Northwest from Jelling is **Givskud Løveparken**, an animal park with apes, exotic birds and lions. Visitors can drive through or take a safari bus.

Billund is a very small town with an international airport. It is a central airport for Jylland but its real purpose is to bring visitors to **Legoland**, entirely made of the famous Lego bricks. Start a visit with the Lego train and pass through this world of bricks, from the canals of Amsterdam to the Mount Rushmore presidents, from Amalienborg Palace in Copenhagen to the Statue of Liberty. There is a Wild West town where visitors pan for gold, a children's driving school using minicars, and a children's theatre. Many activities have

THE EGTVED GIRL

Egtved, to the southeast of Billund in Mid-Jylland is best known for the Egtved Pigen, the Egtved Girl. She was found in a hilltop grave in 1921 and brought widespread fame to the village.

Probably aged between 8 and 16, she was buried around 2,500 years ago. Somehow, the grave remained intact. What made the find really exciting is that the clothes that the Egtved Girl had been buried in were still intact, some of the best-preserved examples of Bronze Age clothing ever found. How they survived has not been well explained. There were other finds in the oak coffin, including some jewellery and a very beautiful belt buckle.

The finds are now in the National Museum in Copenhagen but the reconstructed burial mound looks as it was when first discovered on the hilltop at Egtved. A statue of the Egtved Girl shows her wearing the clothes she was found in, with the jewellery and the beautiful belt buckle.

a slant on learning, which is part of the Legoland philosophy. The museum building has a marvellous collection of toys, but pride of place goes to Titania's Palace built by Sir Neville Wilkinson in the early 1900s and bought by Legoland at a Christie's auction in London in 1978.

Billund's **Center Mobilium** houses three interesting museums: **Danmarks**

Legoland can claim to attract more visitors – not just youngsters but their parents too – than almost anywhere else in Denmark. They come to marvel at a miniature world, made out of the toy building bricks, invented by a Billund manufacturer.

Flyvemuseum with aircraft including a Spitfire and a DC-3; **Danmarks Bilmuseum** with 75 classic cars; and **Falck Museet** full of shiny red fire engines with ambulances, frogmen and much more.

In addition to this concentration of amusements, the area offers some fine scenery, interesting ruins, trails and walks, golf and fishing.

Gateway to the West

Esbjerg is Denmark's main west coast port, with a ferry link to Harwich and Newcastle in Britain, and to the Faroes, via Norway and Iceland. A hundred years ago, Esbjerg was just a handful of houses but the 1864 war with Germany led to its swift development. Now there are 70,000 inhabitants, and there is all the excitement of an active harbour and a lively town.

Twenty minutes away by boat is the old seafaring town of Nordby, on the lovely island of **Fanø**. Fanø was once the home of great sailing ships, and at the southern tip, **Sønderho Kirke** has votive ships decorating the church. Fanø was already a community in the 13th century, and its golden age came after Fanø people bought their island for 6,000 Rigsdaler in 1741. Now, this quiet island holds fast to its own culture, with a unique costume still used for festive occasions.

Nordby, the ferry terminal in Fanø, has typically narrow streets and small houses with pretty painted doors. There are 14km (11 miles) of beach down the west coast, along with camping sites and cottages. Though Fanø is now a holiday island, Nordby has reminders of its seafaring past in **Sømans Kirke**, a typical seamen's church, and a museum.

But **Sønderho** in the south is the pearl, an idyllic village, its lanes lined with thatched cottages with brass lamps, shipping mementoes, figureheads and china figures gracing the windows. **Sønderho Kro**, now in the care of Denmark's National Trust, was opened as an inn in 1722. It has a marvellous view over the tidal flats and is a good spot for birdwatching. **Sømans Kirke** is half a century younger, and **Hannes Hus** is a museum.

To the north of Esbjerg is a long, open coastline, with dunes and marram grass, endless blue sea, seals lying on sandbanks, and people doing the same on the beaches and swimming in the shallow waves. In winter, this can be a rough place with a piercing wind sweeping in from the sea.

As a port, **Esbjerg** is a town where different nationalities come and go, with excellent shops and pavement restaurants. But the sea and its uses are the main attraction. Get up early and the fish auctions are absorbing and, in a town with several hundred fishing boats, it is interesting to visit the yards where they are built. The main landmark, **Vandtårnet** (water tower) shows Germanic influence, and the tourist office is in the old gaol! **Fiskeri og Søfartsmuseet** (Fishing and Maritime Museum) has in part an open-air setting with fishermen's cottages. The saltwater pools of **Saltvandsakvariet** (Aquarium) hold fish and shellfish galore and at the **Sealarium**'s large pool, seals laze and play. There is a daily feeding session and a seal rescue service is run from here.

East Across Jylland

It takes around one and a half hours of leisurely driving to cross Jylland to the east coast and the bridges to Fyn, but you will almost certainly want to stop along the way, so allow plenty of time. Instead of going straight for the bridge, detour off the main road (E20) where it crosses the big north–south route (E45) and turn into

Kolding. Until 1864 and the war with Germany, Denmark's southern boundary passed through what are now the town's southern suburbs.

The frontier was the reason for **Koldinghus**, which has been the site of a castle since 1268. Its fine buildings include the great hall, the chapel and the library. **Koldinghus Museum** has exhibitions including one of the 1848-50 Slesvig War. Throughout the castle some stunningly beautiful restoration work was completed in 1989. The Giant's Tower gives a magnificent view of the town, the fjord and over to Fyn.

Other places not to miss are **Den Geografiske Have** (Geographical Gardens), 30 acres with 2,000 tree and shrub species, gathered worldwide and laid out in geographical groupings, together with some 5,000 roses; and **Kunstmuseet Trapholt**, the latest museum of modern art in Denmark, its building the result of an architectural competition.

Just before the bridge, at the railway junction south of **Fredericia**, detour north into the main part of this fortified town founded by Frederik III in 1650. **Fredericia Vold** dates from the 17th century and has some of the best-preserved ramparts in northern Europe, with eight magnificent bastions, surrounded by the old moat. The bastions give superb views of the fjord, forest and fields.

Fredericia was once a tobacco town and **Fredericia Museet**, housed in five old buildings, recalls a trade that only ended in the early 1980s; it also holds memorabilia of the town's large Jewish community. The old **Lillebælt Bro** (bridge) which dates from 1935, gives a fine view of the newer motorway and railway bridges taking visitors on to Fyn and, eventually, Copenhagen.

South Jylland

No area of Denmark has been fought over so fiercely in the past, or so recently, as South Jylland with its border to Germany. In early times, the Danes built the Dannevirke, a great wall, to keep out invaders from the south. In the 19th century this area was beset with two wars over Slesvig-Holsten (Schleswig-Holstein) and much was lost to Prussia after the great battle of Dybbøl. This land was only recovered in 1920 when the matter was finally settled. Now, all is peaceful.

South Jylland is largely flat country with wide marshlands and dunes in the west where the sea flooded regularly until both Denmark and Germany built dykes. There are forests too, some natural and many planted woodlands which the Danes call *plantage*.

Just south of Esbjerg is Denmark's oldest town, **Ribe**, going back at least to the ninth century, and some claim to the eighth century after excavations revealed coins from that age. Much of the centre of the town is a conservation area with a unique atmosphere of the past. There are more half-timbered houses here than anywhere else in Denmark and Ribe preserves the custom of a night watchman. Each summer evening around 10pm a **vægter** (watchman) tours the streets, singing old songs, telling stories, making sure that all is well and the citizens can sleep secure. He is usually accompanied by a group of visitors.

Ribe became a Bishopric in 948AD and the **Domkirken** (Cathedral), dating largely from 1117, dominates the town. A fine example of Romanesque architecture, the chancel of this old building has modern paintings and mosaics by Carl-Henning Pedersen. One survival from the days when the sea flooded regularly is the bell in the

15th-century tower which rang out when danger threatened. Another is the town's flood marker. The cathedral's Cat's Head Door, is said to be for use by the Devil.

Skt Catherinæ Kirke og Kloster was the only one of the four original abbeys to survive the Reformation and you can tour the medieval cloisters from the church, though not the abbey itself. **Quedens Gaard** is one of three buildings which house the **Ribe Antiquarian Collection**; **Det Gamle Rådhus** is the old Town Hall and **Hans Tausens Hus**, the old bishop's palace, has an exhibition of 60,000 Viking Age finds. Ribe harbour, long silted up, is suitable only for small pleasure boats.

Offshore is the tiny island of **Mandø**, with an inn and a kirk, and around 100 inhabitants. It is reached by a tractor-drawn postal bus at low tide. To the south, the bigger island of **Rømø** has been linked to the mainland and the town of Skærbæk since 1948 when a 9km (5.5-mile) embankment was built. It is possible to drive a car across. This has long been a seafaring island, which at one time provided some 50 commanders for Dutch whaling vessels off Greenland. The wealth they brought in is evident in **Nationalmuseets Kommandørgård**, once the home of a well-to-do commander (as the Dutch called them). It has music and folk-dancing displays in the summer.

Rømø also has Denmark's oldest and smallest school at Toftum, which once had 40 pupils. **Rømø Kirke** is appropriately dedicated to St Clements, patron saint of seafarers, and **Tønnisgård** is an 18th-century sea-captain's farm, now a visitor centre and home of the tourist office. All along the west coast there is a beautiful white shore.

Rømø is linked by boat to Sylt, the next island south, a long thin strip of an island which belongs to Germany. **Vadehavet**

The harbour at Ribe, Denmark's oldest town. The harbour can now only be used by smaller boats, as it has been silted up for many years.

(the Wadden Sea), which lies inshore of this line of islands starting with Fanø off Esbjerg, and the beaches around it, is a unique wildlife area. Scientists have identified 500 lower animal species in the tidal waters, and more than 20 types of plants not found anywhere else, while the embankment and the various dykes make the sandflats near Rømø one of Europe's most important sites for wading birds.

146

hawkers'. The town also has a horse fair and a street festival.

Tønder, a port before the dykes were built, gained its charter in 1243 and has magnificent old merchant houses. Tønder is also known for its goldsmiths and silversmiths, and particularly for lacemaking. Consecrated in 1592, **Kristkirken** has a very richly adorned interior.

A walk along the cobble-stoned village street of **Møgeltønder**, with its thatched houses, is said to be a walk through Europe's most beautiful village and the claim is strong. Also have a look at the newly restored murals in **Møgeltønder Kirke**, where the organist still plays on an organ dating from 1679.

South of Kolding, **Christiansfeld**, a little way inland, is a distinctive town founded in 1773 by Moravian immigrants who sought religious freedom. The huge Moravian church, **Brødremenighedens Kirke** can hold a thousand people and the distinctive houses, with their beautifully painted doorways, have a pleasing slightly un-Danish air. The great food speciality is gingerbread, often made in unusual shapes. **Søsterhuset** (Widows' House) is now a museum and in **Gudsageren** (the graveyard or God's Acre) the graves lie in the traditional Moravian way: men's to the west, women's to the east.

Some 13km (9 miles) from Christiansfeld is **Skamlingsbanken**, the national monument which celebrates the Danish reunion of 1920, with a fine view of the surrounding country restored to Denmark at that time. West of Christiansfeld, the small town of Jells is the home of **Orion Planetarium**, a planetarium and observatory with exhibitions on space travel and astronomy as well as an experimental section.

Even away from the coast, most of this central area of South Jylland has a feeling

In Denmark's southwest corner, **Markslandet** is marshland set between Højer, on the coast, Tønder to the south, and to the northeast **Løgumkloster**, a monastery town with a famous market. The abbey church was founded around 1173 and is reckoned to be one of the most beautiful brick-built churches in northern Europe, with the curious tradition of holding a special service for its market 'pedlars and

Rømø on Jutland's west coast, provides kilometre upon kilometre of sandy beach with enough space for everyone.

of the sea with sandy soil and inland dunes. Small towns and villages are dotted throughout the luxuriant beech woods, lakes and flowering meadows. Two good fishing rivers meander past Gram, southeast of Ribe, and the woods around many of these communities are full of mushrooms and berries for berry-picking afternoons. One distinctive feature of Gram is **Gramslot**, a 500-year-old castle with an idyllic lake and park. Its ghost, the 'White Lady', is said to be a member of the Schack family, the castle's owners for 300 years. In one castle wing is **Midt-sønderjylland Museet**, with local geology and natural history.

All this country is ideal for outdoor activities but **Vojens** claims to offer more sports for the young and active than anywhere else in the area, whereas **Toftlund**, towards the southwest, is peaceful forest land for walking, with horse-drawn carriage tours a speciality.

Haderslev has a cathedral from 1250 and many well-preserved town houses. Early 18th-century riding stables are now **Hesterkøretøjmuseum**, a carriage museum, and **Hertug Hans Sykehus og Apoteket**, an old hospital and apothecary, dates from the 1550s. Haderslev is not only history but also natural history. **Dampark** (town lake) is a waterbird sanctuary and Haderslev has an important archaeological museum.

The golden age of **Aabenraa**, on the fjord of the same name, was during the 17th and 18th centuries when this early fishing village grew into a shipping centre with a big fleet of sailing ships. That it now concentrates on energy is clear

HÆRVEJEN – THE OLD MILITARY ROUTE

The ancient military road through Jylland used to stretch from Viborg in the north as far as the present border with Germany and beyond. It was as much a drove road as a military road and the old drovers, bringing their cattle down from the farmlands to the markets, earned it the alternative name of Oskevejen (oxen road).

Today, many stretches have been lost: cut into by other roads, converted for motor use or simply built on. But a relatively intact section starts at Immervad Bro (bridge) just south of Haderslev. The bridge was built in 1776, cut from a single block of stone.

Going south, much remains, including one of the oldest rune stones from 900AD, stone wayside markers and Stenvase, an old cobbled stretch. There are also the remains of a customs house where the drovers had to pay the local duke for the right to move their cattle, and a beautiful old stone bridge at Bommerlund where the inn once served Bommerlund *schnapps* to the drovers, cheerful at nearing the end of their long journey. Now, alas, the *schnapps* is made in Flensburg. Also along the way are the inevitable sites of historic fights and killings, and ancient burial grounds.

Most moveable remains are now in Aabenraa Museum, but many walkers are eager for Hærvejen to be restored. It would make a marvellous walking path along its old route from the border as far north as Viborg.

from the power station and large oil storage tanks, but there is fine yacht harbour at Lystbådehavn, and wonderful horse-riding along the shoreline. The countryside around the fjord is forest with sandy coves and winding flower-lined roads. **Aabenraa Museet** has a marvellous collection of some 200 ships in bottles and concentrates on local shipping history.

Further south, visitors cross the border from Germany at Kruså, often to head for the island of **Als**, leaning out into Lillebælt towards Fyn. Almost on the border is **Frøslevlejren**, a Nazi concentration camp for Danish resistance members in 1944 and 1945. Some 12,000 Danes were interned here, and 1,600 of those were later deported to the horror camps of Germany. The old barrack rooms on view in Hut H2, which look more orderly than they can ever have done in World War II, and the main watchtower, both tell of camp life. Other huts have exhibitions of the Danish Home Guard, the Red Cross, Amnesty International, and other relief organizations.

Gråsten Slot lies on the coast road north of the fjord through which the border also runs. This centuries-old castle has been the home of many noble families and, in 1935, became a royal summer palace. It has a lovely chapel, all that is left of the original 1709 building after a fire some 50 years later, with an altarpiece reaching from floor to ceiling. When the royal family is not in residence, the chapel and parkland are open to the public.

Just before Sønderborg, the main town of the island of Als is one of Denmark's most important national monuments. **Dybbøl** was the scene of a fierce battle in 1864, which lost much of South Jylland to Prussia for more than 50 years, until the 1920 settlement. Dybbol is now a national park, which includes the ten redoubts, the earth fortifications and Dybbøl Mølle which stood on top at that time. Cannons and other military memorabilia of the battle are kept in **Historiecenter**, a restored mill.

Sønderborg itself has a wonderful position on both sides of the narrow Alsund (strait) that separates Als from the mainland, facing the Baltic. Excellent for sailing and water-based activities, it is a lively commercial town of 30,000, only minutes away from forest and beach. **Sønderborg Slot**, built by Valdemar the Great around 1150 has the oldest Lutheran royal chapel in northern Europe, dating from the mid-16th century. There is also a magnificent baronial hall, and a museum featuring the often wartorn history of this part of South Jylland, including the Danish–German wars of 1848 and 1864, as well as World Wars I and II.

On North and South Als, which lie between the fjords and Lille Bælt, the main road to Fyn comes to a halt at Fynshav, where the ferry leaves for Bøjden, not far from Fåborg on Fyn. Another ferry sails from Mommark, further south, to Ærø the nearest island of the Fyn archipelago. Als has woods and open country and, looking at a map of the area, it is easy to see that all the way round are beaches for swimming, windsurfing and the rest. It is an island for relaxation.

Jylland's Wonderful West Coast

North of Esbjerg, Denmark's beautiful west coast has been formed by the ever-changing sea. Its miles and miles of long white beaches, and dunes with clumps of marram grass, all come from the waves that curl in from the west. In some places they have slowly shifted the sand dunes and changed the shape of the coast, sometimes turning a fjord into a lake.

In summer, the sea can be calm and blue and full of swimmers, in winter the wind can be biting as waterproofed walkers stride along the edge of the tide, their heads bent against the cold. On some stretches, dykes have been built to stop the sea flooding in, and small communities that were once on the coast have moved inland. Away from the beaches the clumps of planted forest, called *plantage* by the Danes, are home to wildlife. The dunes are full of summerhouses and campsites.

Højer has been working to tame the sea since the first floodgate and dykes were built in 1556. Vidå floodgates, the most recent, were built in 1982, forming a saltwater lake. There is an exhibition here about Vadehavet and its fauna. One side benefit of these dykes is that they create large areas of lake and marsh, ideal habitats for waders and other sea birds. There are nature reserves all the way up coast.

Vejers Strand, Henne Strand to Nymindegab

On many maps this coast is outlined with the thick blue line used to indicate safe, clean bathing beaches – the choice is almost limitless. Inland, as a change from the shore, Oksbøl has **Aal Kirke**, built around 1150, with grand murals, including the Knights' Frieze, which shows Danish warriors from around 1200. Further on, the pretty 15th-century town of Varde has an amusement park, **Sommerland**, with 40 activities in a lovely river setting. More for the mind is **Varde Miniby**, a walk-around model of the old town as it would have been around 1800, all to scale. From Henne Strand to Nymindegab, the road runs alongside Blåberg Plantage, which is a national forest, open to the public.

To the west of Nymindegab, **Tipperne**, on the southern edge of Ringkøbing Fjord, is a famed bird sanctuary, with large flocks of geese, swans and duck. It is open on Sundays only. Further east along the fjord, Skjern Å (river) is one of the best salmon rivers and there is a nature trail running along one bank with the tempting title of **Odderstein** (otter path). In many nature reserves around the fjord ranger services arrange walks and tours covering birds, mushrooms, flora and fauna, and beaches; ask at tourist offices.

Ringkøbing Fjord to Agger

The fjord today is really a saltwater lake, separated from the sea by a narrow strip of sandhills with a road on top. Once it was open to the sea at the northern end but the shifting sands reduced the entrance to a narrow channel halfway along the sandhills. This has happened all along the coast but **Ringkøbing** is the largest. The old port of **Ringkøbing**, dates back to 1250 and still has much of the atmosphere of the days when it was one of the coast's busiest ports.

South of the road bridge over the sandhills channel, near Håvring, **Abeline's Farm**, built in 1871 but no longer farmed, is a memory of the life of the people here before it became so popular for holidays. Near the channel at Hvide Sande, **Fiskeriets Hus** illustrates the history of west coast fishing. The *St George* **Museum** has more than 1,000 finds brought up by divers from the wreck of the *St George* which ran aground in 1811. Many of the small communities along this stretch have attracted craftworkers who have opened workshops and shops.

North of Ringkøbing Fjord, a detour right will take you to Stadil on Stadil Fjord. **Stadil Kirke** is one of only two churches which still have 'golden altars' from the 13th century. Children may prefer a visit to another Sommerland, a little further west; there is also an animal park. At Ferring, the long road beside the white sand and marram grass can be interrupted for **Jens Søndergaards Museum**, once the summerhouse of the painter Jens Søndergaard and now a museum with 70 of his works. Inland again, Lemvig has a beautiful position on its own small inlet and a strange trail, **Planetstiern** (Path of the Planets), a tour on foot or bike of the solar system along the edge of the fjord. To the south, Klosterheden is one of the largest planted forests in Denmark.

From Ferring, the sand dunes narrow to a ribbon of land at Thyborøn, from where a ferry takes around ten minutes to reach the narrow northern peninsula of Agger Tange. Between the ferry quay and Agger, the dunes protect another area of water with wading birds. West of Agger is the village church, **Vestervig Kirke**. In 1150 this was a church and abbey, and it has a rich interior decorated with granite sculpture. The church looks out over the water to Nissum Bredning, the western entrance to Limfjorden.

Limfjorden to Hanstholm

From Agger it is possible to go directly north to Hanstholm. From the fishing village of Vorupør, where the fishermen still drag their boats up onto the beach, the coast road runs through *plantage* areas such as Tvorup Klit. North from Vorupør the scenery becomes more spacious, passing through Hansted nature reserve, a wide heath with birds and other wildlife. It is not open during the birds' breeding season.

Limfjorden is a fascinating jigsaw of a fjord, with dozens of offshoots, peninsulas and islands, linked by bridges and ferries, so mixed together that it is often hard to know which is which. The largest island is Mors but there are also Fur, Livø and Venø, all of them magnets for sailors, and sailing is undoubtedly the best way to explore Limfjorden.

Around the fjord, the main towns are Struer and Skive, each on its own inlet,

Nykøbing on Mors, and Thisted. But there are small settlements and campsites lying around this marvellous fjord with its limpid views. It would take a lifetime to get to know the whole area.

East from Agger and Vestervig Kirke, near Hurup, **Ydby Hede** is a prehistoric burial ground with some 200 barrows and 30 burial mounds on a heather-clad moor which is now a conservation area. The ferry to Mors only takes around five minutes, for a visit to **Jesperhus Blomsterpark**, south of the island's main town, Nykøbing. This flower park has some 500,000 plants, as well as bird and butterfly parks. Nykøbing is home to **Morsland Historic Museum**, housed in Dueholmkloster. On the north side of Mors, the remarkable 61m- (200ft-) high **Hansklit** is a cliff of white clay, with black layers of ash from long-extinct volcanoes.

Thisted, on the Thy peninsula of the mainland and reached from Mors via Vilsund Bridge, has a core of delightful squares and old houses and is a centre for trade and education. The Gothic church gives the name of Thisted's earliest known citizen: for those who cannot read the runes, he was 'Thor Amdissøn'. There is also a regional museum. From here the road north also leads direct to Hanstholm, but circling round the fjord gives the chance to visit **Bygholm Vejlerne**, 5km (3 miles) inland from Øsløk. With small lakes and dykes, this conservation area is one of the best breeding grounds for wading and sea birds, with many others resting here on migration.

On the southern side of Limfjorden, west of Lemvig, **Struer** is a largely industrial town beside Venø Bugt, looking out to the island of Venø, and with the largest marina on the fjord. There is a ferry from here to Venø. East of Struer, **Hjerl Hede** is some of Denmark's finest natural scenery, and including a bog area. Apart from the bogland conservation areas, **Den Gamle By** (Old Village) has a large collection of historical buildings and also **Skovbrugsmuseet** (a forestry museum).

Northeast on the Salling peninsula, the town of **Skive**, on yet another arm of the fjord, has the beautiful **Krabbesholm** manor. It dates from the 16th century, and is built on a lovely spot between Krabbesholm Skov (forest) and the fjord. It has long been a Folk High School. There is also **Spottrup Slot**, northwest of Skive. **Skive Museum** has a large collection of amber and a fine selection of modern Danish painting and sculpture from 1920 to the present day.

Hanstholm

The town is one of Denmark's largest fishing ports with a fleet of modern North Sea trawlers, and a ferry to the Faroes. Vigsø Bugt is a wonderful wide sweep of sea for swimming and surfing. In World War II, **Vigsø Batteriet** (battery) with its huge gun emplacement helped to turn Hanstholm into a fortress. A bunker is now a museum. From a much earlier age is the Viking burial site, with around 100 mounds and several burial stones laid out in the classic ship design.

Hanstholm lighthouse was built in 1843 and at that time was the most powerful beacon in the world. There is a panoramic view from the top of its 65m (213ft) tower. The museum gives chapter and verse of the harbour construction, the fishing industry, and the geology and natural history of the area.

From Hanstholm, the north coast is one long strip of shore, sand dune, marram grass and *plantage*, to the port of Hirtshals 133km (100 miles) northeast, and then it goes on to Skagen and the Nordic Light.

*T*hink of Norway and think of mountains and fjords, scurrying rivers and waterfalls pitching down bare rock. It is a long narrow country, at one point only 10km (7 miles) from the Swedish border to the sea. If you stick a pin into Oslo and pivot the whole of Norway round, northern Finnmark will stretch as far as Italy. The land changes constantly, from mountains sweeping down into the fjords, to lakes, glaciers and forests where deer and elk roam. Further north there are reindeer, still herded by the Sami people. The geographical centre of Oslo is in a forest, but all the smaller cities of Norway – Bergen, Trondheim, Stavanger – seem to be part of the sea; it is no wonder that Norwegians have been great sailors since Viking days. Today, summer means boats, fishing and the water. In winter, the skis come out with magnificent slopes all around, so large they rarely seem crowded. Ski tracks wind through the forests and every Norwegian youngster's ambition is to ski-jump. It is a land of magnificent space.

Stave church at Ringeby

A City for All Seasons, with its own Surrounding Garden

A winter city and a summer city, a Viking city, a 19th-century city, and a weekend city where people seem to be able to stay up all night and still manage to get out to the great outdoors the next day, to walk or ski, or to swim or sail. Oslo is all these things and more, in a beautiful setting with uplands and forest to the north and islands and boats to the south.

Oslonians never tire of telling you that Oslo is one of Europe's biggest capitals, the size of Los Angeles. But this is just a little tongue in cheek, since much of Oslo is woodland and moor, and the geographical centre is in the heart of a forest.

Central Oslo, on the other hand, is easily covered on foot, with museums and other places of interest close together. To give Oslo the best of both worlds, it has a good integrated system of trams, buses, local trains and ferries which make it easy

Since Norway regained its sovereignty in 1905, the country has made much of its monarchy. The Palace Guard is a popular sight for visitors too.

to reach these hills, forests and fjordlands. Oslo is also a green city – motorists have to pay to bring a car into the centre and an underpass system keeps through-traffic off the city streets.

As in all Scandinavian capitals, the sea and a busy harbour are never far away. In summer, the many small islands and beaches snuggled into the fjordside are thronged with swimmers and sun worshippers, and the water is dotted with sails, small boats, and ferries.

In European terms, Oslo is not old, though hunters, traders and later farmers were making use of this safe fjord as long as 7,000 years ago. Harald Hårdråda built the first Oslo in the 11th century. Two hundred years later, Håkon Magnusson built a fortress where Akershus Slott now stands, and made Oslo his capital.

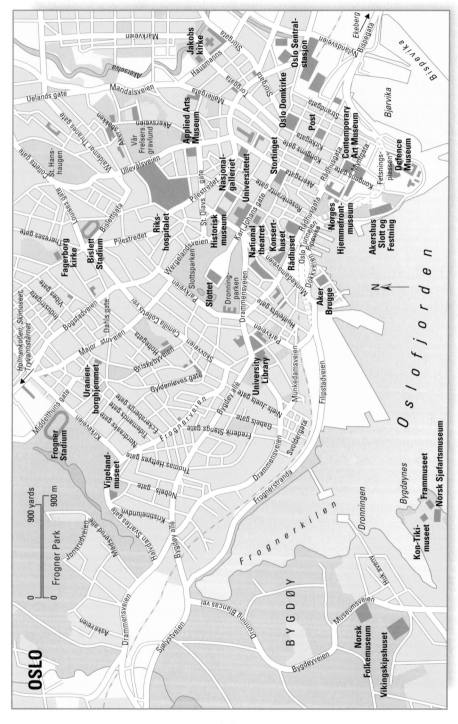

In 1624, the old wooden city burned to the ground and the Danish king, Christian IV, who had a liking for building towns in the Norwegian part of his kingdom, raised a new city under the walls of Akershus Slot. Called Christiania, its lattice of streets form the basis of modern Oslo. Later, the 19th-century city, freed from Danish rule, spread west beyond the new Storting (parliament) and Royal Palace to leave a legacy of beautiful 19th-century buildings. Today, modern Oslo has changed from a sleepy small capital to a bustling end-of-the-century city, which stays open late.

Coming from the Jernbanetorget end of the street, a right turn takes you to the colourful market stalls, with every sort of flower, that fill **Stortorvet** outside the **Domkirke**. The cathedral was consecrated in 1697 and has Norway's oldest tower clock from 1718. The lovely bronze doors are by Dagfinn Werenskiold from 1938.

Inside, the Domkirke was restored in 1950 in beautiful blues, greens and gilt on white. The ceiling's biblical scenes were lovingly laboured over between 1935 and 1950 by Hugo Louis Mohr and the stained glass windows are the work of Emmanuel Vigeland, brother of Gustav (see p.164).

Karl Johans Gate and the Centre

Most routes in Oslo come back to **Karl Johans Gate**, the centre of a 19th-century grid system that makes it easy to find your way around. This wide street links Jernbanetorget and Oslo Sentral railway station to the east and the Royal Palace and Slottsparken in the west. Karl Johans Gate and the roads parallel to it are crossed by others running down to the sea. Between them are the grass, flowers and trees of gardens such as **Studenterlunden**, where cafés and restaurants move outside in summer.

Karl Johans Gate is largely car free, with shops and stalls to interest browsers.

O slo's main street, Karl Johans Gate, is named after the man who became monarch under the joint Norwegian-Swedish Constitution of 1814. Today, largely pedestrian, it is a favourite place to stroll, shop, eat, and meet friends.

*T*he interior of the
Domkirke (Cathedral) has
traditional Scandinavian colours of
blue, green, and white, with delicate
gilt. On the ceilings are scenes from
the bible by Hugo Louis Mohr
which took 15 years to complete.

Much older is the lovely organ front from
1729. Behind is Domkirkeparken, a small
garden where you can drink coffee outside, screened from the main street by
Basarhallene, a semi-circular wall of galleries, cafés and shops.

 Nearer the centre of Karl Johans Gate,
Stortinget (Parliament) was built in the
1860s. When Parliament is in recess (mid-
June to late-September), daily guided tours
help to explain the Norwegian system.

Three of Oslo's famous old hotels stand
in this area. The **Grand Hotel** has a
ground-floor restaurant with a fascinating
long mural which shows the playwright,

Henrik Ibsen, coming through the door for
his noontide aperitif, his Bohemian
friends already waiting. Just around the
corner, **Hotel Bristol** is famous for its
store koldtbord. The **Hotel Continental**'s
Theatercafeen, standing opposite the National Theatre, is a haunt of people from
the theatre and the arts.

Nasjonal Teatern, very much looked
on as Ibsen's theatre, has a statue of him
outside, and also one of Bjørnstjerne
Bjørnson, poet and politician, who wrote
the Norwegian national anthem. The beautiful building has a magnificent auditorium
with portraits of famous artists. In summer, there is a guided tour. Though most
productions are in Norwegian, the theatre
provides simultaneous translation.

On the far side from Nasjonal Teatern
is **Oslo Universitet**, where the Great Hall
of the University hosts the Nobel Peace
Prize ceremony each December. It is also
open in July for visitors to see the celebrated Edvard Munch murals. In the street
behind, the University's **Historical Museum**, has ethnographical, numismastic

and antiquities collections, the last in-cluding a Viking hall and treasures from the stave churches (see LEISURE ROUTES). Not far away is **Nasjonal Galleriet**, with a wealth of examples of the National Romantic movement fired by the nationalism of the 19th century. One room devoted to Norway's most celebrated modern painter, Edvard Munch, includes *The Scream*, stolen and retrieved in 1994. A short walk leads to St Olav's Gate and the **Kunst Industrimuseet** (Museum of Applied Art), best known for the 13th-century Baldishol tapestry, found at Nes in 1879.

At the western end of Karl Johans Gate, the **Royal Palace**, surrounded by parks and a statue of King Karl Johan, is not

*T*hough the Royal Palace in Oslo is not open to the public, when the Royal Family is in residence, the daily Changing of the Guard always attracts the crowds.

open to the public, but there is a daily Changing of the Guard at 1.30pm. When the King is in residence, the Band of the Royal Guard plays on weekdays.

Down Universitets Gate, which crosses Karl Johans Gate, towards the sea is **Råd-huset**, the City Hall. This huge rust-coloured structure was built in 1931. Its front steps down to Fridtjof Nansens Plass have a magnificent swan fountain and a cascade of water and, on both sides, the carved Yggdrasil Frieze depicts Norse mythology. Inside, Rådhuset is as much a gallery as City Hall, with frescoes and paintings from Norwegian art in the first half of this century.

Behind Rådhuset is **Pipervika,** from where most sightseeing boats and some ferries leave. The Tourist Information Office is in the yellow building to the right, towards the glass and steel of **Aker Brygge**, built onto the disused wharfhouses that stand along the quay. It follows the modern style of having shops, restaurants and theatres under connecting roofs,

*O*slo is famous for warm summers, and café life is lively. In the background is Rådhuset, the 20th-century City Hall.

excellent for sitting outside in summer, pleasant under the glass in winter. The long-term plan is to make Aker Brygge a community where people also live. But Aker Brygge is new-style Oslo which, if it is not to spoil this compact small city, calls for a very careful marriage with the past.

*T*he old Aker Brygge (wharf) and its houses have been successfully converted into restaurants, theatres, houses and shops, many of which are linked by useful glass corridors.

Christiania and Old Oslo

After medieval Oslo burnt down in 1624, the builder king, Christian IV, set about designing a new, fireproof capital for his Norwegian territories. Set below Akershus Slott, its buildings were stone-built or half-timber only, and the 15m (49ft) wide streets were planned to act as firebreaks. More than 300 years on, this plan still forms the foundation for central Oslo.

From Rådhuset, it is a short walk along Rådhusgaten to Myntgaten and **Høymagasinet** (hay barn), a long, low building which holds **Christiania Bymodell**, a complete model of Christian's city in 1838, some 10m by 15m (33ft by 49ft) in size. With a 20-minute multi-media presentation tracing Oslo's progress to 1840, it is an absorbing history lesson.

Only a few minutes away is the gate to **Akershus Slott**. Set beside the parade ground is a statue of a gigantic woman and a small man within the circle of the earth. This monument to the victims of World War II, by Gunnar Jansson, symbolises his death and her continuing life of struggle.

Nearby, **Forsvarsmuseet** (Armed Forces Museum) traces Norwegian military history, with intriguing exhibits such as the old Buick in which Crown Prince Olav (later King Olav) toured Oslo when he returned to a triumphal welcome at the end of World War II.

Christian IV also restored Håkon V Magnusson's old fortress as a royal castle. Akershus is in very good condition today, with a tower at each end. Olav's Hall was used as a prison for Norwegian resistance members in the last world war, and the royal mausoleum has the tombs of the modern monarchy, starting with King Haakon VII in 1905, alongside that of Håkon Magnusson.

The absorbing **Hjemmefrontmuseum** (literally Home Front Museum) documents five hard years of occupation and an heroic resistance. Next to it is the memorial to 42 resistance members who were executed there. At the end of World War II, Norway briefly restored the death penalty, and the traitor Vidkun Quisling was sentenced to death and shot in Akershus. Where he is buried is not public knowledge.

17th MAY – NATIONAL DAY

It is still possible to come across one or two very old Norwegians who can just remember Norway becoming independent in 1905, and this may be the reason that Norwegians celebrate 17th May (the day the Eidsvoll Constitution was signed) with such overwhelming zest.

Unlike many similar events in other countries, Norway parades without a weapon or a fighting man, just thousands of the red, white and dark blue national flags, carried by children, with many of the marching crowds in the traditional costumes of their own district.

Every small community will have its own celebrations but Oslo's is the most magnificent, the streets crammed with walkers, and with much singing of Bjørnstjerne Bjørnson's national anthem and other patriotic songs. The focal point of the celebrations is the Royal Palace at the end of Karl Johans Gate. It takes hours for the procession to file past the king and royal family.

At the same time as the king reviews his parade, all over the country, even in the northern places where the snow is still lying, Norwegians are celebrating in the same way, and all with the underlying seriousness of an old nation but a young state.

Close by Akershus along Myntgaten is **Den Gamle Logen**, used for entertainment over the last 150 years and now a concert hall. Bankplassen holds the beautiful building that was once the Norges Bank headquarters, now **Samtidskunstmuseet** (Museum of Contemporary Art). Opened in 1990, it has the post-war collections from the Nasjonal Galleriet and the State Travelling Gallery, showing the works of modern Norwegian painters, of whom Arne Ekeland is considered the most important.

Other places not to miss are **Børsen**, the 1820 Stock Exchange, which is still in use today, and **Det Gamle Raadhus**, the original city hall – then a court, dungeon and assembly halls, now a good restaurant specialising in fish and shellfish. Just across the road is **Café Celcius**, the oldest surviving Christiania house. Situated round a courtyard, it is a pleasant place to eat. Inside, the café has two long rooms, much as they might have been a couple of hundred years ago, with bare floors and wooden tables. The building also holds the Oslo Art Association, and NORLA (Norwegian Association for Literature Abroad), with public galleries above.

For a good look at Old Oslo, drive, walk or take a bus east to **Bispegate**, past the quays of Bjørvika and Bispavika, to **Oslo Gaten**. Here are the ruins of **Skt Hallvard Kyrke** and **Bispegård** (Bishop's House). **Ladegård** was added in the 1720s above the arched 13th-century cellars of Bispegård. Its restored reception rooms have antique furniture and paintings, with models of Oslo in the Middle Ages. **Minnepark** at Sørenga, not much more than a stones throw away under a tangle of bridges, has the ruins of **King's Castle** and **Skt Mary Kyrke**.

Bygdøy and Other Museums

Oslo is very much an outdoor city, and some Oslo museums are outdoor too. In good weather, to go to the Bygdøy peninsula by ferry from Pipevika sets the scene for a day largely devoted to the sea. There is also a bus to, and around, Bygdøy.

However, the first museum up the hill from Dronningen, where the ferry lands, covers land not sea. The **Norwegian Folk Museum** is a whole village of dark wooden buildings, some with carved outside galleries and stairs, from 20 different areas. They are all authentic, brought together since 1894 when rural life was only just beginning to change. There is one of the finest stave churches, from Gol in Hallingdal (see LEISURE ROUTES), and groups of the various buildings – stores, kitchens, living rooms, lofts, dairies and byres – that made up each farm, every district with its own characteristics. Often there are dancing displays in regional costume. A visit here could easily fill a whole day.

Bygdøy has much else to offer. Norwegians learned more about their Viking past from the **three longships** found just over 100 years ago in the Oslofjord than from most other finds. They are the Tune ship, found 1867, the Gokstad ship, 1880, and the Oseberg ship, 1903, the last probably the oldest, built around 800AD. All ended their lives as burial ships and held the wealth of jewels, weapons and household implements with which the Vikings ensured a welcome for their dead in the afterlife.

The best-preserved, the Gokstad ship, held the skeleton of its royal chief. The slightly smaller Oseberg ship, luxurious enough to be royal too, held two women, probably Queen Åsa, the only known Yngling queen, and her bondswoman. The

*B*ygdøy, with (above) the Norwegian Folk Museum, which provides colourful folk dance displays (right); and the magnificent Viking Ship Museum, specially built to hold three Viking ships (below).

Tune ship was little more than a skeleton itself when raised, but the original wood of the other two ships was found during the excavations and a naval engineer, Frederik Johannessen, painstakingly rebuilt them. Today, their specially built **Viking Ship Museum** shows to perfection their sleek lines, designed for speed.

Close by Bygdøynes on the far side of the peninsula, the schooner *Svanen* is not just a museum but a floating centre for youth clubs and school groups. The polar vessel *Gjøa* was Roald Amundsen's vessel for his three-year journey to the Northwest Passage.

Here, **Norsk Sjøfarts Museet** (Norwegian Maritime Museum) tells the long story of the importance of coast and sea in Norwegian history: from a model of the Kvaldor dugout canoe from 600AD, to the *Kong Sverre* at 3,500 tons the largest wooden warship ever built in Norway, and a modern tanker. The **Kon-Tiki and Ra Museum** is a tribute to the two adventurous journeys of Thor Heyerdahl and his crew. On the *Kon-Tiki*, he sailed across the Pacific in 1947, and later built *Ra II*, a reed boat, and used it to test his theory that a similar boat could have sailed to the West Indies long before Columbus reached America.

It is hard to imagine the well-painted little *Fram* in its smart museum, caught in the Arctic ice. Yet she is sturdy enough to have made three testing voyages: on Nansen's first voyage she spent three years in the pack ice; with Otto Sverdrup she was north of Arctic Canada; and in 1910, Amundsen used *Fram* for his successful expedition to the South Pole. But pictures show the immense ice, and to scramble over the decks and visit the cabins, some still with the old names, brings it all to life.

Before the return ferry arrives at Bygdøynes, there is time to see the **Joseph Grimeland's Memorial** to 4,500 who died at sea during World War II, and the nearby **Mine Box** which remembers the dead of World War I.

Vigeland Sculpture Park, in Frogner Park to the west of Oslo, sums up the work of early 20th-century sculptor, Gustav Vigeland. From the big gates, a bridge ahead is lined with 58 bronze statues of human figures, leading to a great bowl of a fountain, held up by six main figures. The central hill, circled by stone steps and statues shows the stages of human life. Vigeland's master work, *Monoliten*, is a tall granite column, carved with a throng of figures struggling upwards. The park is completed by the *Wheel of Life*, a group of seven huge figures. All this was donated by the sculptor to Oslo in return for a studio, which is now the nearby **Vigeland Museum**, well worth a visit.

Not far outside the gates, **By Museet** (City Museum) is housed in the lovely 1790 Frogner Manor, with photographs, drawings and documents showing Oslo's recent progress from little more than a village of 10,000 people in 1814, to 150,000 by 1900, and a population of 460,000 today.

Few would argue that Edvard Munch is Norway's greatest painter of the late 19th to early 20th centuries, with a prodigious output, most of it housed and shown in changing displays in **Munch Museet** in

*T**he giant stem of Gustav Vigeland's statue*, Monoliten, *is eye-catching from every part of Frogner Park. The park also has many other statues by this prolific sculptor.*

Oslo's Toyen area. Munch's gloomy nature – he had a mental breakdown early in the century – shows in many paintings, such as *The Sick Child*, inspired by his sister's early death. Throughout his life he returned to many of the same themes which means there are similar paintings with similar titles in different galleries. One of the most striking is his *Death of Marat* but there are many more and this is a gallery to return to again and again.

There are paintings, too, at **Botanisk Hage** nearby, such as the botanic art of Dagny Tande Lids. The gardens, with mountain plants, waterfalls, trees and flowers, are a peaceful place, and the glasshouse is full of exotic plants.

Outdoor Oslo

Oslo is very much an outdoor city and for Oslo people that means the **Marka**, the swathe of forest, lake, hill and upland moor that circles central Oslo. Cross-country skiing is a national winter sport and – whatever happens on Fridays and Saturdays, Oslo's party nights – on Sundays whole families are out in the Marka,

even tiny children on skis or babies secure in a *pulk*, a sort of pram-sledge on skis towed behind a parent. In summer, this is the place to walk, canoe and fish.

The most accessible is the **Nordmarka**, some 20–30 minutes by bus or car, or better still take the tram-train to Frognerseteren station, a journey that gives a marvellous view of Oslo falling away behind. This is the station for the **Holmenkollen Ski Jump**, the venue for Norway's oldest ski event each March. To get a feel for it, but only if you have a good head for heights, take lift and stair to the top and marvel at how the ski-jumpers ever have the courage to launch themselves down.

Even higher is **Tryvannstårnet**, Oslo's radio and telephone tower, with an observation platform some 118m (387ft) above the ground. The lift takes only 11 seconds to reach the top and leaves the stomach far behind. At some 558m (1,929ft) above sea level, this is the best view in southern Norway: over to Sweden in the east, with the city and fjord below, it goes on for ever.

Below Holmenkollen Ski Jump is Ski Museet, tracing the history of skiing back to the earliest skier (a copy of the 4,000

HOLMENKOLLEN

In winter Norway, it sometimes seems that every Norwegian child is banking up existing bumps on the snowy slopes to act as ski-jumps, and it is no wonder that the Holmenkollen Ski Festival is the oldest in the world – and, many claim, still the greatest.

By the 1760s, the Norwegian military were already holding skiing competitions, and an existing competition in Oslo moved to Holmenkollen in 1892. This is no slick standardized festival confined to top skiers. The week includes children's competitions, the Guards' Race and, most surprising of all, a race for Members of Parliament. Holmenkollen Sunday attracts some 8,000 skiers for 43km (26 miles) cross-country, ending right under the big jump.

On the Big Ski-Jump Day, it is the top-class international ski-jumping that counts, from the distant high platform, where the tiny figures wait for the launch, to the great leap and flying descent. Today, the longest jump is over 110m (360ft). The applause builds to a crescendo and, wrapped up warmly, the spectators rise from their seats to greet the winner. Holmenkollen, it seems, is far too exciting for anyone to feel the cold.

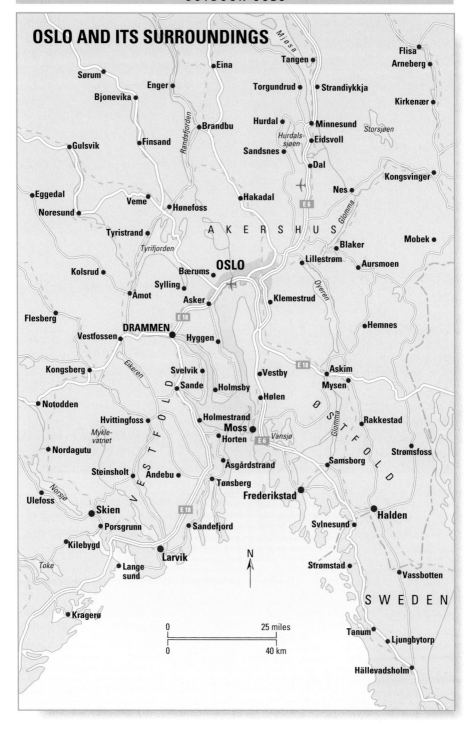

OSLO AND ITS SURROUNDINGS

*H*olmenkollen in the
*Nordmarka is the outdoor
paradise closest to Oslo, where
Oslonians spend their free time
skiing or walking. The traditional
Holmenkollen Hotel is a good
place to end a day in the fresh air.*

Tableaux illustrate Nansen's crossing of
Greenland on skis in 1880, and Amundsen's 1910-12 expedition to the South Pole,
with everything authentic except the explorers' clothes. At the side of the ski-
jumpers' landing place (a summer lake)
that lies between ski-jump and auditorium
(used also for summer concerts) is a statue
of the great skiing monarch, King Olav V.
He was a formidable ski-jumper and an
Olympic sailor with his constant skiing
companion, his dog. Until his death in
1991, King Olav rarely missed a Holmenkollen ski-jumping event.

year-old rock carving of a skier from
Rødøy in Nordland) and to the father of
modern skiing, Sondre Norheim (see p.81).

Island Idylls in Oslofjord

Summer means sailing, swimming and picnicking in Oslofjord and every sort of craft, from inflatable to big cargo ship, passes up and down. The islands provide many wonderful places for swimming; the sheltered waters are warm and safe unless a firm notice indicates *nej* (no).

Six islands are quite close to the mainland, ideal for a day or half-day tour. Some have *hytter*, wooden summerhouses, some are largely uninhabited but can be reached by ferry. Few people except wardens and caretakers live all year round on the islands. The nearest, Hovedøya, and the furthest out, Langøyene, are probably the two most popular with visitors. The a/s *Oslo Ferjene* (ferries) leave from Vippetangen, on the point of Akersnes. The ferry visits the five innermost islands, alternating its journey clockwise and anti-clockwise.

For the best overall view of the fjord, take the route that finishes with Hovedøya. A half-hourly service allows passengers to get off at any island that takes their fancy and pick up a later boat. Schools and clubs make early summer trips, followed later by swimmers and sun-worshippers, when the picnic-basket-laden queue may be long, mostly heading for Langøyene.

Nakholmen, Lindøya and Bleikøya

In the off-season, only a few passengers who live on Nakholmen and Lindøya board or disembark there. In summer, many more visit their *hytter*, which you also find on Bleikøya.

Gressholmen

This is really three islands in one with a narrow neck of land linking Gressholmen to Rambergøya in the south. The huge bay between them contains a shooting range. Another neck of land leads west to Higgholmen which has a lighthouse. A long coast and sheltered beaches make the island popular, so does its café.

Langøyene

The island has clean sandy beaches and a huge southwest facing bay for good, safe bathing. Round the headland on the southeast coast is a nudist beach. Campers are welcome to bring tents and stay overnight but the ferry here runs only at the height of summer, early-June to mid-August.

Hovedøya

Closest to the mainland, Hovedøya has a sailing harbour and is historically the most interesting. Monks lived here near a thousand years ago, and in the 18th century the islanders built the biggest sailing ship in Denmark-Norway. It was also an army base, and the two-storey, timber-framed building at the jetty, **Lavethuset**, housed gun carriages. Inside are fine timber beams and lots of models of Oslo.

Up the first hill lie the ruins of an 11th-century **Cistercian cloister**, its outlines showing clearly, with some walls and its precarious-looking steps, well-preserved. Close by is **Klosterkron**, the Cloister Inn, which serves meals in summer and at weekends. The former commanding officer's house nearby is now a remarkable puppet theatre, **Arjuna Dukketeater**, formed in 1972. Daily, from mid-May, it uses a cast of beautiful puppets to retell old tales. It is only open on Sundays during September.

You can walk up to the remains of **Krutthuset**, an old ammunition and powder house, where the view sweeps over the fjord. One fascination of all these islands, but especially Hovedøya, is the vegetation, which grows undisturbed so that plants regenerate naturally. The soil is good, temperatures are slightly higher than they are in Oslo, and species no longer found in Oslo have survived in this naturalist's paradise. Nobody is allowed to pick flowers or plants on Hovedøya. The flora is *fredet*, protected.

But the island night-of-the-year is *Midsommer* on 23rd June. On this lightest night, Oslonians flock to the islands to enjoy bonfires and festivities that include drinking, eating, traditional dancing and games.

Hinterland and Fjord

The three *fylker* (counties) close to Oslo and touching Oslofjord are Akershus, Vestfold to the west, and Østfold on the east side of the fjord, lying along the border with Sweden. They provide a rich variety of places to visit and explore, either as an expedition by car, bus, coach tour or perhaps boat, or as somewhere to stay awhile. From the peaceful village of Åsgårdstrand, where Edvard Munch lived and painted one of his most famous works, *Three Girls on a Bridge*, north to Eidsvoll, where the Norwegian constitution was agreed, there are many places to enjoy.

Akershus

Akershus, circling the city, could almost be called Oslo's 'Green Belt', except that central Oslo is so green. It runs as far north as the southern end of Lake Mjøsa, touches the Swedish border for a short stretch in the east, and takes in the northern end of Oslofjorden. The result is a cross-section of southern Norway with farmland, forest, fjord and hill country, no large towns, just a series of small towns and villages.

Eidsvoll built in the 1760s, lies some 80km (50 miles) northeast of Oslo on the E6 road. This lovely white manor house was the home of Carsten Anker, one of the main proponents of Norway's Constitution. It housed the meeting of delegates which produced the Constitution on 17 May (now Norwegian National Day) in 1814. The house remains unchanged from Carsten Anker's time. Also in this area, **Eidsvoll Bygdetun** is a rural museum, showing both a small farming community and a *seter*, mountain farm. An old paddle steamer, the *Skiblaldner* also calls at Eidsvoll for cruises on Lake Mjøsa.

Where the river Vorma to the southeast meets one of Norway's longest rivers, the Glomma, are the ruins of **Nes Kirke**. There has been a church here since the 11th century. It was last rebuilt in 1697. **Gamle Hvan** is a farm museum with old buildings and an ancient courtyard tree. At Stein close by is the extraordinary **Fairy Tale School**, designed in 1912 by author Ingeborg Rofling Hagen and teacher Erling Elverhøy, to bring the arts to the people. In use until the 1970s, it attracted many artists who have left a legacy of decorated doors, walls, ceilings and furniture.

South, on the Glomma, **Akershus Energivert** at **Rånåfoss** (waterfall) has supplied energy to the area since 1921. It now has **Energy Forum**, a permanent exhibition describing progress from the waterwheel to solar energy, and offers guided tours. Close to the same river, **Urskog-Hølandsbanen** is a narrow-gauge, third-class railway, known as Tertitten. Once used for passengers and goods, it is now a railway museum which runs each Sunday, stopping at old Bingfoss station, much as it was in the railway's heyday.

On Oslofjorden at Høvikodden, and not far from Oslo's Fornebu airport, is the

Henie-Onstad Art Centre. This collection of Norway's, or perhaps the world's, most famous skater, Sonja Henie and her husband Nils Onstadt, holds 8,000 20th-century paintings, sculptures and graphics, including works by Matisse, Picasso and Miró. The centre holds exhibitions, and also hosts concerts, ballet and theatre performances.

Also in the Bærum and Asker district to the west of the city is **Tanum Kirkeområde**, one of Norway's finest churches from the Middle Ages, set in lovely surroundings which also hold several large Iron Age grave mounds. **Bærum Verk Senter** is a traditional ironworks now open to the public, and its Vertshuset Restaurant has been an inn since 1640. A little further south **Asker Museum** is based in the home of the artists Otta and Tilla Valstad, surrounded by an exotic sculpture garden.

Along Oslo's eastern fjord (Bunnefjord) is **Uranienborg**, Roald Amundsen's home at Svartskog, where he lived from 1908. The house is as he left it in 1928 when he set out to rescue his friend, the Italian explorer Nobile, from which he did not return. Arne Vigeland's statue of Amundsen stands by the fjord.

Østfold

Inland, Østfold is a land of countless lakes, rivers and canals, where wildlife flourishes. Parallel to the Swedish border, **Halden Kanal** has the tour boat m/s *Turisten*, and still operates a manual lock at Ørje, where there is a famous **Kanal Museum.** In the north, **Mormatten Trotting Track** in Mysen lures many addicts from Oslo.

Østfold has always been a trans-Scandinavian route and today Swedes and Norwegians pass through to Sweden on the E18 Oslo–Stockholm road, or drive over the Svinesund Bridge close to Halden

and **Fredriksten Slott**, where the Swedish King Karl XII was killed in 1718, the end of Sweden's era as a great power. The fortress is in fine shape, floodlit at night and with museums and guided tours.

Northwest of Halden, **Sarpsborg** is thought to have been founded by St Olav in 1016. The king sailed up the river Glomma to **Sarpsfossen** (waterfall) and built a church and castle there, and so began the town. Østfold everywhere celebrates St Olav's Day on 29 July, but nowhere better than at Sarpsborg's **Borgarsyssel Museum**, with music, dance and *bunader* (national costume). The museum occupies the site of the ruined Skt Nikolas Kirke and is a group of old buildings with a display of medieval art.

Present-day **Frederikstad**, at the mouth of the Glomma, is a preserved fortress town from the 1660s, when prisoners laid the cobbled stones in Gamle Byen's old streets. Today guides take visitors around the narrow lanes and to the dungeons where the cobble-laying prisoners eked out their lives. The big cathedral also has Norway's largest church organ, with 4,000 pipes. Roald Amundsen's birthplace at **Tomta** is now a museum.

All along this coast, sailing and motor boats take to the water and the royal yacht lies at **Hankø**, a great regatta centre. There are tour boats to the fjord islands and on Østfold's canals. The northernmost coast town, **Moss**, has ferry links to Denmark, and a boat service across the fjord.

Like many Østfold towns, Moss has a flourishing timber industry which started as early as the 16th century. On market days, **Dronningengate** is thronged with shoppers. Many artists and craftworkers come to join the town's traders, and Moss's **Galerie F-15** now has a recognized international reputation.

Moss's greatest historic moment came in the early 19th century. With Norway free of Danish rule, the Swedes and Norwegians were arguing about the future. Norway had already agreed its Eidsvoll Constitution but, faced with overwhelming numbers of Swedish troops, it was forced to agree to a meeting with Sweden which took place in Moss. The result was a compromise that made King Karl Johan joint-monarch of Sweden and Norway but left the Eidsvoll Constitution intact. It was signed in Moss in 1814.

Vestfold

Linked by ferry from Moss to Horten, Vestfold is Norway's smallest *fylke*, stretching down the fjord to Larvik. Ships and ports are vital here and much of the Norwegian merchant fleet is registered in Vestfold. **Horten**'s main industry is ships and shipbuilding, with an excellent **Sjøfarts Museum** (Maritime Museum).

Everywhere in this long-inhabited fjord there are signs of the past. St Olav also came to the fjord's west side, and some 5km (3 miles) north of Horten, are **Skt Olav's Spring** and **Skt Hallvards Kirke** on Løvøya. Horten's nearest national park has northern Europe's largest collection of old Norse royal graves. Heading south, Borre's medieval church is rich in baroque decoration. **Åsgårdstrand** on the coast has Edvard Munch's primitive little house where he painted some of his best works (see p.164), making this pretty town very well known.

Between Åsgårdstrand and **Tønsberg**, Norway's oldest town, founded around 900AD, is **Slagen**, where 19th-century archaeologists could scarcely believe their eyes when Oseberg Haugen (mound) revealed the most important Viking discovery to date, the Oseberg Viking ship,

now in the museum on Bygdøy (see p.162). Not far away, similar excavations revealed the Gokstad ship.

Tønsberg shows its Viking past in graves discovered along the main street, Storgaten. Now under glass, they are incorporated into the ground floor of the library. Other interesting relics are **Slottsfjellet** (castle hill), nicknamed 'the acropolis of the north', the ruins of **Magnus the Lawmaker's Castle** and Håkon Håkonsson's **Bredstue** (hall).

Sandefjord depended on whaling and has a **Whaling Museum**, and a whaling monument by the sculptor Knut Steen. **Larvik**, Vestfold's southernmost town, is a trans-Scandinavian terminal from Norway to mainland Europe, and not far away is Norway's largest beech forest.

Larvik was home to two famous seafaring men. **Larvik Ship Museum** includes a special division devoted to Colin Archer, the Scots-Norwegian boatbuilder and designer of the Polar ship *Fram*, whose distinctive boats are known and prized far and wide. His first home was at Tollerodden on the fjord. Another seafarer whose home was Larvik was Thor Heyerdahl, famed for the *Kon-Tiki* and *Ra* voyages (see p.164). From earliest times, Vestfold and the sea have been inextricably linked.

Lillehammer and the Heart of Norway

Lillehammer, Norway's ski town which held the 1994 Winter Olympics, is around a couple of hours north of Oslo, at the northend of Lake Mjøsa, Norway's largest lake, with Eidsvoll (see p.170) at its southern tip. From Lillehammer, through Oppland, one of Norway's most famous valleys, **Gudbrandsdal**, heads north-west, leading eventually to Oppdal and Trondheim. Closer to the Swedish border, a parallel valley, Østerdalen, travels on to Røros (see p.219). Many smaller valleys follow the same north-west slant or branch off the main two.

To the west lies the great mountain massif, Hardangervidda, on the main railway line between Oslo and Bergen, a fact that makes it very easy to reach by the hundreds of mountaineers and walkers, who come to tackle peaks such as the highest mountain, **Glittertinden**, (2,472m, 8,110ft). To the south-west of this huge area, and not far from the distant Hardangervidda, is another of Norway's favourite southern winter sports centres, **Geilo**, which is very popular for cross-country skiing.

Over Lake Mjøsa sails the *Skibladnner*, the world's oldest paddle steamer, launched in 1856. It skims along at 14 knots, and takes only some 11 hours to cover the round trip from Eidsvoll in the south to Lillehammer in the north and back. Even a shorter journey reveals Mjøsa's beauty.

Lillehammer became a town only last century and the main street's pretty, gable-roofed wooden houses are well-preserved. Good for younger visitors are a quarter-size version of the town in 1900, Lilleputhammer, and Humderfossen family park, not far away, with the largest troll in the world. He is as ugly as most trolls, Norway's small, mythical creatures, easy to imagine in the strange shape of mountain rocks. Long ago, people believed they came out at night to do their mischief. **Maihaugen** is one of the best of the open air museums, and Norway's biggest with more than 100 buildings.

Lillehammer was always a good skiing area but the Olympics have brought superb new downhill runs, skating rinks, bob-sleigh tracks and ski-centres, as well as new hotels, and an exhibition centre at Maihaugen. This has a concert hall and permanent exhibitions of Norwegian history. Nearby **Sjusøen**, a cluster of *seter* (mountain farms) is a great all-year centre, with sleigh rides through the woods, eerily lit in winter.

Heading north to **Gudbrandsdalen**, the main road (E6), following the railway, goes through **Ringebu** with its stave church (see p.68) Vinstra, and Fagernes. But off that road is the Per Gynt Way, named after the legendary braggart and ski-runner. His family farm at Hågå nearby is now privately owned, though the cemetery at Sødorp, a mile away, holds his statue. His life was commemorated in the celebrated play by Henrik Ibsen, with music by Edvard Grieg, *Peer Gynt*. A little further west, **Golå** has excellent skiing and all this area north is good for cross-country skiing and ski touring.

East of Lake Mjøsa, **Østerdalen** lies almost parallel to Gudbrandsdalen, and **Glomdal** has a big outdoor museum, with an indoor section and exhibition of agriculture and the life of the area. All around the land makes good skiing and further north-east from Elverum, close to the border, **Trysil** in Hedmark *fylke* is Norway's oldest ski centre, with the oldest club, the Trysil Shooting and Skiing Club, dating from 1861. Summer has every sort of sport, from mountain and canoe tours to para- and hang-gliding.

Distances in the heart of Norway are enormous. Apart from the fact that Oppland, Hedmark and Rondane (with a superb mountain park) are huge areas, roads may have to skirt mountains and make other detours. The scenery is magnificent and everywhere, as the heart of Norway slips imperceptibly into Sør Trondelag and on to Trondheim, this beautiful Norwegian territory is dedicated to the 'great outdoors.'

Endless Coastline, Rich Farmland, and Hidden Upland Valleys

This is the area of Norway that is closest to the rest of Europe, and it shows in the easy friendliness, contradicted by the close little communities that Henrik Ibsen portrayed in some of his plays. For visitors it is an easy way of life and, southerly though it is, this is the part of the country that brought modern skiing to Norway.

Sørlandet, the southland, is where the Norwegians take their holidays. It has a gentler climate and terrain than most of Norway, though that does not make this land of great variety either flat or uninteresting. The choice is between the long serrated coast curling round from Flekkefjord where southern Norway meets western Norway; lake, hill and forest in Telemark; or the deep inland valleys such

*S*ørlandet, Norway's southland, which lies to the west and south-west of Oslo, is a fine mixture of mountains, rolling upland valleys and plains, with a fine coast. This is Flatdalen, near Vradal in Telemark.

as Setesdal. In its northernmost area, the south stretches to the foothills of the great bulk of the Hardangervidda.

This is the part of Norway closest to mainland Europe and the coastal communities show the influences of many cultures. The lovely sheltered town of Flekkefjord has the nickname of Hollenderbyen (the Dutch town), a legacy of the days when many Dutch settled here. Against that, some southern valleys were Norway's last secret places. Almost until this century, the inhabitants lived out their lives cut off from the rest of the country.

Telemark is best known for two things: it is the place where Sondre Norheim founded Telemark skiing (see p.181), and it was the scene of the daring World War II act of sabotage to the heavy water plant at Rjukan, by Norwegian resistance fighters.

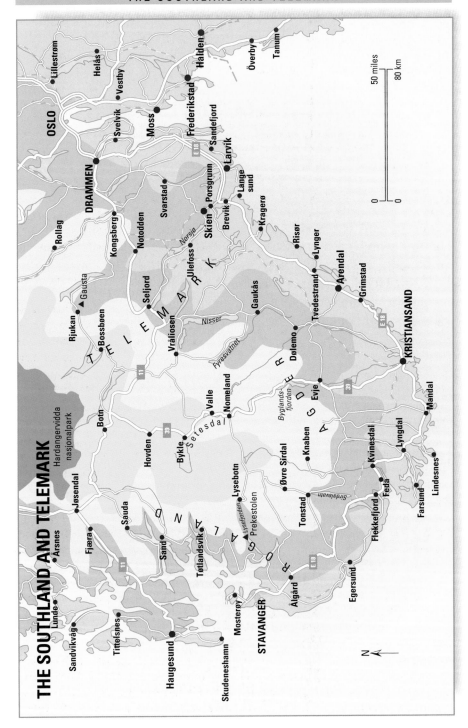

THE SOUTHLAND AND TELEMARK

50 miles
80 km

OSLO

DRAMMEN

Lillestrøm
Helås
Vestby
Svelvik
Moss
Frederikstad
Halden
Överby
Tanum
Sandefjord
Larvik
Porsgrunn
Langesund
Brevik
Kragerø
Skien
Risør
Lynger
Arendal
Grimstad
KRISTIANSAND
Svarstad
Norsja
Rollag
Kongsberg
Notodden
Ulefoss
Seljord
Gaukås
Tvedestrand
Gausta
Rjukan
Bossbeen
Vråliosen
Nisser
Dølemo
Evje
Mandal
Fyresvatnet
Hardangervidda
nasjonalpark
Botn
Valle
Nomeland
Byglands-
fjorden
Lyngdal
Kvinesdal
T E L E M A R K
S E T E S D A L
Hovden
Bykle
Knaben
Øvre Sirdal
Feda
Lindesnes
Jøsendal
Arsnes
Sauda
Øvre Sirdal
Tonstad
Sirdalsvatn
Flekkefjord
Farsund
Fjæra
Sand
Totlandsvik
Lysebotn
Prekestolen
Lysefjorden
Egersund
Sandvikvåg
Tittelsnes
Mosterøy
Ålgård
STAVANGER
Haugesund
Skudeneshamn
Lunde
R O G A L A N D
N

Made famous in the film, *The Heroes of Telemark*, this courageous deed undoubtedly shortened the war.

Norway has several towns and districts founded by King Christian IV of Denmark-Norway, who seemed determined to perpetuate his name; Sørlandet's principal town is Kristiansand which is also one of the largest ferry ports. Built in 1641, some of the oldest parts of the town still survive. By road, the coast is circled by the far flung E18, which stretches from Stavanger in the west of Rogaland, east to the porcelain town of Porsgrunn, and Skien in Telemark, on to Oslo and eventually to Stockholm. All along this popular sailing coast, almost every town has a guest harbour.

Telemark

Over the years, Porsgrunn and Skien, Telemark's two largest and most easterly towns, have grown steadily towards one another, so that now they are almost one. **Porsgrunn** is best known for beautiful porcelain, made in a factory close to the river that leads to the fjord. It has guided tours and a factory shop.

Skien goes back a long way and at one time was a town built of wood in southland style. Few of those original buildings remain because the wooden heart of Skien has burned down every hundred years or so since the 17th century. The last fire in 1886 destroyed the whole town centre. Skien is probably best known as the birthplace of the playwright Henrik Ibsen. The small-town life of that community did much to influence his later writing. Perhaps that is why, once he left Skien, Ibsen never went back. **Nodre Venstøp** just north of Skien, where he lived between the ages of seven and 15, is open to visitors,

and still has the windowless attic which he used in *The Wild Duck*.

Below Porsgrunn and Skien, the fjord is famous for ocean fishing and two idyllic small towns, **Langesund** and **Breik**, are at the heart of the sport. Dedicated fishers assemble each year for the largest ocean fishing competition in northern Europe, with new records attained every time.

A little to the south, the town and district of **Kragerø** doubles and trebles its population in summer when the 2,000-or-so *hytter*, scattered around the archipelago, fill up with visitors, as does the harbour. Edvard Munch proclaimed Kragerø 'the pearl' of this coast. Here, he painted the famous sunrise which now hangs in Oslo University's Aula.

Inland from Skien is the **Telemark Canal**, which 500 men hewed out of sheer rock, taking five years to cut the 110km (77 mile) canal from the foot of Hardangervidda to Norsjø, and eventually to the sea. Opened in the late 19th century, its main purpose was to transport timber.

Today, ms *Victoria* carries passengers from Skien along the canal's calm waters and through numerous locks. The Nome district, an early industrial area centred on Norsjø, holds all the locks on the Norsjø to Bandak stretch, the finest being Vrangfossen, with six locks and a rise of 23m (75ft). Many people tour on a passenger boat like *Victoria* but there are houseboats to rent and even canoes to paddle. At the end of the canal's western arm, **Hotel Dalen**, built in 1894 but still welcoming visitors, is one of Scandinavia's largest wooden buildings, with a dazzling glass ceiling in the lobby.

The town of Notodden at the end of Lake Heddal is the end of the Telemark Canal's eastern arm, and has the beautiful **Heddal Stave Church** (see p.69) built in

1240. This magnificent stave church of towers and spires is Norway's largest.

Not far from the coast begin some of Telemark's splendid walking districts: Dragedal, Nissedal and Fyresdal. It is also home to mines, offering mineral and precious stone hunting. This natural landscape, dotted with lakes, and divided by the River Nissa has a wide range of wildlife – beaver, grouse, elk and reindeer – and the **South Norway Ecology Centre** at Hauggrend escorts special nature excursions.

To the north lies one of Telemark's most famous valleys, **Morgedal**, where the young farmer, Sondre Norheim, invented modern skiing. His skis and especially their bindings gave skiers a control that had never been known before, and Norheim and his friends perfected new techniques.

The Sørlandet Coast

As Telemark moves west into Aust Agder, the small coastal towns continue to attract sailors and other visitors from many lands. The white town of **Risør** has some of the *fylke*'s best-preserved wooden architecture, and has become a strong artistic and cultural centre, with many good eating places. Its annual Wooden Boat Festival brings in thousands, and Risør has its own

*T*he Telemark Canal, *once an integral form of transport for the flourishing timber industry of the area, now makes an excellent way of seeing the landscape on ms* Victoria *or a rented boat. This is one of the best stretches, Vrangfoss (waterfall), which has six locks, near Ulefoss.*

'watchmen' who lead groups on town walks. Sailing trips on the newly restored fishing smack *Risør*, another boat built by marine architect Colin Archer (see p.172), are very popular.

Tvedestrand, a few miles away, also has typical white-painted houses, and is popular with boating folk. **Nes Verk** has some of the oldest workers' houses still in their original form, and glassblowers at **Glasshytta** demonstrate their art and make lovely glassware for the shop. In 1991, **Lyngør**, set on one of the many small islands, was elected Europe's best preserved village, the happy result of now-justified neglect during the 1950s and 1960s. Its authentic pilot and customs houses, lighthouse and homes have become a treasure.

However, the sea is not the only source of sport here. Just inland, **Nes Golf Park** is Norway's largest golfing complex, with 18-hole and 9-hole courses. Also nearby is **Nes Jernverkmuseum**, a unique industrial site which, until 1959, made elegant cast iron stoves. Now a museum, most of its production plant is still intact.

The coast continues with **Arendal**, a favourite for children because of its good beaches, and **Grimstad**, which once had as many as 40 sailing shipyards and continues ship- and boatbuilding today. It also has Dømmensmoen, an interesting school of horticulture based on traditional methods, in a beautiful area full of burial mounds and other prehistoric relics. But Grimstad is best known as the home of Norway's two greatest writers. Knut Hamsun spent his early life in **Nordland**, which was the prime influence in his early novels but, from 1918, Norholm Farm became his home, where he wrote his last work, *On Overgrown Paths*.

Henrik Ibsen came from Skien as a young man, and Grimstad watched his metamorphosis from apprentice chemist to playwright. There is much of Ibsen's life still in **Ibsenhus**, where he lived, and **Grimstad Museum** has the world's largest collection of Ibsen memorabilia. Outside the chemist there is an Ibsen bust and the **Gallery and Cultural House** attracts many theatre groups and an annual meeting of film-makers.

King Christian IV built the town of **Kristiansand** for defence. Though no gun was fired in anger until 1940 in World War II, the old **Kristiansand Fort** is in fine condition. Another memory of war is **Kristiansand Cannon Museum** with an original giant German gun, and to the west at Søgne is the German coastal fort Ny Hellesund.

Kristiansand has benefitted from its military past in nature parks such as **Baneheia** which extends right into Kvadraturen in the very heart of the town, and **Ravnedalen Nature Park**. Both owe their origins to General Wergeland and his troops stationed in the town, who planted them up between 1870 and 1880. Baneheia was used as pasture and for woodcutting, and now has wonderful walking and cycling trails, and swimming and fishing pools. In Ravnedalen, Wergeland turned marsh and swamp into a haven of plants and trees, where in summer there are now concerts, festivals and theatre performances.

For children, and many of their parents, the favourite visit is to Kristiansand **Dyrepark** which has both Nordic animals in home surroundings as well as exotic species. But it is much more than a zoo. **Kardemomme By** brings to life the town and characters created by Norwegian children's writer Torbjørn Egneras, such as *Captain Sabletooth* and *Tobias' Tower*. With the flume and other rides, superb swimming and shows in the amphitheatre, a day slips past in no time.

With a population of 67,000, and another 24,000 inhabitants in the three burghs close by, Kristiansand is Norway's fifth largest town and, with its ferry harbour, the main trade and communication centre in Sørlandet. Yet it still has some ten streets of white, wooden, low-level houses characteristic of Sørlandet in **Posebyen**, the biggest collection in Scandinavia. A trotting track is another sign of the Norwegian way of life.

To the west of Kristiansand is **Mandal**, Norway's southernmost town, with an archipelago packed with white beaches, the most famous being Njervsanden, with campsites, holiday cottages and flats. Each summer Mandal is filled to bursting with visitors to the **Shellfish Festival**.

The best way to travel the last miles to **Flekkefjord** from Mandal is to forsake the impersonal carriageway of the E18 and turn onto the smaller road that zigzags up and down the fjords, 'the road through the skerries'. A peninsula or two further on, **Lindesnes** is Norway's most southerly lighthouse. A notice states boldly that it lies 2,518km (1,765 miles) south of Nordkapp (North Cape). Next to Kristiansand Dyrepark, its wonderful view and unique position make Lindesnes Sørlandet's most popular visiting place. At the fjordhead, the best boat journey from Lyngdal is to **Sælør**, the island where St Olav wintered with his fleet in 1028. The island is developing a coastal culture centre based on Sælor's old school and there are other 11th-century relics within the wider area.

Farsund, southwest on the Lista peninsula, was the privateers' base during the 1807-14 Napoleonic wars, and **Kaperdagene** (privateers' festival) is part of every summer. The whole Lista peninsula is a fascinating mix of flat cultivated land and rugged mountains, known for its special quality of light which attracts many artists. It also attracts birds, particularly during the migrations. At Lista lighthouse, in operation since 1834, **Lista Lighthouse Gallery** gives details about lights around the coast, and the **Lista Ornithological Station** has an information centre with details of the area's nature reserves and bird populations.

Havika has marram grass and sand dunes and is an important wintering place for migratory birds. **Einarsneset** is another plant and bird sanctuary where, in

---

SONDRE NORHEIM

Judging by a rock carving from Nordland, now in Oslo's Skimuseum, Norwegians have been skiing for around 4,000 years. But this was simply getting around on snow in the easiest way. Stylish, modern skiing came into being in the mid-1890s, thanks to a farmer and ski-maker, Sondre Norheim, from Morgedal in Telemark. He designed ski bindings, changed the shape of the actual ski, and devised new techniques for turning and stopping that became known as Telemark skiing, a graceful style using only one ski-stick.

Inspired by their success, Norheim and his farmer friends put on their skis and skied all the way to Oslo (then Christiania), later opening Norway's first ski school there. The new style and ski schools proliferated all over Norway, and spread further.

Today, Telemark skiing has had a revival, and can be seen again on many ski slopes with its own competitions. Norheim's methods were devised for heavy skiing and tackling deep snow. The present Telemark on prepared downhill tracks may not be quite what he would have expected, but it does keep alive the name of Sondre Norheim as the 'father of modern skiing'.

winter, red-throated divers, cormorants and many diving ducks swim among its shallow sea waters.

Fedafjorden, further west, is a wonderful fjord some 15km (12 miles) long, and **Feda** is Vest Agder's best preserved village. From the 17th century, it was a shipping and postal station, with long narrow streets and old houses, and the village still has its own cooper's workshop. The view of the fjord itself is best seen from **Utsikten**, a viewpoint close to the highest stretch back on the E18 at Kvinesheia. The area of Kvinesdal was a centre for the great 19th- and 20th-century emigrations to North America, and each year thousands return to **Sarons Dal** for an emigrant festival and religious celebration.

Flekkefjord town is well sheltered between Grisefjord and Flekkefjord. Its fine wooden architecture is a reminder of the days in the 1820s and 1830s when Flekkefjord was the heart of the wealthy herring fisheries, and also made its money by sending timber to the Netherlands. This is how the old part of the town became 'Hollenderbyen' or Dutch town. **Fedrenes Minne** tells something of the area's maritime past.

This last stretch of the Nordsjøen (North Sea) coast road is not for those in a hurry but nowhere gives a better sense of contrast between Sørlandet (the south land) and Vestlandet (the west land): the typical, white, wooden Sørland houses of the coast, and the magnificence of west Norway's mighty mountains which seems to slope straight into the sea.

The Inland Valleys

Inland, Sørlandet has several long valleys running from near the coast north into the mountains. Kvinesdal and Sirdal push north into the highlands of Vest Agder. Some 65km (43.5 miles) into Kvinesdal, **Knaben** was once a flourishing mining community with houses and schools. When the mine closed in the 1960s, almost everyone left the area and today Knaben has only a couple of permanent inhabitants along its empty ways. Upper Kvinesdal is a lovely natural mountainous area.

Sirdal on the border to the west is surrounded by mountains and reindeer but its main wealth is sheep. One of the biggest attractions is the September sheep drive when thousands are brought down from the mountains. There are wilderness walks, camping trips, and opportunities for joining the shepherds in hill-work. Another fine tour from Sirdal is to drive (or walk) down the amazing road from Øvre Sirdal to Lysebotn on Lysefjorden, past the famous high shelf of **Prekestolen** (the Pulpit) rising above the fjord, or make a round trip by driving south through Sirdal to Tonstad by Sirdalsvatnet and on to the coast.

But the most famous valley of all is **Setesdal**, right in the heart of Sørlandet. People have lived here since Viking days but it was only in the last 100 years that Setesdal came into the modern world. Not long ago, it was one of the most remote of these secret valleys, where people preserved the old ways of speech, dress and food, and nowhere has a better selection of the old cog-jointed wooden houses, stores and churches.

In Setesdal, the brilliant *bunad* (traditional costume) of the valley is so distinctive that it is often chosen to represent Norway abroad. Today's dialect is also unique, and the valley is the home of many folk musicians who make its old music popular still. Silversmithing is also a local craft, making beautiful traditional jewellery to be worn with the colourful dress.

In **Valle** close to the Otra river, many jewellers welcome visitors to watch them at work. Nowadays, they are working not only to traditional designs but are producing inventive contemporary silver jewellery. Other skills are woodcarving and *rosemaling*, the distinctive rose-painting on furniture, plates, bowls and walls that is typical of Norway. Among many other wooden buildings, Rygnestadloftet in Valle has the oldest pillared storehouse in Setesdal. It is nearly 500 years old and in August each year sees a folk music competition with costumes and old music.

The remarkable mountain road that connects Setesdal to Sirdal reaches a height of some 1,000m (3,300ft) over land inhabited by reindeer rather than people. The more usual route from Kristiansand is road 12 through the busy, small town of **Evje** and north along **Byglandsfjorden** with its mountains and waterfalls. This part of south Setesdal is rich in rare minerals. Some mineral collections are open to the public, and **Setesdal Mineral Park** is well worth a visit, as is **Evje Mineralsti**, an open mineral path leading to several mines. With a mineral card from the tourist office, a visitor may look for minerals, the most highly prized being the blue-green amazonite.

Nearer the north end of Setesdal, **Bykle Kirke** is one of Norway's smallest and most richly decorated churches. In contrast, some of the great dams and power stations are very impressive. Not so long ago, the old travellers' way, **Byklestigen**, was the only route into Bykle, and still makes a good day's walking. Close to the northern boundary of the *fylke*, **Hovden** is surrounded by mountains up to 1,250m (4,000ft) high, and is a first-class wintersports centre for alpine and cross-country skiing. Now almost as popular in summer

---

ROSEMALING

A favourite memento to bring back from Norway is one of the characteristic wooden plates or bowls, usually red, dark blue, or a mixed bluey-green, with a stylized design of leaves and flowers.

Rosemaling is a traditional Norwegian rural craft, going back to the days when people would carve and paint under dim candle and rush lights in the dark hours of winter.

The oldest examples go back to around 1700, but paint fades and the craft could have started earlier, a natural outcome of the decorated wooden panels and walls of some old Norwegian churches. Later, *rosemaling* expanded beyond bowls and platters, and you may come across hanging cupboards, chests, china racks and bedheads with this sort of decoration in museums and some lucky households.

By the end of the 19th century, it seemed that *rosemaling* skills were dead. Then, in reaction against the modern standardization that crept into many cultures in the second half of the 20th century, *rosemaling* began to enjoy a quiet revival. Made mostly in small workshops or privately, it is now on sale again in many craftware shops.

---

are hunting and shooting, and **Hovden Badeland** offers good year-round open-air and indoor swimming.

Of all the mountains here, and in Telemark, that bring in the climbers and mountain-walkers to this rugged part of Norway, the most famous is **Gaustatopen**, from where, on a clear day, you can see one-sixth of Norway: to Oslo in the east; to Rogaland in the west; over the whole of Telemark, and to the Setesdal moors. These small communities of Hoveden, Rjukan and Rauland are also the gateway to Hardangervidda, Europe's largest mountain plateau, and one of Norway's most magnificent national parks.

BERGEN AND THE FJORDS

Norway's Fjord Capital and its Kingdom of Blossom, Waterfalls and Winter Snow

Think of Norway and most people think of the fjords. In many ways, these awesome feats of nature, with their steep sides plunging into the deep water, sum up this northern land, moulding its history and people. Along these dramatic waterways, waterfalls cascade down from the rock sides in May and June when the water reflects the delicate colours of the blossom. In autumn, there is a last blaze of yellow, orange and brown, before the still white of winter comes, with skeleton trees outlined against the snow. Even then, the Gulf Stream keeps the seaward harbours ice-free so that the life of fjord, coast and islands continues.

The main fjords, starting in the south, are Lysefjorden with Stavanger at its gateway; Hardangerfjorden which is probably the best known (see p.191); Sognefjorden, further north and the longest fjord; and Nordfjord. Beyond Nordfjord are many more, such as Romsdalsfjorden and Tingvollfjorden cutting into the heights of Møre og Romsdal, which stretches almost to Trondheim. Its main coastal towns are Ålesund, Molde and Kristiansund. The three other fjord *fylker* (almost too large to translate as counties) are Rogaland in the south, Hordaland and Bergen, and Sogn og Fjordane bordering Møre og Romsdal.

There are dozens of smaller fjords and offshoots, some like Nærøyfjorden so narrow it is hard to imagine a ship turning there. Others push far inland, such as Geiranger famed for its calm beauty. On the coast, it can be hard to decide among the jumble of island chains whether a community is on the mainland or separated by sea.

Beautiful fjords are high on the list of Norway's claims to fame. They stretch north from Stavanger to Trondheim and beyond.

Bergen and its Islands

The best view of Bergen is from the top of Fløyen, one of the town's seven hills.

185

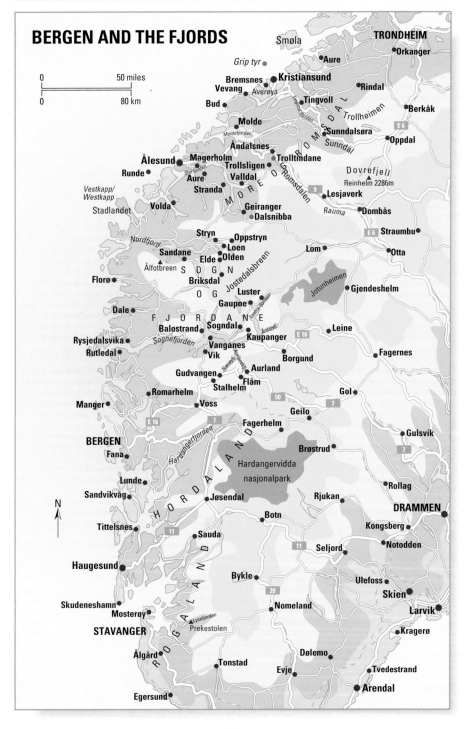

BERGEN AND THE FJORDS

0 —— 50 miles

0 —— 80 km

Smøla

Grip tyr •

TRONDHEIM
• Orkanger

• Aure

Bremsnes • **Kristiansund**
Vevang • Averøya

Rindal

Bud •

Tingvoll •

Berkåk

Molde •

Trollheimen

Moldefjorden

• **Sunndalsøra**

E6

Åndalsnes

• **Oppdal**

Sunndal

Ålesund
Runde • **Magerholm**
Trollsligen • • **Trolltindane**

Storfjorden

Aure **Valldal**

Dovrefjell
Reinhelm 2286m

Vestkapp/
Westkapp

Stranda

9

Geiranger • **Lesjaverk**

Stadlandet

Volda •

• **Dalsnibba**

Rauma

• **Dombås**

Stryn

E6 • **Straumbu**

Oppstryn

Sandane • **Loen**
Elde **Olden**

Lom •

• **Otta**

Ålfotbreen

S O G N

Jostedalsbreen

Floro •

Briksdal

Jotunheimen

• **Gjendeshelm**

O G

Luster

Dale •

Gaupne

F J O R D A N E

Balostrand **Sogndal**

Leine •

Rysjedalsvika •
Rutledal •

Sognefjorden

Vanganes
Vik

Årdalsfj.

Kaupanger

E16

Borgund

Fagernes •

Gudvangen

Aurland

Nærøy

Flåm

Manger •

Romarhelm
Stalhelm

Gol •

Voss

E16

50

7

Geilo

BERGEN

7

Fagerhelm

Gulsvik •

Fana

Hardangerfjorden

Brøstrud

7

Lunde •

Hardangervidda
nasjonalpark

Sandvikvåg •

N ↑

Jøsendal

Rjukan

• **Rollag**

H
O
R
D
A
L
A
N
D

Botn

DRAMMEN

Tittelsnes •

11

Sauda

Kongsberg

11

Seljord

• **Notodden**

Haugesund •

Bykle •

Ulefoss •

39

Skien

Skudeneshamn •
Mosterøy •

R
O
G
A
L
A
N
D

Lysefjorden

Nomeland

Larvik

STAVANGER

Prekestolen

Dølemo •

• **Kragerø**

Algård •

Tonstad

Evje •

• **Tvedestrand**

Egersund •

• **Arendal**

NYNORSK – THE OLD LANGUAGE?

The fjords and mountains, cutting off valleys and separating communities, sometimes make it seem that Norway has almost as many languages as it has valleys. This has been complicated further by the long years of Danish rule, when the very similar Danish tongue became the official and written language.

After the end of Danish rule, and with the coming of the 1814 Eidsvoll Constitution (see p.52), came a great wave of all things national. There was a strong call for a Norwegian language, and that inspired school teacher Ivar Aasen, from the Ålesund district, to travel and collect dialects and original Norwegian words. In 1853, he launched a dictionary of Landsmål, now Nynorsk, largely an amalgamation of west Norway speech and old Norwegian.

Many writers of that time, and later, published books in the new language which, from its antecedents, really should be called 'Old Norwegian' and there was much argument about the choice. Since 1884, Nynorsk has been one of the two official languages.

Today, the debate about which to use has cooled. As a general rule, Bokmål, largely based on Danish with a Norwegian variation and pronunciation, is favoured in the southeast, and Nynorsk is heard most often in western Norway. Nynorsk is in the curriculum of Norwegian schools, and NRK (Norwegian broadcasting) must broadcast a certain percentage of programmes in Nynorsk. In the 1990s, just under 20 percent claim the old, new language as their native tongue.

Rising steeply from the centre, it shows a wide sweep of sea, islands, hill and harbour, with ferries, cruise ships and other vessels criss-crossing the calm water or lying alongside the quays, and Bryggen's beautiful, old wooden harbour buildings.

Everywhere the sea is part of Bergen, cutting into the land, spreading the city across islands, now mostly linked by bridges though some still need a ferry. Bergen's hills once cut off the city from the hinterland, and to travel meant a steep climb or a boat but, today, there are road and rail tunnels.

This fjord capital, a maritime city, centres round its harbour, **Vågen**, where King Olav Kyrre founded Bergen in the 11th century. A century later, King Øystein Magnusson built a large wooden castle on Holmen; the town grew along the wharf below, and became united Norway's first capital.

Torget, the harbour square, has had a fish market since the 16th century. Today, it has expanded into flowers and fruit, but early morning still sees Bergensere (Bergen people) examining the catches with expert eyes. Torget is also popular with visitors, and stalls sell fresh salmon rolls, useful for those who do not want to stop for lunch.

The **Hanseatic Museum** was once a typical Hanseatic merchant house, furnished inside just as it would have been around 1700. Fear of fires which could devastate whole areas meant that the luckless merchants and their young apprentices could light no fires here. The only heating was in **Schøtstuene**, behind Bryggen, whose warm rooms were the social centre of German life, with fires, flowing beer and music. It was also the apprentices' school. The nearby Tourist Information Centre will help with queries, leaflets, some bookings, tickets and tours.

Though **Bryggen Museum** now shelters the remains of the first city, the wharf itself is a monument to the German Hanseatic traders who, from medieval times, lived in their cold wooden houses and controlled trade far along the coast. These beautifully preserved wooden houses, divided by narrow closes, form the laticework of old buildings, now workshops, small shops and eating places, that have made this a UNESCO World Heritage Site.

Bryggen Museum stands along the seaward end of the wharf, over the excavations of the town's earliest buildings, and also has collections describing life in the Middle Ages. The solid, high tower nearby is the 1560s **Rosenkranztårnet**, built by Scottish builders for Bergen's Danish Governor, Erik Rosenkranz. **Håkonshalle** dates from the 13th-century reign of King Håkon Håkonsson, and has a huge interior, often used for concerts.

On the far side of Bryggen Museum, the 12th-century **Mariakirken** (St Mary's Church) is Bergen's oldest building. The baroque pulpit alone would make it worth a visit. In the old streets inland from Torget, **Domkirken** (Cathedral) is a blend of styles, explained perhaps by the great

cannon ball still lodged in one wall from an especially turbulent period. Also 12th-century is **Korskirken**, although little remains of that period and its architecture is predominantly 17th-century Renaissance.

The harbour is a centre for restaurants and eating, often outside. When she is in harbour, the elegant sailing ship *Stadsraad Lehmkuhl* rides at anchor a little way out. Torget is also the berth of *The White Lady*, who passes the sailing ship, cruise ship and ferry terminal, and the old waterside warehouses on her sightseeing voyages. Up above the Holmen peninsula is the site of Øystein Magnusson's **Sverresborg** (castle). Its 17th-century successor, with the old cannon that once

T he best view of Vågen, Bergen's harbour, is from Fløyen, high above the town. Here the sailing ship Stadsraad Lehmkuhl *rides at anchor in the calm waters.*

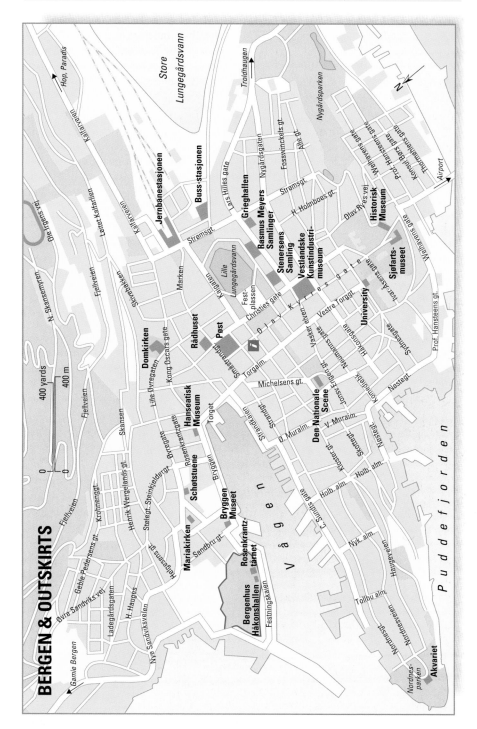

BERGEN & OUTSKIRTS

hammered a British fleet, is again open to the public in a lovely natural area. Further seawards, **Gamle Bergen** is an open-air museum with 35 18th- and 19th-century Bergen houses, laid out as a community.

Vågen is also the terminal for the streamlined hydrofoils that take less time to reach Stavanger to the south than the journey by road. Further along behind the wharf is **Tollboden** (Customs House) from 1744, and **Nykirken**, with beautiful galleries, and the waterside Hotel Augustin. On its inland side, the hotel faces on to **Strandgaten**, one of Bergen's best shopping streets which, heading for Nordnes Point, becomes a long pedestrian street, surrounded by a maze of old buildings that was once Bergen's working class district, with the homes and warehouses of traders from many lands.

In every direction, you seem to face the sea, and narrow streets such as Knøsesmauet plunge down towards the water. At the point is **Bergen Aquarium**, with a large collections of seals, sunning themselves or plunging into a pool that has glass viewing sides below the water. **Nordnes Sjøbad** nearby is one of Bergen's best swimming spots, and also has a heated outdoor pool.

Central Bergen

Torgalmenningen, the big square just up from Torget, is the hub of shopping streets, hotels, restaurants and cafés. One of the best shopping centres is **Galleriet**, with some 70 shops, from a silversmith to sports shops and places to eat, all under cover. Early evenings usually mean live music.

Torgalmenningen is also close to the parks, bandstand, museums and galleries. Cutting through from the square to Lille Lungegårdsvann, a pretty lake with a central fountain, you pass one of Bergen's

best-loved hotels, **The Norge**, with a statue of the famous 19th-century violinist, Ole Bull. He was a close friend of the composer Edvard Grieg, whose own statue is but a stone's throw away, near the bandstand.

In three fine buildings to the southwest of the lake are the Bergen **Billedgalleri** (Municipal Art Museum) showing Norwegian painting from the last 150 years; the **Steneresen's Collection** with 250 works by modern artists from Picasso to Klee and some excellent examples of Edvard Munch's works; **Bergen Fine Arts Society Gallery**, with alternating exhibitions of contemporary art; and **Rasmus Meyer's Collection**, also with Norwegian artists, such as J.C. Dahl, who was born in Bergen, Harriet Backer, and more Munchs.

Just to the right of these museums is **Grieghallen**, Bergen's concert hall. The building echoes the shape of a grand piano and has a superb acoustic. It is the home of Norway's oldest symphony orchestra, the Bergen Philharmonic founded in 1765. On the far side of Lilla Lungegårdsvann, **Jernbanestasjonen** (train station) is a grand, early 20th-century building, also good for shopping and eating, as is the bus station.

Up Torgaten, the steep, cobbled hill from Torgalmenningen, is the unmistakable red brick and copper steeple of **Johanneskirken** in Nygårdshøyden, an area built at the end of the 19th century. Behind the church are the **Historical**, **Natural History**, and **Maritime** museums and the **Botanical Garden**, where Bergen University had its birth. The view reaches over to the next big harbour inlet. On the far side is the lovely 18th-century manor house **Damsgård** (easily reached by bus), once the most opulent in the city and now restored as a museum to an age when Bergen merchants grew rich. It also has lovely period gardens.

Excursions from Bergen

Very few cities are as well supplied with tours as Bergen, not just within the city itself, but immediately outside its wide boundaries where city slips imperceptibly into rural areas, with special tours such as **Norway in a Nutshell** (see p.194). It is also a centre for the southern fjords, and for trips by fast boat north to Sognefjorden and Nærøyfjorden.

Bergen offers tours by coach, train, ship, yacht, car, mountain bike or simply on two feet, sometimes with permutations of most of them, with or without a guide. A fun way to see the best-known sights is the little red train, **Bergens Expressen**, which tours from the fish market around the city and part-way up Fløyen for a panoramic view. A popular evening visit is south to Fana, for **Fana Folklore** – a traditional meal with west Norwegian music and dancing. Good well-integrated public transport also makes independent touring easy to plan.

A favourite visit is to Edvard Grieg's lovely summer home at **Troldhaugen**, which in recent years has also had its own concert hall built into the hillside. Opened here in 1995 is a new **Edvard Grieg Museum**, not far from Grieg's working *hytte* above the fjord, where he spent many hours in composition. Another excellent visit is to **Lysøen**, violinist Ole Bull's last home, a venue for recitals during the Bergen International Festival.

Rosendal is Norway's only baronial manor from 1665, surrounded by Renaissance gardens and now in the care of Bergen University. Boats going south and north thread their way through the islands of **Sunnhordland**, or visit **Nordhordland**, with its new bridge or the inland

GRIEG AND BERGEN

Though one of his best-known pieces of music, *Per Gynt*, is set in eastern Norway, the composer Edvard Grieg had his closest ties with the western side of the country. He was born in Bergen in 1843, the grandson of a Scottish merchant who emigrated from Aberdeen in 1779. Later, Grieg spent his last 20 summers at Troldhaugen, his Bergen home, overlooking a lake on the edge of the city.

At that time, a composer had to tour to promote his works. Grieg and his wife, the singer Nina Hagerup, spent their winters on demanding European concert tours, where he was always rapturously received. Back in Norway, Troldhaugen was a working retreat.

Grieg was a strong voice in the tide of Norwegian culture which swept Norway after 1814. In his earlier life, he had been much encouraged by the violinist Ole Bull, who was also from west Norway. Later the two would tour Hardangerfjorden, and other fjord areas, absorbing the old Hardanger fiddle tunes and traditional music. Grieg transcribed much traditional music for the piano, showing a rare understanding of these folk melodies.

In 1907, he died at Troldhaugen, living just long enough to see Norway become independent. Troldhaugen has become something of a shrine to this most famous of Norwegian composers, and is visited by thousands every year.

island of **Osterøy**. Hardangerfjorden is probably the favourite, using a mixture of boat and coach, or independently by car.

Hardangerfjorden

Hardangerfjord is a legendary name, inspiring the best-known picture of the 19th-century painter Hans Gude. *Bridal Journey in Hardanger* shows a traditional bridal-boat crossing the fjord and it now hangs in the National Gallery in Oslo. The fjord also gave its name to Norway's national

B *lossom time is lovely in the fjords, as the orchards wake from their winter sleep. Nowhere is the blossom more abundant than in the beautiful Hardangerfjord.*

musical instrument, the eight-stringed Hardanger fiddle, which aroused an interest in traditional music for the composer Edvard Grieg during his regular walking tours with the violinist Ole Bull.

The poet Henrik Wergeland probably contributed most to Hardanger's fame when, in the 1830s, he wrote of 'wonderful Hardanger'. Not only Norwegians but Europe's great and good came to explore and, when the Bergen steamer started in the 1860s, a host of wealthy travellers followed. To this day, regular boats still sail to Hardanger. There are also excellent coach tours but independent travel calls for car or boat.

The fjord's deep waters push far inland. Many people still work fruit and other farms though a few small factories and workshops make furniture and other specialist goods. Tourism is important and Hardanger folk look after their guests well. Some old farms have become holiday villages, and Hardanger is a good place to find traditional music and costumes.

The road from Bergen is the E68 from **Nestun** at the south of the city, at that stage signed for Voss. It climbs to **Kvamskogen**, a favourite Bergen skiing place. At **Steindalsfossen** (waterfall), you can walk a little way up the hill and duck under the falls for a fine sense of their volume and power. In the nearest lay-by, coffee and *vaffler* (waffles) in the small café are a treat. Many think waffles are North American but it must have been Scandinavians and Germans who took them there.

Norheimsund on the northwest side of the fjord gives glimpses of the **Folgefonn** glacier opposite, which has a summer ski-centre and an exciting new road from

Jondal along the fjordside. Many Hardanger peaks rarely lose their snow, small farms perch on the mountain ledges, and the waterfalls are at their height in May and June, when the fjord sides are covered in the pink and white blossom of cherry, apple, pear and plum. In summer and autumn, the trees are heavy with fruit.

Norheimsund has an interesting waterside workshop: **Hardanger Fartøyvern Senter** (Ship Preservation Centre) restores and reproduces the famous wooden Hardanger boats. It welcomes visitors and has completed some remarkable reconstructions, such as *Svannen*, a three-masted schooner belonging to Norsk Sjøfartsmuseum at Bygdøy in Oslo.

Northeast along the fjord is the **Ingebrigt Vik Museum**. A cabinet maker's son, Vik turned to sculpture and Bergen has many of his best-known works, such as his 1917 statue of Edvard Grieg. This museum has 83 statues and casts. In nearby Øystese, the **Hardangerfjord Hotel** is the start for a cruise up the narrow Fykesund, north to the roadless hamlet of Boten at the head of the fjord, stopping for coffee and a local *lefsa* pancake.

The road clings to the fjordside through Alvik and past the ferry terminal for Utne at Kvanndal, then on to Granvin. **Granvin Kyrke** from 1726 has the oldest Norwegian church bell still in use. From here, the smaller road, 572, branches right through woods and fine scenery on the old post road to Ulvik.

Even turning inland, it is hard to get away from water and **Ulvik** stands on its own tranquil stretch. Long popular with foreign visitors who come for walking, sailing, fishing and outdoor pursuits, Ulvik is also favoured by many artists, and has several permanent exhibitions. The 19th-century church has wonderful

rosemaling (rose-painting), and Lars Osa's 1923 paintings follow the characteristic colours of flowers and whirls. **Brakanes Hotel**, over 130 years old, has a perfect view along the fjord. Its own seaplane gives guests an eagle's view of fjord, mountain, and **Vøringfoss**, and the shiny glacier on the edge of the Hardangervidda. Ulvik Fjord Pensjonat has beautiful woodlined rooms and a superb old collection of stuffed local animals and birds.

Before taking the road down the fjordside towards Bruarvik, a short detour up the amazing mountain road to **Osa**, at the end of the next finger of water, gives a fine view of the fjord spread out below. Back to Ulvik the road down runs through Bruarvik and the 7km (4.5-mile) Vallavik Tunnel leading back to the E68, Kvandall, and the ferry to Utne.

Utne on the east side of Hardangerfjorden is an old-established village. The Utne Hotel opened in 1722, and the village was the first to have post and telegraph offices, in 1836 and 1876 respectively.

A bygone cluster farm with all its outlying buildings is now the **Hardanger Folk Museum**. It has an orchard with varieties of fruit once commonplace in Hardanger, now rare. Inside are beautiful Hardanger costumes, traditional rose-painting, wonderful old photographs and, a museum treasure, the oldest known Hardanger fiddle, made in 1753 by Isak Nielsen Skaar, one of the early fiddle-makers. Along the fjord, old boathouses hold the long, narrow boats of the area, and a village shop has many goods used by Utne folk until recently. It is still open in summer.

Utne Hotel has been owned and run by five generations from the same family (though now it has new owners), gaining its international reputation at the time of

NORWAY IN A NUTSHELL

West Norway's most famous tour not only covers a changing panorama of land and water but gives a good insight into the way that the Norwegians get around their dramatic mountains, fjords and valleys.

In summer, the train leaves Bergen around 10am, via a tunnel through the hills that used to cut the city off from the hinterland. On the far side, the track to Dale runs alongside the peaceful waters of Sørfjorden, where birch and conifer cling to steep rock faces above small, fertile fields full of rangy sheep.

From Dale, the train turns northeast to Voss, the centre of rich farming lands, famous for winter and summer sports. After Voss, the train plunges into the Gravhals Tunnel, emerging some 5km (3 miles) later to climb up to Myrdal. The trains may seem to travel slowly but, in fact, they cover the ground quickly and tackle some remarkable gradients along the way.

From Myrdal, a special small train winds down Europe's steepest gradient (for a non-funicular train) to Flåm, nearly 850m (3,000ft) and 6km (4 miles) below on Aurlandsfjorden. This is one of the innermost of Sogn's many fingers, and is more than 146km (97 miles) from the sea.

The Flåm line is an engineering marvel, snaking down the narrow length of Flåmsdalen. A vivid impression of wild beauty appears and disappears in a flicker of slatted light, as the little train plunges under snowsheds which are very necessary in winter. At Kjosfossen (waterfall), at its height in May, great spouts of creaming water cascade from ledge to ledge through a dark ravine. Passengers pile out, cameras at the ready.

A break at Flåm gives time to wander down to the fjord's edge, or to stand below the small terminus to watch the train as its sets off back up the steep climb to Myrdal, the sound of its hooter a mournful echo against the hard rock. There is time too for lunch at Hotell Freitheim before the ferry moves off along Aurlandsfjorden for a two-hour voyage.

On both sides, mountains swoop close to the water and every flat piece of ground or ledge, however small, holds a cluster of wooden houses or a tiny farm. The biggest community is at Aurland, famous for making shoes. Next comes Nærøyfjorden, where the mountains' height is double the width of the fjord, seeming almost to close in on the boat.

From Gudvangen, huddled below the mountains, a coach heads into Nærøydalen, up the hairpin bends of Stalheimkleiven (gorge). The route was built as long ago as 1849, when pack horses and traders waited for the snows to melt before they started their slow, laden journey. It has two fine waterfalls, Sivlefossen, named after the poet Per Sivle, whose early home is nearby, and Stalheimfossen.

Peaceful today, the gorge was the scene of fierce conflict in World War II, when Norwegian troops held out in the Stalheim Hotel at the top. A few traces of battle and occupation remain in the caverns below the terraces, overlooking the gorge. There has been a coaching inn here since the 17th century and the hotel carries on that tradition. It is also a good place for authentic mementoes of the tour.

The arrival at Voss allows little time to explore, just a quick coffee before the train leaves for Bergen. It arrives back there around 8pm at the end of a day that gives an excellent flavour of this part of Norway. The tour can be booked through Bergen Tourist Information Office.

Torbjørg Utne (1812-1903). She was known as Mor (Mother) Utne, and her picture hangs in the sittingroom.

From Utne, the next stop south along the fjord is Jondal. On the way there, take time at **Herand** to look at the Bronze Age carvings on the peninsula to the right. Jondal has the area's largest church, known as the Hardanger Cathedral. The Folgefonn glacier road also starts here.

After the short ferry crossing from Jondal to Skutevik on the west side of Hardanger, road 551 goes left for Strandebarm, which has **Eikenes Herregaard** (Eikenes Manor) now an excellent hotel. Continuing to just before Mundheim, the road turns north and winds along the water's edge to rejoin the E68 at Tysse. From there it is but a short drive back to Bergen at the end of a fine introduction to Hardanger.

There is, however, much more to see and many more detours to make off this route, notably from Utne down the east side of Sørfjorden to **Aga**, and the old farm of Agatunet, or by crossing from Utne to Kinsarvik and pursuing the old pack horse route up Måbødalen, past the great **Voringfoss** (waterfall). **Kjeåsen Mountain Farm** was once reached by foot only from Eidfjord at the bottom of Måbodalen, but it is now possible to reach it by car through the remarkable steep S-shaped road tunnel which goes up to Sima Power Plant. The plant is built inside the mountain and is open to visitors.

The Hardangerfjord's possibilities are many and very varied but it all takes time. Nobody could get to know this great fjord in a couple of days.

Stavanger and Rogaland

Stavanger has long been a lucky city and goes back to early Norwegian history. **Domkirken** (Cathedral) was built between 1125 and 1135, and is one of the best preserved medieval cathedrals in Europe. Today, this robust cathedral has massive pillars but elegant arches and a beautiful 16th-century baroque pulpit. The spectacular stained glass windows, by Victor Sparre, are at their best with the morning sun shining through them.

For centuries, Stavanger depended on maritime trade and the rich agriculture of Rogaland. When shipping and sea trade began to dwindle in the mid-19th century, a providential abundance of brisling (sardines) appeared and the city took on the permanent, heavy scent of hot fish oil from dozens of canners – the 'smell of money' said the Siddis, the colloquial name for a Stavanger citizen. That lasted until after World War II, when Stavanger began to face a thin future. Then, in the 1960s, a new crop was discovered – oil.

Oil has brought prosperity and a massive building programme for the many international oil company headquarters and personnel, which have in turn brought with them eating houses and shops, good hotels and foreign schools. Oil has also given Stavanger the money to restore and reuse many of the old warehouses that once lined the harbour.

But the city's greatest restoration is **Gamle Stavanger** (Old Stavanger), behind the west side of Vågen. The collection of 150 white, wooden houses from the 17th and early 18th centuries line cobbled streets, lit with old street lamps. The houses are not a museum but are privately owned and lived in, though strictly protected.

The sardine era is remembered at the **Canning Museum**, in the last of the city's 70 canneries. The big ground floor has curing ovens and threading rods, where men and women worked long, tedious hours threading, smoking and packing sardines that went all over the world, their colourful labels almost an art form in their own right.

Maritime trade and the shipping industry are remembered in three old mercantile houses. This **Maritime Museum** with exhibits from the times of sailing ships to oil platforms, also contains a general store full of goods sold before World War II, a merchant's office as it must have been when last used in the 1930s, and the dwelling house of a 19th-century shipowner, his prosperity clear in the heavy, stuffed furniture.

Further into the centre, **Breidablikk**, built in the 1880s by the shipowner Lars Berentsen, is another indication of earlier wealth, and not far away, **Ledaal** was the home of the Kielland family. Its best-known member is the writer Alexander Kielland, who vividly described Stavanger life. Ledaal is now the King's residence whenever he visits Stavanger, but it is open at other times. Earlier times are also remembered at **Ullandhaug**, a few kilometres southwest of the city, the reconstruction of a 1,500-year-old farm, excavated in the 1960s, with original houses, authentic tools and materials. Southwest of Stavanger is the site of the Battle of Hafrsfjord, where King Harald Hårfagre (Fairhair) brought unity to Norway by defeating the warring minor kings. On the fjordside are three enormous sword sculptures, points sticking straight down into the ground.

From the southernmost harbour town of **Egersund**, its summer yachts best seen from the top of the lighthouse, Rogaland claims the mildest climate in Norway, and to be the biggest producer of dairy goods, poultry, eggs and meat. North from Egersund, a coastal strip has become **Jærstrendene Protected Landscape Area**, with natural bird and botanical reserves and fine white sand bathing beaches. Near the coast is a typical wooden vicarage, **Hå Gamle Prestegård** from 1780. Now a museum with art and other exhibitions, it lies along the North Sea route (road 44). For children the best treat must be **Kongenparken**, a huge leisure park further north near the small town of Ålgård. It has an enormous Gulliver figure, full of unexpected playthings, and a long bob-sleigh ride.

Stavanger's main fjord is **Lysefjorden**, some 40km (25 miles) long, a dramatic high-sided cleft into the land. Its most spectacular feature is **Prekestolen** (the Pulpit), a flat slab sticking out some 600m (250ft) above the fjord, it is reached via a hard scramble up through steep heather moor, or by horseback on guided riding tours. Looking down from the slab is a spectacular experience, as is the remarkable road up to **Lysebotn Power Station** at the inner end of the fjord, which snakes up through 27 hairpin bends to some 750m (2,500ft).

Lysefjorden can also be reached by boat, and boats go to many islands to the north of the city. Mosterøy has **Ulstein Kloster** (monastery), not a ruin but a well-preserved cloister, where concerts are held on summer nights. The big island of Karmøy has **Skudeneshamn**, a delightful preserved village, with little white wooden houses, galleries, arts and crafts shops, and a small factory making reproduction foghorns from sailing ship days. **Museum Mærlandsgården** tells the local history. On the main coast from Karmøy, **Haugesund**, is an old fishing and shipping centre, and today a busy seaway between Stavanger and Bergen, and to the islands. Its harbour, lined with warehouses, is also filled with pleasure boats. Today, Haugesund is also popular for congresses and festivals, the main annual event being the Norwegian Film Festival.

Inland from Bergen to Voss

There are many roads inland to reach the heights and the small towns and villages of the upland valleys, though mountain roads like this may be closed in winter. The train on the great Bergen–Oslo railway line invariably gets through and makes Voss, which lies between Norway's most famous fjords, Hardangerfjord and Sognefjorden, a year-round place to visit.

Settlers came to **Voss** as long as 3,000 years ago to hunt and farm this fertile, green valley. A reminder of King (St) Olav's visit in 1023 to convert the villagers is **Olav's Cross** in the town centre.

In winter the area is home to skiing and winter sports, and the lake, **Vangsvatnet**, has excellent ice-fishing. In summer, the thrill is to see hang-gliders hovering gently like huge birds off the top of the mountains, which also make marvellous walking and mountaineering terrain, and the lake is full of boats and windsurfers. Close to the lake is a **War Memorial**, not to the last world war but to the people of Voss who took part in the war against Sweden, from 1808-14, which started the long road to Norway's statehood in 1905. The World War II memorial is not far away at Bømoen military camp.

Beside the station is one of Voss's oldest and best-known hotels, **Fleischer's Hotel**, opened in 1889 for the rich, aristocratic and royal, and still owned and run by the Fleischer family. In the small station garden, a bronze relief of a traditional Voss

T he fjord waterfalls are at their height in May and early June, after the spring thaw. Tvinnefoss, on the way to Voss, is a delight at this time of year.

bridal party is by Brynulf Bergslien. A monument to the sculptor, also dedicated to his brothers the painters Nils and Knut, stands behind the church. Its creator, the sculptor Magnus Dagestad, has an arts and crafts museum named after him.

In the town centre, the thick walls of the church, **Vangskyrkja**, were built by King Magnus the Lawmaker in 1277. Inside are rich medieval and Renaissance decorations. The octagonal steeple is unique in Norway. By a miracle, the church escaped the heavy bombing at the start of World War II which is the reason for the rest of the centre of Voss being largely modern.

Summer or winter, the way to the top of the town's main mountain and ski-centre is **Hangursbanen**, with two gondola cars, Dinglo and Danglo, taking just four minutes to climb from the centre more than 660m (2,200ft), and giving a spectacular wide-angled view. A chairlift runs up a further 800m (2,500ft). This first stop has a platform and restaurant, which moves out of doors in summer, with even better views of paragliders soaring on the thermals over Vangsvatnet. Hill walking here calls for stout boots, a sweater and an anorak.

Also visible from the cable car is **Mølstertunet**, a collection of 16 old buildings in a traditional arrangement around a grassy square. Once two farmsteads on their original sites, the oldest, with an open hearth and primitive kitchen, dates from the early 17th century. All the old farm implements and furniture were in use here until 1927, when the last family left. Here too is a carved version of the Voss bridal party, which Gudleik Brekkhus based on Bergslien's bronze relief at Voss station. The bride, in a distinctive headdress, rides with her father and her retinue, including the traditional fiddler and toastmaster of a true Voss wedding. If you are very lucky, you may still see a Voss bridal party just like this.

This is all part of the long artistic tradition of Voss which, for a town of 6,000, has produced a remarkable number of Hardanger fiddlers and other musicians, artists and craftworkers in wood, silver and textiles, whose monuments are everywhere. It is also one of the best places to see Norway's old dances performed in rich and beautiful *bunader* (national costumes), and to visit farms where the old ways are still followed. This tradition makes Voss an excellent place for searching out Norwegian mementoes of all sorts, and the local silversmith sells exquisite jewellery to go with the *bunad*, and other silverware.

Sognefjorden to Nordfjord

When winter looses its grip on the fjords, the spring air is full of the sound of tumbling water as mountain ice melts and waterfalls drop into the fjords below. Nowhere is this more true than in Sognefjorden and Nordfjord, and the land between. At 220km (150 miles), Sognefjorden is Norway's longest and deepest fjord, leading to the country's greatest mountain massif, Jotuneheimen (home of the giants) and Europe's largest glacier, Jostedalsbreen.

Features like these made Sognefjorden a favourite with 19th-century visitors, and European royalty such as the British Crown Prince, later Edward VII, and the German Kaiser, Wilhelm II. That popularity has not changed. Though the fjords no longer act as Norway's main roads, cruise boats and smaller vessels make their way far inland to ever-narrower waters, and intrepid drivers tackle the high mountain roads.

Sognefjorden

One of the best-known villages is **Balestrand** on the northern shore, which has been popular for over a century, especially with the British, whose presence is remembered in St Olav's English Church, founded by an intrepid Victorian lady. It still holds summer services.

Balestrand has always attracted artists, and Germans from the Düsseldorf Academy added to its early charms by building Swiss-style houses, decorated with dragonheads in tribute to their hosts' Viking past. The climate here is remarkably mild, ideal for the exotic trees planted by a local pastor, who was also a botanist, at **Dragsvik**, just across a small inlet. Also

Since the 19th century, the little town of Balestrand on the Sognefjord has been a favourite, particularly with British people.

here is an enamelling workshop, open to visitors, and a few evocative old hotels.

To the north, **Jostedalsbreen** covers some 1,200 sq km (463 sq miles), and no less than 24 of its long ice-white glacier arms have their own names. From Balestrand, the nearest way to the glacier is via **Fjærland** on a narrow side fjord. From here, daily tours, led by guides, head

*N*orway is famous for its stav kirker *(stave churches) built of upright split-timber walls. They have unusual sloping roofs and, often, dragon decorations. One of the best-known is Borgund, easily reached from Flåm on the Aurlandfjord.*

off for the awe-inspiring sight and seeming permanence of all that ice. There are also glacier walks and courses for experienced, well-equipped walkers. Fjærland is a farming village with a small farm museum and a collection of implements, all explained by the owner.

Sogn og Fjordane has three glacier centres. On the Sogn side, in Fjærland's **Norwegian Glacier Museum** a big glacier model allows visitors to see a glacier from the inside, and there is a film about Jostedalsbreen. Further west at Gjerdein Jostedalen, the **Glacier Centre** covers 20,000 years of the history of the glacier. **Jostedalsbreen National Park Centre** at Oppstryn on the north side has botanical gardens and natural science exhibitions.

All the high ground to the north of Sognefjorden offers fine mountain walking. From Høyanger to the west of Balestrand, you can also visit the **Water Power Museum**, which explains the importance of water to fjord life. Water leisure activities alone include fishing, rowing, waterskiing, swimming, sailing and exploring. From Balestrand, there are round trips and ferries to the fjord's eastern end, to the four stave churches (see p.68), and links to Flåm, the Stalheim Gorge, and more, which give an idea of the long importance of the fjords to transport.

East from Balestrand, towards Leikanger, the great arc of the **Kvinnfoss** (Lady's Waterfall) lies close to the road at Hella, which runs through the fruit and berry lands of **Leikanger**, the county town, linked to Bergen by the Expressbåten hydrofoil. **Sogndal** is the main town of Inner Sogn, the heart of a farming district, with Sogn's four stave churches (see p.68). This town has a population of around 3,000, a number that swells enormously in term time for this is the fjord's main educational centre; pupils come in from distant valleys to board at one of the five university-level establishments. Sogndal also has Norway's oldest **Folk High School**, part of the long Scandinavian tradition of adult education.

Sogndal's open-air museum, at nearby **Kaupanger** is one of Norway's oldest, with some 32 houses and farm buildings, and a living museum with its own animals. Summer brings lively evenings of traditional music and dancing. On the southern side of this inlet, a stone marks the Battle of Fimreite in 1184, when the peasant Birkebeiner, clad in birch bark boots, helped King Sverre defeat King Magnus Erlingsson and the nobility. Further inland, the dog-leg of **Lustrafjorden** offers boat-trips on its icy-green waters, before it pushes its way northeast to the high peaks of Jotunheimen, with Gaupne and Luster easy gateways to the glaciers Jostedalsbreen and Niggardsbreen.

To the south, Sognefjorden ends in two more fjords and valleys. Årdal, finally meets its match in the bulk of **Jotunheimen**, and Lærdal runs south to meet **Lærdalselva** (river) and ends at **Borgund** with its stave church (see p.68) and **Sjurhaugsfossen** (waterfall) nearby. Both valleys are good for walking and riding, and Årdalen's great waterfall pours some 1,000m (3,330ft) into **Tynin Power Station**.

On the south shore, almost opposite Balestrand, **Vangsnes** and **Vik**, a few miles inland are encircled by beautiful snow-capped peaks. This farming area supplies most of Norway's *gammelost*, a tasty, mature cheese. It also holds not only **Hopperstad Stavkirke** (see p.69) but **Hove Steinkirke**, Norway's oldest stone church, built in 1150 and only 20 years younger than the stave church. The towering statue of the Viking hero, Fridtjhof, 26.5m (90ft) high, was the generous gift of a man who loved Sognefjorden, Kaiser Wilhelm II.

East of Vik, the long inlet of Aurlandsfjord leads to Sogn's innermost recesses: **Aurland**, home of Norway's best agricultural shows in an area of small mountain farms; and **Flåm**, terminal of the steep mountain railway (see p.194). Its side fjord is the famous **Nærøyfjord**, part of the most dramatic fjord cruise in Norway, ending at the village of **Gudvangen**, and the long climb to **Stalheim** and **Voss** (see p.197).

Nordfjord

The coast between Sognefjorden and Nordfjord is stippled with islands, and bisected by many more smaller fjords cutting deep into the land. Nordfjord also has its own small glaciers, **Ålfotbreen** and **Gjegnalundsbreen**. Each road junction has a small village but there are few main roads and the only community big enough to merit the term town is **Florø**. Right on the edge of the sea, its 19th-century growth came from herring, but it is now part of the oil industry. All along this coast, fish-farming has brought new wealth to village and island, and Florø alone registers more than a thousand pleasure craft.

Nordfjord, under its own name, stretches inland only as far as the district town of **Eid**, but its many inner side-fjords, valleys and lakes such as **Hornindalsvatnet**, Europe's deepest and clearest lake at 514m (1,700ft), where water flooded the valley thousands of years ago, lead into the mountains. This is the home of the sturdy Norwegian fjord horse, the *fjording*. Cream-coloured with a darker upstanding mane, in the past it pulled the two-wheeled *stolkjerre*, which every farm used for transport. Today, one of the favourite horse-drawn journeys is up to Briksdalsbreen,

through Oldedalen. All around the farming land of these inner fjords, communities have held onto their traditions of handcrafts, music, dancing and costume.

Nordfjord Folk Museum dates from 1920, when little had changed over the centuries and it was easy to find original structures. It has 32 buildings, including barns, cowsheds, lofts, and a mountain *seter* or *støl*, the old summer farm where cows enjoyed fresh grass, and women and girls spent their summers milking and cheese-making. The museum is at the end of Gloppenfjorden at **Sandane**, which has an energetic adventure centre offering everything from canoeing to mountain-biking.

There are many of these open-air museums in inner fjord villages, and opportunities galore for outdoor activities. Summer skiing is best at the eastern end of the Nordfjord system at **Stryn** and **Loen**, the northwest edge of Jostedalsbreen. Stryn's summer skiing is spectacular, with Jostedalsbreen National Park Centre (see p.201) at nearby Oppstryn. One of the furthest northwestern spots in Sogn og Fjordane is **Vestkapp** (West Cape) in the Selje area. It is mainland Norway's western edge, not as famous as Nordkapp but a fierce, windy coast where the closest land is Shetland, which some claim to have seen on a clear day.

Møre og Romsdal

Like most of the fjord country, Møre og Romsdal owes its long history to the sea, set as it is amongst a network of fjords, and hundreds of islands and skerries. Its three main towns have been on the Hurtigruten (the coastal route) for a hundred years. From fishing to maritime engineering, and ships and shipbuilding, the sea has set the pace.

Ålesund, the southernmost town, is the country's biggest fishing community, and the gateway to Storfjorden and to Geirangerfjorden, probably Norway's best known fjord. Ålesund itself spreads out from the mainland to the islands of **Nørvøya** and **Aspøya**, and is surrounded by more, best viewed from **Aksla**, reached by 418 steps from the town park. At the top, **Aksla Fjellstua** (mountain lodge) revives breathless climbers (there is also a road) and the panorama from its terrace gives a wonderful view of sea and islands. The harbour is a bright squeeze of fishing boats, and the pier is *the* place to buy fresh seafood, even though Ålesund has now also moved into fish-farming and processing. There are many fish restaurants and visitors and locals alike spend a lot of leisure time on the water.

Turning inland, where half the ground lies above 600m (1,800ft), the elegant shapes of the **Sunnmøre Mountains** peak up to 1,800-1,900m (6,000ft) and more. Their first climbers, mostly from England, came around the turn of the century. Joined today by many other nations, climbing has continued from small communities like **Ørsta** and **Volda**, south of Ålesund, the whole great series of peaks easily reached by way of fjord and mountain road.

Yet it was tragedy that made Ålesund what it is today when, in 1904, a fierce fire destroyed over a thousand buildings. Ålesund was fortunate to be so popular with foreigners including, once more, Kaiser Wilhelm II, and help came from many sources. With *jugend* the style of the moment, within three years Ålesund had risen again, with all the typical details of *art nouveau* – turrets, stonework decoration, and delightful front doors. The best idea of how the town looked before the fire can be gained from a model in **Ålesund Museum**.

At Borgund, some 5km (3 miles) inland is **Sunnmøre Museum**, close to the site of **Borgundkaupangen**, one of the county's two ancient market centres, at their height from 1000-1500AD. There are some 50 old houses, and a collection of around 30 working boats, once used by the coast's intrepid fishermen. **Skt Peterskirke**, from the old market centre, now forms the cross nave of **Borgundkirke**.

The Norwegian skill at building tunnels is well illustrated, with islands and mainland all linked. The spectacular connection to Ålesund airport goes down to some 140m (465ft) and is 11km (7 miles) long. Another favourite island is **Giske**, a small community that still clings to the coastal way of life, with a 12th-century marble church. Here the beaches are white sand and teeming with birds. One of the best places for birdwatching on this coast is the famous bird-island of **Runde**, now reached by two bridges but more fun by boat. Some 170,000 pairs of seabirds nest each year, making this Norway's third largest bird-cliff. Some years ago, divers also found a hoard of gold from the Dutch ship *Akerenedam* off Runde, and are still searching for the Spanish galleon *Castillo Negro*.

Geirangerfjorden

Many cruise ships travel inland to Geirangerfjorden but, by road and ferry, the most direct and interesting way is south on road 60, taking the ferry between Magerholm and Aursnes, through Sykkylven – the surprising home of several leading furniture manufacturers – to the southern end of the fjord, and the world's shortest salmon river, Straumjerde, which abounds with fish. The road climbs Strandfjellet, which is fine mountaineering country with winter skiing, to Stranda, with Stranda Skisentret. South through Strandadalen, still on road 60, the road ends at Hellsylt where Geirangerfjorden begins and the cruise boats cluster in Norway's most beautiful fjord. There is also a car ferry to Geiranger.

There is nothing of the sea in this beautiful, narrow fjord. It feels secret and enclosed, protected by high mountainsides, reflected in the mirror-still waters. The sun turns the waterfalls into sparkling lace, so beautiful that they have names such as the **Bridal Veil** and the **Seven Sisters**. In some places along the formidable walls, triangles of green indicate small farms clinging to the ledges, some still in use, others deserted, no more than a memorial to the hardships of times gone by.

The best way to see Geiranger is to travel to the inner end by boat, with waterfalls so close it seems they must fall on to the deck. A summer alternative is the path stretching under the high southern wall. **Geiranger** village at the eastern end is a cluster of buildings protected by a half-circle of mountains. Half way up the winding road **Hotel Utsikten Bellevue** has an apt name. High above the hotel, the road passes **Dalsnibba**, at 1,495m (4,600ft) one of the best viewpoints of the area, and connects into the inland alternative route north.

From Ålesund and Molde, it is possible to take tours by coach and ferry to Geiranger, but to make the best of independent travel by car it is sensible to spread these inland tours over several days, staying along the route.

Molde

Molde, further north on a south-facing hillside at the entrance to **Romsdalsfjorden** is a green town, which has earned the name 'The Town of Roses' from the luxuriant gardens around its remaining original small wooden houses – bombs destroyed many in 1940. Another reminder of that time is **Kongebjørka** (the King's birch), said to be the place where King Håkon VII and Crown Prince Olav sheltered from the bombers. Once Molde depended on timber, then on fish and herring, and the first visitors discovered this pretty town at the end of the 19th century. Now, there are also electronics and engineering.

The *Little Rose Seller* statue presides over the market which sells many roses alongside other flowers and fruit. Jazz has now moved in and the annual **International Jazz Festival** in August brings musicians and audiences from many countries onto the streets to stroll and play. Not far from the town centre, the **Romsdal Museum** has buildings from the whole area. Its display of *bunader* (local costume) is particularly fine. **Hjertøya**, Molde's favourite swimming island, has a **Fisheries Museum** clustered around a small coastal lagoon. Modern life includes a good sports stadium with running tracks, an all-season football ground, indoor sports centres and swimming pools.

From Molde's best viewpoint, **Varden**, locals claim that on a good day you can see 87 Sunnmøre snow-capped peaks, and as far as the wide mouth of Romsdalsfjorden towards Åndalsnes. To reach Åndalsnes from Molde entails road and ferry, in two beautiful routes alongside the fjord. On both, the view across water and islands to the mountains is magnificent.

Åndalsnes has one of the finest positions of any Norwegian community, on a small peninsula encircled by fjord and mountain. The small town raises its eyes to peaks and sheer cliff walls that have attracted climbers of many nationalities since the 19th century. One of the most spectacular of these, **Trollveggen** (Troll Wall), has more than 1,000m (3,300ft) of overhanging and vertical rock, and was not climbed successfully until 1965. Dedicated climbers still find new routes every year.

Trollveggen is part of the massive crags of **Trolltindane**, rising from the valleys in the east. On its less testing side, the average mountaineer can get to the top though it is not a route for a novice and calls for boots and good climbing gear. This does not mean that non-climbers cannot get a feel of these magnificent mountains. **Troll-stigen**, the road through Isterdalen between Trolltindane and the even higher peaks of **Bispen**, **Kongen**, and **Dronningen** (the

*O*ne of the most dramatic roads in Norway's fjord region is Trollstigen, which crosses the massive crags of Trolltindane, as they seem to rise straight from the fjord near Åndalsnes.

Bishop, King and Queen), climbs in 11 gigantic zigzags up the bare mountain. Halfway up, the spray from **Stigfossen** (waterfall) blows across the bridge, and every June there is a ski race on the glacier near Trollstigen. The road reaches its highest point at 852m (2,840ft), and then heads downwards for Valldall and Geiranger.

Åndalsnes is also the terminus for the railway, **Raumabanen**, that leaves the main Oslo–Trondheim line at Dombas some 100km (60 miles) southeast, and follows the course of the Rauma river along Romsdalen. This is one of the best ways to arrive, with passengers craning their necks to get a full view of the great rock faces and stark peaks. **Romsdalshorn**, 1,852m (6,100ft) was conquered in the 1880s by famous climbers such as William Slingsby, Johannes Vigdal and Carl Hall, though it had been climbed 50 years earlier by two local farmers. The Rauma is a superb salmon river.

North from Molde, the adventurous route for Kristiansund is via Bud and the Atlantic Toll Road. **Bud** was a major trading centre in the Middle Ages and, in 1533, held the last Norwegian parliament until 1814. Ergan coastal fort is a reminder of World War II. Fishing is important here, with good sea-angling for visitors. The village of **Vevang** lives on commercial fishing but also has an excellent scuba diving centre.

Vevang is also the start of **Atlanterhavsveien** (Atlantic Ocean Road) which crosses the sea to Averøy. Relatively new but already famous, it is like driving over the sea as the road jumps from islet to islet out in the ocean. Sometimes, there are huge waves, at others just a quiet movement on the water. **Averøy** was one of the earliest settlements after the last Ice Age, and in 1909 archaeologists found remains of the Fosna culture from around 7,000BC. From a later past are the old wooden **Kverneskirka** (church) from 1300, and **Horg the Viking Farm**. Here Harald Hårfagre, who had vowed to leave his hair untouched until Norway was united, had his famous fair hair cut and washed after the Battle of Hafrsfjord. The ferry from Bremsnes to Kristiansund takes 15 minutes.

Kristiansund

Kristiansund, the 'ocean town', where the Atlantic waves pound the rocks below, stretches over three islands linked by bridges and was the fishing capital of west Norway. Like several others, Kristiansund was named after a Danish King, this time Christian VI. Previously it had been called Fosna, from the area's earliest settlers. But the advantage of town status, which was granted by the King, meant that Kristiansund was responsible for its own affairs and trade, instead of being controlled from Trondheim.

The merchants grew rich, their names curiously commemorated in somewhat primitive stone monuments: the **Hagbart Brinchman Monument** to the engineer responsible for the town's water supply; the **Moses Monument** to the memory of merchant John Moses, who was Kristiansund's delegate to the Constitutional Convention at Eidsvoll in 1814; and **Christian Bræin's Monument** to the organist, composer and father of Kristiansund's musical and opera life, and also to his musical son and grandson, both Edvard. Similar merchant names, such as Christie (almost certainly from Scotland) are still seen in fine houses such as the 18th-century **Christiegården** which is open to visitors.

Though Kristiansund has only 18,000 inhabitants, like Bergen, long contact with the outside and the foreign merchants who lived here has made it a cosmopolitan town with many restaurants and good shops. **Festiviteten**, built as the town's social, concert and theatre hall, in *jugend* style, escaped the World War II bombing. Today it stages opera as well as theatre, a tribute to the musical Bræien family.

Kristiansund's main church was a victim of the 1940 German bombing, and has now been replaced by a new church, designed by architect Oddøsby, who named it 'Rock Crystal in Roses'. **Kirkelandet Kirke** was dedicated in 1964, and it is impossible to ignore this stark white building, with a 30m (100ft) high choir wall of 320 stained glass panels. They rise from the sombre, dark colours of earth at the foot to eternal light at the top. An even newer building is **Vardetårnet** (Varde Tower). As long ago as the Napoleonic wars, Kristiansund had erected a simple watch tower on Varde Hill. In 1892, for the town's 150-year jubilee, a new tower was raised, and now a third tower has been built.

For a general impression of Kristiansund, take *Sundbåten*, the harbour boat which sails around all three islands. On Innlandet island, close to the Sundbåt quay, **Den Gamle Byen** is the oldest part of the town, much of which miraculously escaped the 1940 bombing. Here are the old customs house, the first hospital and school. **Sjursvika** on the east side of the island has some fine old warehouses.

Mellomverftet was once a shipyard beside Vågen on Kirkelandet. Now it is preserved as part of **Nordmøre Museum** and continues to build and restore beautiful old ships and boats in traditional style. Another part, **Woldbrygga**, a coopers' workshop, with the original machines and tools, makes barrels in the old way. This wharf also displays rope-making, herring salting, and some lovely old work boats.

Hjelkrembrygga, from 1835, has a *klippfisk* museum. Kristiansund has been a *klippfisk* town for some 300 years, a major exporter of Norwegian dried cod to all parts of the world. The original export of *klippfisk* was to Spain and Portugal, which has had two curious results. In the town's excellent fish restaurants, *bacalao* is now the favourite party dish. A more bizarre result comes from the 19th century when sailing ships on the way back from Spain sometimes used Spanish soil as ballast. Much of it was dumped on Gomalandet, site of an old cemetery. So, many people from this northern town lie buried in Spanish soil!

Excursions from Kristiansund

Kristiansund is the last town in Møre og Romsdal and various routes lead either out of the county or form round trips. Southeast is the island of **Frei**, and at **Krifast** is the start of one of Norway's largest road projects: a 52km (32-mile) undersea tunnel, and a floating bridge over Bergsøysundet.

It leads to Tingvollsfjord and **Tingvoll** which has Nordmøre's oldest church, with stairs and tunnels built into the thick medieval stone walls. Further south on the other side of the fjord is **Nesset Prestegård**, where the Norwegian patriot and poet, Bjørnstjerne Bjørnson grew up. Author of the national anthem, much of his later writing was inspired by the mountains: 'some standing white, others standing blue, with jagged, competing, agitating peaks, some marching along in ranking rows'.

The road continues along the fjordside to **Sunndalsøra**, dominated by a large aluminium plant, but surrounded by mountains with deer and other wild animals. From here Sunndalen (road 16) squeezes between the great **Trollheimen** massif to the north and **Dovrefjell**, peaking to over 2,000m (6,600ft) to the south, for Oppdal and Trondheim. A second way to Trondheim is through Surnadalen direct to Trondheim along the north of Trollheimen. Both run through the **Nordmøre Wilderness**, where small farms in narrow valleys provide excellent grain for the whole country. More than that, it is fine walking country, with energetic routes and mountain *hytter*.

Another favourite route from Kristiansund is to **Grip**, an island to the north. Once 400 souls survived on this small island. Today, it is occupied only during the summer, perhaps because of ferocious winter weather. In 1796, a nor'wester washed away 100 houses. Further north, on little **Kuløy**, off the big island of Smøla, is the **Kuli Stone**, dated to around 1015AD, both Norway's oldest Christian monument and the first known relic on which the world 'Norge' appears. From **Smøla**, the fjords widen and the land turns into islands, where the remnants of the old farming-fishing way of life remain, as Møre og Romsdal merges into Sør-Trøndelag.

Hurtigruten – The Great Coastal Voyage

The changing view as the ship leaves Bergen at 10pm sharp is one of the finest of this sea city. In the cold of winter, the lights of Bergen seem to climb up its encircling hills. The spring brings the first blossom and a sudden surge of colour. In summer, water and hills glow under a late sun, striking an occasional flash of light from glass and metal; by autumn, the trees are turning rich oranges and yellows in a final blaze.

This is one of the most beautiful voyages in the world, along a dramatic coast. Though Hurtigruten (literally 'the swift route'), goes far north, there are rarely very rough seas or ice. For most of the time, the ship weaves in and out of the sheltering islands that line Norway's west coast, and a benevolent Gulf Stream keeps ice away from all but the narrowest of the fjords.

Hurtigruten, the coastal voyage, has been taking place day-in and day-out for over a hundred years. In those early years, voyage by sea was the easiest way of getting from community to community along the coast and to the many islands. In winter, it was the only way, other than on skis and at that time the ship's purpose was to transport passengers and cargoes. Although today it has become much used as a holiday journey by visitors, the original purpose still remains, with every sort of cargo, even perhaps a family dog or a prized calf.

There are 36 stops, a few at bigger ports such as Ålesund, Trondheim, and Tromsø, but most are village harbours where the ship is particularly important. Some people come down to the wharf just to watch because the ferry's arrival is part of the community's diary. Except for the larger places, stops vary on the northern and southern journeys.

The first organized time ashore heading north is at Ålesund, the *art nouveau* city built after a disastrous fire early this century (see p.203). Here, there is time for a walk up Aksla Hill's 418 steps for a view of the sea, fjords and mainland. At the old capital of Trondheim further north (see p.211), a tour takes passengers to Nidaros Domkirke and one or two other places of interest. On the return journey, in summer, a midnight tour goes to the top of a local mountain.

Not far north of Trondheim is the Arctic Circle. In summer, this means a ceremony on deck with 'King Neptune' handing out certificates. In winter, it is more informal, but passengers can have a certificate to show they have crossed this magic circle.

The journey through the islands of Lofoten and Vesterålen, where the ships stop at several harbours, is stunningly beautiful with peaks rising straight from the sea. For most of the way along the coast mountains loom, many high enough to have snow caps much of the year. In winter, with the short-lived sun streaking the tops red, they look for all the world like ice-cream cones with a

A favourite stop on Hurtigruten is Trondheim, the old capital with Nidaros Domkirke (Cathedral).

All along the north-western coast, Hurtigruten passes lovely coastal mountains.

dollop of raspberry sauce on top. But the temptation of the winter deck is probably strongest of all for bird watchers. The islands and cliffs have some wonderful bird colonies and the small harbours are often full of colourful ducks. Favourite of all are puffins.

Tromsø, where the ship sails right into the fjord behind the main island (see p.232), gives enough time for a tour and the chance to take the cable car up Storsteinen, one of the peaks that circle Tromsø, looking towards the Lyngen Alps and the fjord. In the summer months, the ships begin to take on aspects of a cruise ship, and a treat is a detour into the Trollfjord, so steep and narrow that no large cruise liner can enter it.

At Hammerfest, most passengers go ashore to see this northernmost town (see p.242), and particularly to gain the coveted certificate which proves they have been there. But, almost certainly, the favourite tour is to the massive rocky headland of Nordkapp (North Cape), where Hurtigruten makes a short detour so that passengers can reach this brooding land by coach from Honningsvåg (see p.243).

From here the ships turn east and sail along the northerly coronet of land, with small ports such as Vardø, and on to Kirkenes, almost on the boundary between Norway and Russia. For days now, in summer, the sun has never set which has the curious effect of confusing night and day in everyone's mind.

At Kirkenes, many join who have chosen to fly north and use the coastal steamer in one direction. A few others leave, usually locals. The two-way journey takes 12 days; one way the best part of six or seven. But whatever way one travels, the Hurtigruten voyage, will be a time out of the ordinary.

209

Norway's Ancient Capital – Mountains and Modern Technology

On the long journey north in Norway, it comes as a surprise that the ancient capital of Trondheim is only one-third of the way north on the fjord coast. Northerly as it seems, it is then almost as much of a shock to realise that the valleys and hills of the Trøndelag region around Trondheim, are a rich grain-growing land. Nord-Trøndelag starts just north of the city, and Sør-Trøndelag covers the country to the south and west. To the south, the Oppdal district, is the size of Luxembourg but with only 6,000 inhabitants. This is one of Norway's better skiing areas and in summer is always alive with climbers and walkers.

Trondheim

From the observation platform of Tyholttårnet, the city's communication tower, some 124m (500ft) high, it is easy to see that Trondheim has all the things that a city should have: a magnificent cathedral, a university, a fortress, a beautiful old bridge, mountains, a palace, colourful old wharf-houses interspersed with bright new buildings, parks, a river and the sea with yachts and pleasure boats. The heart of

Much of the beauty inside Nidaros Domkirke, former coronation site for Norway's Monarchs, comes from the soft, grey-green of the soapstone.

Trondheim lies on what is virtually an island between the **Nidelva** (river) which winds through the city, and **Trondheimsfjorden**. It is joined to the mainland by a narrow neck of land to the west, where **Skansen**, once the fortress that guarded the city gate, is now a fjordside park.

Trondheim's life is firmly interwoven with the sea. Out in the fjord, the grey shape of **Munkholmen** was once an 11th-century Benedictine monastery and, even earlier, a place of execution. At the harbour is **Ravnkloa**, the fish market and, around 9am every day, out on the long harbour arm, the Hurtigruten ship (coastal express) ties up for a few hours. For over a century, the Hurtigruten ships have been the link on this jagged coast where, certainly when winter closed the mountain passes, it was easier to get about by sea.

TRONDHEIM AND CENTRAL NORWAY

0   50 miles

0   80 km

N

Trofors

Skillebotn

Svenningdal

Hommelstø

Tosaunet

Vennesund

Børgefjell nasjonalp

Smalåsen

Terråk

Djupvik

Namsskogan

Kongsmo

Gjersvik

Garstad

Kolvereid

Abelvær

Flått

Skorovatn

Skogmo

Skjellbreissund

Namsos

Grong

Nyneset

Formofoss

Gressåmoen

Gressåmoen Nasjonal- park

Osen

Brørs

Hammer

Snåsa

Storvik

Veldemelen

Momyr

Steinkjer

Harsvik

Arnes

Mørreaunet

Svellingen

Grønsjøen

Verdalsørn

Stiklestad

Kallsedet

Levanger

Vaterholmbru

Opphaug

Åsen

Sandvika

Kallsjön

Berge

Fillan

Rissa

Medstugan

Sandstad

Stjørdal

Sunde

Rørvik

Hell

Meråker

Duved

Flak

TRONDHEIM

Storlien

Änn

Stemshaug

Børsa

Orkanger

Selbusjøen

Selbu

Vinjeøra

Rollset

Ås

Rindal

Rogstad

Gåre

Skei

Soknedal

Haltdalen

Stugudal

Storsjön

Berkåk

Reitan

Aursunden

Sunndalsøra

Gjevilvatn

Nåvseter

Røros

Steinsåsen

Funäsdalen

Oppdal

Yset

Tolga

Femund- marka nasjonalp

Drivstua

Töfsingdalens Nat. park

Motrøen

Seter

Namdalen

Snasavatnet

Beitstadfjorden

Trondheimsfjorden

Frøya

Hitra

Orkdalsfjorden

Gaula

Gaula

Trollheimen

Dovrefjell

SØR - TRØNDELAG

SWEDEN

*A*lmost an island, with
the Nidelva river running through
the town, shipping has long been
important to Trondheim. These
colourful warehouses go back
several centuries.

Now, there is also a network of air routes
to bring the communities together.

Trondelag was already a centre of power
when in 997AD, King Olav Tryggvason
founded a small trading town, built a
palace, and made Nidaros his capital. From
here he ruled an empire that stretched from
the White Sea in the east to western Europe, Iceland, Greenland and even touched
North America. But the king who made
Nidaros famous was King Olav Haraldson,
who introduced Christianity and, in
1030, fell at the Battle of Stiklestad.

Shortly after the King's death, reports
began of miracles connected with his resting place. A stream began to flow nearby
and the sagas reported that 'men were
healed of their ills by the waters'. Olav was
declared a martyr and became St Olav. His
body was moved and the saint's nephew,
Olav Kyrre, built the great stone church
that became **Nidaros Cathedral**, over his
new grave. Nidaros became renowned in
the Middle Ages as a place of pilgrimage,
many making the long journey on foot
through Sweden, others arriving by sea.

Nidaros Cathedral is a glorious building, with wonderful stained glass windows. The rose window over the west
door is particularly famous. It is a 1930s
work by Gabriel Kjelland, with the organ
below. Inside and out, there are many

Nidaros Domkirke (Cathedral) was built by Olav Kyrre, in honour of his uncle Skt (King) Olav Haraldson. In later years thousands of pilgrims came to visit his tomb.

statues of saints and kings but the beautiful effect of the grey-green soapstone interior needs little decoration.

Norwegian monarchs have been crowned in the cathedral since ancient times and the custom was revived after 1814, when Norway became free from Danish rule. The modern monarchy has done away with a formal coronation but the present King Harald received a blessing here and, since 1988, the cathedral has housed the Crown Jewels, a simple but beautiful regalia, displayed during the summer months in the North Chapel.

Close to the cathedral is the 12th-century **Archbishop's Palace**, one of Scandinavia's oldest secular buildings. It was the archbishop's seat until the Reformation and later became the residence of the Danish governor. The North Wing, the oldest

part, is used for official receptions. The palace also contains **Rustkammeret**, an army museum. **Hjemmefrontmuseet** has displays giving a picture of the activities of the local Home Front Defence, from sabotage to intelligence, from 1940 to 1945.

In 1681, Trondheim was devastated by one of the great fires that were a hazard to any wooden city, and much of today's city owes its shape, particularly its military remains, to General Johan Caspar de Cicignon, a military architect from Luxemburg, who was responsible for planning and building. **Den Gamle Bybro**, the old town bridge, was first built in 1681 when de Cicignon's men were constructing **Kristiansten Festning**, a fort on a hill then outside the city. The bridge as it is today is a later vintage, built in 1861, but Kristiansten Festning makes another good city outlook and it is a pleasant walk up, not far from Tyholttårnet. From here, you can pick out **Vår Frues Kirke** (the Church of Our Lady), near the main city square. Parts of the church go back to the 13th century though it was restored in 1739. Nearby on Munkegate in the old town, **Stiftsgården** is Scandinavia's largest timber mansion, built in the 1770s and now the King's official residence in Trondheim.

The citizens of Trondheim have not made the mistake of moving ever outwards, and this is a walking city with many people still in the centre. Two districts to tour on foot are **Hospitalsløkka**, set around the old Trondheim Hospital, dating from 1277 and now a home for elderly people. Its grounds hold an octagonal church, built in 1705, and the district is full of old wooden houses, carefully restored.

East of Nidelva, not far from the old town bridge, **Bakklandet** was once the great working-class district, along with **Mollenberg** and **Rosenborg**. These areas were restored more recently than Bakklandet, but again with the same loving care. **Sukkerhuset**, the sugar factory, not far from Trondelag Teater on Sverresgate, was built in 1752 and it was a brewery until 1984.

Trondheim today is a highly modern, technological city with the Institute of

T rondheim has a wealth of timber buildings and Stiftsgården, the Royal Palace when the King visits, is Scandinavia's largest timber mansion, built in the 1770s.

Den Gamle Bybro was first built in 1681 by the military architect, General Caspar de Cicignon, who was responsible for much of the city's architecture. This bridge replaced it in 1861.

Technology part of Trondheim University. There is a great emphasis on environmental research and the university also has, among other disciplines, a faculty of medicine, the Royal Norwegian Society for Science and the Humanities. The University Museum, founded 1760, is Norway's oldest scientific institution. Here also is Scandinavia's largest scientific and industrial research foundation, SINTEF. This has encouraged many high-tech businesses to open here. Past and present are joined at **Nordenfjeldske Kunstindustrimuseet**, devoted to applied art and craft.

First-class museums range from natural history and archaeology to **Trondhjems Sjøfartsmuseum** (Maritime Museum) plus a fine art gallery and theatre. **Trøndelag Folk Museum** at Sverresborg shows life in local towns and villages from times gone by, with the advantage of The Tavern, an old inn from 1739 which now has a good restaurant and handcrafts shop. There are several more, but one not to be missed is **Ringve Museum**, on the city outskirts, with rare, old musical instruments, brought together largely by the efforts of Russian-born Madame Victoria, widow of the last owner of Ringve Manor. One delightful speciality is that the guides are musicians who are able to demonstrate the instruments. Combined with nearby **Ringve Botanical Gardens**, the world's most northerly botanic garden, Ringve can easily fill an excellent day out.

Trondheim's most recent cultural centre is **Olavshallen** (Olav's Hall), set within Olavkvartalet, a newly restored four-sided block near the Nidelva. It has three halls with superb acoustics now attracting many major orchestras, it also incorporates the modern Grand Hotel, and a large public area with good restaurants and shops, all under cover.

Excursions from Trondheim

Like every other Norwegian city, Trondheim is also an outdoor place. **Bymarka**, agricultural land and moor to the west, is used for skiing and walking. **Gråkallen** (the old man) reaches to 520m (1,700ft) and there are the usual walking trails, alpine slopes, *skistua* (skiing lodges), and the Norwegian youngsters' favourite, ski-jumps. To the east, **Estenstadmarka** has similar open-air activities. Salmon fishing is excellent in Nidelva, and other rivers in the area such as the Gaula are equally good, while the fjord provides sea-fishing.

It is not difficult to get a guided tour around Trondheim and the area. There are city tours, boats along the harbour and out to Munkholmen island, coach tours, and day tours, sometimes by catamaran, out into the fjord, which may include fishing. There is a visit to the **Ski Museet** and summer skiing at the Ski Centre at **Granåsen** for those who like artificial ski slopes, or a hike into the Bymarka. Another tour starts with a catamaran sail along the fjord, then on to the 17th-century manor house, **Austråtborgen**, at Ørland. Close by is **Lundahaugen**, the site of a huge battery of heavy artillery, with a World War II cannon from the battleship *Gneissenau*. Many visitors also enjoy a short leg at sea on the coastal steamer, returning from the next port by train or coach.

Sør-Trøndelag

All Trøndelag has fine fishing, particularly for salmon, extending right into the city from boat or bank, in rivers, lakes and the sea. Two of the best rivers to be found in Norway are the **Gaula**, which rises in the Femundsmarka mountain area near the old mining town of Røros to the southeast, and the **Orkla** which flows into Orkdalsfjorden west of Trondheim. Fishing clubs will help with the fishing card and the small licence fee.

To the west, Sør-Trøndelag stretches through a jumble of small fjords with fishing and hunting, to the islands of **Hitra,** with **Dolmkirke** and **Frøya** and the fishing villages of Sula, Mausundvær and Frøøyene, the last with large seal breeding grounds, and also the windmill at Titan.

Heading south to Oppdal, it is a good idea to forsake the E6, and take road 65 through **Børsa** which has a 12th-century stone church, to the Meldal district. Here **Løkken Gruveland Mine** has a lift and guided tours to almost 1km (0.5 miles) underground. The **Mining Museum** shows old-time tools and methods of production. On Sundays, it is also possible to ride the **Thamshavnbanen** from Svorkmo, on a rare electric railway museum line.

All around Oppdal, the call of the mountains is strong and there are walking and climbing routes suitable for both newcomers and more experienced walkers. Between them, **Trollheimen** and **Dovrefjell** can offer most things that keep an outdoor person happy, peaks and plateaux, wonderful views that go on for ever, and great crags falling sheer to the valley below. Trondheim Tourist Association and others own overnight *hytter* along the way.

Since the 18th century, when Professor C.G. Oeder from Copenhagen University discovered the amazing flora of upper **Drivdalen**, botanists have been ranging over this mountain area and the species list is near synonymous with the entire flora of Scandinavia. Only a few species found in the far north are missing, while the valleys have revealed a few rarities, such as

Primula scandinavica, not seen outside Scandinavia, and a rare orchid, *Nigritella nigra*. Animals are just as plentiful, and there may be a chance to see the rare musk ox, perhaps on a weekend 'musk ox safari', led by experts, to watch them in their natural state.

Oppdal village has around half the population of the district's 6,000, and many more during the skiing season and at the height of summer. As a skiing centre, Oppdal has excellent hotels and shops. A modern gondola cable car takes skiers 1,125m (3,750ft) up Hovden above the village, also good for summer walkers.

Sør-Trondelag's bounty of rivers, lakes, fjords and the sea make fishing one of the most popular attractions. It also costs little for locals and visitors alike.

Not far from Oppdal, off road 16, a path leads to **Vang**, a small, green place with trees and grass mounds, which are Viking

graves. Vang was the centre of the community here until the railway arrived and Oppdal grew around the station. To the west, a track through **Gjevilvassdalen** to its lake runs through beautiful open land. Last century, Anders Rambech, a lawyer who was a negotiator of the 1814 Constitution at Eidsvoll, built **Tingstua** here. Now this wooden house, in its perfect setting, is a popular summer inn, and the base for many mountain expeditions. As Crown Princess, Queen Sonja, a skilled mountain walker, used it as a favourite base.

Røros

To the southeast of Trondheim is Røros, until 1972 the centre of this great copper mining area. At a bleak 600m (2,000ft), slag heaps, poor mining houses and a smelter did not exactly make this company town beautiful but the authenticity of the thousand-or-so preserved buildings has gained it a place on UNESCO's list of World Heritage Sites. **Røros Museum** in the smelting works shows mining, crushing ore and smelting copper, with exhibitions on the area's cultural and natural history.

A highlight is the stone church with its white steeple. At the height of the town's activities, Sunday worship included prayers for the company, and its importance also shows in church paintings, not just of clergymen but also of company officials. **Olavs Gruva** (Olav's Mine), some 12m (8 miles) east of the town is the only mine still open out of 40, and has guided tours through 500m (1,640ft) of galleries, 50m (160ft) below ground. With tools and machinery still in place, the mine looks as though it were waiting for the next shift. A **Mining Museum** stands by the pit entrance.

Another fascinating museum is the **Fjell-Ljom Newspaper Museum** with a preserved newspaper press where the writer Johan Falkenberget learned his trade. Falkenberget made this whole mining area famous. He grew up not far away from Røros and worked in the mine for 20 years. Like D.H. Lawrence, he took his characters from the lives of his own people and his novels tell of the struggles of the mining families just to make a living.

Returning to Trondheim, take the small unnumbered road east past **Aursundet** (lake), and the three smaller lakes, north to the Tyndal area, close to Nesjøen. The **Dyrhaug Ridesenter** is a good riding centre for short or longer excursions. There is

The old mining town of Røros was once the centre for copper mining in this area. Nowadays you can visit the Roros museum.

a 1696 church at **Eidet**, and at 90m (300ft), **Henfallet** is the region's highest waterfall. Nearer to Trondheim is a chance to see and buy first-class Norwegian craftwork at **Selbu Husflidsentral**, which specialises in typical Norwegian goods. Selbu, beside Selbufjord, also has an open-air museum, **Kalvaa Bygdetun**.

Nord-Trøndelag

Trondheim's airport, Værnes, to the north of the city lies in Stjørdal, which has always

been a four-way crossroads. Today, the E6 north meets the E75 here, the latter heading east along Stjørdalen and into Sweden. Nordlandsbanen (railway) also keeps company with the E6 and, just before it meets the E75, a branch line heads west to one of the best-known stations in Norway, Hell. Tickets are a collector's item.

Everywhere rock carvings indicate how long this area has been inhabited. At **Steinmohaugen** early inhabitants carved two big reindeer figures into the rock some 5,000 years ago. Further on, the **Leirfall** site is one of the biggest, showing more than 300 figures going about their daily lives when this valley must have been a social and cultural centre.

Not very far from the airport, in 1985, **Værneskirke** celebrated its 900th anniversary, a record few Norwegian churches can match. Building started in the reign of Olav Kyrre, only a few decades after St Olav's death at Stiklestad and before Nidaros Cathedral was built. It has beautiful white walls and a unique roof construction, a tribute to the 12th-century carpenters. Close to the church is **Stjørdal Museum**, with farmhouses, barns and Værnes old vicarage as its centrepiece. Beautifully restored inside, the garden has majestic trees and fine plants.

Just before Leirfall is **Hegra Fortress**, built in 1908, when the new state was feeling the need to protect itself, because this area had always been vulnerable to Swedish attack. In fact, it was not used until 1940 against a different enemy, when 250 Norwegian resistance fighters held out for a month against massive German attack. Today, the now peaceful fortress still contains the elderly guns that performed so well. In the centre of Hegra is **Vekvetloftet** where seven weavers work under the charge of designer Heidrun Kringen. She specialises in both traditional and contemporary designs, always inspired by the culture and nature around her. The workshop was once the old village schoolhouse, with one room retained as a classroom of 100 years ago.

Back on the E6 heading north, the road passes close to **Fættenfjorden** where the German warship *Tirpitz* sought shelter in World War II. The ship survived many air attacks and an attempt to use miniature submarines against her, brought in by the resistance hero, 'Shetlands' Larsen. Eventually she was sunk at Tromsø, further north, but at Fættenfjorden, it is still possible to see where she was moored.

At Verdalsøra, a side road to the east leads to Stiklestad, where King Olav Haraldson died in July 1030. **Stiklestadkirke** was built about a century later and every year, in and around Trondheim, St Olav's death is marked by special days known as *Oslok* days. On the anniversary of the battle, a huge cast of actors, singers, dancers and musicians recreate the events of that momentous day in Stiklestad's lovely open-air theatre.

Steinkjer, some 90km (55 miles) into the innermost end of Trondheimsfjorden, (now Beistadfjorden) has been a trading centre on the main south–north route for a thousand years and, judging by the many rock carvings in the area, was inhabited even further back. Nevertheless, Steinkjer bears little resemblance to its past because it was destroyed by German bombing in World War II, and almost everything is new.

Half way along the southeast side of the narrow waters of Snåsavatnet towards Snåsa is **Bølareinen**. Here is a magnificent reindeer carving 6,000 years old. **Snåsa** itself is a cultural centre for the South Sami (Lapps) with a school and museum. To the east, **Gressåmoen National Park** has dense Trondelag forest stretching towards Sweden, with peaks rising over 1,000m (3,300ft), and many lakes. Rejoining the E6 at Snåsa, the next stop, **Grong**, is an excellent wintersports centre, another crossroads town, and the meeting place for two excellent salmon rivers. The **Namsen** runs down west to Namsos, on the coast, and the **Sandøla** heads south to **Formofoss** (waterfall) not far below the town. Heading north up Namdalen, the Namsen's waterfall is the dramatic **Fiskumfoss**.

Through Namdalen, road and train keep each other company until Nørd-Trondelag slips into the next *fylke* of Nordland. **Børgefjell National Park** bestrides the boundary. Its tall mountains, streams and tree-lined lakes are a delight for walkers and climbers, who move backwards and forwards from central to northern Norway without ever noticing the difference.

Norway's Narrow Northern Neck

There are islands to the west, mountains and Sweden towards the east, much of the untouched land protected as national parks. In the past, when the easiest way to get around was by sea, this narrow coast had a bigger population than it has today, and traces of old communities lie on many islands. Now it is a place to linger, with no need to hurry, and endless diversions along fjordsides. There will be surprise finds too of small communities and big caves.

The first thing to remember is the sheer distances involved in this long narrow strip of Norway, leading to Nordkapp (North Cape) in the west, and Kirkenes on the Russian border. From Nordland's southern border, it is some 1,350km (around 860 miles) to Nordkapp and 1,630km (some 1,000 miles) to Kirkenes in Finnmark (see p.239). But the main roads make for easy driving, and a memorable journey through stunning scenery. There are many

Many of the lovely Lofoten towns, like Reine, an old fishing, shipping and trading centre, sit not on one but several small islands, linked by bridges.

contrasts, from the surprisingly gentle coast, warmed by the Gulf Stream, and the drama of the Lofoten and Vesterålen islands. East towards the border with Sweden are wide open spaces, highlands and mountain peaks. Here on this narrow neck of land Norway is sometimes no wider than a few kilometres between coast and Swedish border.

Apart from the faithful E6, heading north, there are few big roads, except for an occasional road crossing west to east. Out on the coast, the alternative route north as far as Bodø (road 17) clings close to the sea, with bridges and skerries between the dozens of islands. It is a beautiful way to wander rather than hurry.

NSB's Norlandsbanen also travels north to its terminus at Bodø, and trains are

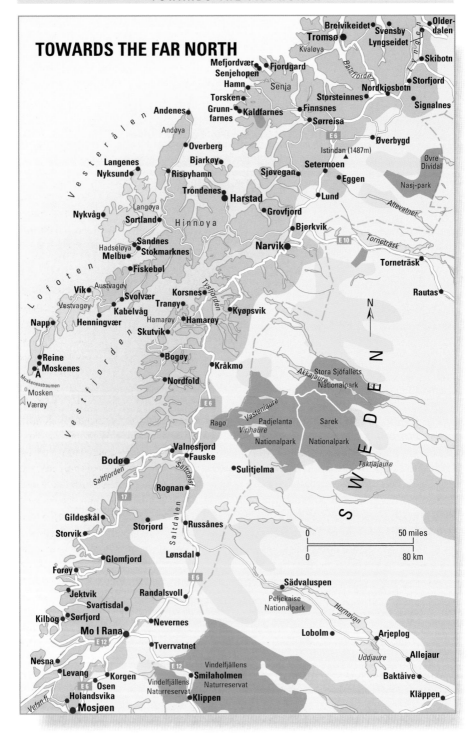

TOWARDS THE FAR NORTH

Brelvikeidet • Svensby • Olderdalen
Tromsø • Lyngseidet
Kvaløya
• Skibotn
Mefjordvær • Fjordgard
Senjehopen
Hamn • Senja • Storfjord
Torsken • Nordkjosbotn
Storsteinnes • Signalnes
Andenes • Grunn- Kaldfarnes • Finnsnes
farnes • Sørreisa
Andøya • Øverbygd
• Overberg
Istindan (1487m)
Langenes • Bjarkøy • Setermoen • Øvre Dividal
Nyksund • Risøyhamn • Sjøvegan • Eggen • Nasj-park
Tröndenes • Trøndenes Harstad • Lund
Nykvåg • Langøya • Grovfjord • Altevatnet
Sortland • Hinnoya
• Bjerkvik
Sandnes
Hadseløya • Stokmarknes • Narvik • Torneträsk
Melbu • E 10
• Fiskebøl • Torneträsk
Vík • Austvagøy • Rautas
Svolvær • Korsnes
Vestvagøy • Tranøy • Kyøpsvik
Kabelvåg • Hamarøy
Napp • Henningvær Hamarøy • Hamarøy
Skutvik
• Reine • Bogøy
• Moskenes • Kråkmo
Å • Stora Sjöfallets
Moskenesstraumen Akkajaure Nationalpark
• Mosken • Nordfold
Værøy
Vastenjaure
Rago • Padjelanta
Virihaure
• Nationalpark Nationalpark Sarek
Valnesfjord
• Fauske Taktjajaure
Bodø • Sulitjelma
Saltfjorden
Rognan
17
Gildeskål
Storvik • Storjord • Russånes
0 50 miles
Glomfjord • Lønsdal 0 80 km
Forøy •
• Jektvik Randalsvoll • Sädvaluspen
Svartisdal • Pelickaise
Kilbog • Sørfjord • Nationalpark
Mo I Rana • Nevernes • Lobolm • Arjeplog
E 12 • Tverrvatnet Uddjaure • Allejaur
Nesna • Vindelfjällens
• Levang • Korgen E 12 • Smilaholmen • Baktåive
E 6 Osen Vindelfjällens Naturreservat
Holandsvika Naturreservat • Klippen • Kläppen
• Mosjøen

SWEDEN

N

popular, full of climbers and backpackers who set off on foot along a fjord or up a mountain, or by Norway's comprehensive bus service to more remote areas. All along the road it is simple to find campsites and groups of *hytter*, which drivers and walkers use as bases to explore the area. There are many more on lakes, fjords and in the hills. The third way to reach Nordkapp is by Hurtigruten (the coastal route) which, when it started a century ago, was often the only winter way to travel.

Nordland

Mosjøen is largely industrial with a big aluminium works, but it is beautifully sited at the head of the sheltered waters of Vefnesfjorden. On the way north, just past Trofors, the road has already discovered Laksfoss (waterfall), a favourite place for salmon. From Mosjøen the road begins to climb into the mountains, and there is a fine *utsikten* (viewpoint) just past Osen, and many more along this fine road to Mo-i-Rana. Also an industrial town, it is wonderfully close to the dramatic **Svartisen** (glacier).

The summer way to the glacier is via Røssvoll, a 20-minute boat trip across Svartisvatnet, and a 3km (2-mile) path up Østerdalsisen. Boots are best and, in winter, Svartisen is for experts only. **Grønliggrotten** is a lit cave, with an exciting guided summer tour as lights bounce off the roof stalactites. The white marble **Sættergrotta** also has guided tours but is unlit and calls for some caving experience.

In **Mo-i-Rana** itself, **Rana Museum** leads to a good understanding of the many cultures that have lived in Nordland, and the **Nordland Museum of Natural History** gives an insight into the varied wildlife of

the area. Some 8km (5 miles) west along road 12 towards Nesna is **Stennesetby Museum**, with 18 buildings from 1700-1800, and **Nesna** itself has a village museum.

Now comes the exciting climb to the Arctic Circle – the Polar Circle to Norwegians – the invisible line that marks the passage from everyday life to the mysterious north. On a ship, there is inevitably a ceremony and few people cross the Circle anywhere without a sense of excitement. From Mo-i-Rana, road and rail climb slowly towards the heights of **Saltfjellet** as the high valley grows more wildly magnificent, and suddenly the **Arctic Circle** is there, lying at 650m (1,950ft). There are official markers and a remarkable number of rough cairns built by people who felt the need to mark the spot. More recent is the **Arctic Circle Centre**, a striking, mushroom-shaped building, etched against the bare landscape. It has exhibitions, a cinema, a souvenir shop with north Norwegian articles and a cafeteria. Just north of the Circle, the road reaches its highest point, 717m (2,340ft).

The way down runs through Saltdalen, with Saltdalselven (river) never far from road and rail, as trees and plants begin to reappear. Just before Storfjord, the road right (77) through Junkerdalen is the historic **Silver Road**, which carried silver mined in these hills through Sweden to Arjeplog and on to the Gulf of Bothnia at Piteå.

The road from Rognan to Fauske earned a more sinister name, the 'Blood Road', during World War II. Built with slave labour, more than 1,600 prisoners did not survive. Mostly Yugoslav and Russian, they are buried at Botn, just north of Rognan. Northern Norway has too many of these large graveyards where the fighting men of many nations lie, a hard reminder of how the people of this northern land suffered under occupation.

Fauske lies at the centre of a quarry area most famous for the rare and beautiful pink marble known as 'Norwegian Rose' and used for the United Nations building in New York. Here the road for Bodø turns off west. But first, an interesting detour runs east to **Sulitjelma**, which opens its copper mines to the public and has a **Mining Museum**. Part of the attraction of taking this mountain road, which replaced an earlier railway, is its wild beauty, with the **Sulitjelmabreen** (glacier). Nordland depends on hydro-electric power and has many power stations, some from the 1920s, which also offer tours.

Bodø, with a population of 37,000, is northern Norway's second largest town. It looks new – it was bombed almost flat during the dark spring of 1940. But Bodø has not looked back and is now Nordland's administrative, service and communications centre. It is an important Hurtigrute port, and the gateway to Lofoten, the famous fishing isles, their fortress peaks rising out of the sea to the west. From early June to around 10 July, Bodø is the first town north where the sun never sets, the glowing red ball resting just above the sea horizon at midnight. The place to watch this remarkable sight is from the heights of **Rønvikfjellet**, some 3km (2 miles) from the centre.

Bodø **Domkirke** (Cathedral) is a 1956 building, with an old-style detached bell tower. The ceiling stretches wide and has no pillars, and the 12m (40ft) stained glass window above the altar is eye-catching. In contrast, **Bodin Kirke**, some 3km (2 miles) east of Bodø escaped the bombing and dates back to the 13th century, the centre of a vast parish which then stretched between the Atlantic and the Swedish border. It is full of valuable pieces such as a Renaissance altar from 1650 and a baroque altarpiece. **St Eysteins Kirke**, close to the airport, built in 1981, is one Nordland's two Roman Catholic churches.

Nordlandsmuseet occupies one of Bodø's few older buildings, Prinsensgate 116, with exhibitions describing the old way of life of the fishermen and women, and the Sami, while **Bodøsjøen Friluftsmuseum**, the open-air section some 3km (2 miles) away on Saltenfjorden, has a big collection of distinctive Nordland boats.

Bodø is a good centre for expeditions: north to **Kjerringøy**, an old trading post as it was a 100 years ago, or south to **Saltstraumen**, a powerful maelstrom, caused by ferocious tides fighting to get through a narrow channel and creating great whirlpools. Full of fish, it is a favourite with both anglers and birds, and the birders who watch them. This south coast is mild enough to grow orchids at Inndyr.

From Fauske, the road north clings close to the fjord with tunnels reducing the twists and turns, and shortening distances. On the right, peaks with names such as **Lappfjellet** and **Siidasjiekna** indicate the two languages of the area. At more than 1,100m (3,700ft) they are part of **Rago National Park**.

Well known among the coastal islands is **Hamarøy**, the birthplace of the Norwegian Nobel Prizewinner for Literature, Knut Hamsun. Though he moved south, Hamsun wrote vividly of the hard life of his own people in books such as *Pan*, but he is best known for his novel *Hunger*. Hamsund, his childhood home, houses the **Hamsun Museum**, and **Tranøy** exhibits the illustrations of Hamsun's books by Karl Erik Harr. National interest in Hamsun has recently been rekindled, leading to the start of a **Hamsun Cultural Centre** at the home farm, Skogheim. Every second year, Hamsun Days celebrate the writer.

To the north of Hamarøy, the lighthouse **Tranøy Fyr** provides one of the finest views of this land and seascape. **Sagelv** has rock carvings of reindeer, some 7,000 years old and, not far north, **Korsnes** in Tysfjord is one the largest rock carving areas, with more than 40 different subjects. World-wide, good climbers know the strenuous 1,390m (4,600ft) of **Stetind** as 'The Anvil of the Gods'; it was first climbed in 1910. In his irritation at a failed 1880 attempt, William Slingsby described lovely Stetind as 'the ugliest mountain I ever saw'.

Narvik, at the innermost end of Ofot-fjorden, gained its *raison d'etre* from deep fjord water and iron ore carried over from

*A*bove the cluster of fjords leading to Narvik, great cliffs rise from the water, interspersed with rocky beaches. The scenery attracts many artists and sculptors; this sculpture is Heaven on Earth *at Strømstad, just south of Narvik.*

northern Sweden by rail. A century ago, this line made Narvik the first Nordland town with a railway, built by the Rallare, hard-living navvies. Each March, Narvik remembers their achievement in a special festival.

During World War II, Narvik suffered badly in the bombing and fighting, when the town changed hands twice, and in the great naval battle of Ofotfjorden. This dangerous time is commemorated in the **Nordland Red Cross War Memorial Museum**, and in the rows of graves in new Narvik cemetery. Older graveyards, such as Håvik, remember earlier conflicts on what has often been a troubled border.

Now Narvik has become active in win-tersports and the north's finest alpine cen-tre, with ski lifts and *løyper* (ski runs) high above the town. Narvik is only a 45-minute drive from the Swedish border and the best way to see the dramatic views of fjords and mountains is by cablecar, looking over to the peaks of Beisfjordtotta and many oth-ers rising over 1,500m (5,000ft). From the E6, Nordland ends at Bjervik, just north of the city but, to the west, is a world of is-lands, fjords and mountains still to explore.

Lofoten and Versterålen

In the south, Lofoten rises sheer from Vest-fjord in a solid wall of jagged mountains, visible along miles of the Nordland coast, which shelter both coastline and islands from the worst of the winter Atlantic. The sea has always spelled danger for the is-landers. In days gone by, many lost their lives at sea and some small communities have special days of remembrance. The survivors of foreign ships also left a legacy. In **Unstad**, the village has a hint of north German style, said to be the result of a Ger-man wreck. Turning potential danger to good use, these huge Vestfjord waves may make this the site of Norway's first com-mercial wave-power generating station.

In the 11th century, Lofoten's fishing waters already attracted fishermen. For hundreds of years they used handlines, *jukse-fiske*, in simple Nordland boats, catching cod from January to March. At its height, some 6,000 boats and 30,000 men arrived and, as long ago as 1908, Sørvågen Radio became the first com-mercial radio link, connecting islands to mainland. Fishermen crammed into the old wooden *rorbuer*, simple cabins by the waterside, which are now beautifully re-stored and make fine, rented houses for to-day's visitors. Fishing has now changed to an all-season fleet, with sturdy boats set-ting out in a cloud of seabirds. **Vesterålen** still has some 10 groups of *rorbuer* and *sjøhus* (harbour houses) to rent, and Lo-foten has at least four times as many.

All these islands have great seabird colonies, nowhere better than **Værøy** and **Røst** for cliffs laden with seabirds. Almost all birdlife is protected and nest sites are sacrosanct. But there are still hunting sea-sons for species such as cormorant, eider, kittiwake and ptarmigan, to provide rare delicacies for bold appetites.

Lofoten and Vesterålen have many car and passenger ferries, from Bodø, Narvik and Skutvik, and both are on the Hur-tigruten. Beyond **Moskensøy**'s southern tip is Moskenstraumen, the maelstrom mentioned by Jules Vernes, and once the terror of the fishermen in their delicate wooden boats.

From Moskenes, it is worth detouring south both to the maelstrom and to the town with the shortest name in Norway, Å (pronounced 'awe'). One of the few old fish-trading posts that has kept its original

style, Å gives an authentic feel of what Lofoten life must once have been like. **The Stockfish Museum**, demonstrates the process of stockfish production.

From Moskenes, the road north runs through the two island chains, via bridge, ferry and tunnel to the north end of Andøya in Vesterålen. It passes through every sort of magnificence, with great peaks growing out of the valley floor close to the water to protect the little towns and bays. Everywhere is sea. **Reine**, a trading centre since 1743 has a rare beauty with arching bridges touching down at smaller islands against a background of cone-shaped mountains. An underwater tunnel at Napp links Flakstadøya to Vestågøya. **Flakstadøya**'s long, sandy beaches are warm enough for paddling, and an 18th-century church has an unusual onion-shaped dome.

Along the Nordland coast one stunning view follows another in bewildering succession. The same is true for the island groups, Lofoten and Versterålen, but, even with all the competition, Utakliev on Lofoten is something special.

Many of these small communities offer something peculiarly their own: **Sakrisøy** has **Dagmar's Doll and Toy Museum**; **Sund** is well known for its artistic blacksmith who makes bird statues in metal, especially king cormorants, and has his own small museum of marine engines; at **Vikten** is Tangrand's glassblowing workshop; and **Vestågøy Museum** depicts the fishermen-farmers' lives.

Though Vesterålen is better known for artists and craftworkers, Lofoten is catching up, and on Austvågøy, the **Karl Erik Harr Galleri**, at Henninsgvær is the studio of the celebrated Nordland artist. Kabelvåg, further up the east coast has the **Espolin Johnson Galleri**, a collection of the works of Nordlander Kåre Espolin Johnson. **Lofoten Museet** is in an old manor house near the remains of the medieval town of Vagar, which is being excavated by a team from Tromsø Museum. Kabelvåg's most recent acquisition is the **Lofoten Aquarium**, a small fishing area with wharves, many fish, and a seal tank. Lofoten's capital, **Svolvær** has the **Nordland Centre of Art** on the islet of Svinøya and in the same building, **Studio Lofoten**.

From Fiskebol in the north of Lofoten, a ferry sails to Melbu on Hadseløy in Vesterålen, with the **Vesterålen Museum** housed in grand style in Rødgården, an old manor with 19th-century buildings and a park. It hosts cultural events. The **Norwegian Fishing Industry Museum**, also in Melbu, concentrates on herring oil and herring meal production in the old Neptun herring oil factory. Between Melbu and Stokmarknes further north, **Hadsel Kirke**, from 1824 with a fine wood interior, stands on what has been a church site since the Middle Ages.

Stokmarknes was an 18th-century trading post. Its great claim to fame is as the birthplace of the Hurtigruten, created by the Vesteraalen Steamship Company over 100 years ago. It now has a **Coastal Steamer Museum** with many mementoes of the past.

The elegant Hadsel Bridge carries the main road north to the next island of Langøya, rising to mountains on its western leg. On this west coast is **Nykåg**, a small, photogenic fishing hamlet with a large bird cliff, and to the northwest **Hovden** which cannot be bettered for viewing the midnight sun, except perhaps by **Langanes** at the north of Langøya, which also has a 16th-century church. The deserted fishing village of **Nyksund** with its unique architecture speaks poignantly of a time when these islands could keep and feed a much larger population.

Langøya's commercial centre is Sortland. Nearby Jennestad was a trading post in the 19th century and it still has an old shop with original stock. Knut Hamsun, who spent two years in Vesterålen as a teacher and country policeman, mentions Sidpollen, south of Sortland, in his writings. **Bø Village Museum** at Parkvoll Farm has records of his time here.

Sortland Bridge leads to **Hinnøya**, Vesterålen's biggest island, part of which lies in the next *fylke* (see p.231). The northernmost island is Andøya, with **Andøy Museum** at Risøyhamn, housed in a 250-year-old building and with *Fembøring*, a large turn-of-the-century Nordland fishing boat. As the road runs east of the island, it passes a distinctive octagonal church at **Dverberg**. At the northern tip, in addition to a whale safari, Andenes has a harbour **Whale Centre**, and a memorial stone to fishermen lost at sea. **The Arctic and Fisheries Museum**, has exhibits from expeditions to Svalbard (Spitzbergen) and the North and South poles.

Troms

Troms lies between Narvik and the small community of Alteidet, not far from Øksfjordjøkulen, the coastal glacier that marks the beginning of Finnmark. East of the road through Troms, mountain clusters stretch north from Øvre Dividal National Park, many looming to 1,500m (5,000ft). In the west, where the long coast curves gently east, much of Troms is of the sea rather than the land. The large islands of Senja, Kvaløya, Tromsøya – the last two hold northern Norway's biggest town, Tromsø – and Ringvassøya, shelter the coast's peninsulas and narrow necks of land.

Northwest of Narvik, the sea town of **Harstad** on the east of Hinnøya, has a fine harbour, fishing for coley and cod, and some light industry. It also has a large fleet of leisure craft, including the schooner *Anna Rogde*, launched in 1868 and owned by three generations of the Rogde family. She was the last Norwegian sailing ship to leave active duty and now carries visitors for voyages that vary from day trips to tours of Lofoten.

Harstad has developed around the sea and the 18th-century wharves at **Hemmestad** in Kvæfjord are now a museum to this way of life. In summer, the long gentle fjord slopes are sunlit for most of every 24 hours, and Kvæfjord produces wonderfully sweet strawberries. A reminder of a long and continuing religious tradition is **Trondenes Kirke**, built in 1250. Temporal pleasures have also long been important and the old restaurant, **Rokenes Gård**, was first granted an alcohol licence in 1776.

North of Harstad, the small island of **Bjarkøy**, linked by a bridge, was a Viking settlement with many Viking graves, and an old stone church from 1250. Bjarkøy also claims Tore Hund, who slew King Olav Haraldson at Stiklestad, and has decided to revive this Viking past. Every year since 1991, they have performed an open-air saga play about Tore Hund, timed around *Midsommar* (midsummer's day). There is also a private museum collection of more than a thousand species of stuffed birds and mammals. For those looking for the real thing, at Sundsvoll Sound, Bjarkøy has a large nesting colony of kittiwakes.

After the occupation in 1940, the Germans built a huge fortification at **Trondenes** to cover the shipping lanes into Narvik, with some of the biggest guns Krupps ever made. One remains, the so-called 'Adolf Gun', which fired shells weighing a ton each, and needed 68 men to fire a single shot. Building the fort cost the lives of some 800 Russian prisoners-of-war, commemorated in a monument in Harstad. It is possible to see this military monster but, as this is a military area, only with a guide.

Harstad's newest acquisition is **Kulturhuset** (Culture House) opened in 1992 as a long awaited venue for concerts and theatre performances, along with a hotel, all very important during the annual arts festival held at the end of June.

Climbing out of Nordland, the first place north of Narvik is the military town of Setermoen, with **Bardu Kirke**, a large octagonal church, built in 1829 by settlers from the south as an exact copy of Tynset Kirke, south of Trondheim. From the late 18th century, all this area was settled by farmers, many from Gudbrandsdalen, who brought their memories and customs with them. **Bardustua**, at Eggen Farm is a log cabin from 1791 with mementoes of the settlement days. The statue, *The Settler's Wife*, at Lapphaugen, dedicated by the late King Olav V, commemorates the bicentenary of the settlement of Målselvsdalen, a valley stretching towards the east.

Best reached via Elverum is **Malselvfossen** (waterfall), only 22m (73ft) high but a 600m (800yd) long thundering torrent of white water.

The mountain area of inner Troms is excellent for walking and climbing, river rafting, canoeing, caving, pony trekking, winter skiing and dog sledging. For the best view, make a bid for the summit of **Istindene**, at 1,490m (5,900ft), before Elverum. Fitness, but no climbing skills, are necessary. Much of the country is a military area and the **Forsvarsmuseum** (Military Museum) gives an excellent view of military history. There are many more monuments to war, such as the Fleischer Monument at Lapphaugen, where German troops suffered their first World War II defeat.

Norway's second largest island is **Senja**, reached via Sørreisa from Bardufoss and the bridge to Finnsnes. Islanders divide into those from Yttersida and those from Innersida, and are as different as chalk and cheese. **Innersida**, the sheltered side facing the mainland, is wide and well-cultivated, given over to agriculture, trade and small industry. **Yttersida** faces the ocean, the Arctic Ocean pounds the land, and earning a living means 24-hour-a-day fishing, with nets and lines, wet boots, and black coffee to keep out the winter gales. The rocky mountains rise in peaks and slope sheer from the sea. In the south, **Ånderdalen**, a national park, winds gently across south Senja, and some of the pines are so large that three people holding hands have a job to encircle them.

Finnsnes, a port of call on the southbound Hurtigruten makes an ideal base for touring. One astonishing drive is from Fjordgård, via Senjahopen to Mafjordvæar, which involves mountain tunnels and a famous panorama of the island's Nordlandet peaks. An alternative is to drive across

Svandalen, from Svanelvmoen to the wild west coast, and turn south (left) past the **Huldlerheimen Art Centre**, and an enormous troll, **Senjatrollet.** This children's delight is a troll-shaped building with an adventure playground in its stomach!

In contrast, **Hamn**, further south is a place of ocean beauty, where the historic buildings of the fishing station have been restored, with places to stay and a visitors' marina. Here too are the remains of a nickel foundry started by an English company in 1872, and a hydro-electric power station. At **Torsken**, the church dates back to 1784 but has many earlier contents, and there are *rorbuer* to rent.

On the southwest point of this peninsula, reached via the southern route from Svanelvmoen, is **Grunnfarnes**, and **Flagstadvåg**, one of the smallest villages, well known because of the 17.5m (57ft) yacht *Angelica*. Built in north Norway nearly a century ago, she is the ideal craft for adventure cruises off the Senja coasts, when no excitement can quite match the surge of wind in her 163 sq m (1755 sq ft) of sail.

Back on the mainland, the E6 now bypasses Storsteinnes, in Balsfjord, famous for its goat cheese and fertile farm land. At Nordkjøsbotn, the east–west E78 between Tromsø and Finland crosses the E6.

Tromsø

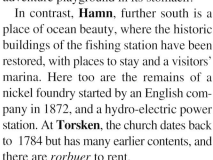

Tromsø celebrated its bi-centenary in June 1994, the anniversary of the granting of city status when the inhabitants were offered a number of privileges, such as tax exemption for the first 20 years of their living in the city. This brought new inhabitants, not just from Norway but from many parts of Europe. Some newcomers sent their children back to be educated in their home country and, even today, Tromsø has unusual family names, and the local tongue uses words of foreign origin.

It also has the world's northernmost university, founded in 1972, both to enable young Nordlanders to study in their own area and to expand the study of polar conditions and the northern environment. This carries on a long tradition that began when Tromsø boats sailed north each year for hunting, sealing, whaling and trapping in the far north, leading to a strong local scientific interest in the Arctic.

Today, Tromsø has a curiously cosmopolitan outlook that shows in many ways: in the varied nationalities of its origins and now its student population; in 16 fine restaurants, several members of the *Chaines des Rotisseurs*; some 79 licensed premises and 16 nightclubs. This may explain why summer Tromsø never seems to go to bed. Though the 24-hour light is a constant presence everywhere in the north, it is somehow easier in Tromsø to find

yourself turning night into day. Expeditions often begin and end in what is technically the middle of the night and that does not seem strange. Be it 2am or 4am, Tromsø is full of people strolling about as though it were daytime.

A cable car rises 420m (1,400ft) to **Storsteinen**, a main outlook point, to reveal that Tromsø spreads over two islands and across another arching bridge to the mainland, and the great white, shiny triangle of the **Ishavskatedral** (Arctic Cathedral). The Cathedral has a huge stained glass window,

*T*romsø sits on an island and spreads on to two more, with one bridge leading to the remarkable Ishavskatedral (Arctic Cathedral), built in glass to reflect nature both literally and metaphorically. It also has Europe's largest stained-glass window.

which glows brightly when there is daylight behind. Looking further afield, deep fjords push their fingers between the mountains, still tipped with snow even in summer, and islands in their hundreds stretch away in a protective ring around the city. The *fylke* of Troms has some of the best fishing on a coast long famed for fish, and Tromsø itself has four fish-processing plants, and the famed Mack brewery, maker of Arctic Ale.

It is a pleasure to walk around this well laid-out city, or to sit outside one of the harbour-side restaurants and inns, watching the daily arrival of the Hurtigruten ship, with passengers pouring off for a tour of the town. Tromsø's **Domkirken** (cathedral) is one of Norway's biggest wooden churches, close to the central Town Square, which sometimes sprouts a few market stalls. A sign of the times is that several of them are now Russian. There are also good museums including **Bymuseum** (City Museum) at Skansen, with historic displays shown in the old customs house, on a site which had been a fortress since 1250. Also good value is **Polarmuseet** which celebrates the Arctic, and explorers such as that most single-minded man, Roald Amundsen, who beat Scott to the South Pole, and died seeking his fellow explorer Nobile over the North Pole. The museum shows many aspects of the north, including a big section on the ancient Sami inhabitants.

Not far from the Arctic Cathedral, a recent **Defence Museum** is gathering artefacts from World War II, when Tromsø saw the German battleship *Tirpitz* sunk some 16km (12 miles) from the town centre. There is also Tirpitz Minnesmerke (memorial) on the nearby island of Håkøya. **Nordlysplanetariet** (Northern Lights Planetarium) means you can see the Northern Lights whatever the time of year: you lie back in reclining seats as they streak across the domed roof. In winter the real thing zigzags mysteriously through the long nights.

Excursions from Tromsø

Tromsø is the starting point for many expeditions: to the islands at each end of the fjord that screens the city; to other small islands such as Sommerøy; or across to the mainland to lunch in a Sami *lavvu* (tent). Many Sami bring their herds south from Finnmark for summer grazing. A few settled families live locally all year round, and the *lavvu* is used only on the autumn journey north, which can last two months.

Inland from Tromsø, on the long peninsula that separates Ullsfjorden and Lyngenfjorden, are the nearest mountains Norway has to a row of Alpine peaks. They are known as the **Lyngen Alps**. These sharp peaks, always scattered with snow, rise to over 1,500m (5,000ft) and **Jiekevarri** is 1,822m (6,000ft), a largely undiscovered paradise for glacier-trekking, mountaineering and similar pursuits. A good starting point is **Jæger-vatnet** (lake) for one of the widest alpine views, surrounded by jagged tops and small glaciers. The view from a plane coming into Tromsø is glorious.

A spectacular way back to the E6 is to head north on road 91 for Bredvikeidet, crossing by ferry to Svensby on the main Lyngen peninsula, then on below the mountains to Lyngseidet, and over Lyngenfjorden itself to rejoin the E6 at Olderdalen. On the ferries look out for *seivøa*, a school of coalfish, the Troms fjords are full of them, or take part in a fishing expedition. As always in Norway, this is fine country for wild berries, of unusual varieties as well as old favourites, and north Norwegians go berry-picking at any time in the endless daylight.

SVALBARD – NORWAY'S POLAR ISLANDS

The Dutch explorer, Willem Barents, looking hard for a way north of Russia to China and the east, landed on Svalbard in 1596. He named it Spitsbergen because of the spiked mountains. But Svalbard (the name of the whole archipelago) may well have been visited by Vikings as early as 1194 and many nations have since hunted here for bear, whale and seal.

Since 1920, Norwegian law has ruled Svalbard (which lies only 1000km/600 miles from the North Pole), from its main community, Longyearbyen, with 1,100 inhabitants largely employed in mining. There is a small former-Soviet community at Barentsburg. Mostly Ukrainian and also miners, they eke out a frugal life, almost out of touch with their changed native land.

Svalbard is now a mecca for cruise ships which circle the islands, and there is a daily flight from Tromsø. Nearer-to-nature visitors tour on smaller working boats, to visit the cliffs, crammed with breeding birds. There are also the remarkable remains of earlier explorers, Nobile, Amundsen and the Swede, Andrée, and the old hunters' huts, well preserved by the cold.

Most of all, people come to Svalbard for the wildlife and nobody settles until the first polar bear lumbers into sight looking creamy-yellow against the ice. Binoculars are always at the ready for the tough little Svalbard reindeer, not much bigger than a large dog, white arctic foxes, the great curved back of the walruses, and over 150 bird species that have been seen here. Under its brief summer covering of small arctic plants, Svalbard is a natural laboratory, and all over the remote islands, parties of scientists study everything from the nymphs of some exotic fly to the effects of global warming. Svalbard is unique.

North from Nordkjøsbotn

The main E6 north from Nørdkjosbotn, where the road to Tromsø branches off, also has places to visit. In Signaldalen, off Storfjord, is an early settlers' wooden house, at the foot of the peak of Ottertind. Here the land on both sides of the fjord rises high, and people from far and wide used to gather at **Skibotn**, on the edge of Storfjord, for the oldest market in Nord-Troms, still a market today. It is also exciting to walk in country such as the high plateau above **Kåfjorddalen**, a mixture of old mining roads, great rock clefts and the river banks of Ørndalen.

Sami people have lived in northern Troms for hundreds of years and various sites are part of the ecological museum. **Nord-Troms Sjøsamiske Museum**, which shows the life of the early Sea Samis. Holmenes, inland from Birtavarre,

has a farmhouse, a woodshed, a stable, a well, a barn and a cowshed, surrounded by a long summer meadow. There are also implements and tools used for skills such as the weaving of *grene*, a multi-purpose covering which came from Asia Minor.

Birtavarre itself has the Sea Sami boatsheds where voyages began, and the outbarns in Kåfjorddalen. Eastwards is **Reisadalen National Park** with huge pine forests and remarkably rich vegetation for so far north. Here too is **Mollisfossen**, where water gushes over a 269m (900ft) drop, close to the smaller **Imofossen**, and traces of the many Finnish settlers who headed west for a new life in Norway.

To the west of the road is a vista of mountain tops, fjords and islands. After Alteidet, just before Troms ends, a small road heads west for the **Oksfjordjokullen** (glacier). It carves down into the sea below, and has the boundary with Finnmark running at its foot.

Sagavegen

From Norway, this long route runs from northwest to southeast, crossing the Swedish border at Skalmodalen, and continuing over Sweden to Örnsköldsvik on the Gulf of Bothnia, a favourite destination for Norwegians. The Saga Way is named for a rich crop of legends which emanate from this ancient part of Norway, known as Helgeland, where people have lived for thousands of years.

The road starts at Brønnøysund on the Nordland coast, and at first follows road 17, which makes use of many bridges and ferries to cross the sea along this marvellous northern stretch of coast and islands with the mountains behind. From Sweden, the official Saga road terminus is Dønnefjellet on the island of Dønna, but by starting at Brønnøysund, the route includes much more of this lovely and ancient coast. The Norwegian part of the route, which is described here, is around 250km (150 miles).

On the way to Brønnøysund from the E6, (road 76 which has a 6km (4-mile) tunnel) the energetic might like to arrange a tour of Tosenfjell's famous caves, particularly Vattenhullet which has one of northern Europe's longest subterranean lakes (guided tours only). Also near this road, the 1674 Nestvik Kyrke is northern Norway's oldest wooden church.

Brønnøysund is a lively small port, surrounded on three sides by sea and islands, with a population of 4,000. It is perfect for sailing and fishing, with the unmistakable tall peaks of the Seven Sisters (De Syv Søstre) visible from almost everywhere. As a point of call on the Hurtigruten it has a busy harbour, a good place for a leisurely outdoor meal, on a coast with a mild climate and fertile land.

To the south, Torghatten is an island mountain with a huge hole right through it, 35m (115ft) high and carved out by an ancient sea. Torghatten takes some 20 minutes to climb on a steepish path, well-worn because thousands make the 160m (520ft) climb each year. At Tilrem, north of Brønnøysund, Hildur's Urteranium (herb nursery) has 100 different old roses, against a background fragrance of some 200 herbs and spices.

The same distance to the northeast, off road 17, Skaren Monsenhulen (cave) has 4-5,000-year old wall paintings. The steep walk up takes a half-hour. Avoid spring-time when the thaw can cause landslides.

Holandsosen and Kjellerhaugvatnet on the island of Vega are two fine marshes for birds in an area famed for its puffins and white-tailed eagles. There is also a varied flora and fauna. In the past, most islands had busy trading posts and fishing villages. Many, such as the fishing hamlets of Skævær and Bremstein, seen on a Vega skerries cruise, are now abandoned. Rørøy trading post has a lively market and Vegstein is well preserved but closed. Gladstad's wooden church dates from 1864 and Vega Museum of Local History is housed in what was the old parsonage. On Yylvingen, just off the coast, bunkers and cannon bases are reminders of World War II.

Forvik has a busy market at the ferry landing on Velvestad, and its buildings date from 1792. The 1796 wooden church has reredos painted by the Italian artist Piascani. A museum includes farms and farm buildings.

Reached by ferry from Forvik, the whole Tjotta area has many graves and burial mounds. It is said to be the home of Hårek, yet another chief who, reputedly, helped in the killing of King Olav at Stiklestad. Two more recent graveyards are the Russian Cemetery where some 7,500 who died as prisoners-of-war to the Germans are buried, and Riegel Cemetery which holds Russians, Czechs, Poles, Germans and Norwegians who drowned when the prison ship Riegel was sunk by Allied aircraft, unaware that they were on board.

At the south of the island of Alsten, 12th-century Alstahaug Kyrke became famous because of Norway's poet-priest Peter Dass, who lived there from 1689 until his death in 1707. The vicarage has several exhibits connected with the poet, such as artist Karl Eris Harr's illustrations of his prose. Sandnessjøen has been a trading post for some 300 years, and today it is good for fishing, sailing and boat tours out to sea.

The island of Donna has its own Nord Kapp (North Cape) where the road ends at the Dønnesfjell (mountains) in the northwest, with one of the best views of the Seven Sisters, and a café on top. Dønna was once a prosperous manor and the 13th-century Dønnes Kyrke holds the family mausoleum. The island also has a cultural trail through a large burial ground, with an unexpected marble phallus from 4-500AD.

The many relics show that, when the best way to travel was by sea, these now empty islands were once vigorous centres of population. South of Dønna

and linked by bridges, Herøy is a former Viking settlement with a 12th-century church, Helgelander Cathedral. Herøy also has the house where Peter Dass was born in 1647, and a museum with some 3,000 exhibits.

Over the ferry from Sandnessjøen to Leindesodden, road 810 leads to Mosjøen on the main E6. Whole areas here were destroyed by an avalanche in 1890 and it is now largely an industrial town in beautiful surroundings. But not all was lost. Some 19th-century farmyards remain, now home to the Museum of Local History. Sjøgata's 18th- and 19th-century buildings are also well preserved, and Dolstad cruciform church dates from 1735.

Inland Helgeland has wonderful salmon rivers, mountains for the energetic, and many possibilities for the popular pastime of berry- and mushroom- picking. On the way south to Trofors, the raging rapids of Laksfors (literally 'salmon waterfalls') have a 16m (43ft) salmon ladder and lie on Norway's largest salmon river, the Vefsna.

After Trofors, the road left continues to follow the river to Hattfjelldal, where in good weather you can book a sight-seeing flight by small aeroplane. Hattfjelldal is a centre of Sami culture. The Sitji Jarnge Sami Centre has a library and exhibits of the Lule and Southern Sami, and is a good place to buy Sami handcrafts. From here, there are three choices: southeast for the border at Skalmodalen and the long run through Sweden to Örnsköldsvik on the Gulf of Bothnia; south into Borgefjell National Park, and a visit to Svenskoll Gård Farm (village museum) at Susendal; or return to Trofors and the E6 north or south.

Ancient Land of Endless Summer Daylight

This large empty province holds Europe's northernmost point at Nord-kapp (71°10'21"N), the country's most easterly boundary with Russia, and Vardø, Norway's only community set in the Arctic climate zone. Finnmark is Norway's largest *fylke*, all 48,000 sq km (18,500 sq miles) of it, with only 75,000 people to occupy that great space. Thanks to the Gulf Stream, the ports at Hammerfest, Alta, Vardø, Vadsø and Kirkenes, and the smaller harbours on the northern coronet-shaped coast, can wel-come Hurtigruten ships at any time of the year.

Four cultures meet in Finnmark – Sami, Norwegian, Finnish and Russian – and some of the earliest remains have been found here, from as far back as 8,000BC when the Komsa people are believed to have arrived. There are also rock carvings thought to be between 2,000 and 6,000 years old. Samis came some 2,000 years ago and five Finnmark districts have both Norwegian and Sami as official languages. Norwegians moved in from the 13th century, and in the 18th and 19th century, many Kvens – from northern Finland and Sweden – moved west. Towards the end of the 19th century, more than a quarter of Finnmark's population was of Finnish descent, and Vadsø earned the name of 'the Kven capital'. Today, there are many Finnish family names in eastern Finn-mark and a strong Finnish culture shows in language and architecture.

At the end of World War II, in their re-treat from the liberating Soviet army, the Germans applied a 'scorched earth' policy to Finnmark. They burnt more than 10,000 buildings, from homes and schools to churches and hospitals, and sank much of the fishing fleet. The urgent need to rebuild fast has, even today, left some of these northern communities with a curiously un-finished appearance. Vadsø, Finnmark's administrative capital has the *Rebuilding*

Some 3,000 reindeer, owned and herded by Sami people from Karasjok, roam Magerøya (close to Nordkapp) each summer. To reach the grazing grounds, most adults swim the Magerøy Sound.

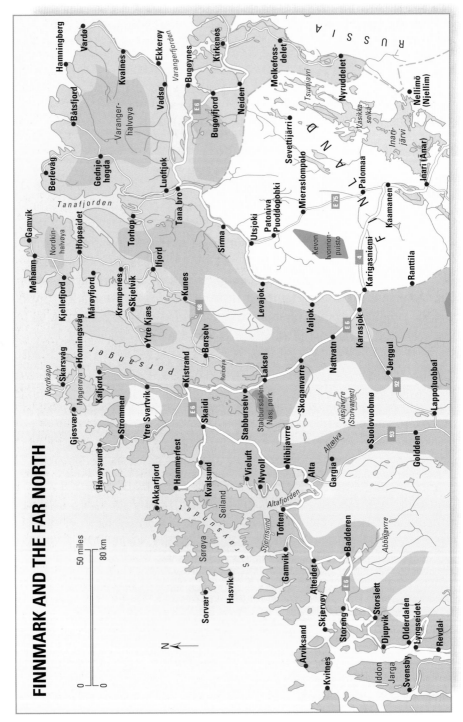

FINNMARK AND THE FAR NORTH

R U S S I A

Hamningberg
Vardø
Kvalnes
Ekkerøy
Kirkenes
Melkefoss-delet
Nyruddelet
Nellimö (Njellim)
Bugøynes
Varangerfjorden
Vadsø
Bugøyfjord
Neiden
Tsurajarvi
Vasikkä selkä
Inari-järvi
Inari (Änar)
Båtsfjord
Varanger-halvøya
E6
Sevettijärri
F I N L A N D
Berlevåg
Gednje hogda
Luoftjok
Mieraslompolo
Palomaa
Kaamanen
Hopseidet
Tana bro
Torhop
Sima
Utsjoki
Patoniva
Puoddopohki
Kevon Ivonnon-puisto
Karigasniemi
Ranttila
Tanafjorden
Nordkin-halvøya
Gamvik
Mehamn
Kjøllefjord
Ifjord
Kunes
E75
Mårøyfjord
Krampenes
Skjelvik
Ytre Kjæs
Levajok
Valjok
Karasjok
Jerggul
Nordkapp
Skarsvåg
Honningsvåg
Kafjord
Giesvær
Strømmen
Ytre Svartvik
Kistrand
Børselv
Reinoya
Laksel
Skoganvarre
Nattvatn
Jiesjavrre (Storvattnet)
E6
Lappoluobbal
92
Magerøya
Porsanger
98
Stabburdalen Nasj. park
Skaidi
E6
Havøysund
Akkarfjord
Hammerfest
Kvalsund
Vieluft
Nyvoll
Nibijavrre
Gargia
Alta
Suolovuobma
93
Goldden
Sørvær
Hasvik
Soroya
Seiland
Altafjorden
Stjernsund
Toften
Gamvik
Lapunsbojes
Abbojavrre
Badderen
Arviksand
Skjervøy
Storeng
Djupvik
Storslett
Olderdalen
Lyngseidet
Revdal
Kvitnes
Alteidet
E6
Iddon
Jarga
Svensby
Soravik

50 miles
80 km
0

N

Monument by Thor Sandber, to commemorate this desperate time in Finnmark's demanding history. Another legacy is that, before the Cold War ended, Finnmark retained a more cordial attitude to the Soviet Union than was usual in the West.

But none of this destroyed the wonderful flora of low-growing shrubs, berry-rich bushes and brilliant small flowers that greet the short summer on the mountain *vidda* (plateau) and deep valleys. There are summer birds galore, and hunting for ptarmigan, hare and elk. Fishing is good, with the Tana and Alta among the world's best salmon rivers. In winter, the temperature can go down to –50°C (–70°F) but in summer it can easily touch over 30°C (around 80°F) and from early May to the end of July the sun never sets.

In winter, skiing is paramount, with thousands of miles of marked trails, many lit and best in the spring-winter (March to May) one of the eight Sami seasons. Ice-fishing, dog sledges and snow scooters are also popular and people who arrange tours normally supply the special thermal clothing necessary for spells out of doors.

Alta

Immediately past the southern border, the ground starts to lose height in a wide, empty landscape, though to the west, mountains and islands continue to rise. The first town from the south, and Finnmark's biggest, is the port of **Alta** on Altafjorden with 16,000 inhabitants and a superb setting between Finnmarksvidda and the fjord.

Alta makes a good base, summer and winter, but its most renowned feature is prehistoric **Helleristningene** (rock carvings) at Hjemmeluft. Discovered as late as 1973, they are Scandinavia's only prehistoric monuments on the UNESCO World Heritage List. The four main sites lie close to the fjord in a park with the **Alta Museet**. The carvings eloquently show Stone Age life – hunting, fishing, men, women and children, in procession and dancing, with musicians and symbols, and many skin boats, large and small. Sometimes the panels tell stories, almost like cartoons.

Wooden paths lead the way from the museum building, cleverly divided into different routes – from a quick 30 minutes for those in a hurry to a whole day for addicts. There are also guided tours. But the museum ranges wider than the carvings themselves and has five exhibitions on the Alta area, past and present. It is easy to linger. The main museum, not far from the E6 just before the town centre, has several offshoots such as the first **Northern Lights Observatory** built in 1899 on the summit of **Haldde** (Holy Mountain) at 1,000m (3,300ft) above Kåfjord. This was another World War II casualty but two buildings have now been restored and make an excellent target for a four-hour hill-walk for the reasonably fit.

Alta is also the jumping off point for tours on **Finnmarksvidda**, from summer walking and horseriding to winter dog-sledging and skiing, sometimes to the central lake, **Jiesjavrre**. The name indicates that this is Sami country, with the the main centres at **Karasjok**, east of the *vidda*, and **Kautokeino**, close to the Finnish border. Alta also has a tremendous canyon at **Sautso** on the Alta river, reached by boat, or in an energetic four hours, by car and on foot, via Gargia.

North of Alta, the lonely E6 runs through some 90km (60 miles) to Skaidi. Almost the only human mark on this immense landscape is **Samikapellet** (Sami Chapel). Elsewhere, the land is given over to great reindeer herds. Another Sami legacy is **Stalloen**, a big stone close to the road, which was a place of early Sami sacrifice. In Sami, *skaidi* means 'where the rivers meet'; **Skaidi** itself is a good base for summer and winter outdoor activities, and is the junction with road 94, for Hammerfest.

port. But Hammerfest has not escaped destruction. In 1890, the wooden town was nearly burnt out by fire, and it was a mere shell at the end of the German occupation of World War II, when the only building to survive was the cemetery's burial chapel.

In 1891 the town was the first European town with electric street lighting. From 1816 to 1852, the best astronomers in Russia,

Hammerfest

Far out into the northern sea, **Hammerfest** is the world's northernmost town, where 7,000-or-so inhabitants traditionally made their living from fishing and polar hunting. Its sheltered waters and the Gulf Stream have long made it the north's best ice-free

On the sea side of the island of Kvaløya (island), linked to the mainland, Hammerfest is so far north-west it is almost in the Norwegian Sea. It is either reached by a very beautiful scenic road, Hurtigruten, or by air.

Norway and Sweden pooled their efforts, personally encouraged by their monarchs, to determine the exact size and shape of the earth and the **Meridian Monument** recalls this survey. **Ishavsportalen**, on the town's sheltering escarpment, is known as the midday pole because at noon its shadow falls directly on the Meridian Monument. Ishavsportalen is topped by a cannonball left over from the time when British warships attacked and plundered Hammerfest during the Napoleonic wars. Hastily, the military built **Skansen** in 1810, but this was something of a case of shutting the stable door after the horse had bolted, for the fortress guns have never fired a shot in anger.

It was renewed for the 1989 bicentennial celebrations, which also gave the town some new places of interest, such as the **Music Pavilion**, its shapes and colours representing the best of old Hammerfest architecture, and **Ishavesskute i Skru-Is** (Polar Vessel in Pack-Ice) an acknowledgement of the origins of the town – polar hunting and fisheries.

Hammerfest Kirke, built in 1961 and designed by Oslo architect Hans Magnus, has something of the feel of Tromsø's Ice Cathedral, with a tall narrow turret, like an inverted triangle, echoed in the main building. The beautiful stained glass triangular window is by Jardar Lunde, who was responsible for all the church's new decorations, though an altarpiece and one or two other items go back to Hammerfest's first church, built in 1623. The town also has a Catholic Church.

But the main target for visitors, whether they arrive by road or pour off Hurtigruten which calls every day, is **The Royal and Ancient Polar Bear Society** in Hammerfest **Rådhus** (Town Hall). They visit, of course, for the interesting museum with exhibitions of Arctic hunt-

ing but value even more membership of the Society and the certificate that verifies it, and graces many a wall around the world. It can only be gained by going to Hammerfest to collect it in person.

Nordkapp (*North Cape*)

For many, the need to get to the northernmost, southernmost, highest or lowest is always a target and Nordkapp is an *idée fixe* for many visitors. Back on the E6, the road runs for a few miles north, then the E69 takes a left turn along the west side of Porsangen. It is by far the largest of the fjords separating the coronet of peninsulas that form the top of Norway, some 118km (70 miles) from Lakselv in the south to Honningsvåg on Magerøya, and Nordkapp. The road stops at Kåfjord and in summer it can be a longish wait for the ferry to **Honningsvåg**. From there, Nordkapp is a further 35 km (21 miles) of stark, treeless scenery.

In 1523, this ancient landmark was given its name by the English explorer, James Chancellor, Captain of the *Edward Bonaventure*, seeking a new route to China. He did not achieve that aim but his name will always be connected with North Cape. Visitors today have an easier road than the first passengers from the *Prinz Gustav*, who rowed ashore in 1845 to tackle a 300m (1,000ft) cliff. The intrepid King Oskar II faced the cliff in 1873, and it was not until 1880 that a path from Horn Bay below, with a fragile handrail, helped visitors to the top.

Nordkapphuset in Honningsvåg was opened in 1956, at the same time as the road from that small community to Nordkapp. It is usually open from 1 May to mid-October. There is a fee for each

visitor to the Nordkapp seaward plateau, which can seem a little overcrowded. A hall, **Nordkapphallen**, is open from 9am to 2am during the season. Cut into the rock, right inside the mountain, the cave-like amphitheatre has a panoramic window to the Arctic Ocean, a wrap-around video-graph, North Chapel, and ancient grottoes. Above are such modern amenities as a souvenir shop, post office, restaurant, cafeteria and information office.

Outside, with the cliff falling 307m (1,000ft) into the sea, the great Arctic Ocean is the most striking natural monument, but a significant human one is presented by the **Children of the Earth**, seven large disks set on their sides, designed and made by

*N*ordkapp is everyone's goal, Europe's most northerly cape on Magerøya. The many modern amenities here sit rather strangely with the grandeur of the cliffs and the magnificence of the natural world all around.

*T*here are a lot of 'northernmosts' in Finnmark, and Porsanger is the world's northernmost archipelago, a wild mixture of sea and island, with a unique flora and an exciting birdlife (right).

seven children from seven different lands, who lived together for seven days on Nordkapp in 1988. They symbolise Hope, Joy, Concord and Friendship.

Once on Magerøya, few can resist a first rush to Nordkapp but the island also has some 5,000 deer on summer pastures, and a wonderful island nature reserve, **Gjesværstappen**, off Gjesvær. This lies on the western side, reached by the island's second road, and boat. The birdrock is especially famous for sea eagles and a huge puffin colony. On the other side of the island, a marked path from the small fishing community of Skarsvåg takes some 15 minutes to reach **Kirkeporten**, a strange rock formation which gives a fine view of Nordkapphorn. **Honningsvåg** has long been a fishing village and an important pilot station and several other

communities still fish, but many now provide boat and fishing tours, and one or two have interesting workshops.

Porsangen and the Sami Towns

There are so many 'northernmosts' in Finnmark that it is no surprise to find that **Porsangen** is the world's northernmost archipelago with thousands of islands and skerries, where the endless flow of water comes into the fjord from mountain streams and waterfalls, and also from the abundant sea tides. There are several fine natural areas and nature reserves: the wetland, **Reinøya**, near Borselv, with unique flora and fauna; **Trollholmsund**, on the opposite bank, with columns of stone close to the

THE SAMI

The Sami people have wandered through the north of Sweden and Norway – and into Finland and Russia too – for hundreds of years. These nomadic people still follow their reindeer herds on the endless quest for pasture in summer, coming back to stay in one place when winter closes in.

It is a life of eight seasons, closely linked to the life patterns of the reindeer. Only about a quarter of the Sami population still follows this way of life and those that do now use modern equipment such as snowmobiles, radios, and motorcycles and dogs for the great reindeer round-up. The Sami skill with a lasso among the careering reindeer is marvellous to see, as they divide the herds and mark the calves during a busy three weeks in summer.

There are also Sea and Forest Sami and though the Sami culture has been neglected (if not suppressed) for a long time, there has been a recent revival with the advent of Sami schools, and the *joik*, a strange mixture of story-telling and singing, once more looked on as an artform. Many still live in Sami towns, a grouping of settlements with common interests, but the old Sami *kätor* (tents) are only used when moving the herds. Sweden's great Sami area is Jokkmokk with a famous market each February (see p.323), and Arvidsjaur with Lappstaden. In Norway, Karasjok has the Sami Parliament and a joyful Easter Festival. Kautokeino is the centre of Sami culture .

water, said to be night-time trolls, surprised by the sun and turned to stone; and, on the west (E6) side, **Stabbursnes Nature Reserve**, part of Stabbursdalen National Park, is largely marshland with wonderful birdlife, as well as many interesting plants.

Stabbursnes Naturhus og Museum in the shape of a Sami *lavvu*, is an information centre for Finnmark's nature and culture, with excellent exhibitions, guided walks and marked footpaths.

South of Lakselv at the inner end of Porsangen, the E6 heads for **Karasjok**, one of the two main Sami towns, on the eastern side of Finnmarksvidda, and a junction for routes east, west, north and south. Here is **Samelandsenteret** (Samiland Centre), a modern wooden building with everything Sami, including tourist information and handcrafts. Outside is a Sami camp with reindeer and gold panning.

Sametinget is the Sami Parliament, which has 39 members and meets four times a year. At this stage, its role is advisory only but it is a symbol of the new recognition given to Sami people and culture. Inside, are tall wooden *lavvu*-shaped walls and red, blue and yellow Sami colours. The **Sami Museum** has exhibitions of many sorts, there is a **Sami Library** with a unique Sami collection in several languages, and the **Art Centre** has a workshop and shows the work of Sami artists in changing exhibitions. Not far from the town centre, it is possible to visit a *lavvu*, surrounded by reindeer, and to eat lunch there with the owner, herdswoman Kerstin Berit Gaup, who is also an expert at *joiking*, something between singing and telling a tale.

Karasjok also has Finnmark's oldest church, built in 1807, and the only town building to escape the 'scorched earth' fires. The greatest time to visit this Sami town is for the Easter Festival, with reindeer racing, a market, concerts, exhibitions, religious services, sports and everything else that sums up Sami life, including weddings and confirmations.

Karasjok is a good place to learn about Sami culture but so too is **Kautokeino** to the southeast, almost on the Finnish border, also reached direct from Alta on road 93.

Kautokeino is the largest *kommune* (municipality) in Finnmark but the whole area has only 3,000 inhabitants. It is best during winter when the nomadic, reindeer-herding Samis are in town. It has become a centre for Sami culture and particularly for education, with the **Nordic Sami Institute** and various colleges of education, culture and research. A large collection of workshops and craftworkers have made their homes here, and the **Cultural Centre and Museum** includes a **Sami Theatre**.

Kautokeino's Easter Festival is also a very big occasion, with the same activities as you find in Karasjok. It is so popular that visitors need to book almost a year in advance, and it is a busy time for Bajos, the company which is responsible for the reindeer-herding trade.

Towards the Russian Border

Back to the crossroads at Karasjok, the E6 almost immediately turns northeast close to the Finnish border, running alongside the great fishing river, the Tana, for some 180km (110 miles). It is another long road with few buildings but it is worth stopping at the **Lavajok Mountain Chapel**, where the Levajokka (river) joins the Tana. As the road nears the first bridge at **Tana Bru**, the 1853 **Polmak Kirke** on the far side has an altarpiece from 1626, and was one of the few churches left standing after World War II. Tana itself has an excellent museum largely devoted to salmon fishing, and also arranges tours to Polmak Kirke.

Leaving Tana Bru gives a chance to head towards Finnmark's northern coronet, and to the municipal centre of Vadsø, on the north side of Varangerfjorden, and Vardø (see p.248). The main E6 continues

east for Kirkenes and the Russian border. The Finnish influence is strong in this empty area. **Burgøynes**, an old fishing village on a peninsula sticking out into Varangerfjorden, escaped destruction in World War II and retains its Finnish architecture and some 350 Finnish-speaking inhabitants. It is also a starting point for the 90-minute walk to the great seabird rock, **Ranvi**. Heading south, the old trading centre, Burgøyfjord, is best known as the birthplace of the Sami artist, John Savio.

Neiden, only some 8km (5 miles) from the Finnish border, is a cultural melting pot, with the Lutheran **Neiden Kirke**, and a 16th-century Greek Orthodox church dedicated to St George, where a distinctive Sami branch, the Skolte Sami, worship. **Labhagården** is a restored Finnish immigrant farm, part of **Sør-Varanger Museum**, which has its main building in Strand, which lies some 40km (30 miles) from Kirkenes.

Kirkenes is the last town in Norway before the Russian border, marked by the Pasvikelva (river). The main crossing place at **Storskog** is some 3km (1.5 miles) to the east, with an old Russian-style inn, **Solia Gjestgiveri**, only some 300m (328yd) from the border, for an overnight stay or a meal. There are also various viewpoints into Russia, such as **Skafferhullet** looking over to Boris Glebe, and **Grense Jakobselv**. This is Norway's easternmost tip, where Oskar II emphasized Norwegian sovereignty by building **King Oskar's Chapel** in 1869. Further south, a narrow pocket of Norwegian territory hangs down, like a horse's leg, into Finland and Russia. This is the route to **Ovre Pasvik National Park**, the largest untouched pine forest in Norway, a wonderful wild area, part of the Siberian Taiga. The famous **Pasvik Taiga** is an old *fjellstue* (mountain lodge) and there are also *hytter* and camping sites.

Kirkenes was bombed over 300 times in World War II, an unwished-for record exceeded only by Malta, and the population spent much of its time underground. You can visit one tunnel, **Andersgrotta**, a great cavern in the centre of the town, a tribute to the human will to survive. Rebuilt as quickly as possible, it is no surprise that Kirkenes still shows some of the results of that need for speed. The town was liberated in 1944 by the Soviet army, and its people have never forgotten the debt. They built a memorial to the Red Army and liberation, and there have always been comings and goings across the border.

Norway's Northern Coronet

From **Varangerbotn**, which has a good, small **Sami Museum**, road 98 takes the north side of Varangerfjorden. The adminstrative centre of Vadsø shows its links with the Arctic in **Polar Galleriet**, which deals with polar expeditions that started from the town. **Luftskipsmasta** is the mooring mast used in 1926 by Roald Amundsen's airship *Norge* and, in 1928 by his Italian colleague Umberto Nobile and the *Italia*, to set off for the Pole.

Vadsø Kirke built in 1958, has two towers like iceblocks outside the front door, put there as shelter from the wind by the architect Magnus Paulsson. There are also two **Kongesteiner** (King's Stones), one with the signatures of King Olav, Finland's President Kekonen, and King Carl Gustav of Sweden, to commemorate a visit in 1977. The later stone is the result of a royal visit in 1992. **Invandrermonumentet** (Immigrants' Monument)

commemorates the early 19th-century Finnish immigrants. **Vadsø Museum** also has exhibits of the two communities, Finnish and Norwegian.

Like the rest of Finnmark, this whole northern coronet, which might be thought of as the remotest of places, has long been inhabited by different peoples, and there are many archaeological remains. Handily placed close to the E6 on the coast north of Vadsø is **Ekkerøy**, said to be Finnmark's only birdrock which can be reached by car and a chance for everyone to see some of the province's magnificent wildlife. Next comes **Kibergnesset**, a huge gun site from World War II, and on to **Domen**, said to be the witch mountain, where witches met the devil for special ceremonies. Today, that is mere legend but between 1621 and 1692, no less than 80 unfortunate women were condemned and burnt.

Vardø is set on an island reached by **Ishavstunnelen**, some 3km (1.75 miles) long, and offers a tunnel certificate to prove you have travelled under the Barents Sea. The oldest area, **Brodtkorbsjåene** has kept its 19th-century waterfront charm and gives guided tours into the past. **Gamle Skole** is the old wooden school of the same period. This northerly town dates back to 1789, when King Christian VII of Denmark-Norway signed its charter. **Vardøhus**, an octagon-shaped fortress, was built in the 1730s, succeeding two earlier fortresses going back to 1300.

All this may seem surprising enough so far north but, after a strange journey through the moonscape-like territory, the road ends a few kilometers further on at **Hamningberg**, an abandoned fishing village, left with its old architecture and church. It is a Finnmark irony that this church was one of the few *not* to have been burned at the end of World War II.

*T*ravelling across Sweden, it does not take long to notice the huge skies – great stretches of light from one horizon to the other with changing cloud formations and a pure clarity. In the far south, Sweden is farmland which melts into forest and is dotted with the eyes of thousands of lakes, until it reaches the great lakes between Gothenburg and Stockholm. To the east is the longest inhabited part of Sweden, the land of Svear. Further north, Dalarna, more than anywhere else, has retained Sweden's past in custom and costume, particularly around Lake Siljan. Then comes the long road and rail track north, up through the land of the Sami people, and the warm coast of the Gulf of Bothnia. Stockholm is a city of lake and sea, and Sweden's smaller cities are never far from harbour and coast. Like all the Scandinavian countries, Sweden may be one of the most modern places in the world, but life out of doors in a simple summerhouse is still the idea of heaven for most Swedes.

Traditional Swedish winter woodpile

City of Sea and Lake in the Land Where Sweden Began

Stockholm is a water city, based on 14 islands and started by early Baltic traders. It is a busy port, where the sun sparkles off the lake and Stockholmers can safely bathe and fish close to the centre. With every sort of museum and theatre and a beautiful opera house, Stockholm is the essence of Sweden and the area round it – from Uppsala to Lake Mälaren is the cradle of the Swedes. Above all, Stockholm is a successful city, and has trebled in size this century, with a standard of living higher than almost any other city in the world.

Stockholm

Stockholm started life on one of the islands huddled along the old trading route which threaded its way from the Baltic through the archipelago to the interior where Sverige (the kingdom of the Svear people) began. Today, fresh and salt water are divided by the great lock gates of Slussen,

A *ll Scandinavians love the traditional open-air museums which bring together traditional buildings from different parts of the country. Stockholm's Skansen was one of the first, opened in the late 19th century, when many old buildings were still in use.*

into Saltsjön on the seaward side, and Lake Mälaren to the west. Slussen also links one of the biggest islands, Södermalm, to the island where Stockholm began, now known as Gamla Stan.

From any of the many bridges or, best of all, from the height of the observation platform (150m (500ft) up the Kaknäs television tower), sea and lake below sparkle summer blue against the muted reds of older buildings and the white and glass of the modern area, with a patchwork of green trees, gardens and parks, busy quaysides, and hundreds of small boats moored along inlet and island.

On the seaward side big Baltic ferries and other working ships line the quays. In summer both lake and sea are dotted with smaller ferries and the bright triangles of sails, and where else could you find a

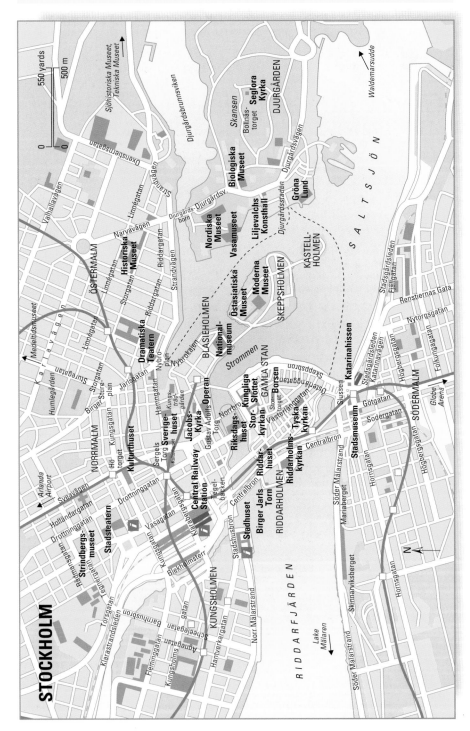

capital with 14 beaches where Stock-holmers swim or sun on the smooth rocks?

The heart of Stockholm lies around five main areas: Gamla Stan, Norrmalm, Öster-malm, Djurgården, and Södermalm. It is all compact enough for walking but, for a first view, what better than a sightseeing boat, sliding past the familiar buildings of the centre: the Royal Palace, parliament buildings, and Rådhuset, the city hall, then on further east and west where Stockholm has spread out along the waterside.

Gamla Stan

Stockholm had its birth some time before the 13th century as a small trading settle-ment and a natural fortress to guard the en-trance to Mälaren. It was the first landing point for traders from west and east and, on Gamla Stan today, the lanes and wynds of the Middle Ages, where the seamen of old carried their goods, have changed lit-tle. Now traffic-free, they are a mecca for seekers of silver, glass, antiques, rugs and wall-hangings, or just a place to stroll and enjoy the summer sun.

If you reach Gamla Stan by Riksbron (bridge), the route runs right through the **Riksdagshuset** (parliament building). Be-low the Riksdag terrace is **Medelstids-museet** (Medieval Museum) with the city's 1530 wall, the town gallows, and various shop cellars, discovered during ex-cavations in the 1980s when the Riksdag needed a new car park. Another part of Gamla Stan's past was discovered under **Hotell Victory** in Lilla Nygatan. It is now

*R*iksdagshuset, the *Parliament building, has a wonderful setting very close to Gamla Stan. A few years ago, building excavations beside parliament revealed part of old Stockholm, now Medelstidsmuseet (Medieval Museum).*

protected by heavy glass which forms part of the restaurant floor.

The unmistakable outlines of **Kungliga Slottet** (Royal Palace) lie ahead. It stands on the site of an earlier and more warlike castle, the Tre Kronor (the three crowns which are now Stockholm's symbol). With 608 rooms, today's palace claims one more than Buckingham Palace in London, but it is no longer the royal family's main home. There are five different museums, with some beautiful Gobelin and Swedish tapestries.

A favourite with visitors is the **State Apartments** including **Oskar II's Writing Room** brought alive by its homely 19th-century furniture and the King's desk that stands as it did in his lifetime. Below the main palace are the **Royal Armoury**, with the stuffed horse and armour of the great warrior, King Gustav II Adolf, and a display of the **Crown Jewels**, which are beautifully lit. The other museums include **Skattkammaren** (Royal Treasury) and **Slottsmuseum**, the ruins of the earlier palace. Each summer day, the Royal Guard parades on horseback down Hamngatan in Norrmalm, and over the bridge for the Changing of the Guard at noon (1pm Sundays).

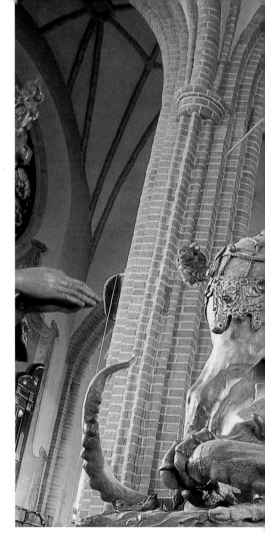

Gamla Stan's centre is **Stortorget**, once the scene of the macabre Stockholm bloodbath of 1520. At what was supposed to be the end of one of the continual wars between Sweden and Denmark, the Danish King Kristian II, known as The Tyrant to the Swedes, had invited the Swedish nobles to a banquet. Despite a guarantee of safety, he then killed 80 people, both nobles and humbler citizens. Today, the peaceful square's cobbled stones have a weekend market and summer benches full of people pausing to open lunch packets or just to sit in the sun and watch life go by. On one side is **Borsen** (Stock Exchange) where the Swedish Academy decides the winner of the Nobel Prize for Literature.

Stortorget leads to many of the favourite shopping streets, such as Västerlånggatan and Österlånggatan, which follow their medieval routes. **Mårten Trotzigs Gränd**, at the southern end of Västerlånggatan, sets the cameras clicking. More a stairway than a lane, it is less than a metre wide. For many, the way to explore Gamla Stan is to wander and find their own special places, but there are guided tours available.

Storkyrkan (Cathedral) is both parish church and place of ceremony. Thickset pillars, stripped back to their original brick, hold up the high ceiling of this big Gothic church. Its best-known statue, **St George and the Dragon**, was carved in wood in 1489 by the medieval sculptor Bernt Notke. Five hundred years later, its original colours survive. Storkyrkan is Gamla Stan's oldest building, rivalled only by **Tyska Kyrkan**, the German Church, not far away, built by medieval German traders. Every four hours, its bells send two alternating hymn tunes floating over Gamla Stan.

*N*ot to be missed in Storkyrkan (the Cathedral) is the fine statue of St George fighting the Dragon, by Bernt Notke from the 16th century. Today, it still glows with it's original colouring.

Turning west, a short bridge leads to **Riddarholmen** and the distinctive lattice-work spire of the 700-year-old **Riddarholmskyrka** (Church of the Nobility),

255

*R*iddarholmen, the
*nearest island to Gamla Stan. This
'island of the Knights (Nobility)'
has Riddarholmskyrka and the old
Riddarhuset, once the
Parliamentary Chamber of the
Nobles, now abolished in ultra-
democratic Sweden.*

with the tombs of every Swedish monarch
since Gustav II Adolf. Close by is **Riddarhuset** (House of Nobility) which has a
grand chamber where the nobles once de-
liberated, and a fine view of Lake Mälaren.

Norrmalm

Norrmalm is Stockholm's commercial
centre with many hotels, restaurants and
stores such as Åhlens and NK. There is
also the central station, **Kungliga Operan**
(Royal Opera House), with its well-known

Opera Källaren restaurant and Café Operan, and **Kungliga Dramatiska Teatern**,
where actors such as Max von Sydow and
Greta Garbo made appearances.

Though many older buildings survived,
as with most European cities in the 1960s,
Stockholm felt the urge to pull down old
stone and put up modern concrete. Norrmalm became the poorer for it. All that
stopped when Stockholmers rebelled and,
climbing the trees in **Kungsträdgården**
(King's Garden), a pleasant square off the
main street, Hamngatan, they dared the
treecutters to cut them down.

*R*ight *in the heart of
Stockholm, Kungliga Dramatiska
Teatern was founded by that
patron of the arts, Gustav III.
He also commissioned the first
play in Swedish there in the late
18th century.*

This happy defiance left Kungsträdgården as the open-air heart of Norrmalm, with flowers, trees, seats, games and a big outdoor café and bar, surrounded by restaurants and small galleries. It comes into its own when the sun begins its rapid rise up the summer sky and Stockholmers take to the open air. In winter, Kungsträdgården becomes an outdoor skating rink. On one side, **Sverigehuset** (Sweden House) has a tourist information office and a booking centre, the starting point for many excursions.

A memorial to the demolition period is Sergels Torg, a huge square at the top of Hamngatan with a giant glass obelisk, lit up at night. Opposite, **Kulturhuset** is a modern cultural centre and meeting place. Below Sergels Torg lies a lower level of walkways, a place for street musicians and artists, and covered shopping arcades such as **Gallerian**. Many shops, such as NK, have entrances at this lower level as well as from the street.

For a taste of one of Stockholm's popular street markets, walk along Sergelsgatan, past five ugly glass tower blocks which dominate the area, to **Hötorget**, a large colourful market with flowers, vegetables and fruit. Here too is **Konserthuset**, the home of the Stockholm Philharmonic Orchestra, and a venue for concerts, from classical to rock. In front of this fine building, the lovely **Orpheus**

Stadshuset (Town Hall) on the water's edge at Riddarholmen was built in the early 20th century in the popular Natural Romantic style of the period. With the three golden crowns (Tre Kronor) on top of the tower, the interior is ornately decorated, including this ceiling in the Council Chamber.

Fountain is by Carl Milles, one of Sweden's most famous sculptors (see p.268).

To the west, Norrmalm finishes at Tegelbacken, with a good view of **Stadshuset** (City Hall), just across the bridge on the next island of Kungsholmen. From anywhere in the south of the city, it is hard to miss the massive square tower, 105m (450ft) high, under the shape of a huge harbour light and Tre Kronor, the golden crowns of the city. Inside, Stadshuset gleams as brightly. The Golden Hall, all marble and gilded mosaics, is the venue for the equally glittering Nobel Ball. The Blue Hall, its wide staircase inspired by the Doge's Palace in Venice, hosts the Nobel Dinner. The tower is also open for public viewing. Below Stadshuset is the departure point for Mälaren's sightseeing boats.

UNDERGROUND ART GALLERY

Below Stockholm's wide streets is a remarkable art gallery, started in the 1940s, when Stockholm began to build Tunnelbanan, the underground rail system. Some 70 artists have created mosaics, paintings, engravings and sculpture on half of the 90-plus stations.

Station walls become rural scenes or take on fascinating patterns. Going down an escalator can seem like entering a cave, and the great T-Centralen station, at the centre of the network, has more decoration than anywhere else. Solna Centrum is a highlight, with a mural of hill and forest set against a red sky.

Most Stockholmers have their own favourite motifs but most agree that the Akalla line (line 11) is high on the list. Not only does it stop at Solna Centrum but Västra Skogen has a huge human profile, picked out in terrazzo tiles and cobbles. Children love the decorated beetles in their glass cases at Gärdet (lines 13 and 14).

ALFRED NOBEL

Born in 1833, Alfred Nobel, the inventor of dynamite, was also one of the first internationalists, running his companies even then as a worldwide group.

One reason could have been that the Nobel family moved to St Petersburg in Russia when he was only nine, and then moved between several different countries. Nobel spoke, read and wrote five European languages, and there is a fine collection of his letters in Swedish, Russian, English, French and German to prove it.

The subjects of his prizes are physics, chemistry, physiology or medicine, and literature. The idea of a peace prize was undoubtedly stimulated by his friend, Austrian Baroness Bertha von Suttner, who was already holding peace congresses in Rome and Berne. She won the Peace Prize herself in 1905.

Literature was Nobel's private predilection. He read a lot – Byron and Shelley were his favourite English-language poets – and wrote too, saving little except a long autobiographical poem in English. But, throughout his life, however at home he seemed in other languages and other lands, this early internationalist never gave up his Swedish citizenship.

Djurgården

Djurgården, once a royal hunting park, has retained its rural atmosphere. The island lies on the Saltsjön side of the city on the edge of Östermalm, one of Stockholm's smartest areas. By bus, or on foot, the way to Djurgården from Nybroplan (at the foot of Hamngatan) is along Strandvägen waterfront, past the dignified buildings where Östermalm begins.

In summer many prefer to take a ferry from nearby Nybrokajen, or from Slussen at the southern end of Gamla Stan, through the harbour with its small boats moored

*N*ot many cities have a youth hostel as elegant as the Af Chapman, *an old sailing ship moored in Saltsjön, on the seaward side of the capital.*

*O*ne of Stockholm's most *famous hotels is the Grand Hotel at Blailsieholmen, looking over to Gamla Stan and the Royal Palace.*

around the islands or heading out into the archipelago. The first sight is the graceful silhouette of the sailing ship *Af Chapman*, now an unusual youth hostel. Next comes Kastelholmen, a fortress island used by the army; then Skeppsholmen and **Moderna Museet**, with a big 20th-century collection which includes Dali, Matisse, Picasso and Warhol. Also on this island is **Östasiatiskt Museet** (Museum of Asiatic Antiquities), a large collection of Chinese and Asian art and crafts.

Blaisieholmen, now more a peninsula, is the northernmost of the three islands, all linked by bridges and reached on foot

from the centre. Here is Sweden's national collection, **Nationalmuseet** (National Art Museum), with great Swedish painters such as Anders Zorn and Carl Larsson. Also on the island is one of Scandinavia's finest hotels, the Grand.

For most people, Djurgården means **Vasamuseet** and **Skansen**, the open-air museum which founded this Scandinavian tradition when, in 1891, Artur Hazelius, decided to preserve the familiar Swedish way of life, by gathering in old buildings and crafts that were then beginning to die out. The great arch of the scenic railway and the Ferris-wheel of **Grona Lund**, a 19th-century amusement park, are another essential side of Djurgården.

The 17th-century *Wasa* warship was built for the warrior king, Gustav II Adolf, as the pride of his growing fleet. On its maiden voyage in 1628, out in Saltsjön, the great ship keeled over and sank, watched by the horrified king, his court and many Stockholmers who had come out to celebrate. Few on board escaped. In the 1960s, *Wasa* was discovered by a determined marine archaeologist, Anders Franzén.

The best way to reach the old Royal hunting ground of Djurgården is by the colourful boat from Slussen, which gives the chance to pass other islands as well.

Thanks largely to his efforts, the ship was brought up a decade later in a complicated naval exercise. Piece by piece, over the next 30 years, marine specialists patiently restored her. Now, in her own museum,

Djurgården's Wasa Museum houses a most remarkable recovery of an old ship. Gustav II Adolf's warship, Wasa, had lain under Saltsjön's waters for over 300 years when it was discovered in the 1960s. After 30 years of reconstruction, it is now beautifully displayed (following pages).

opened in 1992, the *Wasa* is a glorious ship with gold leaf on her bow and stern, and the heavy bronze guns which many say caused her to capsize, all easily seen from several cleverly designed open floors.

Skansen has recreated an old village where present-day craftsfolk demonstrate the traditional skills and where visitors can sample old sweets and *bullar*, traditional spicy buns. When the bakery is making them, the enticing smell alone is enough to attract an eager queue

Djurgården has two excellent museums: **Nordiska Museet** has displays of Nordic life from the 16th century; **Biologiska Museet** shows Nordic animals against dioramas based on works by Sweden's best natural history artist, Bruno Liljefors.

Along with its old buildings, Skansen practises many traditional crafts, from lace- to pipe-making and beautiful old-fashioned baking.

They form a naturalistic habitat for dancing cranes and displaying black cocks. The delightful **Hotell Hasselbacken**, quite recently built onto a famous 19th-century restaurant, is an added asset to Djurgården's lovely surroundings.

Nor is art forgotten. **Liljevalchs Gallery** has a big spring exhibition of modern works, and the **Thiel Gallery** was once the home of banker Thiel, and a meeting place for early 20th-century artists. A gem of a museum at **Waldemarsudde** was the home of the painter-prince Eugen, brother of the late King Gustav V. This beautiful house, with lakeside gardens, holds the Prince's collection, including many of his own large landscapes.

Lake Mälaren and the Archipelago

Most Stockholmers divide sharply into those whose summer weekends mean the lake, and those who travel out to some of the 25,000 islands of the archipelago. Both have their own special delights.

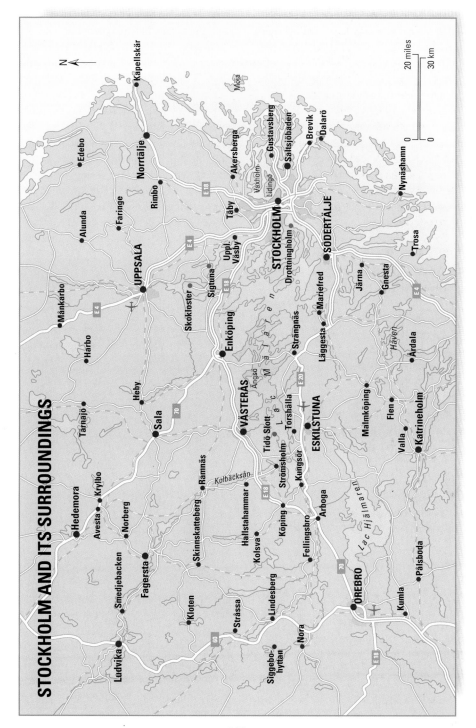

STOCKHOLM AND ITS SURROUNDINGS

20 miles
30 km

N

Kapellskär
Möja
Gustavsberg
Saltsjöbaden
Brevik
Dalarö
Edebo
Norrtälje
Åkersberga
Nynäshamn
Faringe
Rimbo
Vaxholm
Lidingö
Täby
SÖDERTÄLJE
Alunda
STOCKHOLM
Trosa
UPPSALA
Uppl.
Väsby
Drottningholm
Mariefred
Järna
Gnesta
Månkarbo
Skokloster
Sigtuna
Enköping
Strängnäs
Läggesta
Årdala
Harbo
Mälaren
Håven
Heby
Ängsö
VÄSTERÅS
Torshälla
Malmköping
Flen
Katrineholm
Tärnsjö
Sala
Tidö Slott
ESKILSTUNA
Valla
Krylbo
Rämnäs
Kolbäcksån
Strömsholm
Kungsör
Hedemora
Avesta
Norberg
Skinnskatteberg
Hallstahammar
Köping
Arboga
Fellingsbro
Lac Hjälmaren
Pålsboda
Smedjebacken
Fagersta
Kolsva
Kloten
Strässa
Lindesberg
ÖREBRO
Kumla
Ludvika
Nora
Siggebo-
hyttan

Lake Mälaren

Mälaren stretches some 100km (60 miles) west and holds many islands. Some are famous, such as Lovön, with Drottningholm Slott (Royal Palace) reached by vintage steamer from Stadsbron quay, or by car, Tunnelbana or bus. The steamer voyage takes 50 minutes, past islands with evocative names such as Fågelön (bird island) or Kungshatt (King's Hat, from its shape). Sun-worshippers on rocks and beaches, and sails by the hundred make it hard to believe that on this journey, the boat never leaves the city boundaries.

Lovön has been a royal island since the 17th century and the palace here is now the royal family's main home. Its lovely garden gives it the nickname of 'Versailles-in-miniature'. Not to be missed is **Drottningholm Kungliga Teater** (Royal Theatre), built in 1766 by Queen Louisa Ulrika, mother of Gustav III, Sweden's great patron of the arts and founder of Swedish theatre – his reign introduced a blossoming of Swedish arts.

In summer today, there are performances in this exquisite little theatre, still with the original backdrops and most of its 18th-century equipment. In the auditorium's dim light, it is possible to work out the names of court officials on the seat backs. There are also daily guided tours. Another reminder of Gustav's lavish court life is the royal folly of **Kina Slott** (Chinese Palace) with pagoda roofs and balconies.

Gustav III was assassinated at a masked ball in 1792 – an event which inspired Verdi's opera *Un Ballo in Maschera* – and the lights went out on Sweden's flourishing new arts scene. The court theatre was forgotten until the 1920s, when Professor Agne Beijer pushed open a door and found the 18th-century theatre, intact and undamaged by the passing years.

Further to the west is **Björkö**, once the Viking Birka and Sweden's oldest settlement. Little remains above ground, but between 900 and 975AD Birka was a trading

*T*he formal gardens of Drottningholm Royal Palace, on the island of Lovön in Lake Mälaren have earned it the nickname of 'Versailles in Miniature'. The Palace is the permanent home of the Swedish Royal Family.

centre for some 40,000 people around Mälaren, at a time when nothing stood between the island and the Baltic. Travellers and traders sailed in from faraway Russia and Arabia, and from Europe came Skt Ansgar, bent on conversion. The 1930s chapel is dedicated to the saint.

Stockholm's Archipelago

Some 14,000 islands and skerries lie off Stockholm, reaching 40 miles into the Baltic, unbeatable for sailing, canoeing, windsurfing, swimming, fishing, bird-watching and wildlife. Year-round, only 150 islands are inhabited. In summer many visitors live in simple summer houses, hostels and cabins. Cycling is a good way to get around the bigger islands; some hire out bikes and boats. The islands are reached by scheduled boat services, special day excursions, and private boats. The main shipping company is Waxholmsbolaget but you can also book through the Excursion Shop at Sweden House (Sverigehuset), Stockholm's main tourist informtion centre.

The great archipelago's inner islands are Lidingö, Vaxholm, and Fjäderholmarna, a group of four only 20 minutes by boat from the city. You can also reach **Lidingö** by

*N*ot many capitals can
boast 14 bathing beaches within
the city boundaries, but Stockholm
is lucky. In summer, Stockholmers
catch the sun, and swim from both
smooth rocks and sand.

Tunnelbana and bus, but a boat on a warm
day sets the mood for Millesgården, the
summer home of the sculptor Carl Milles.
Here, he spent his time reproducing the
statues that had made him famous. Set on
steep terraces, the figures seem to fly.

Vaxholm is just an hour from the centre of Stockholm and is the best place for
swimming, canoeing and windsurfing. It
has a long tradition of rowing, thanks to
the Vaxholm oarswomen who plied their
boats between island and city until a road
was built in 1926. Today, the oarswomen
have been replaced by boats with engines.

The 16th-century **Vaxholm Slott** was
built by Gustav Vasa to safeguard the
city's sea route. Summer Herring Picnics
are held at the fortress. There is Vaxholm
Slott Hotel and Rådhusbodarna sells handcrafts. The **Homestead Museum** is
housed in a fishing cottage, and there is an
old **Customs House**.

Though close to the city, only 20 minutes by boat, **Fjäderholmarna** (Feather
Islands) are genuine archipelago islands.
They have a Baltic fish aquarium, a
smokehouse, a boat museum and an inn.

Grinda is a small, green island of
meadows, paths and lanes, some two
hours from the city. Swimming is good,
there are boat hire agents, a small summer
shop and a simple campsite.

Three hours out, **Möja** is some 4km (3
miles) across, with 250 residents, many of
whom farm and fish in traditional ways.
Berg community has a church, a museum,
a bakery and a restaurant. Just northwest
of Möja, there are three small, linked

islands known as **Finnhamn**, ideal for swimming, with smooth rocks and small beaches. The archipelago's biggest hostel is here and there are also *stugor* (summer houses) or tents to rent and boats for hire.

Sandhamn on Sandön has the archipelago's best harbour, attracting hundreds of summer yachts and other boats, doubling the 100-or-so population. The village cemetery has the graves of seafarers, and there is a restaurant dating back to 1762. Fine sandy beaches are ideal for swimming and scuba diving.

Utö in the southern archipelago has everything: a hotel, a hostel, a restaurant, swimming, fishing, camping, cycle hire and a guest harbour. It is also home to the oldest iron mine in Sweden. You can look down the mine shaft, visit the small museum, and see the 18th-century miners' houses and a windmill.

Scarcely known to overseas visitors, despite a daily summer boat, Stockholmers prize the northern archipelago islands of **Svartlöga** and **Rödlöga** for peace and quiet, fine landscapes, swimming, sunbathing and sailing.

The seaward island of **Bullerö** is part of a nature reserve of 900 islands and skerries. There is a small archipelago exhibition in a former hunting lodge which was once owned by the famous nature artist, Bruno Liljefors. It is an ideal place for naturalists and birdwatchers, with a small overnight guest hostel. Many islands here are rich in wildlife, with elk, deer, otter, badger, and occasional mink; plus whitetailed eagle, gulls, ducks, swans and wading birds galore.

Out into the Baltic, **Huvudskär** were fishing islands in the Middle Ages. Red fishing huts, now disused, are scattered along the cliffs. Boats run from Dalarö, on the coast southeast of Stockholm.

Old Sweden

Stockholm sits at the eastern end of three provinces: Uppland, with the old capital Uppsala, Södermanland, and Våstmanland where Sweden's history began.

Uppsala

There are three huge 5th-century grave mounds at **Gamla Uppsala** (Old Uppsala), just north of the present city. These are the burial sites of the ancient kings, Aun, Adils and Egil, and a reminder that this was once a heathen capital, which left dead animal sacrifices swaying from the holy trees. But Uppsala became Christian early on and today it is the seat of Sweden's archbishop, and has Scandinavia's largest Gothic cathedral, some 118m (340ft) high.

Gustav Vasa's 16th-century **Uppsala Slott** also dominates the city skyline, and Uppsala has Sweden's oldest university with many fine buildings such as the **Anatomical Theatre**, once used to demonstrate operations to medical students. The university and its students have always been important in the life of the city and, today, streets and cafés have a busy and sometimes noisy student population, particularly during Walpurgis night (30th April), a traditional student celebration.

The names of the university's many illustrious *alumni* include Carl von Linné (Linnaeus), the botanist who devised plant classification, and Dag Hammerskjöld, peacemaker and poet who, as Secretary General of the United Nations, was killed in a yet-to-be-explained air crash in Africa.

The famous botanist left **Linnéträdgården** (Linné Garden) as a beautiful city oasis of lovely plants, and a museum. His summer home **Hammerby**, south of Uppsala, has a fine, small botanic garden, which also delights plant lovers and gardeners.

Just off the E4 route to Uppsala from Stockholm is the village of **Sigtuna**, with traces of ruined monasteries as a reminder that this was Sweden's first town. Further north, in a cluster of lakes is **Skokloster**, the seat of an important family, the Wrangles, who once ruled over much of Scandinavia.

One of the most peaceful and restful ways to reach Uppsala is by boat, along a route that uses Mälaren and then sneaks through the countryside by a mixture of inlets and lakes, a continuation of the days when water was the only route for the many people who lived and traded around Mälaren.

Around Lake Mälaren

When water meant transport, many great families chose to build their castles close to Lake Mälaren. Many houses and castles remain, such as **Gripsholm Slott** (see p.71), close to the idyllic little town of Mariefred, not far from Stockholm on the south side of the lake.

Nearest of the lakeside towns to Stockholm, **Mariefred** is linked to the city by a leisurely steamboat, and also by today's excellent road system which makes public or private transport very simple. Another delight is **Östra Södermanlands Järnväg**, a magnificent steam railway between Mariefred and Läggesta.

Strängnäs, a little to the north, was a 12th-century bishop's see, and the vast Gothic cathedral recalls those important times, as do some fine old town buildings. Lake sightseeing boats also leave from the harbour at Strängnäs.

Further west, the town of **Eskilstuna** had its birth in the great days of steel and iron, and the **Rademacher Smithies**, founded in 1658, are now an industrial museum. Eskilstuna is still important for

engineering, and also has a popular zoo park with a pride of white tigers.

The easiest way across the lake is to return almost to Strängnäs, and head north by route 55, over bridges and islands to Mälaren's northern bank. From here, a side road leads to the old estate of Ängsö Slott (see p.70). The next town west on E18 is **Västerås**, an early trading centre. There is a fine castle and **Domkirkan** (cathedral) holds the tomb of King Erik XIV. Västerås has one of the lake's best leisure sailing harbours, linked to the capital by ferry. Nearby **Anundshog** has Sweden's largest Iron Age burial mounds and ship tumuli.

At the western end of Mälaren, where the road merges into the E4 from the south side, **Arboga** is one of the best preserved old towns in Sweden. In 1435, it was the historic meeting place for what eventually became Sweden's first Riksdag (parliament) when the patriot Engelbrekt Engelbrektsson was elected Captain of the Realm.

To the west, the ground rises to the mountainous area of Bergslagen (see p.73) and, at **Örebro**, at the western end of the smaller Lake Hjälmaren, the famous Swedish steel industry came into being in a marriage of water, ore and lake transport. Three places locally show that way of life: the old **Strassa Gruvor** (mines) allow visitors to go underground in original mining carts, **Lilla Nora** is a well-preserved 19th-century wooden village of houses where steel workers lived, and **Siggebohyttan** has a manor house, the home of a rich mill-owner.

The most romantic way to travel around Mälaren is by steamer or ferry boat; road travel is also simple on quiet roads through lovely country. But whatever way a visitor chooses, this historic lake never lacks charm, beauty and interest.

A Talent for Invention

Most people know that Sweden gave the Nobel Prizes to the world, as a result of Alfred Nobel's bequest. Not so well known is the fact that his country has also produced many other discoveries and discoverers worthy of the acclaim.

Nobel was only 29 when, in 1866, he made his best-known invention, dynamite, in a form that was stable enough to be handled without exploding. He followed this with the later inventions of safety fuses and smokeless gunpowder. He ended his life famous for two apparent contradictions. He was both a huge armament manufacturer and the founder of the Nobel Prize for Peace. Though the prize is also awarded for physics, chemistry, literature, medicine and economic sciences, it is best known for the Peace Prize.

Another anomaly about the Peace Prize is that, though the other prizes are decided by the various Swedish academies, and awarded in Stockholm, the Nobel Prize for Peace is decided in Oslo, which at the time of Nobel's death was still part of a joint Swedish-Norwegian monarchy under the Swedish king.

The Swedish flair for scientific invention could be said to have had its birth in 1739 when the Royal Academy of Science was founded, though there was already an Academy of Sciences at the old University of Uppsala. By that time also, Swedes such as Carl von Linné (Linneaus) were already travelling and meeting like-minds overseas, and had discoveries and inventions to their credit, such as Olof Rudbeck the Elder's discovery of the human lymph glands nearly a century before.

Carl von Linné's famous classification of plants, animals and minerals is still the basis of today's systems, and he travelled the world in his search for new species and specimens. He worked mainly at Uppsala, where his garden and museum and the botanic garden in

The early botanist Carl von Linné's house and garden in the old city of Uppsala, north of Stockholm, makes a gardener's dream visit, full of plants and its own museum.

his summer home, not far away, are still in existence (see p.269). A little earlier, the astronomer and mathematician, Anders Celsius, had invented the centigrade thermometer, with its new scale of temperature units, used today all over the world.

Despite this early flurry of invention, late industrialization meant it was well on in the 19th century before Swedes began to produce the sort of inventions that led to the country's astonishing industrial success in the 20th century.

An early invention, which brought great prosperity to what became the big dairy equipment manufacturer, Alfa-Laval, now Tetra-Alfa-Laval, came in 1878. The cream separator was invented by Gustaf de Laval, who also designed an early milking machine and many other machines. Another engineer, Nils Gustav Dalén became interested in acetylene for lighting and, as chief engineer of AGA in 1906, he made several inventions connected with maritime safety such as a sun switch which automatically turns beacons on and off at nightfall and dawn. In 1906, he was an early winner of the Nobel Prize for Physics.

Even earlier, in 1844, Gustaf Erik Pasch had received a patent for the safety match, with which two other inventors Edvard Lundström, and Alexander Lagerman later started a match factory in Jönköping, at the south of Lake Våttern, (see p.285). It began production of Pasch's safety match, and to turn out boxes of his matches by the hundreds of thousands.

As a young man in 1921, the scientist Baltzar von Platen designed a refrigerator without moving parts which became the basis of the great Electrolux electrical appliances empire. Later he made the first synthetic diamonds, and in the 1940s Arne Tiselius discovered electrophoresis, a method of protein analysis, for which he received a Nobel Prize in 1948.

Sweden's invention, just after World War II, of the ball-bearing, is an invention with all the simplicity of genius. Sven Winquist's spherical ball-bearing led to a revolution in mechanical design. As one of a nation where inventors were not prone to waste their inventions, Sven Wingquist founded the company now known as SKF, the world's leading producer of industrial bearings. In turn, it was engineers from SKF, who started the now huge car manufacturer, Volvo, backed by SKF in the first instance.

Many more inventors founded Swedish companies now known worldwide. As far back as the 1870s, Lars Magnus Ericsson and a partner had founded the company that became L.M. Ericsson, and were manufacturing telephones by 1878. Though he ran into competition from America, Ericsson has had overseas subsidiaries since 1890, and was himself responsible for many developments in switchboards and telephone networks.

Another inventor-industrialist was Jonas Wenström, the father of the alternating systems of electricity, as well as a classic direct current generator, and other items connected with electricity. He founded the now multinational company ASEA (today also a half-owner of the Swedish-Swiss ABB) which expanded fast, thanks to the large sums of patent money Winquist earned from his three-phase electrical system.

The Hasselblad, a single lens reflex camera invented in 1948, has remained at the top for more than four decades, despite the worst that miniaturization and automation could throw at it. It is still in a class of its own, well known as the camera used by the astronauts on the US space voyages to the moon, and the camera's superb body system that keeps the Hasselblad factory busy in Gothenburg today.

These examples of inventions omit many more, equally valuable, such as the screw propellor for ships invented by John Ericsson, and Johan Peter Jahansson's monkey wrench – the universal spanner that deals with any kind of nut. They also raise two puzzling questions. Why has this small country of only eight million given birth to so many inventors? The second is why Swedish inventors, unlike so many others, have had the practical realism to make use of their inventions and turn them to their own benefit. This strong entrepreneurial skill sits uneasily with the stereotype of the absent-minded scientist.

Part of the first answer could be the backing and enthusiasm that various monarchs and governments gave to science and the inventors early on, and the acclaim many of the discoveries earned abroad. This, in turn, brought foreign scientists into Sweden to meet Swedish scientists who themselves travelled overseas, and so were long aware of the worldwide potential of their inventions. In the second case, a late industrial revolution may have given Sweden the opportunity to consider what other countries had already done, and the already established wave of industrialization made it more natural that Swedish inventors should think of their 'brain-children' in industrial terms.

Nor has the trend faltered. In the last 40 years, many new ideas have come on to the commercial market, though now the invention, as it is everywhere, is more often collaborative than the complete work of one person. Ruben Rausing developed the revolutionary packaging for liquid foodsuffs, such as milk and juice, called Tetra-Pak. It had been created first by Erik Wallenberg, a member of the great banking and business family, which collaborated with Rausing to found the Tetra-Pak (later Tetra Laval) Group which includes Tetra Pak and Tetra Laval food units. Goran Lundahl and Oscar Persson developed a technique for quick-freezing vegetables which, as Flofreeze, now holds 60 percent of the world market.

Today, few people in the queue outside a Cashline machine realize that the fact they are waiting is due to Leif Lundblad, who invented a machine for automatic cash handling. Today, Leif Lundblad and his fast-developing company, Inter Innovation AB, are concentrating on a new invention called SealFax, which folds and seals confidential fax messages so that the address is still showing.

The Swedes have never been confined to any one specialization. At ABB a team led by Tore Nordin invented a means of stopping tractors from slipping, which has been incorporated into tractors sold all over the world. The turbo-charged engine used today, for example, in another Swedish car, Saab, was invented by Bengt Gadefelt in 1976.

Nor have Swedes been slow in the medical field. They are prominent in the areas of intravenous nutrition, beta-blockers, local anaesthetics, kidney dialysis and the artificial kidney, and ultrasound for medical examinations. This was originally an area of research of the Austrian, Helmujth Hertz, for which he became famous throughout the world. Eager to devise a non-invasive method for heart examinations, a Swedish doctor, Inge Edler, contacted Hertz. The two men collaborated for years to introduce echocardiography, which revolutionized ways of diagnosing heart problems. They both received the award of the American equivalent of the Nobel Prize, the Lasker Prize in 1977.

Swedes, it appears, have lost none of the inventive skills of the 17th-century Olof Rudbeck, and his contemporary Christopher Polhem, an astonishing universalist, who not only invented his machines – from lathes to tools and clocks – but made them himself. Today's Swedish inventors are still following that example, on a grand scale.

Sea, Sun, Castles and Ripening Corn

Travelling through the south of Sweden, it is no surprise to learn that this fertile land is known as 'Sweden's granary'. Everywhere you look there are rich fields, the corn ripening fast under a gentle sky. In the people, and certainly in the voices, there is a subtle difference from the rest of Sweden in this southern corner, so near continental Europe and part of Denmark until 1658. Every year more than 25 million people cross the sound between Denmark and Sweden, and even more may make the journey when the proposed Öresund bridge is complete – provided that conservationists' doubts about water flow into the Baltic can be satisfied.

Skåne is Sweden's most southerly province. Tiny Blekinge to the east is one of the smallest, with many lovely beaches. It is home to Sweden's great naval base at Karlskrona. Bright roadside verges and leafy woodland give this area the title 'Sweden's garden'. Halland lies to the northwest of Skåne, a favourite for families, with sandy beaches and seaside towns. Inland, Halland too is fertile farming country.

*F*åro *lies off the north end of Gotland, a dream Baltic island, with beaches, Fårökirka and these strange raukar, natural stone statues. Day tours from Gotland cross the Fårösund.*

The rich farmland disappears the further east you go, and Småland in the southeast has miles of heath and forest with hundreds of lakes dotted among the trees, and a beautiful coast along the Baltic. Only in the north, nearing Jönköping and Gränna, beside Lake Vättern does the land become fruitful again.

Sweden's main Baltic islands are Öland and Gotland. Öland is long and narrow, a few miles out into the Kalmar Sound on the Småland coast. Kalmar, the nearest mainland town, is connected to Öland by one of Europe's longest bridges. Further north, Gotland is the Baltic's biggest island, 120km (90 miles) long and 40km (30 miles) at its widest. The old town of Visby, once the main Baltic base of the German Hanseatic traders, is circled by sturdy 12th-century city walls.

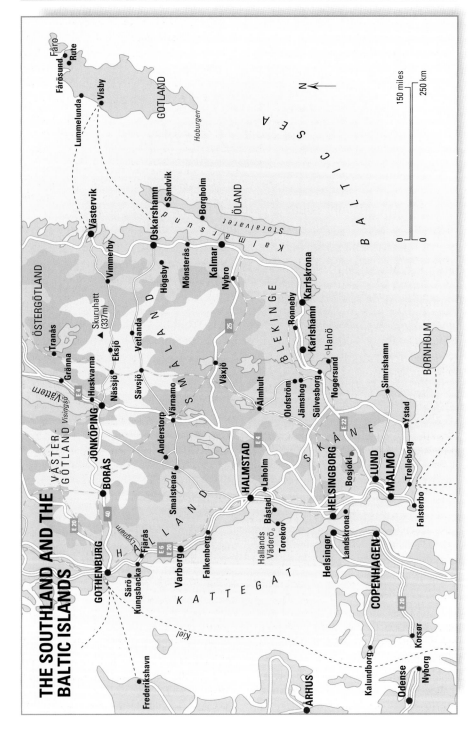

THE SOUTHLAND AND THE BALTIC ISLANDS

Fårö
Rute
Fårösund
Visby
Lummelunda
GOTLAND
Hoburgen

BALTIC SEA

150 miles
250 km

Sandvik
Oskarshamn
Borgholm
ÖLAND
Storalvaret
Kalmarsund

Västervik
Vimmerby
Högsby
Mönsterås
Kalmar
Nybro
Karlskrona

ÖSTERGÖTLAND
Tranås
Gränna
Skuruhatt
(337m)
SMÅLAND
Vetlanda
Karlshamn
Ronneby
BLEKINGE
Hanö

Vättern
Visingsö
Huskvarna
Nässjö
Eksjö
Sävsjö
Växjö
E 25

JÖNKÖPING
E 4
Anderstorp
Värnamo
Älmhult
Olofström
Jämshog
Sülvesborg
Nogersund
Simrishamn
BORNHOLM

VÄSTER-
GÖTLAND
BORÅS

SKÅNE
Ystad
E 22

Smalstenar
HALMSTAD
Laholm
E 4
Bästad
Bosjökl
LUND
Trelleborg
MALMÖ
Falsterbo

HALLAND
Fjärås
E 6
E 20
Varberg
Falkenberg
Hallands
Väderö
Torekov
Helsingør
Landskrona
HELSINGBORG

Lygnern
E 20
40

GOTHENBURG
Särö
Kungsbacka

KATTEGAT

COPENHAGEN
E 20

Kiel
Frederikshavn

Kalundborg
Korsør
Odense
Nyborg

ÅRHUS

N

Until the 18th century, much of this land was Danish. The frontier, the present-day border between Blekinge and Småland, was alive with skirmishes and more serious strife. Kristianopel, once a Danish fortress is a reminder of this period which continued for hundreds of years. Then, first King Gustav II Adolf regained some of the southern provinces, then in the fierce winter of 1657-8, King Karl X Gustav regained the remainder under the Treaty of Roskilde.

Skåne

Skåne has Sweden's best farmland, a patchwork of green and yellow fields outlined by trees and hedges. Although popular belief has it that this is flat country, a short cycle tour will quickly scotch that illusion. Skåne undulates, rising to higher ground as it reaches Småland, with some 800km (560 miles) of good, marked cycles routes.

The province supplies much of Sweden's best food, and is famous for its gastronomic traditions. In days gone by, well-off peasants underlined their wealth by impressing friends with the richness of their *smörgåsbord* (cold table) and, even today, it is sometimes just possible to detect a little of that old sense of pride at table. There are many *smörgåsbord* specialities, culminating in a Skåne *spettkaka*, made from dozens of eggs and best cooked on an open fire.

The Skåne coastline is as fine as the food. Many of the small coastal towns have good, clean swimming beaches, with first-class sailing and fishing. All along the stretches of sand and rocky promontories there are people with binoculars, for this is also fine birdwatching country, as are inland lakes such as **Ringsjön**, northeast of Lund.

 One of the best spots is the **Bjäre peninsula** to the northwest. Here are **Hovs Hallar**, rocks shaped like statues, and more spotless sandy beaches. Fishing villages such as **Torekov** have kept a feeling of the past. Also on Bjäre, **Båstad**, still a fashionable resort, is now a tennis centre. It hosts the international Båstad Open and the Donald Duck Cup, the biggest tournament for the 11-15 age group, where many of Sweden's champions made a start. Båstad encourages social players too. There are idyllic offshore islands and Torekov is the harbour for **Hallands Väderö**, an island nature reserve.

Many *herrgård* (manor houses) and castles hint at Skåne's long prosperity; some are now open to the public as restaurants and hotels, or for concerts and events. One of the most beautiful is the 12th-century monastery and chapel of **Bosjökloster**, with its red roofs and white walls, northeast of Malmö (road 23). Here you wander through the scent of rose and herb and marvel at a thousand-year-old oak. **Sinclairsholm**, some 50km (35 miles) further north, just off the same road, is still owned by the original family. Baron Barnekow is happy to escort visitors and tell them about the estate, which is one of Sweden's largest asparagus producers.

Many buildings remain from the hundreds of years when warring powers fought over the south. Helsingborg's medieval keep, **Kärnan**, is the only one of its kind in Sweden; the citadel of Malmöhus dates back to the 15th century; **Landskrona** has **Citadellet** built in 1549; and 15th-century **Simrishamn** is one of Scandinavia's best preserved early fortresses, set round a wide courtyard.

From Landskrona, you can visit the island of **Ven**, almost halfway to Denmark and the home of the Renaissance astronomer Tycho Brahe. Simrishamn itself, in the popular artists' area of Österlen, has many small galleries and, at Easter each year, an artists' open-house week. This southwest peninsula has fine scenery and two friendly resorts, **Falsterbo** and **Skanör**.

Many Continental visitors arrive at **Trelleborg** on the south coast by ferry from Travemünde, Rostock and Sassnitz in Germany. Further along, **Ystad**'s old houses look almost Tudor. The town is the terminal for a ferry to the Danish isle of **Bornholm**. Reminders of early days are the **Ales Stenar** (standing stones) from Viking times. To the east is a land of fruit farms and orchards that seem almost Danish. The coast is magnificently rocky, the loftiest rock being **Stenshuvudet**.

Malmö

Malmö, on the west coast, is Skåne's biggest city, with a population of some quarter of a million. Yet it retains the friendly atmosphere of a much smaller town. Many nations have passed through this busy port, each adding to the diversity, and making Malmö a cosmopolitan, lively city, where one in five residents has a foreign background.

Malmö's heart is its central square, **Stortorget**, with an impressive **Rådhus** (Town Hall). One of the longest surviving buildings is the 15th-century **Jorgen Kockshus**, which can claim 'King Gustav Vasa slept here'. **Malmöhus** goes back to the last decades of Danish rule and was built by King Kristian III. It is now a museum. **Skt Petris Kyrka**, one of Malmö's loveliest buildings, is 14th century though its greatest treasures came later.

Malmö is a city of squares, many with colourful street markets such as **Lilla Torg**, a beautiful small cobbled square, with stalls selling jewellery, handcrafts and pottery. **Möllevångstorget** is heady with the scent of flowers, fruit and herbs.

Scented in a different way, **fiskebodarna** are small fishing huts near the water, the best place to buy freshly caught morning fish. Malmö is full of parks and greenery, **Pilldammsparken** being Sweden's largest landscaped park, with an amphitheatre for summer performances. Marvellous for children is **Aq-Va-Kul**, an indoor water park, with water at 29°C all year round, and plenty of pools and whirlpools.

The city is very much a cultural centre and **Malmö Festival** in August packs the hotels and **Konserthuset**, home of Malmö Symphony Orchestra, and **Konsthallen**

(City Art Gallery). Another favourite is the theatre where the famous film-maker, Ingmar Bergman, was director.

Also in August, the highly innovative **Equestrian Weeks** bring showjumping right into the city, to a suitably prepared Stortorget, with dressage and trotting events in the park. This whole area is devoted to the horse, with nearby **Jägersro**, Sweden's only combined trotting and race track, in use since 1907, and now the home of the Swedish Derby.

All these events are well publicized through the city and well run. Bus 20 has

S tortorget, literally meaning the 'Big Square', is the centre of Malmö. The city goes back to the days of Danish rule in Skåne, with many 14th- and 15th-century buildings.

information boards to show visitors where they are, what they can see, and how to get there, and Malmö tourist office runs special guided tours.

Lund

Some 27km (19 miles) east of Malmö, the city of **Lund** has winding, cobbled streets and old buildings, appropriate to a community that dates from 990AD. It was founded by Sven Tveskägg. The Danish king, Canute, who also reigned over England, later designated Lund as a religious, political and cultural city. The university was founded in 1666 and the towering Romanesque cathedral was consecrated in 1145. At that time, Lund was the Nordic region's religious capital, and the archbishop's see covered all Scandinavia and Finland. The cathedral has a fine 15th-century altarpiece and a beautiful **Astronomical Clock**, which shows the movement of the heavenly bodies and, when it chimes, the story of the Three Wise Men.

Lund Universitet is surrounded by lovely gardens with a big stone fountain. The 30,000 students are an important part of Lund's 90,000 population, much to the fore on student occasions such as Walpurgis night. The university also ensures good museums and **Lunds Konsthall** (art gallery), **Historiska Museet** and **Kulturhistoriska Museet** (Museum of Cultural History) are popular with visitors.

Under its everyday name, **Kulturen**, this is among Sweden's biggest and best open-air museums, with the advantage that some of its old farms and big houses stand on their original sites at Gammel (Old) Lund, to give a true sense of authenticity.

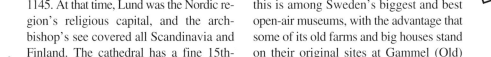

*T*he University and Cathedral city of Lund (right) is one of Scandinavia's oldest, dating back to the 10th century. At one time, the Archbishop's See included all of Scandinavia and Finland. The Cathedral treasures the Astronomical Clock (above).

Halland

Northwest of Skåne, Halland's long beautiful coast stretches as far as the outskirts of the port of Gothenburg, Sweden's second city. To many Swedes, the province is one long and beautiful beach, but Halland has much more. Inland, woods and countryside make for fine walking; there are many recognized cycling routes such as Ginstleden, named after Halland's symbol, a special flowering broom. Many rivers flowing through Halland are ideal for canoeists and anglers. Canoeing is also popular on inland lakes, such as Lake Bolmen in the Hylte district, or the Fegan area close to the Småland border, with the added bonus of wonderful wildlife.

From the south, **Laholm**, just inland on the Laganälva (river) is Sweden's oldest town, founded in 1231 in the beautiful countryside that still surrounds it. **Halmstad** is the province's main town, famous for the Halmstadgruppen (Halmstad group) of artists and, in particular, for Carl Milles' statue *Europa and the Bull* in the main square. It is also a busy port with sea links to Grenå in Denmark.

Some of Halland's seaside towns have been favourite summer resorts since the last century. **Gamla Stan** (Old Town) in **Falkenberg** is well preserved and the town has Sweden's oldest pottery, and good fishing in the Åtran near the customs bridge. **Varberg** is another old seaside resort with public baths and **Societetshuset** from the 19th century, the last traditional seaside pavilion on this coast, which still provides nightly summer concerts. The coastal archipelago starts here, with many islands heading north, and Varberg is ideal for sailing and fishing.

North Halland is different from the rest of the province. Behind **Kungsbacka**, on the coast, is **Fjärrås Bräcka**, a great ridge caused by ancient glaciers, which looks over Lake Lyngern, once part of the sea, now cut off by the ridge, which has large Bronze and Iron age grave fields. The market town of Kungsbacka is surrounded by fertile ground, best known for Fjärrås radishes. Here too is **Tjlöholm** castle, built at the turn of the century in an eccentric mock-Tudor style.

This coast was once a playground for royalty and the rich, who patronized Varberg's Societetshuset. Traces remain in other seaside towns such as **Sarö**, near Kungsbacka, where Gustav V and Oskar II played tennis. In summer, the town is still a playground for Gothenburgers.

Blekinge

The four main towns of Blekinge – Sölvesborg, Karlshamn, Ronneby and Karlskrona – all lie on the southern coast of this tiny province. Between them are old fishing villages, some still used commercially to catch fish, many more now peaceful places where visitors come to fish and sail around Blekinge's lovely southern archipelago.

Inland, Blekinge is a sweep of lush green with plain, river, lake and forest. When Blekinge was ruled by Denmark, this forest was a safe hideout for many an outlaw and it is still dotted with secret small villages. Other survivors of those times are castles and ruins, such as 13th-century **Sölvesborg Slott** overlooking Sölvesborg Bay. **Sölvesborg** town is medieval, with streets and buildings to match. Several nearby fishing villages have busy, crowded harbours and curing sheds and one, **Nogersund**, is the ferry terminal for the archipelago island of Hanö. It has one of northern Europe's tallest lighthouses, and a British cemetery from the Napoleonic Wars.

In the last century, Blekinge was spa country, attracting people from many parts of Sweden. Some spas remain, such as **Jämshog**, close to Olofström, away from the coast on the Skåne border. There is an interesting old water- and sawmill on **Lake Halen**, which is also fine for bathing. Other spas have become hotels and conference venues, such as Ronneby Brunn, Sweden's largest conference, recreation and golf centres. It is well used, for Swedes have taken up golf with all the zest they earlier brought to tennis. **Ronneby** town has **Blekinge Naturum**, which holds exhibitions on the area's natural life, and the long-distance walking trail, **Blekingeleden**, which winds through the woodlands of Brunnskog. From nearby **Ekenäs**, the *Karöline* ferry leaves for **Karö**, a gentle island with near sub-tropical vegetation.

River fishing is at its best in Blekinge. Just inside the border, **Morrumån** is one of Sweden's finest salmon rivers, drawing fishers from near and far. Morrum gives a chance to see salmon at close quarters in **Laksaqvavariet** (salmon aquarium).

Built on 30 islands, Blekinge's biggest town, 17th-century **Karlskrona**, has long been connected with the Swedish navy. Its wide streets, old buildings and fortresses have a flavour of the sea, and the sail-training ship *Jarramas* is tied up at a quay. **Marinmuseet** (Maritime Museum) has a splendid collection of ships' figureheads, and Karlskrona is also excellent for hiring boats, fishing and swimming.

Many of the people who left Sweden for North America in the last century and in the early decades of this one, boarded their ships along this coast and in Gothenburg. **Karlshamn** has a touching **Emigrants'**

Monument, known as *Karl-Oskar och Kristina*, a tribute to the million who left their homes for a brave new world.

Småland

Despite its name, Småland is the biggest province in the south, a land of 5,000 lakes and as many islands along a magnificent coast. There are great forests with elk, small farms, and many wonderful areas for walking and wandering, and fine too for the annual ritual of berry-picking.

In the past, it was hard to make a living from these croft farms and a big proportion of Karl-Oskars and Kristinas, who emigrated, came from Småland. **Utvandranas Hus** (House of the Emigrants) in Vaxjö has a large archive on emigration with 2,000 Swedish-American church and other records, and a library of more than 250,000 books, much used by returning North Americans of Swedish descent and of great interest generally as a slice of history. Among the collection's founders was Wilhelm Moberg, who chronicled this Swedish exodus in his *Emigration Trilogy,* later made into two films with Liv Ullman and Max von Sydow. Växjo itself goes back further than the emigrations, to Viking times, and also has a good **Glassmuseum**.

The life of hard work and ambition that helped the emigrants also bred a talent for commerce. Two of Småland's most successful businesses are furniture-making and timber housing, both of which make use of the forests. IKEA furniture is one of the greatest success stories. Its founder, Ingvar Kamprad, opened his first shop in Amhult, where he grew up. Now, there are IKEA stores all over Europe.

At the other end of the province, Jönköping on the south of Vättern, one of the two Great Lakes, is best known as the place where the safety match was invented, its history told in **Tändsticksmuseet**. Not far away is **Huskvarna** where the smiths of old made weapons. Today, Huskvarna is a household name for domestic appliances and lawn mowers, and the old smithies are now an arts and craft centre.

The Heart of Småland

Småland's geographical centre lies somewhere in the upland country of lake and forest between Vaxjö and Sävsjö, Vetlanda and Nässjö, in the Småland highlands. Many areas have the remains of mines and ironworks and, to the west of Växjö, the best known is the 17th-century **Huseby Bruk** with ironworks, a farming museum, a natural history centre, a mill and sawmill. Most popular of all is the beautiful white castle, built by the ironworks' owners in 1844, its perfect reflection shining up from a lake. In the highlands to the north is **Kleva Gruva**, an 18th-century mine in surroundings that have changed little. Inside is **Malmkyrkan**, the ore church, and **Labyrinten** which calls for strong nerves.

Northwest of Växjo, the market town of **Värnamo** at the north end of Lake Vidösten has an open-air museum of fine old buildings, and the furniture workshop and home of the world-famous designer, Bruno Mathsson, which are open to the public. You can also board the *Vidfamme*, a Viking ship reconstruction, and sail on Lake Vidösten. Northwest, near **Anderstorp** is Småland's wild west at **High Chaparral**, a ranch-style forest park. To the south, close to Lake Draven and almost on the border with Halland, are **Smålandstenar**, five 2,500-year-old standing stone circles, claimed to be an ancient court of law.

In South Småland, the great conifer forests give way to oak and beech woods, with lush undergrowth and southerly farms reminiscent of Blekinge. Near Almhult, the turf-roofed **Råshult**, where the botanist von Linné (Linnaeus) grew up, has been restored to its original 18th-century style. With his herb garden and rich meadows thick with plants, it must have given him his first inspiration. This is marvellous waterway country with lakes, rivers and wetland where, in early summer, the calls of flocks of cranes greet the morning. Very early or at dusk, you may well see the bulky shape of an elk come down from forest to roadside. Elk safaris are run from places such as **Emanate** to watch, not shoot, the kings of the forest.

The Småland Coast and Kalmar

There are some 5,000 islands along the Småland coast, most of them on the **Blue Coast**, the northern archipelago where Småland shades into Östergötland. With fishing villages and small coastal towns, it is superb for watersports and usually easy to hire a boat.

The colourful harbour market on **Västervik**, once one of Sweden's biggest ports, is full of vegetables, flowers and newly smoked fish – a place to dawdle and meet friends. It is also a good starting point for deep-sea fishing, and has a popular **Ballad Festival** in summer. To the south, **Oskarshamn** is Småland's main ferry port to Gotland, and a shipbuilding centre. **Mönsterås** is a picturesque, old-fashioned small town, its main street laid with paving stones.

Inland, there are characteristic vast woodlands, lakes and leafy valleys, fine places to walk. North of the inland town of Högsby, a unique rock formation, **More Kastell** forms a deep ravine 10km (7 miles) long. **Aboda Klint** is the Småland coast's wintersports centre. Between central

The old city of **Kalmar** was first mentioned on an 11th-century rune. **Gamla Stan**, popular with visitors, is one of several well-conserved areas that have twice gained the city the coveted Europa Nostra award for city preservation. Kalmar is dominated by the formidable 12th-century **Kalmar Slott**, built to watch over the narrow sound between the mainland and Öland. These safe waters made Kalmar an important Baltic port for the German Hanseatic League – it was once the third largest Swedish city – and, in the time of the Vasa kings, it was the 'Key to the Realm', Sweden's southernmost fortress.

The red stone battlements and round towers now house **Slottskyrkan** (chapel) which sometimes offers a glimpse of a wedding party making use of a castle room. The castle is also the resting place of the remains of the royal ship *Kronan*, sunk in May 1676 when fighting a Dutch-Danish fleet, largely because its admiral, disturbed at lunch, turned his ship too quickly. As water gushed in, the magazine fired. Out of a crew of 842, only 41 survived the inferno. A diving team found *Kronan* in 1980 and has gradually brought up treasures such as cannon, the ship's bell, compasses, wooden statues, and homelier items such as an officer's box with his uniform intact, and some 300-year-old brandy, which bring the scene to life. The team has also made a huge find of golden coins. The divers continue to dive every year and the treasure trove is still growing.

*D*ifferent areas have their own customs, and this couple in Västervik in Småland have followed the tradition of a black wedding dress worn under the white of the wedding veil.

Pippi Longstocking Country and the North

Astrid Lindgren, author of *Pippi Långstrumpor*, to give the story its original title, was born in **Vimmerby** in the northeast of Småland. So popular are these

Småland and Kalmar on the coast is the **Kingdom of Glass**, Småland's best known asset, with some 19 glassworks lying on and around the 80km (60-mile) stretch between Växjö and Nybro to the east (see p.71).

stories that Vimmerby has become something of a place of pilgrimage. **Astrid Lindgrens Värld** (world) is made up of miniature buildings from her books, a fine way to get to know more about her characters in their authentic setting. Near Vimmerby are the settings for the *Emil* films, based on her books, and Saga Town's miniature train stops at Emil's House. Her childhood home at Näs also has exhibits.

West of Vimmerby, Eksjö town exhibits some 400 years of different architectural styles and its marvellous central buildings are now national monuments, which means that not so much as a window or cobblestone can be changed. Nearby the great **Skuragata** ravine, carved into the rock, was once known as the home of the trolls, a place where it was never warm, and now a popular walk on a hot summer day. **Nässjö**, a little further west, has the remarkable **Barkeryd**, a combination of agricultural school and glassware museum in a fine collection of typical buildings. The story is told of the local emigrant-millionaire, Sven Magnus Svensson, who made a fortune as a rancher in Texas, and named his ranch Barkeryd.

At the northernmost tip of Småland, fertile farmland edges Lake Vättern, and **Jönköping**, once a small trading post, is now the capital of northern Småland, with a busy airport. The city that invented the match (see p.272) is a modern shopping centre, the Saturday morning market place on **Västratorget** full of colour and atmosphere as well as bargains. More recent shopping palaces have grown up in the town, the most intriguing being **A6**, once the home of an artillery regiment, now dedicated to shops, boutiques and cafés.

On the east of Lake Vättern is the little town of **Gränna**, where it is worth sampling the specialities: luscious pears and *polkagrisar*, red-and-white striped, peppermint flavoured rock. Demonstrations of the process of making the sweet are given at one of the bakeries. From here, it is a short boat ride to the long narrow isle of **Visingsö**, where horse-drawn carriages take visitors up to the ruins of the 16th-century **Visingborg Slott**. There are also two churches, **Brahekyrka** and the 12th-century **Kumlaby Kyrka** with fine murals.

Småland ends at the town of **Trånas** on Lake Sommen, which offers good sailing, and tours by an old steam boat, *Boxholm II*. Also popular is the **Musik Runt Sjön Sommen** (Music Round Lake Sommen) festival in August with parades down the main street of Trånas, where visitors sit and watch from pavement cafés.

Öland

Twenty-three thousand people live on the long, narrow island of Öland, linked to Kalmar by a four-mile-long bridge. Nearly half the population are farmers, successors to some of the ancient people who have left traces in chambered tombs and other relics from 4,000 years ago. Öland is a world of its own, with a mild climate and a base of limestone that, in places, has pushed upwards forming a plateau; **Stora Alvaret** is a botanist's dream, with many rarities such as a special island potentilla, *Ölandstok*, and some 40 species of orchid.

Öland is also famous for birds, with **Ottenby Observatory** at the southern tip one of Europe's liveliest, particularly during the migration periods, when honey buzzard and clouds of other birds wing past in huge numbers. Inland, in early summer, nobody should miss the flocks of long-legged storks, grazing in fields almost like a herd of farm animals.

From a later period than the chambered tombs is the fortified village of **Eketorp**, painstakingly restored to show the life of a busy community between 300 and 1300AD. The ruined walls, some 8.5m (25ft) high, of **Gråborg**, an Iron Age fortress, are enough to indicate how big it was in its heyday.

Borgholm, the first island town over the bridge and **Borgholm Slott** are worth

*T*he long, thin island of Öland lies close to Kalmar, linked by a very long bridge. Travelling it, Borgholm Slott is the first place over the bridge and merits a visit.

lingering over. Here too is the well-known *Ölandsflickan* (Öland girl) statue, by the Swede Arvid Källstron, in front of the Town House. **Öland Zoo**, lying just below the bridge, has pony-rides and a fun-fair, as well as animals. A little to the south, the royal family's summer home, **Solliden**, opens its grounds to the public from June to August.

But Öland's most potent skyline symbol is the windmill. Once there were 2,000, now some 400 remain, including **Sanvik**, a large Dutch mill, with eight floors. Built in 1856 in Vimmerby in Småland, it was later dismantled and transported to the north of Öland. Visitors can now view the skillful engineering, and there is an unusual restaurant and café.

Gotland

Gotland's beaches are splendid, some 100km (60 miles) of fine, warm sand along the 670km- (400-mile-) long coastline, where the summer heat lingers longer on the calm Baltic waters. But Gotland has much more. Everything grows on this big island, called the 'Island of Roses and Ruins', with deep red roses in bloom as late as November. In Visby, **Almedalen** was once the Hanseatic harbour with a monopoly of Baltic trade. Now it is a wonderful garden park with aquatic plants in reed-lined pools. In summer, the harbour is stiff with the masts of visiting boats.

Visby has been an important trading centre through the centuries, which has left unexpected relics such as Byzantine painting in **Gardakyrka**. But its great trading days came during the long Hanseatic period, clearly seen in the town's architecture. An incredible 3km (2 miles) remain of the medieval walls, and there are 44 towers. By contrast, the Gothic **Church of St Catherine** is now a ruin. Within these old walls, Visby still seems medieval, full of step-gabled houses with red pantile roofs, small squares and narrow streets, with intriguing old buildings such as **Gamla Apotek** (old chemist) and the three towers of **Domkyrkan Skt Maria** (cathedral). To gain an idea of medieval Visby, have a look at the large paintings in **Fornsalen** (Gotland's museum), and at details of the island's dramatic history after the Danish King Valdemar Atterdag conquered it in 1361.

Crafts such as knitting have been part of the life of Gotland women since the Middle Ages, when they set off to sell their bundles of garments in Sweden. Today, knitting continues in sophisticated forms, and gold- and silversmithing, glass- and watchmaking, and more are carried out all along Visby's old streets. Each August, Hanseatic times are remembered in **Medeltidsveckan** (Medieval Week) when Gotlanders emerge as monks, merchants and high-born ladies, to dance, sing and visit the theatre. Gotland still has some 90 medieval churches, a tribute to the wealth of the early farmers.

Most of Gotland, like Öland, has a limestone base with the same rich plant life. In particular, the island's large limestone plateau, some 80m (250ft) high, has good soil for farming with Gotland farmers specializing in vegetables, particularly carrots, and cattle. The island has no less than four nature reserves and the **Lojstaskogen** forest is home to a herd of unique wild ponies, with two toes. Called *Russ*, they are believed to have come from Russia (*Russland* in Swedish).

Tourism is an important industry in Gotland and mainland Swedes, as well as overseas visitors, love it. Driving is easy and cycling an even better way to get around, with much to see. **Lummellundargrottorna**, north of Visby, are magnificent coastal caves with huge stalactites. Another strange rock formation off the south coast is **Hobburgsgubben** (Old Man of Hoburg), and there are two good bird islands south of Visby.

Fårö, off the north of Gotland, is a military zone but, since 1992 it has been open to tourists, apart from its southernmost tip. From Rute in Gotland you must go straight through to Fårö Kyrka, but can then roam freely. This is where Gotland has really kept a landscape that goes back into the past, with fields much as they must have been in the 17th century, animals grazing through the open pine woods, and tiny fishing hamlets. Time seems to have stopped.

Sweden's Second City and Scandinavia's Biggest Port

In this huge area, city life is contrasted by that of the small harbours and towns of the coast and the wide expanses of water of the Great Lakes, almost like seas in their own right. Not far from Denmark and mainland Europe, the west coast has always had a cosmopolitan feel and many family names date back to the days when they were brought in by a merchant or ship-owner who came to stay – even the accent is different.

More than 300 years ago, Gothenburg (*Göteborg*) was already the gateway from Sweden to the rest of the world, and to arrive by sea is still the most spectacular route into Scandinavia's biggest port. More than four million passengers a year sail through the islands of the archipelago and into the river, past Nya Elfsborg Fortress, with the Älvsborg Bridge ahead. On each side big cranes angle upwards over the cargo and passenger ships loading and un-

*G*othenburg's newly built Opera House was opened in 1994, not far from the harbour, where a decline in ship-building has brought lively new uses for buildings, and interesting sculptures.

loading at the quaysides, and an occasional small boat draws a white pencil wake across the surface. Night-time is even lovelier, the harbour buildings picked out in lights, the bridge a coloured necklace, as rhythmic flashes warn of rock or island.

Yet year by year, the harbour is changing. Faced with a decline in European shipbuilding, many old yards have closed or been altered. Today, dockside buildings have become houses and offices, and it is impossible to miss the most conspicuous new building, the 86m (300ft) red and white tower, a bit like a ship's funnel, that is Skanskakrapan. A commercial building, it also has Utkiken (lookout) on the 22nd floor, gazing wide over city and sea.

Much more elegant is Göteborg's Operan, the beautiful new opera house on the other side of Lilla Bommen harbour,

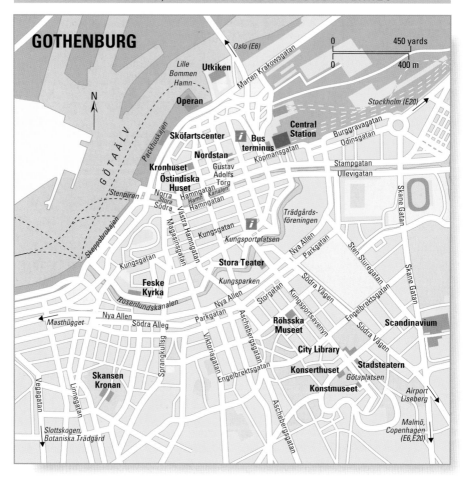

GOTHENBURG

0   450 yards
0   400 m

Oslo (E6)

Lille Bommen
Hamn~
Utkiken
Marten Krakowsgatan

N

Operan

Stockholm (E20)

GÖTA ÄLV

Packhuskajen

Sköfartscenter   **i**   Bus terminus
Nordstan
Kronhuset   Gustav
Östindiska   Adolfs
Huset   Torg
Stenpiren   Norra   Hamngatan
Stora   Hamn   kanalen
Södra   Hamngatan

Central Station

Burggravagatan
Odinsgatan
Köpmansgatan
Stampgatan
Ullevigatan

Skane Gatan

Skeppsbrokajen

Magasinsgatan
Västra Hamngatan
Kungsgatan
i
Kungsportplatsen

Trädgårds-
föreningen

Kungsgatan

Stora Teater

Nya Allen
Parkgatan
Sten Sturegatan

Skane Gatan

Feske Kyrka
Rosenlundskanalen
Nya Allen   Södra Alleg
Masthügget
Parkgatan
Nya Allen

Kungsparken

Storgatan
Södra Vägen
Kungsportsavenyn
Engelbrektsgatan
Södra Vägen

Röhsska Museet

Scandinavium

Sprangkullsg
Viktoriagatan
Engelbrektsgatan
Aschebergsgatan

City Library

Skansen Kronan
Vegagatan
Limegatan

Konserthuset
Götaplatsen
Konstmuseet

Stadsteatern

Airport
Liseberg

Aschebergsgatan

Malmö,
Copenhagen
(E6,E20)

Slottskogen,
Botaniska Trädgård

opened in October 1994. At Packhuskajen nearby, the Sjöfartscenter (Maritime Centre) will eventually have 20 historic ships, as part of Sjöfarts Museum. Today, they include the destroyer *Småland* and the submarine *Nordkaparen*.

Gothenburg:
Gustav Adolf's City

A statue of the man who founded this maritime gateway, King Gustav II Adolf, stands in the square that bears his name,

a stocky figure in his familiar wide-brimmed hat. There had been an earlier community to the north, in the shelter of the powerful Älvsborg fortress, but the Danes had captured that in 1612. By the time Gustav Adolf had amassed enough money to pay the one million Riksdaler ransom six years later, old Gothenburg was nearly derelict.

Gustav Adolf decided on builders from Holland, who built a Dutch-style city with canals, two of which remain, threading their way through the old centre. From **Kungsportplatsen**, the shallow Paddan

290

Boats, give a fine tour of the city's older areas and then move out for a harbour tour. Vintage trams are also a good way to get a first impression. In general, Gothenburg is compact and uncomplicated for getting around on foot or by the well-used buses and trams.

Gustav Adolf would recognize little of his city, near-destroyed three hundred years ago by a ferocious fire, which only the stone of the old city wall, two forts and a few buildings could resist. Part of that thick wall is still visible at **Bastion Carolus Rex**, at Kungsgatan.

Kronhuset was built in the 1640s, between the Lilla Bommen Hamn (harbour) and Gustav Adolfs Torg. In 1660, it knew a brief glory as Sweden's House of Parliament, when Karl X Gustav died suddenly in the city and his four-year-old son was proclaimed King Karl XI there. It is now **Stadsmuseet** (City Museum), and has two long 18th-century buildings (erected as city artillery workshops).

Gustav Adolf's Torg is dominated by the statue of the king who founded the city. At one side of the square, and elsewhere, a canal indicates his choice of Dutch builders.

Now **Kronhusbodarna** these attractive, turn-of-the-century shops and workshops sell craftware, old-fashioned cakes and buns, and spices, a reminder that Gothenburg was once a great importer for the spice trade.

Skansen Kronan, one of the surviving fortresses, stands in the old workers' district of Haga, some 2km (1.5 miles) from the centre, with imaginatively restored wooden houses. It is now the **Military History Museum**, filled with military memorabilia, and with a fine view of the harbour in a city famed for viewpoints. **Sjöfarts Museet** at

Masthugget traces the area's maritime history. Outside, the 44m (142ft) **Sjöfartstornet** (tower) is topped by the statue of a sailor's wife gazing far out to sea.

Gustav Adolfs Torg is also home to **Rådhuset** (City Hall) from 1672, and **Borsen**, the old Stock Exchange, now used for city functions. It is edged by the first of the big canals, Stora Hamn Kanalen, lined with fine buildings from the mercantile past. On the canal's north side, **Östindiska Huset**, the Swedish East India Company's House, has three museums: **Arkeologiska Museet** covers 9,000 years in western Sweden, while

Like many Scandinavian cities, early Gothenburg, built mainly of wood, was not exempt from devastating fires. Only Gustav Adolf's fine stone buildings and part of the wall remain today.

Etnografiska Museet and **Historiska Museet** cover Gothenburg from the Middle Ages to the turn of the century.

South of the canal, close to Lilla Torget, the 20 shops in the **Antique Market** stock collectibles from pewter to porcelain, and are also ideal for hunting rare stamps. In contrast, not far east of Gustav Adolfs Torg is **Nordstan**, one of Sweden's largest shopping centres. Here, all kinds of shops sit under an arcade over an old street which leads to Central Station and the main bus terminus.

Kungsportsavenyn

There is something very French about **Avenyn**, a broad tree-lined boulevard, with shops, hotels, cinemas and restaurants spilling out onto the wide pavement. It starts at **Kungsportsplatsen**, a big open junction with a statue of Karl IX outside Gothenburg's main tourist office. Opposite is **Saluhallen**, a market hall built in 1888, with food shops and four good cafés

selling Swedish specialities. At the far end of Avenyn is **Götaplatsen**, with Carl Milles' famous statue of *Poseidon*, with its big copper fountain. The square itself is a centre of culture, with the **City Library** and **Stadsteatern**, which gives most performances in Swedish. **Konserthuset** is the home of Gothenburg's Symphony Orchestra, and **Konstmuseet** holds an impressive collection of Scandinavian art, including many paintings from the Nordic Light period when young artists gathered at Skagen in north Denmark. P.S. Kroyer's painting of a convivial artists' luncheon *Hip, Hip, Hurrah* sums it all up, and there are many more fine examples.

In between these two squares flows a lot of Gothenburg life, with street traders and musicians entertaining the pavement crowds. Avenyn crosses over the city's second canal, **Rosenlundskanalen**, with the Paddan Boat terminus. **Stora Teatern** specializes in light opera, ballet and musical shows. It is, alas, closed in high summer. Behind the theatre, take a stroll along the banks of the canal in **Kungsparken**. **Röhsska Museet**, off to the right, has an excellent exhibition of 20th-century design and other applied art, and **Lorensberg Teater** on the left is a **Museum of Stage History**.

Liseberg and Other Parks

Liseberg, one of Scandinavia's best parks, celebrated its 70th anniversary in 1993. It was built to coincide with the Gothenburg Exhibition at a time when Scandinavia, already preserving its traditional buildings in open-air museums, took up amusement parks with enthusiasm.

 Lisebergstornet, 146m (485ft) high, gives a wide view of the city and looks down on new rides built for the anniversary. The **Juke Box**, for example, is back to the 1950s with Cadillacs, Studebakers and Chevvies, and music to match. Despite all that is new, it is hard to beat the 20-year-old **Flume Ride**, which has now thrilled more than 20 million yelling human beings as they skim over rapids and races and the last, long free fall. But Liseberg is more than rides: it has stalls of all sorts, good food and drink, concerts, musicians, jugglers, drama and more, usually finishing with fireworks.

 The popularity of **Trädgårdsforeningen**, from 1842, has even given it a nickname – **Trängår'n**. Opposite Stora Teater on Avenyn, the park has more than just beautiful gardens. There are a dozen fine statues by Scandinavian sculptors, **Palmhuset** is an elegant 1878 tropical glasshouse with camellia, water and Mediterranean houses. An outdoor stage is busy in summer, and there is a good restaurant. **Fjärilshuset** is full of tropical butterflies flying free in a lovely warm, moist climate, marvellous on a sharp day.

Botaniska Trädgården (Botanic Garden) is the biggest park, 175ha (400 acres) of greenery across four valleys, with a bamboo grove, rose and spice gardens, and a wonderful rock garden with some 4,000 specimens. Close by, **Slottskogen** (Castle Wood) with trees, hill and grass is home to **Naturhistoriska Museet** (Natural History Museum) and a zoo for children, where they can watch the seals being fed, and an ancient **Deer Park**. A worthwhile stop on the way to or from the parks is **Feske Körka**, a fine fish market housed in an old church, on the north of Rosenlundskanalen, which has an excellent fish restaurant.

Across the river in Hisingen, **Keillers Park**, donated by the wealthy Scottish engineer James Keiller, has a fine view of the city, looking back from its highest hill.

Liseberg, Gothenburg's 60-year-old park, is much more than a simple amusement park, though it has wonderful rides and entertainment. Restaurants, cafés, exhibitions, concerts of all sorts, and more to keep adults and children happy.

Sea and Pool

From Gothenburg you can spend many happy hours sailing in and around the archipelago, and along the coast. As well as Paddan Boat trips, there are longer voyages: to **Nya Elfsborg**, a fortress island,

once the city's main protection from the sea; to **Vinga**, a famous old lighthouse in the heart of the archipelago, with some of the best swimming and sunbathing; or through the archipelago to the island of **Marstrand**, with a history going back to the 13th century (see p.296). Another cruise is north to **Smögen**, with a mainland bridge and a pretty harbour, and the best shrimps on the western coast.

Evening cruises include an unusual steamship tour of the archipelago aboard s/s *Bohuslän*, a seafood cruise aboard m/s *Poseidon*, and jazz cruises wherever the fancy and the music take the ship.

Both within and outside the city are very many bathing beaches. Indoors, try **Valhalla** swimming baths, which have a world-class 50m (137ft) pool, or **Lund-bybadet** on the Hisingen (northern) side of the river, with a 25m (70ft) pool, and waterslides. Lerum's **Water Palace** some 20km (14 miles) away is an exciting adventure pool.

Gothenburg claims to be Sweden's sports capital and it does have some of the best facilities and venues. **Scandinavium** holds 12,500 in indoor comfort and, in April each year, hosts the Gothenburg International Horse Show. Next door is **Svenska Mässan**, the Swedish Exhibition and Conference Centre, booked for international conferences, trade fairs and cultural events. To the east of the city, **Ullevi Stadium** can take 45,000 for events as diverse as European Cup football, athletics, ice-hockey and rock concerts. The area also has 24 golf courses. Trotting, popular all over Scandinavia, is well catered for at **Åby Trotting Track** and is something new to try. A bus there leaves Drottningtorget one hour before the start.

The West Coast and the Great Lakes

In winter, Swedes dream of their summer *stuga* (holiday house), their boats, sailing and swimming, and eating shellfish in a small fishing town. For many, the west coast fulfils that dream, and visitors have not been slow to follow. Gothenburg has a long coast to both north and south.

The West Coast

To the north are the round, smooth-polished rocks of **Bohuslän** along an endlessly varied coast of inlets, bays, islands and

*B*ohuslän's coast has *glorious smooth rocks, ideal for sunning and swimming. The rocks and beaches are also popular with artists, who try to capture the changing mood of the sea.*

All along the west coast are hundreds of islands and small harbours, with dozens of boats and stugor *(wooden holiday houses) – summer retreats for Gothenburgers, this is Ströstad, some 150km (95 miles) north of the city.*

skerries. It stretches from Gothenburg to the **Svinesund Bridge** over the Idelfjord which marks the border with Norway, close to Strömstad. A well-signed cycle track, running north 290km (195 miles) to Svinesund gives a real close up of the countryside.

Marstrand (see p.294), a fishing community with no cars, has a busy summer harbour full of yachts and holiday sailors, and is also a town of craftworkers. For 200 years, Marstrand's **Carlstens Fästning** was a prison, and now, when the island celebrates **Fästningsdagarna** (fortress days), Lasse Maja, one of the best-known prisoners, and other charac-

ters, 'come alive' again. During regatta weeks, the islands really bustle.

Bohuslänsmuseet, in Uddevalla, is a regional museum which covers over 10,000 years of life in the province. Uddevalla's own seaside resort at nearby Gustafsberg started life in 1774, and has 200-year-old seaweed baths, as well as a modern seawater pool. It is well sheltered from the west by two large and long-inhabited islands, Orust and Tjörn. Orust's **Morlanda Kyrka** goes back to the Middle Ages and both islands have beautiful scenery and abundant beaches. The two islands are linked to each other and the mainland by the three Tjörn bridges, arching across calm waters. The great sailing event is **Tjörn Runt** in August, involving more than a thousand boats.

Further north the coast begins to be cut into long narrow fjords, and **Lysekil** is typical, set at the tip of a long peninsula. **Smögen** is among the most interesting fishing villages, with early-evening fish and prawn auctions from Monday to Thursday. Northeast of Smögen, tucked right into the

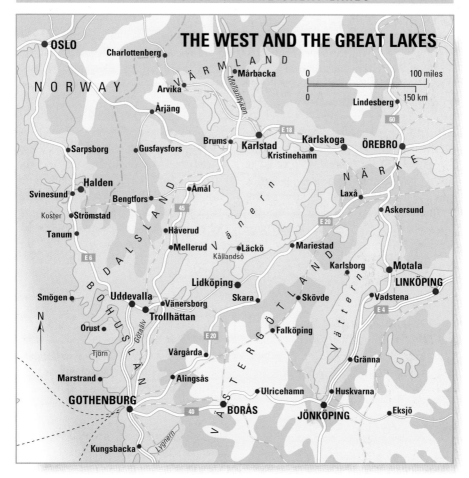

THE WEST AND THE GREAT LAKES

landward end of Åbyfjorden is **Nordens Ark**, a unique sanctuary for threatened species. It is part of Åby Säteri, a 14th-century estate, where you may catch a glimpse of a rare species such as a red panda, a Telemark cow, a forest sheep or even a snow leopard. Binoculars are a must. In all, the province has four major nature reserves.

Bohuslän's long history is proved by its marvellous Bronze Age rock carvings, the largest at Vitlycke. The best way to see these ancient carved figures and symbols is during an evening visit organized by **Vitlycke Hällristningsmuseum** (Vitlycke

Rock Carving Museum), when the characters stand out in an almost unearthly way. Also not to be missed are the sites at Tegneby, Fossum and Tanum, which also has a fine rune stone. Tanumshede has one of Sweden's best-known, and certainly its oldest inn, **Tanums Gestgiveri**, which began to serve travellers in 1663 and is now a member of the distinguished French *Relais et Châteaux* restaurateurs.

Strömstad's harbour is the heart of the town, and easily reached to the west are the isles of Koster, Syd and Nord (South and North), famous for the intensity of the

light bouncing off the sea, and wonderful plants, particularly orchids. Guided nature walks are a good way to learn. The islands are blessedly car free and accommodation is good. Back on land it is not far to the bridge at Halden and into Norway.

Around the Great Lakes

To the northeast of Gothenburg lie Sweden's Great Lakes. **Vänern** at 5,650 sq km (over 2,000 sq miles) is Sweden's largest lake and the third biggest in Europe. **Vättern** at 2,000 sq km (733 sq miles) is Sweden's second largest. The **Göta Kanal** links these two lakes on its way between Gothenburg and Stockholm.

*H*undreds of boats use
the 19th-century Göta Kanal, from
Gothenburg to Stockholm. Built as
a working canal, today the most
nostalgic voyage is on passenger-
carrying vintage boats.

In summer, these vast stretches of water are patterned with the bright shapes of boats, and the smaller dots that are swimmers. The lakes also have fine fishing with superb salmon. Even so far inland, Vänern feels like a sea, and the lake also has some 22,000 islands and skerries. Its centre is a nature reserve.

Dalsland is often called 'miniature Sweden' – a cliché perhaps, but true, for this small province to the west of Vänern varies from well-kept farms and small towns in the **Dalboslätten** area of the south, through forests which hold many elk, too shy to be often seen, and on to the sterner northern areas of **Skigdal** and the border with Värmland.

In the 1860s, the canal builder, Nils Ericsson, responsible for many Swedish railways and canals undertook the building of the **Dalsland Kanal**. In truth, Ericsson's job did not entail a massive amount of digging. It was more an intricate task of devising the best way to connect a multitude of lakes and rivers. His greatest feat was leading the

THE GÖTA KANAL

One of the classic journeys across Sweden is by way of the Göta Kanal, crossing the country between Gothenburg to Stockholm. Various parts of this canal, which flows through lakes and rivers in many places, had been built over the years but it was not until the 19th century that the industrialist Baltzar von Platen succeeded in bringing it all together. Over 22 years, 58,000 men dug out the earth, and built the locks and structures of this magnificent piece of engineering.

Today, it is largely used for leisure and pleasure, with squadrons of small boats moving slowly along its open stretches or waiting at the lock gates. One of the best ways to see the canal is by passenger boat, leaving either from Stockholm or Gothenburg. These elegant boats move gently through changing landscapes: stretches where the banks are so close, you can almost touch the trees, widening out into open country, and taking a course through the Great Lakes and on to Lake Mälaren and Stockholm.

Part of the charm is that these are 19th-century vintage boats in keeping with the canal itself, offering expeditions ashore and a convivial atmosphere on board. Swedes look on it as the holiday of a lifetime. Details from Rederi AB Göta Kanal, Hotellplatsen 2, Box 272, S-401-24 Göteborg, Sweden.

canal past what was then the wild waterfall at Håverud. Today, the canal weaves and winds its way through gentle countryside carrying dozens of summer boats by way of locks and the awesome **Håverud Aqueduct**, a network of road, rail and canal, until it reaches the lake. Håverud now has the **Dalsland Center** and **Kanalmuseet**, with a restaurant and craft shop.

There are no large communities in Dalsland. **Åmal**, on the west side of Vänern, is the only official town. Its Plantager district, between river and lake, is the essence of old Sweden, rebuilt there in 1679 after a great fire. **Stadhotellet** is so typical of an old Swedish town hotel that it has been listed as a historic monument.

Bengtfors has an open-air museum, **Gammelgården**, up the short steep climb to **Majberget** (hill), from where you can see the vessels moving on the Dalsland Kanal far below. **Stenebyskolan** (school) in Dals Långed, further south, is famous for handcrafts and teaches the old strawcraft, a

LAKE VÄNERN – A NATURALIST'S HEAVEN

Lake Vänern's size alone makes it unique in Scandinavia, almost like a sea when you are afloat. On the horizon water meets sky, and the edges give the impression of being coasts. Until 8,000 years ago, when the land began to rise sharply, Vänern was a sea inlet with salt water.

The lake has some 22,000 islands, islets and skerries, their rocky shores and beaches lined with spires of purple loosestrife and bell heather, more usual closer to the sea.

A fascinating plant and animal life on the islands is the most important aspect of the nature reserve; some 70,000 pairs of 62 breeding species of water birds make the most of the sanctuary which covers many of the islands. They include great crested grebe, turnstone and oystercatcher. Arctic terns rise high over the water with their graceful dancing flight.

For greater peace and safety, during the breeding season (1st April-31st July) three areas around the island groups are closed. Boats and people can go no nearer than 100m (110yd) and all the sanctuaries are marked. But that is no disadvantage. A lake like Vänern has islands enough for everyone.

local speciality. **Baldersnäs**, at the south of Lake Laxsjon, is an estate once owned by Carl Frederik Waern, who backed Ericsson's plan for the Dalsland Kanal. Waern planted a garden for the future and his beautiful park has some 240 different species of now fully grown trees and shrubs.

Bengtfors is also the start of a different way to travel. Some 50km (35 miles) of the **Dal Västra Värmlands Järnväg**, is a scenic railway, with special journeys to Håverud and Mellerud. It also offers a chance to try using rail cycles on the track. Pedalling through forests of birch, beech, rowan and aspen is a rare and remarkable experience, and this line goes north to Värmland. North of Mellerud is the more sedate **Pilgrimsleden**, a medieval pilgrim way, leading to Trondheim and the grave of Norway's St Olav the Holy. It now forms a 50km (35-mile) walking route through Dalsland and Värmland.

Along the Norwegian border, Värmland is wild and densely forested. There are few people but great attractions for hunter and fisher, with lakes and rivers full of trout, perch and more. One of the loveliest rivers, **Klarälven**, flows south to join Vänern at the northern town of Karlstad. It is still used to float logs to the mills and one holiday idea encourages visitors to build their own log raft and sail it peacefully down Klarälven to Karlstad. The gentle journey does lack in excitement but Swedish businessfolk swear by it and there is, in any case, white-water rafting and canoeing in plenty around Värmland.

There are many great houses in this area and Värmland can claim two of the best. **Rottneros Manor** on Lake Mellum Fryken is doubly beautiful with a perfect reflection in the formal lake. **Mårbacka** was the home of Swedish writer Selma Lagerlöf (1858-1940), the first woman to receive a Nobel prize, awarded in 1909.

*I*n 1819, the Swedish government began to build Karlsborg Slott, after the loss of Finland to Russia in the 1808–9 war. This massive castle was designed as an impregnable retreat for the Swedish government under a new defence policy. But it was never needed.

To the south of Lake Vånern, Vänersborg is close to the famous falls of **Trollhätten** on the Göta Kanal. On the east bank, **Mariestad** is conspicuous by the towering spire of its 17th-century church. **Lidköping**, the porcelain town, has a famous festival each summer. On Kållandsö peninsula is one of Sweden's finest castles, the 17th-century **Läckö Slott**.

On Vättern's west bank, **Karlsborg** is dominated by a huge early 19th-century fortress, which has **Slutvärnet**, said to be the longest building in Europe at some 680m (2,230ft). The east bank holds Motala, close to the old spa of Medivi Brunn, and the ancient town of the Holy Birgitta, **Vadstena**, with a beautiful 14th-century church. A member of a noble family, Birgitta had married and borne six children before she renounced the temporal life to found the Order of St Birgittine in Rome. After her death, her remains were brought back to Vadstena. Today the spiritual and temporal meet here again, in Birgitta's church and Vadstena Slott, the great fortress built by King Gustav Vasa 150 years later.

They Call it the 'Folklore Country', at the Heart of Sweden

The seven provinces in this chapter cover the true geographical centre of Sweden, though for historical reasons Swedes are inclined to place it further south. It is a broad band from the Norwegian border to the Gulf of Bothnia. Dalarna is often referred to as 'folklore country', because it has clung most strongly to Sweden's old traditions. Here, more than anywhere else, the national costume can be seen worn as a natural way of dressing, and nowhere celebrates *Midsommar* in greater style. Inland, Härjedalen and Jämtland have great sweeps of forest and turbulent rivers. Rising mountains in the west continue the upland ridge that begins in Dalarna.

The whole central area of Sweden is a mixture of landscapes that sum up the country: high cliffs, long beaches, field and pasture, hills and lakes, sometimes dramatic, sometimes calm. The great rivers – Ljusnan, Ljungan, Indalsälven, Ångermanälven – flowing from the western mountains to the Gulf of Bothnia, have long been important for travel and trade, carrying down the timber, ore and other produce which meant prosperity.

With the nickname of the 'folklore country', traditional dress has never died out in Dalarna. Many costumes, and even more the jewellery, are handed down from mother to daughter.

Dalarna – Land of Folklore

The heart of Dalarna is Lake Siljan, which legend claims was created by a meteorite thousands of years ago. Around its calm waters are old lakeside villages of wooden houses, painted a particular dark red. At *Midsommar*, decorated maypoles rise high and local people and hundreds of guests dance through the long light night, encouraged in their revelry by abundant food, *aquavit* and beer.

The old church-boat tradition remains around the lake and, on special summer Sundays, local people in their Sunday dress row church-boats across to **Rättvik Kyrka** at the southeastern end. It is a reminder of the times when worshippers from outlying farms found it the easiest

303

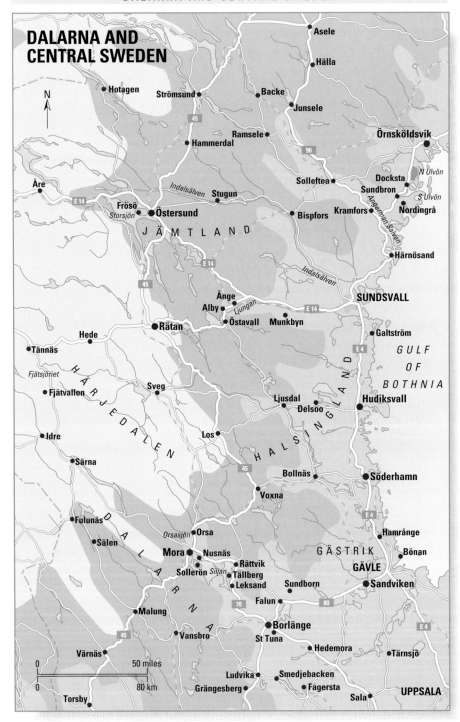

DALARNA AND
CENTRAL SWEDEN

N

Asele

Hälla

Hotagen   Strömsund   Backe

Junsele

45

Ramsele   Örnsköldsvik
Hammerdal

90

Åre   Solleftea   Docksta   N Ulvön
                                                     Sundbron
Indalsälven Stugun   S Ulvön
Frösö   Kramfors   Nordingrå
Storsjön Östersund   Bispfors

E 14

J Ä M T L A N D

E 14   Indalsälven   Härnösand

45

Ånge   SUNDSVALL
Alby   Ljungan   E 14
Hede   Östavall   Munkbyn
Rätan   Galtström
Tännäs
                                                   E 4   G U L F
Fjätsjöriet   H   O F
Fjätvallen   Å   Sveg   B O T H N I A
              R   Ljusdal   Hudiksvall
Idre   J   Delsoo
              E   Los
Särna   D   H
              A   A
              L   L   45
              E   S   Bollnäs   Söderhamn
Fulunäs   N   D   I
              D   A   N   Voxna
Sälen   Orsasjön Orsa   G   Hamränge
              A   L
Mora   Nusnäs   N   A   GÄSTRIK   Bönan
        Sollerön Siljan Rättvik
              R   Tällberg   GÄVLE
              N   Leksand   Sundborn   Sandviken
Malung   A   Falun
                         70   80
                  Vansbro   Borlänge   E 4
Värnäs   St Tuna
                                   Hedemora   Tärnsjö
0   50 miles
                         Ludvika   Smedjebacken
0   80 km   Grängesberg   Fagersta
Torsby   Sala   UPPSALA

304

way to reach the church, built in the 13th century. A test of local knowledge is to try to identify the locations of some of its interesting paintings of biblical characters, in local costumes and settings.

Each one of the lakeside towns has its own character. **Tällberg** stands high, looking out over a sweeping vista of water and mountain. This pretty community also has some of the best-preserved wooden buildings. **Nusnäs** is the home of the ***Dalahest*** (Dalarna horse), a brightly painted, carved wooden horse, which has become almost a symbol of Sweden. Once a peasant craft, they are now handmade in their thousands in a large workshop, open for summer visitors who can watch the carving and painting and take home a shiny, red horse.

At **Mora** on the northern neck of land where **Siljan** joins **Lake Orsa**, **Zorngården** was the home of the 19th-century painter, **Anders Zorn**, a member of the National Romantic movement. His studio is as he left it with a vivid atmosphere of the man. Another Dalarna painter, **Carl Larsson**, lived south of the lake at **Sundborn**, near Falun. He concentrated largely on 19th-century domestic scenes. Many copies of his works hang in Swedish homes all over the country and Sundborn is now a museum. There are guided tours

LAKE SILJAN

True or not, many claim that Dalarna's Lake Siljan was the result of a giant meteorite. According to legend, this monster crashed on the primeval earth, over 350 million years ago, right in the centre of what is now Dalarna.

Siljan holds the island of Sollerön, where the church-boats (see p.303) are made, said to be direct descendants of the Viking longships of a thousand years ago. To the north, Siljan is divided from the next stretch of water, Lake Orsa, by a strip of land where the town of Mora stands, but it seems likely that at one time the two were linked as a single lake.

Gesundaberget, on the west side of the lake, is the best place for a view of Lake Siljan. The typical villages of old Dalarna are scattered round the mountain, the focal point of Dalarna's *Midsommar* celebrations.

It is fair to say that no scientist has yet confirmed this interesting theory of the origins of Lake Siljan, but, if the story is true, Lake Siljan's birth must have been a cataclysm of deafening sound with flying stone and earth, very different from today when everything is peaceful at the heart of Dalarna.

*S*undborn in south Dalarna was where one of Sweden's best-loved painters, Carl Larsson, worked on his distinctive pictures.

of the house, and of **Sundborn Kyrka** and its parsonage. Both also have collections of Larsson paintings.

Borlänge, once full of heavy industry has now turned to high-tech enterprises. It was the home town of the famous tenor, Jussi Björling. In 1994, nearly 35 years after his death in 1960, Borlänge inaugurated an international tenor competition in his honour, and opened a new **Jussi Björling Museum**, with many of his costumes, and a fascinating compilation of early films and tapes. The previous Björling Museum had been part of **Gammelgården**, an open-air museum nearby with

some 30 traditional buildings. Just out of the town is **Stora Tuna Kyrka**, a large, lofty church, built as the cathedral of Dalarna in 1469. It is a marvellous setting for a concert, during the competition week, with members of Björling's musical family taking part.

Siljan's main island of **Sollerön**, which holds some early Viking graves, also builds church-boats. On the western side not far from Mora, the 514m (1,650ft) heights of **Gesundaberget** tower over the lake. Some way up is the unlikely home of **Santaworld**, a mix of animals, toy workshops and a resident Santa.

At the extreme north of the lakes, **Orsa** has **Grönklitt Bear Sanctuary**, in a rising area of trees and rivers. King of these free-roaming bears is the giant Micke, who weighs 450kg (850lb) before hibernation. From a secure footpath and outlook ramps, it is easy to see bears and wolves going about their daily lives in a natural environment, undisturbed despite the visitors' vocal delight at the tiny, playful cubs.

At the southern end of Lake Siljan, **Leksand**'s open-air theatre gives annual performances of *Himlaspelet*, an old mystery play. At the southernmost end of Dalarna, amid a lovely natural landscape, Ludvika and Smedjebacken bring to life the industrial and mining past. One

At one time, bears were relatively common in north Sweden. Today, the best place to see them wild is in a National Park, such as Sonfjället in Härjedalen, or almost wild at Grönklitt Bear Sanctuary in Dalarna, where they roam freely.

example is Grängesberg's recreation of its old harbour, with jetties and warehouses, and **Järnvägsmuseet** (railway museum) with old steam engines that once pulled the heavy iron-ore trains. There are still some opulent mine-owners' old houses around Ludvika, which also has a mining museum. Many of these big houses have been turned into hotels and restaurants giving Dalarna as a whole a fine selection of places to eat.

Though parts of Dalarna are a paradise for industrial archaeologists (see p.74), it is a land of contrasts. Everywhere are huge open spaces, fertile farms in the south and rising hills to the northwest, where **Idre** and **Sälen** are popular for skiing in winter, and for walking, climbing and other outdoor pursuits in summer.

Coast and Countryside

Though Dalarna has the folklore title, Hälsingland, further north, holds Hälsingehambo, Sweden's biggest folk-dancing competition. Every summer hundreds of dancers take part in a gruelling long-distance dance from north of Bollnäs to Järvsö.

*H*ambo dancers dance along a road from place to place. Most remarkable of these long-distance dances is the Hålsingehambo, from Bollnäs to Hårgaberget mountain near Järvsö.

HÄLSINGEHAMBO

All along the route from Bollnäs to Järvsö, hundreds of people turn out to watch the 3,000 dancers, decked out in local costumes, who take part in the Hälsingehambo. But not all of them may know that this happy July event commemorates a much sadder story from bygone days.

Long ago, so the tale goes, at a village festival near Härgaberget, the local mountain, a strange fiddle-player began to wander and play among the crowds. So beautiful was his music that the dancers followed as he led them through the countryside, rather like the Pied Piper of Hamlin.

By nightfall, they were exhausted but still could not resist this haunting music when he took the steep way up to the top of Härgaberget. There they continued to dance, round and round, as the night hours slowly passed. By morning, nothing was left but their skulls. They had danced to the devil's tune and, so they say, all that remains of their whirling bodies is a white ring in the stone, near the summit of Härgaberget.

Hälsingland is the middle of the four coastal provinces. From the south, first comes Gästrikland, very small for Sweden, with its main town, **Gävle**. The town's **Järnvägsmuseum** delights railway buffs, with an 1874 coach of the veteran traveller King Oscar II on display. Some 80km (50 miles) north is the **Jädrås-Tallas** vintage railway, like many others, once used for hauling timber.

This is a land of many industries: timber, mining and, in the south, steel giants such as the world-famous **Sandviken** company, with headquarters here. In Sweden, spaces are so large that industry is almost hidden and does little to spoil the countryside. To a visitor, these central heartlands are simply the beauty of hills, mountains, and farming and forest country, where you can drive for miles in quiet peace.

The simplest way north is the E4 road, heading north along the Gulf of Bothnia, eating up the long Swedish miles. It passes close to **Söderhamn** and **Hudiksvall**, the two main coastal towns of Hälsingland, and on to **Sundsvall** and **Härnösand** on the Medelpad–Ångermanland border. The northernmost town of this part of the coastline is **Örnsköldsvik**, known to its many visitors as Övik. Some 550km (385 miles) north of Stockholm, Övik is, nevertheless, slightly less than halfway up the coast to the Finnish border.

Many small fishing villages offer the great eating delight of Baltic herring, served with dill and boiled potatoes, so beloved of Scandinavia. Not far north of Gävle, herring from Bonan, known as *böckling* takes the prize when smoked over wood to a delicious gold.

Söderhamn started as a 17th-century army town, with an armoury that is now a museum. To the west **Bollnäs** is the home of a favourite sweet, a peppermint once boiled in local kitchens. Today, the factory is as modern as any but visitors can still see sweets boiled traditional-style in the old kitchen.

North from Bollnäs, the Ljusnan valley is the start of the **Hälsingehambo**, which begins early one June morning, and sees some 3,000 dancers rise to take part in this severe test of stamina and feet (see above). There is more music on another occasion, at **Delsbo** a little further north, where hundreds of fiddlers in costume gather together to play at the annual fiddlers' rally, **Delbostämmen**.

Further north is the very centre of Sweden. On the E14, from Sundsvall inland to Ånge, **Flataklocken** rises 465m (1,500ft). There is a road to the top and a wheelchair ramp to the observation tower which enables almost everyone to enjoy the wonderful panorama that stretches for miles around. The village of Munksbysjön, near the foot of the hill, hands out a certificate as proof that you have been to the middle of the country. Another natural feature between Sundsvall and Ånge is the huge cave, **Snödsallegrottan**. The way in is through a deep cavity down to a large cavern with several passages off. Useful assets are good footwear, preferably boots, and a torch. Outside, the view from the top of the cave goes on for miles. To get there, turn north in Tålje. The road is signed.

Not all the things to explore are natural. The ironmasters who prospered in these regions have also left a legacy in many places, such as **Galtström Bruk** (ironworks), also on the Ljungan river to the west of Sundsvall. Galtström was built in 1673 and closed in 1917, and the whole community, from blast furnace and foundry to *herrgård* (manor house) and workers' dwellings, is in fine condition. In fact, Galtström was authentic enough to feature in Swedish television's series *The Timber Barons*.

On the coast, **Sundsvall** is largely stone, the result of the Great Fire of 1888 which destroyed half the town. In the rebuilding, the timber barons determined to show off and built a town that still reflects their wealth. Many of these Gulf of Bothnia towns suffered more from periodic Swedish–Russian conflicts. In 1721, the Russians raided **Härnosand**, at the mouth of Ångermanälven. Few of the original buildings survived except **Östanbacken**'s well-preserved wooden houses. For the best vista of town and harbour, climb **Murberget** (hill), which has a traditional open-air museum, on a par with Stockholm's Skansen, with farm, school, church, store and grazing animals in summer.

Though the mineral and timber industries prospered, they were not exempt from Sweden's 1930s labour troubles. In May 1931, several thousand demonstrated against the hunger and misery of their lives. Very uncharacteristically for Sweden, soldiers fired on the crowd, killing four strikers and a woman bystander. A statue at Lunde, at the southern end of the beautiful Sandbrön (bridge) commemorates their deaths. It was erected in 1981, sculpted by Lenny Clarhall, who began work as a carpenter and is known for his forceful realism.

On the same side of the river, a few miles north, is **Kramfors**. This is Sweden's accordionists' town, with an annual festival, founded by the musician Kalle Grönstedt. It is also the home town of Frans Berwald (1796-1868), one of the earliest Swedish composers, a violinist and prodigy, who played in Stockholm's court chapel when still a child.

A part of this beautiful coast that deserves to be better-known starts at **Härnosand**. The **Höga Kusten** (High Coast) stretches north to Örnsköldsvik, with the **Nordingrå** peninsula at its heart. The simplest detour is probably to turn right off the E4 at Gallsäter into this coast of high cliffs dropping sheer to inlets and bays, with offshore islands. There is fine swimming and in some of the small villages, good homely restaurants serving *husmanskost* (home cooking).

The High Coast ends at Örnsköldsvik (Övik), where **Varvsberget** rises out of the town itself – a hill from which to see great wide stretches of the Gulf of Bothnia and the nearby islands. It is also the start of **Höga Kustenleden**, a 130km (90-mile) long, spectacular walking route south along the High Coast.

Another challenging height is **Skuleberget**, its 300m (1,000ft) rising straight and sudden just before Docksta, in

Skuleskogen National Park. At the foot is **Skula Naturum**, an exhibition and information centre, with a cable car from this southern end to the top. This is the easy way up but Skuleberget is also Scandinavia's only climbing trail, an idea which came from the Alps. The route is for people who already climb and Naturum hires out helmets, harness and safety equipment. The summit café has a fine outlook to the islands and their old villages.

Much of the old fishing way of life has gone from the islands but, from Övik, it is still possible to see some genuine fishing villages on Ulvön and Trysunda islands. They date back to the times when island people worked as fishermen-farmers, and there are a still a few beautiful old fishing chapels with original murals.

Forest, Mountain and River

Härjedalen and Jämtland, with the great rivers that rise in the mountains close to Norway, have some magnificent waterfalls. Most famous is **Tannforsen**, with a drop of 309m (1000ft), a seemingly continuous wall that later becomes Indalsälven. Further north, **Hällingsåfallet** has bitten into its surrounding rock face for thousands of years, to form Europe's largest filled canyon. Many of these northern rivers make for thrilling white-water rafting, with canoeing and fishing on river and lake.

The mountains of Härjedalen and Jämtland offer winter skiing and, in summer, are ideal for walking, mountain-biking, climbing or pony-trekking. Forests are full of delicate small flowers and abundant wild berries – *hjorton* (cloudberries), raspberries, blueberries, lingon – all prized in the great Swedish pastime of picking berries.

But the most thrilling spectacle is the animals, some no longer found in other parts of Sweden, mostly well protected, though controlled hunting is permitted in some areas. Otters and beavers live in river and lake, pine martens in the trees, and well hidden in the remoter areas lurk lynx and wolverines. Birders should look out for ravens, eagles and some unusual species of

310

 owl. **Sonfjället National Park** in Härjedalen, to the west of road 84 and northwest of Sveg, has Sweden's largest population of wild bears, and runs expeditions to see them. King of them all is the elk. A bull, which can weigh up to 500kg (1,100lb), is a magnificent sight but you need to move quietly to get close. More likely is a view from a car, as elk may come

Some of the most beautiful upland scenery lies in central Sweden with the mountains rising behind. Streams and waterfalls bubble down to the rivers. The pine forests are full of interesting animals. It is a paradise for walking, canoeing and camping.

down to the roadside at sunset or sunrise. 'Beware Elk' is a familiar road sign.

Härjejdalen has a lot of 'highests': it is Sweden's highest province, with the highest treeline, the highest village, **Tännäs**, with the highest church, and the highest A-road over the **Flatruet** plateau, at some 1,796m (5,900ft), the highest peak south of the Arctic Circle.

The way into the heights is from the south on road 45, or east–west from Hudiksvall on road 84, along the Ljusnan river. The two roads intersect at **Sveg**, Härjedalen's main town, which has an open-air museum, **Gammelgården**, made up of some 20 old buildings. The railway arrived at Sveg in 1909, marked by the **King's Stone**, and the bridge over the waters of the Ljusnan at Sveg is a masterpiece of railway building. Over these long distances, rail has advantages over road as a relaxed way to travel, with good links from the south. For railway connoisseurs, **Wildmarksexpressen** (Wilderness Express) heads north from Östersund (see p.322).

Storsjön, Sweden's fifth biggest lake, lies right in the centre of a huge area, with the old island of **Frösön** connected by bridge to the main town of **Östersund**, founded by King Gustav III. Frösön was named after the goddess of fertility, Frö or Frej, a reminder that the islanders long worshipped the old Norse gods. At the Frösön end of the bridge, the Vikings left

their northernmost rune stone, some 1,000 years old. **Frösö Kyrka** was built over a sacrificial grove of the ancient Æsir religion. Today, it is popular for weddings. Every summer, Frösön hosts the much-loved open-air opera, *Arnljot*, a Viking story. It was composed by one of Östersund's most famous sons, Wilhelm Peterson-Berger (1867-1942) who lived on Frösön. His other works include five symphonies. Frösön also has 500 animals in a zoo and tropical house. At 468m (1,560ft) above sea level, **Frösö Tornet** (tower) gives superb views of the area all around.

Storsjön is also famous for having its own monster on the lines of Scotland's Loch Ness monster. There have been many claims of sightings but no confirmed proof, despite the possibilities offered by s/s *Thomée*, a coal-fired steamship, to look out for a beast like a snake between 6m (20ft) and 12m (40ft) long, with humps and a small head. **Länsmuseet** (county museum) has a set of monster-catching equipment from the 1930s.

On the western edge, close to Norway, the region's mountains rise to near 1,800m (close to 6,000ft) and give excellent summer mountain trekking, while skiing can last well into summer on the high peaks. Härjedalen has long been a favourite mountain area and has a famous old mountain hotel at **Fjällnäs**, and classic mountain resorts such as **Tänndalen**, **Bruksballarna** and **Ramundberget**, reached via road 84 from Sveg.

More recent is **Åre**, further north in Jämtland, a modern resort where the Swedes were eager to host the 1994 Winter Olympics. Though the Games went to Norway, skiing on the Åre slopes is first class, with **Åreskutan**, 1,240m (4,500ft) towering above the village. A funicular railway takes skiers from the town centre halfway up the mountain, and there is then a cable car to the summit.

All around are white-tipped mountains. Norway to the west is only a couple of lakes and the peak of Skäkerfjällen away. Heading north some 100km (70 miles) as the crow flies will bring you to the Arctic Circle.

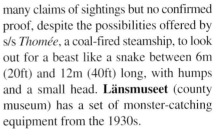

*T*he ancient island of Frösön on Storsjön (lake), close to Östersund, was a Viking stronghold, with a strong tradition of the old Æsir religion. The lake was reputed to have its own monster, like that at Loch Ness, Scotland.

The Long and Lovely Road North

The vast open spaces of Norrland, to use the old name, make up more than a quarter of Sweden, and cover the provinces of Västerbotten and Norrbotten, reaching east to the Gulf of Bothnia and west to the wild stretches of Lappland bordering Norway. A third of the area is beyond the Arctic Circle and the sun never sets for over two months in summer. In winter, midday has a sort of transparent darkness. Before travelling here, it is hard to imagine the remoteness of Norrland, the long moorland miles between small communities, the rail track marching ahead through heathland, scrub and forest. Always, there are lakes, some no more than ponds, others stretching away, with sudden glimpses of mountains to the west, where the great rivers rise before plunging downwards and rushing east to the Gulf of Bothnia.

In this region, larger coastal towns stand at the mouths of the rivers – Umeälven, Skellefteälven, Piteälven, Luleälven, Kalixälven, Torneälven – because fast-moving water was their lifeline, bringing down ore, timber and other materials for the mills. Later, the roads followed the rivers' example.

Today, river, lake and tributary still serve local needs, providing electricity in such abundance that the Umeälven's 17 power stations alone could supply the whole of Sweden for two weeks. But they also give superb sport fishing, canoeing, white-water rafting and more. The sheltered waters of the Gulf of Bothnia, with its islands and headlands, are much warmer than you might expect so far north, and attract visitors by the thousand.

*B*eautiful silver jewellery goes well on the traditional dress worn by this Sami woman. One of the great events of the North is the Sami Market in Jokkmokk each February.

The Gulf's Long Coast

Norrland's biggest town is **Umeå**, the first over the border from Ångermanland to the south. It was another of Gustav Adolf's 17th-century towns, part of his great expansion north. Today, the population is around 70,000 and Umeå is Norrland's only university city. Close by is its port, Holmsund, a terminal for the Wasa Line's

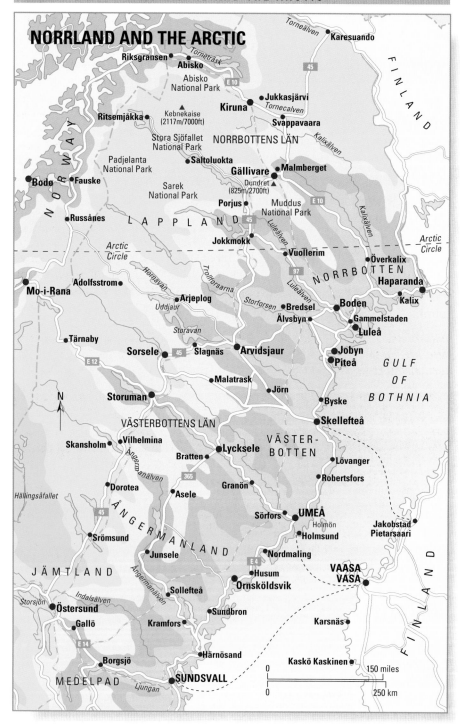

NORRLAND AND THE ARCTIC

Riksgransen
Abisko
Torneträsk
Torneälven
Karesuando

45

Abisko
National Park

E 10

Jukkasjärvi

Kiruna
Tornecalven

Ritsemjåkka
Kebnekaise
(2117m/7000ft)

Svappavaara

Stora Sjöfallet
National Park
NORRBOTTENS LÄN

Kalixälven

Padjelanta
National Park
Saltoluokta

Gällivare
Malmberget

Bodø
Fauske
Sarek
National Park
Dundret
(825m/2700ft)

Porjus
Muddus
National Park
E 10

Russånes
L A P P L A N D

Luleälven
45

Jokkmokk

Kalixälven

Arctic
Circle
Vuollerim
Arctic
Circle

Överkalix

97

N O R R B O T T E N

Adolfsstrom

Hornavan

Mo-i-Rana
Arjeplog

Uddjaur

Trollforsarna

Storforsen

Luleälven

Haparanda

Kalix

Bredsel
Boden

Älvsbyn
Gammelstaden

Luleå

Tärnaby

Storavan

Sorsele
45
Slagnäs
Arvidsjaur

Jobyn
Piteå

GULF

Malatrask
Jörn

OF

N
Storuman
Byske

BOTHNIA

VÄSTERBOTTENS LÄN
Skellefteå

Skansholm
Vilhelmina

Ångermanälven

VÄSTER-
BOTTEN

Bratten
Lycksele
Lövanger

365
Robertsfors

Dorotea
Asele
Granön

Hällingsåfallet

Å N G E R M A N L A N D

45

Sörfors
UMEÅ
Holmön
Jakobstad
Pietarsaari

Strömsund

Ångermanälven

Holmsund

Junsele
Nordmaling

JÄMTLAND
E 4

VAASA
VASA

Husum

Storsjön
Indalsälven
Sollefteå
Ornsköldsvik

Östersund

Gallö
Kramfors
Sundbron
Karsnäs

E 14

Borgsjö
Härnösand

Kaskö Kaskinen

MEDELPAD
Ljungan
SUNDSVALL

0   150 miles

0   250 km

year-round ferries to Vaasa, the nearest town on the Finnish coast.

Like many of these coastal towns, Umeå has had its share of strife. In one of the periodic wars between Sweden and Russia, around a thousand Umeå houses were destroyed and in the 1808-9 war, which resulted in Sweden's losing Finland, Russian soldiers crossed the ice in a surprise attack and Umeå suffered greatly. The nearby harbour of Ratan, popular with visiting boats, still has old bullets and bullet holes stuck fast in its walls. But Umeå's greatest destruction came in the mighty fire of 1888, which nearly wiped out the town. An unexpected bonus from this event is that Umeå then planted avenues of trees as fire breaks, which add to the charm of a city which has interesting architecture in both wood and stone.

Gamlia is one of Sweden's oldest open-air museums. Opened in 1920, it includes **Västerbotten Museum**, with a comprehensive Sami (Lapp) exhibit, and local buildings of note, such as the marvellous Sävar Farm, once involved in the 1808-9 war. It now has a restaurant, a school and a bakehouse. **Helena Elisabeth Kyrka** is an old fishing chapel from 1802, popular for weddings. Holmön, just off the coast, is a large and sunny offshore nature reserve, almost free of cars, and with bicycles to get around. A little to the west, **Stornorrofors** is one of the biggest of the river's 17 power stations, with a drop of 75m (240ft).

Nearby are Våsterbotten's only rock carvings, traced out some 5,000 years ago by an ancient people. Up river, **Klabböle**

*U*meå *was founded by Gustav II Adolf in 1522. Today it has wide streets, trees and fine buildings, and Sweden's northernmost university.*

power station was the first on the river, built in 1899 and still in full operation. It now has an energy centre, to show how the station operates.

As a university city, Umeå is also the area's main cultural centre, and its highly successful **Chamber Music Festival** is now linked with the Finnish Korsholm Festival at Vaasa across the Gulf of Bothnia, and they share a single musical director.

Heading north, the E4 and some of its small side roads lead to many reminders of old industries. Some, like **Robertsfors Bruk** which had its first blast furnace in 1759, have become museums. A preserved section of the 18th-century buildings traces industrial development to today's hi-tech industries such as tool-making, and the manufacture of synthetic diamonds and high-pressure ceramics, which bring prosperity to the small town of Robertsfors.

Church villages date back to the days when parishes were huge and a church might serve several distant communities. Between Umeå and Skelleftea, **Lovanger Kyrkbyn** is a fine example. Its restored church cottages now house visitors, and there is a 17th-century Västerbotten farm.

Skellefteå, mainly industrial, has **Nordanå**, a cultural centre with a theatre, exhibition rooms and, as always, an open-air museum of buildings from the past. There is an outdoor dance floor and summer theatre by the river. Next door is **Bonnstan Kyrkbyn**, a 17th-century church village with 400 rooms, and the summer café at **Kyrkholmen** is somewhere to linger. **Lejonströmbro** (bridge), from 1737, is Sweden's longest wooden bridge, and Skellefteå's old **Landskyrka** is a very large neo-classical church. Its greatest treasure is the **Skellefteå Madonna,** some 800 years old, and one of the few Romanesque madonnas left in northern Europe.

All along this coast, often nicknamed the 'Norrland riviera' for its warm waters and mild summer climate, are many **havsbad**, sea-bathing beaches with good facilities. These are also very popular with northern Norwegians who drive down the old Silver Road (Road 95), which once brought silver ore from Norway's Nasafjäll mines. **Byske Havsbad**, just north of Skellefteå, is one of the best, with a pool and countless activities.

From Skellefteå to **Piteå**, over the border in Norrbotten, the E4 clings close to this beautiful coast, with wonderful views of islands and headlands. Apart from the original peninsula, **Ojebyen**, which has a church village from 1621, Piteå is largely devoted to paper and pulp mills but has good beaches, such as **Pite Havsbad**, with cabins and a campsite.

As a change from the coast, road 474 out of Piteå leads to Älvsbyn, then via Bredsel to **Storforsen**, spectacular falls with an 80m (265ft) straight drop, one of Europe's highest. Back at Älvsbyn, take road 356 to **Boden**, a fortress built after the 1808-9 war and now a large garrison town. **Garnisonsmuseet** (Garrison Museum) is one of the best. Near the border with Finland, parts of Norrbotten are military areas and entry may be restricted. Road signs give details. From Boden, highway 97 follows Luleälven's course to Luleå.

Luleå has a wonderful setting, surrounded on three sides by water, and comes alive in summer when life moves outside, onto the 300 islands of the Luleå archipelago, superb for sailing and watersports. Luleå was also founded by Gustav II Adolf but on a site 10km (6 miles) up the estuary. That first harbour gradually silted up and became too small for the traffic across the Gulf and, some 30 years later, Luleå moved to its present position. **Gammelstad**, on the original site, is now a church village, with 30 old farms and 450 cottages, clustered round a 15th-century granite church.

It goes without saying that wherever you go along this coast or up the river courses, wildlife is all around and **Gammelstadsviken**, 5km (3 miles) from Luleå, is a paradise for ornithologists, with some 200 nesting species. **Ballingeberget Nature Reserve**, 10km (6 miles) away is the same for botanists, with some 200 plant species on its Ice Age moraine and scree. It is particularly famous for orchids. **Selet Mill**, once a busy mill, also has a rich flora and is a haven for many types of owl.

From Luleå, the E4 passes close to the northernmost waters of the Gulf at **Töre-**

*L*uleå today is surrounded by water, boats and islands. The old town, Gammelstad, founded by Gustav II Adolf lies 10km (6 miles) further inside the estuary and has 30 old farms and many cottages.

fjärden with its deepwater harbour, and **Kalix** where the church goes back to the 15th century, though only the altarscreen and font survived a fierce early fire. Close to the border, it was later ransacked by Russians, who stabled horses there in the 1808-9 war. Also from this turbulent time are graves of Russians and Finns, as well as Swedes.

Kalix on Kalixälven, with its archipelago, claims boldly to have some of the best fishing in Europe. Many of these northern rivers could make the same claim, not just for salmon but also for trout, perch, pike and *röding* (arctic char). Kalix also holds **Midnattsolstampen**, an annual cycling event in June, some 150km (105 miles) under the Midnight Sun. North on Kalixälven is the Sami town of **Överkalix** (see p.320). When the treaty that ended the 1808-9 war left Sweden no access to Tornio at the mouth of Torneälven, the Swedes promptly built **Haparanda** on the west bank. For nearly 200 years, it has been Sweden's most easterly town, the gateway to unencumbered freedom in the north of Norrland.

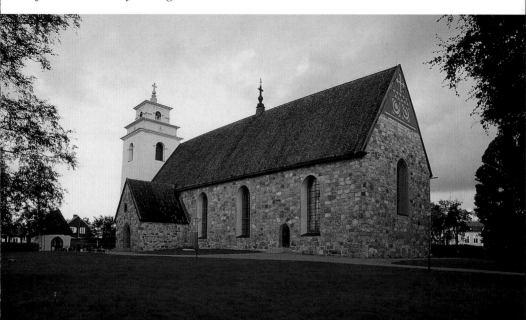

Norrland's Arctic Way – the Gulf of Bothnia to Norway

Almost all this route lies above the Arctic Circle through a terrain and a way of life that is distinctively northern. The Gulf of Bothnia's remarkably warm waters are good for swimming and watersports. Dramatic northern rivers are also fine for sport fishing, white-water rafting and canoeing. Inland, apart from two smallish towns, Gällivare and Kiruna, settlements are small but many have characteristic open-air museums of traditional buildings, similar to Skansen in Stockholm, though usually smaller.

The route starts in Luleå (see p.318) at the northern end of the Gulf of Bothnia, passes through Sami (Lapp) country close to the Finnish border, slants northwest through Lappland to the northern centre of Kiruna, past lake and mountain to Riksgränsen, and on into Norway.

Luleå is surrounded on three sides by water with an archipelago of 300 islands. Norbotten Museum is the area's main museum, well-known for Sami collections, probably the most comprehensive anywhere. Luleå was founded some 16km (10 miles) away from its present site, at a place now called Gammelstad. It is a typical northern kyrkbyn (church village) with a 15th-century church, surrounded by farms and 450 cottages. Gammelstadsviken (bay) is heaven for naturalists and bird-watchers, with more than 200 species visiting at any one time.

After turning away from the coast onto the E10 at Tore, with its deep-water harbour and fine church, Överkalix is typically Sami, with a fine new hotel built in traditional style, a 1940s church, and magnificent 16m (50ft) waterfalls where the rivers Änge and Line meet. The best views are to be had from Brännaberget, and the best taste is braenna (blackcurrant wine), named after the mountain and made in Överkalix.

Gällivare/Malmberget is two communities in one with a huge open-cast mine at Gropen, where a tour drives deep into the awesome, grey pit. The mining museum on site shows 250 years of mining history. Kåkstan, a well-restored area, shows how the first Swedish settlers lived. The view from Dundret at 825m (2,800ft) stretches over this wild area covering one-eleventh of Sweden. Its lower terrace houses a big holiday centre. This far north the sun never sets from May to July.

Take the minor (western) route out of Gällivare for Kiruna. The names show that this is Sami territory, with the old Sami school at Killingi, and Sami cabins where the pupils lived, now used by visitors. Kaitum's Dag Hammarsköld Memorial Chapel commemorates the former UN Secretary General, killed in a mysterious African air crash. This is a good area for watersports such as shooting the rapids and canoeing.

Kiruna is the biggest Norrland town with some 27,000 inhabitants, and a huge mine. Underground bus tours show the machinery at work, like huge dinosaurs. Hjalmar Lundbohmsgården celebrates Kiruna's founder, Hjalmar Lundbohm, who encouraged settlers, planned the town, and educated the children (see p.325). West of Kiruna is Kebnekaise, at 2,117m (7,000ft) Sweden's highest mountain, and the beginning or end of Kungsleden, the 85km (60 miles) walking route to and from Abisko.

A detour to the east of Kiruna takes you to Jukkasjärvi. Jukkasjärvi means 'meeting place' in the Sami language, which it was for travellers long ago. There is an open-air museum on the bank of Torneälven with many old buildings and their contents. Jukkasjärvi Kyrka is Lappland's oldest church, from

1607, with rare paintings. The celebrated old inn offers river-rafting and fine winter skiing (see p.325). After the detour, return to Kiruna.

From Kiruna, the railway has run beside Torneträsk, this most beautiful, long lake, since 1883, but it was another century before the road opened. Either way, the route is magnificent, with mountains and heights, such as Lapporten, the guardian gate of this last outpost.

Abisko Turiststation (Abisko Mountain Station) at the entrance of a big national park, has everything necessary for mountain and outdoor life, including accommodation and guides (see p.326). Abisko is also at one end of Kungsleden. Naturrum, a national park station, explains the local outdoors. Noudlja is the Sami holy mountain, which today has a slightly incongruous cablecar to the top.

Five miles north of Abisko, Låtajåkka is Sweden's highest mountain station and

Fishing of every sort is very popular in Sweden and the magnificent big rivers of the north, make river fishing very special here.

well worth the climb. Björkliden attracts summer skiers from everywhere, to plunge downhill in swimsuits. The caves here are Sweden's largest cave system, and nearby Tornehamn has the Railwaymen's Graveyard, where the early railway pioneers are buried (see p.327).

Riksgränsen is the frontier town on the border with Norway, with midnight summer skiing and a fine photographic studio (see p.327). Narvik is a 45-minute drive (or rail journey) from mountain to sea. By rail, it has long been an important port for Kiruna's iron. The best wide-sweeping view is from the top of Fagernes, 700m (2,300ft) high, reached by cablecar.

The Inland Way

There is a choice of two ways to travel north on Sweden's inland route: **Inlandsvägen** (the Inland Way) starts in Gothenburg, the great road north that has grown out of many old tracks linking the small communities; and **Inlandsbanan**, the railway which reached the Norwegian border a century before the road. Today, they chase one another to the Arctic Circle and beyond, sometimes in sight of each other, and never far away. A car makes it easier to follow a sudden impulse to divert, but Swedes use the train in much the same way, leaving and rejoining it, to walk, ski and fish.

Wildmarksexpress (the Wilderness Express) offers a guided train tour on the regular track from Östersund to Arvidsjaur, some 380km (260 miles) north, with a choice of stops and visits, and unlikely activities such as gold-panning. At Gällivare, Inlandsbanan merges into the great east coast route from Stockholm (around 16 hours, so best tackled with a sleeper) and then goes on to Kiruna and the Norwegian border at Riksgränsen, 440km (310 miles) north.

Taking Östersund as the start, the route to Dorotea (road 45 by car) lies through Jämtland, over hundreds of small islands linked by bridges, past lakes where you may see beaver, with the forest never far from road or track. Almost certainly the train will sometimes have to wait for elk and reindeer to cross and disappear silently into the trees.

Dorotea's old church has sculptures by Carl Milles and in the chapel a separate collection by Björn Martinis. There is a bear statue of Siberian larch in the main square. **Kullerbacken Museum** has brought in buildings from villages all over the area, and **Dorotea Slöjd** has hand-

crafts on exhibition and for sale. Dorotea is typical of most villages between here and **Arvidsjaur**, some 250km (175 miles) north. All give a feel of the past, and all are the focal point for mountain walks or horseback-trails, in lovely countryside full of plants and birds.

Vilhelmina, the main town, started as a church village with some 38 buildings, now mostly converted for the use of summer visitors. It is famous for folk dancing and singing, and July's special festive days include both, plus an old-time wedding. At that time, the train may well pull into a station full of folk musicians playing a greeting and, in minutes, most passengers are out on the platform, joining in. The old parish hall is now Vilhelmina's **Folk Museum**. **Västerbottens Slöjd and Same Ätnam** (Västerbotten and Sami crafts) has demonstrations and sells craftwork.

At **Storuman** on its own beautiful lake with the wooded island of **Lusholmarna**, road and rail cross the Blue Road from Umeå to the border. Its name comes from the many lakes along the way. **Kåtakyrkan** (church) is built in the style of a traditional Sami hut, and the town's **Old Railway Hotel**, a relic of early railway days, is now a library.

Further north, in a car you can divert northwest at Slagnäs onto a minor road that hugs the beautiful waters of Storavan and Lake Uddjaur, to the Sami town of **Arjeplog**. Almost surrounded by water and in a splendid setting, Arjeplog is the junction with the old Silver Road. With silver mines nearby, **Silvermuseet** has a rich collection of Sami silver and many other exhibits of Sami life. **Arjeplog Kyrka**, also with fine silver, was founded in 1641 by Queen Kristina.

From here, comes a chance to use the Silver Road (road 95), a quicker journey to

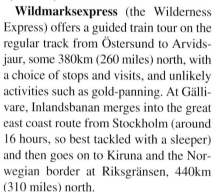

322

Arvidsjaur. This crossroads town, lying at the junction of five good roads, has been a main trading post for the last century. In summer, it is full of young soldiers on military training, which all young Swedish men must take. The wide main street and lake close to the centre make Arvidsjaur an attractive town, home to around 8,000. **Lappstaden** is Sweden's oldest preserved church village with some 80 Sami *kåtor* (houses) and commemorates the Forest Sami who have gathered here for markets and church festivals for hundreds of years. They still celebrate Storstämningshelgen, in late August. A popular outing here is to visit a Sami village and eat supper in a *kata*.

Arvidsjaur's river **Piteälven** is good for canoeing, and in turbulent sections such as Trollforsarna (rapids), is still more exciting for white-water rafting. There are islands too for berry-picking and picnics. The area runs courses in hang-gliding, and a new idea is to hire one of the railway cycles (a grandchild of the old platelayers' trolleys) complete with camping gear, and pedal off along the disused railway to Jörn, some 70km (50 miles) southwest. **Vittjåksfjällen** and **Prästberget** make good summer walking and excellent downhill and cross-country skiing in winter.

North of the Arctic Circle

Road and rail reach the Arctic Circle just before **Jokkmokk Kommun**, some 160km (110 miles) of forest and marshland north of Arvidsjaur. Jokkmokk is Sami country and the great Sami annual event, **Jokkmokk Marnaden** (market) opened in 1605. It has taken place on the first Thursday, Friday and Saturday of February ever since. For these three days in the darkest part of the year, Jokkmokk buzzes. Sami people, traditional dress bright against the snow, come to town to enjoy themselves with relatives and friends. Visitors flock in to savour the atmosphere and buy Sami handcrafts. It is so popular that you must book a year ahead to make sure of a bed, though Sami handcrafts are on sale here at any time of year.

The town's **Áttje**, an evocative museum, covers not just Sami life and culture but also the hard mountain lives of the Swedish settlers who came to better themselves. *Áttje* is Sami for a storehouse and

*T*oday, the Sami people live mostly in houses but still use the lavvu tent for travelling in summer with the herds. Some Sami people invite visitors to see a lavvu.

this is a fine collection that brings it all to life. Southwest of Jokkmokk on road 97, **Vuollerim** is based on excavations of a 6,000-year-old hunting community, with well-preserved Stone Age tools, utensils and displays. Outside, Vuollerim offers the old dish of beaver for the brave of appetite.

The railway's push north at the turn of the century went hand in hand with the development of hydro-electric power, on which Norrland is largely dependant today. **Porjus** power station was a pioneer, built early this century before the roads came. Its purpose was to power the iron ore trains from the open mines at Malmberget and Kiruna, which were growing bigger by the day. It has now been superseded by a modern power station nearby but its huge halls and immaculate generators are monuments to an era of industrial and social history.

However interesting it is to visit places of historic or cultural note, Norrland also means the open air. Jokkmokk Kommun is roughly the size of Wales and four enormous national parks cover this wild country. **Muddus** is the closest to Jokkmokk town. Here also is a wild road, **Sjöfallsleden**, branching west just after Porjus, it runs for some 170km (120 miles) through inspiring scenery, along lakes and tributaries of Luleälven. The road ends high in the mountain gateway to Norway, at **Ritsemjåkka**. From there, it is only an 18km (12-mile) footslog to the Norwegian Sea (Atlantic). From **Saltuluokta**, halfway along the route, a boat also follows Sjöfallsleden, surrounded on all sides by the magnificent wild country of **Sarek**, **Padjelanta**, and **Stora Sjöfallet** national parks.

Gällivare, the next stop north, has an attractive 100-year-old station. The town's life and prosperity depend on nearby Malmberget's **Gropen** – a huge, Dante's

*W*ho said Swedes have no sense of humour? This unlikely statue greets the eye of an astonished visitor to the north of Tårnafjällen (mountains).

inferno hole in the ground, from which comes iron ore. Tour buses circle unnervingly into the grey swirl of the mine. **Gruvsmuseet** goes back over 250 years of local mining history. The early miners lived in **Kåkstaden**, now restored and open to the public from June to August, as is **Disponentvillan**, once the manager's house. **Dundret**, 825m (2,700ft) high, is Gällivare's mountain. The summit view covers one-eleventh of the whole of Sweden. High up one side is a holiday centre, with a restaurant and swimming pools.

All over this northern area, a favourite pastime is panning for gold. A few even

324

visit solely for the purpose of panning and many a tall-tale is told as the evening lengthens – the equivalent of the fisherman's 'one that got away'. Every year in August, Gällivare hosts gold-panning championships.

Road and rail north part company after Gällivare. Rail takes a relatively straight route to Kiruna. Road merges into the E10 for Kiruna via **Svapavaara**, where the original road 45 re-emerges to head northeast for **Karesuando** on the Finnish border. It has the distinction of having Sweden's most northerly church which, with its **Praestgård** (parsonage) and **Laestadiushus**, was once the parish of Lars Levi Laestadius, who later founded the Revivalist movement, Laestadianism. Not many people realize that Laestadius was also a fine botanist and **Laestadius Trädgården**, a botanical garden of Swedish mountain plants, lies close to the Karesuando campsite. There is also **Kaarevaara**, which gives a view of Sweden's only tundra, where birders come from far and wide to study its bountiful birdlife.

At **Kiruna** road and rail meet again though, until 1984, the road stopped here. For most of this century, the only way to Riksgränsen, the border with Norway, was by rail. Now a beautiful open road heads north between the rail track and the waters of **Tornetråsk**, through some of the remotest scenery anywhere.

Kiruna is set between two mountains full of ore, Kirunavaara and Luossavaara, with a lake in the centre. Its population of some 27,000 still lives largely from mining which began last century, first as an opencast mine which has left a great scar. Today, mining is largely underground and a bus tour reveals the drama, with demonstrations by huge machines, lumbering through the caverns like prehistoric monsters.

Not to be missed is **Hjalmar Lundbohmsgården**, the home of the father of modern Kiruna, Hjalmar Lundbohm. In 1889, he took leave of absence from the Swedish Geological Research Institute to become director of Kiruna's newly-formed mining company. Dedicated to making the community a comfortable place for the settlers who came to work in the mine, he planned the town's first houses with meticulous care, showed settlers how to educate themselves and their children, and did everything possible to build a community. All this is shown in the house of this flamboyant man, who was also something of a *bon viveur*, typified by his fine dining room where he entertained his friends.

Jukkasjärvi, some 21km (15 miles) away on Torneälven is completely different, with adventurous white-water rafting in summer and dog-sledging and ski-touring in winter. In Sami, *jukkasjärvi* means 'meeting place' which is how it must have seemed in the olden days to travellers struggling in from the cold. **Lappland Kyrka** is Lappland's oldest wooden church, from 1609, with a brilliantly coloured altarpiece by Bror Hjort from Uppsala, famed for his church art. On the Torne's banks is a small group of old buildings, with many of the original contents.

Winter's oddest attraction here is **Arctic Hallen**, first built of snow by locals in 1991, when the usual January temperatures plummeted, as a meeting place and gallery, with the Ice-Blue Bar. Now, for those who cannot resist something different, each season's Arctic Hallen has become a short-term winter hotel. But local innkeeper, Nils Yngve Bergqvist, whose idea it was, also keeps good warm rooms in Jukkasjärvi Wärdshus.

West of Kiruna, **Kebnekaise** nearly 2,117m (7,000ft) is Sweden's highest

mountain, a challenge for experienced mountain walkers, though the summit need not call for climbing skills. It can also be, literally, the high point of a walk along **Kungsleden**. This 86km (60-mile) walking route to or from Abisko does not demand climbing skills either, and has mountain huts for overnight stays.

From Kiruna, both road and rail to **Abisko Turiststation** (mountain station) follow the same beautiful scenic route,

overlooking the peaceful waters of **Torneträsk**. Of all the mountains, the most noticeable heights are the twin peaks on either side of the gap named **Lapporten**, the entrance to this last wilderness where in summer, from late-May to late-July, the sun never sets.

The term *turist* does not have the same meaning as the English 'tourist'. In Scandinavia, it is used in the sense of someone travelling in remote areas under his or her

Lappland rises in the west on the Norwegian border to high mountains, which are constantly snow-capped, but lower down in the valleys, the lush grass of summer is thick with colour and plants.

self-catering, sports equipment and guides, a shop, and more. Apart from walking, ski-touring, mountain-biking and the like, guides lead specialist weeks on geology, ornithology, botany and railway history. Torneträsk provides first-class sailing, or a chance to just mess about in a boat. Close by, **Naturum**, a national parks' station, has good displays on **Abisko** and **Vadvetjåkke** national parks. A cablecar runs to the top of **Noulja**, once a holy mountain of the Sami people.

Björkliden, 7km (5 miles) north, has Sweden's most northerly and highest mountain station, **Låktatjåkko**. Even at 1,228m (4,000ft), in high summer swim-suit-clad skiers are out on the 15km (10 miles) of still snow-covered trails. Lower down, Björkliden has an abundance of plants, including many rare species, some of which are only found here. There is also one of Sweden's best cave systems, much prized by cavers, and **Tornehamn**, at its height during the great railway-building days, has a graveyard where some of the *rallare* (railway navvies) are buried.

own steam. It is also part of the typical urge to get out into 'nature' which inspired the start of the Svenskturistföreningen, and its counterpart Norskturistföreningen, which run mountain stations all over both countries, and in Sweden are responsible for hostels as well.

Scandinavian outdoor life does not necessarily mean lack of comfort. Abisko has excellent facilities for an active holiday: good accommodation with restaurants or

Road and rail cross the Norwegian border at **Riksgränsen**, only 45 minutes from the Norwegian Sea at Narvik. Riksgränsen is the hometown of a famous Swedish nature photographer, Sven Hörnell, whose first inspiration was the land around him. His studio shows a fine display of his work.

Having a Good Time – Indoors and Out

The cities of Copenhagen, Oslo and Stockholm are cosmopolitan and exciting with every facility for the visitor who wants good restaurants, a lively nightlife and a stimulating cultural scene. The countryside around has such a variety of landscapes that every conceivable sport and pastime can be found through the wide-ranging summer and winter climate.

Sports and Outdoor Activities

Scandinavians are great outdoor people, whether it be on hill and mountain or in and on the water, with coasts, lakes and rivers providing almost endless possibilities for both. One particularly attractive feature of Scandinavia is that even the cities are close to natural surroundings and, in winter, Norwegians and Swedes usually have only a short journey to the ski slopes.

*T*hroughout Norway and Sweden, winter weekends mean winter sports, from downhill skiing to dog-sledging, but cross-country skiing is the universal sport.

Walking and Climbing

In spring, summer and autumn, Swedes and Norwegians take to the hills and mountains in their thousands, opening up *hytter* and *stugor* (cabins) as the winter snows disappear, or they may have remained in use through the winter for cross-country or mountain skiing. In Denmark, city families pour out to the coasts to open up their summerhouses once more, often right down on the beach.

In many mountain areas, special hotels (*fjellhotell* or *fjellstuer* in Norwegian) cater for visitors who walk both in the mountains and along less strenuous routes. In Norway, there are the great *vidda* – Hardanger and Jotunheimen – and mountains such as Dovrefjell, as well as good **climbing** areas like Åndalsnes in the fjord country. There are also special **walking routes** such as the

Kungsleden in Lappland, Sweden, which attract hundreds of walkers every weekend, yet are never crowded. Forest tracks and open land give seemingly boundless space where people can wander and camp at will but must not do any damage. Many routes have basic mountain huts. Elsewhere, it is **wilderness camping** and huge natural areas are designated as national parks.

Horseriding and Pony Trekking

Horseriding holidays over the hills and countryside are becoming increasingly popular and are widely available. Many towns have stables and riding schools, and there are often special treks and journeys usually, though not always, for more experienced riders. These may be for weekends or several days, but there are shorter day or half-day rides too.

Golf

Golf is becoming more and more popular in Scandinavia; Sweden, for example, has over 300 courses. Many Scandinavian courses are owned by private clubs which charge green fees but welcome visitors. Some may have rules that require a visitor to have an official handicap. In northern Norway and Sweden, there is the chance to play golf under the Midnight Sun in summer, a rare thrill.

Tennis

Perhaps it was the Swedish success in the tennis world, but all three Scandinavian countries have woken up to tennis and there are many indoor and outdoor courts for public use. Hotels often have courts.

Watersports

Sailing of all sorts is as popular in Scandinavia as skiing, and with the thousands of islands, small harbours and bays around the coasts, and a large number of inland lakes, the possibilities are almost limitless and universal. In all these places, it is usual to be able to hire both sailing and **motor boats** and there is a range of all-in holidays afloat.

Windsurfing and **water skiing** are good, particularly on the lakes. River **canoeing** and canoe journeys are first-class and further north **white-water rafting** is growing in popularity and can be very exciting.

Swimming

Denmark's long west coast is especially well-known for beaches and bathing, but there are places to swim, in lake, river and sea, all over Scandinavia. The city of Stockholm, for example, has some 18 bathing beaches within the city limits, and Copenhagen and Oslo are also well supplied. This is typical all over Scandinavia and most urban areas have indoor pools for the winter. Many of the bigger hotels have indoor heated pools and often provide sauna facilities and plunge pools as well.

Fishing

The possibilities for fishing are only limited by the waters available and, as there are vast stretches of inland lakes, mountain streams, rivers, sheltered sea and open ocean, fishing is on offer everywhere, from the banks or from a boat. Most fresh water angling requires a permit but sea-fishing is open to everyone.

Wintersports

Low-lying Denmark, further to the south than its sister countries, is not great skiing territory. Norway and Sweden are superb. Here, everyone skis almost from the time they can walk; there are cross-country tracks, and some downhill runs, around every town and city, where Swedes and Norwegians enjoy short winter days.

*D*enmark has
Scandinavia's best beaches. This
beach (above) is in Klampenborg,
Sjælland. Scandinavians at home in
the water (right).

In Norway there is first-class **downhill
skiing** in Lillehammer, which hosted the
Olympic Games in 1994, in Geilo, Voss,
Oppdal and many other places. In Sweden,
the Åre area in Jämtland is one of the best.
Norwegians are fanatics for **ski-jumping**,
and Holmenkollen is one of the world's
most famous ski-jumping competitions.
Ski-touring is also very popular.

For visitors, the great advantage of the
Scandinavian style of **cross-country** ski-

*N*owhere is there finer
fishing than in Norwegian rivers,
unless it is in the streams as here
in Örsta, near Ålesund.

ing, which lives up to its name by covering natural routes and not just circling regular tracks as often happens in continental Europe, is something even a beginner can quickly begin to enjoy. Using special long skis, much lighter and less complicated than the downhill variety, it is a natural way of covering snowy ground in winter.

For details of all these sports, contact the national tourist offices in your own country (see p.32), who can provide information on individual sports and contacts in Scandinavia. Local tourist offices have comprehensive knowledge of their own areas.

Spectator Sports

From tennis to golf, football, boat racing, horseracing, showing and trotting, Scandinavia covers the full range of indoor and outdoor spectator sports, many at international level and with smaller tennis and golf tournaments around the country. Sailing events are often based on one of the clusters of islands around the coasts. For details, the national tourist offices in different countries are helpful and can provide lists of events for the current year. Once in Scandinavia, local tourist offices have detailed information about events in their own areas.

*W*inter is wonderful in Sweden's Jämtland on the Norwegian border, and a snow scooter or skidoo is not just a pastime but can be the easiest way to get around.

Entertainment and Activities

Concerts and Theatre

Scandinavians may be small in numbers but they are three highly cultured nations which are deeply immersed in the arts, with famous companies such as the Royal Danish Ballet in Copenhagen, Operan and Drottningholm Court Theatre in Stockholm, the Munch Museum and Vigeland Park in Oslo. There are events such as the renowned Bergen International Festival which has regularly attracted artistes and audiences from all over the world since it was formed shortly after the end of World War II. In 1994, Gothenburg opened a fine new **opera** house by the harbour. All the main cities have **symphony orchestras**, some very long-established such as the Bergen Philharmonic, founded in 1765.

Many of the more rural areas hold special cultural events, and Sweden in particular has many **music festivals**, such as the Umeå Chamber Music Festival. **Music clubs** and **pubs** are popular in the main cities, with **jazz**, **folk** and **rock music**, and Copenhagen is world-famous for this sort of evening entertainment.

For visitors, there are certain difficulties in that **theatre** performances are usually given in the native language but the National Theatre in Oslo, for example, usually offers simultaneous translation. More difficult is that in summer, most of the regular theatre and concert performances cease during the holiday months, though music often continues **out of doors**. Stockholm holds concerts in Skansen on Djurgården; the winter ski-jump site out at Holmenkollen makes a marvellous venue with its small central lake on the outskirts of Oslo; and Tivoli gives regular concert performances of many different sorts in Copenhagen, as do similar outdoor amusement parks in other cities in all three countries. **Folk** entertainment and dancing is always popular in the summer.

Cinema

Film shows rarely have the difficulty of theatre performances for visitors because almost all foreign films are screened in their original language with subtitles. It can be an interesting challenge to follow a film from the Scandinavian film industry and some may have a synopsis in English. Most cities have a *What's On* guide, free at tourist offices and in many hotels, which will also list nightclubs and discos.

Nightlife

Even 20 years ago in winter Scandinavians went home early, scrambling to be back indoors as the early night closed in. Today, everything has changed, at least in the cities, and the capitals stay up late. There is still an emphasis on the weekend in Scandinavian social life and the **nightclubs** in the city hotels are busiest on Fridays and Saturdays. With that proviso, **restaurants with dancing** and **discos** often stay open until 2 and 3am. In rural areas, almost all late-night entertainment takes place in the bigger hotels.

In all three Scandinavian countries, drink prices are high, slightly less so in Denmark, where the Danes concentrate very much on beer. **Piano-bars** and **jazz** and **rock clubs** are probably the best bargain, but some nightclubs may have what seem to foreigners surprisingly high age limits. With young people in the party, it is a good idea to ask in advance. In a hotel in which you are staying, there should be no problem.

As well as its great water festival, summer in Stockholm is a round of festivals of all sorts; this is the gospel festival.

The Right Place at the Right Price

Hotels in Denmark

Denmark is a country with a variety of places to stay, from hotels to *kro* (inns), self-catering flats, *hytter* and campsites (see p.12, Accommodation in FACTS AND FIGURES).

In Copenhagen there is a plethora of good hotels mostly clustered within walking distance of the central area of Strøget, Tivoli Gardens and Kongens Nytorv though two or three are closer to the airport, which is only some 8km (5 miles) from the centre. In common with other Scandinavian hotels, standards are high at all prices.

Copenhagen hotel charges are usually higher than in other cities and in rural areas but, as many hotels are directed mainly at business guests, at weekends and summer holiday times you should always ask about bargains.

Hotels in Copenhagen

Rates given are approximate and may vary. They are for two people sharing a room at full rates, including cold table breakfast, tax and service.

	Above Dkr1,500
	Dkr900-1,500
	Below Dkr900

Hotel d'Angleterre ||||
Kongens Nytorv 34, DK-1050
Copenhagen K
Tel. 33-12-00-95; fax 33-12-11-18
Copenhagen's 18th-century 'Royal' hotel has often entertained royalty and the famous. Close to Royal Danish Ballet, Nyhavn. Swimming pool. First-class restaurants, pavement café. 180 rooms, plus suites.

Hotel Ansgar |
Colbjørnsgade 29, DK-1652
Copenhagen V
Tel. 31-21-21-96; fax 31-21-61-91
Beautiful 1885 stone building just off a former red-light district which has been well cleaned-up. This is now a quiet area close to train, bus stations, city air terminal, Tivoli, Rådhuspladsen. Courtyard for sitting outside. Modest, comfortable hotel. 87 rooms.

Hotel Ascot ||
Studiestræde 61, DK-1554
Copenhagen V
Tel. 33-12-60-00; fax 33-14-60-00
Central hotel in what was once a famous bathhouse where many political decisions were made. The elegant, high building has a fine main hall, restaurant in the main old bathhouse, and wide city views. An unusual breakfast hotel with 145 rooms, also apartments.

Copenhagen Admiral Hotel ||||
Tolbodgade 24-28, DK-1253
Copenhagen
Tel. 33-11-82-82; fax 31-32-36-07
A well-converted, 200-year-old granary with original beams. High standards. Near harbour. 366 rooms.

Copenhagen Crown Hotel ||
Vesterbrogade 41, DK-1620
Copenhagen
Tel. 31-21-21-66; fax 31-21-00-66
A lovely courtyard entrance and well-fitted rooms. Good view of Copenhagen. 80 rooms.

Copenhagen Star Hotel ||
Colbjørnsgade 13,
Copenhagen V, Tel. 31-22-21-99
Corner site close to Tivoli, station. Good, modern, ground floor renovation with lounge, breakfast room and bar, in lovely late 19th-century building. Courtyard. 134 rooms.

Hotel Esplanaden |-||
Bredgade 78, Copenhagen K
Tel. 33-91-32-00; fax 33-91-32-39
An extremely good reconstruction of a fine old building in quiet square near Churchill Park, Royal Palace and Little Mermaid statue. Good breakfast restaurant in old storage cellar, and courtyard. Comfortable rooms and very service-minded staff. 116 rooms.

Grand Hotel ||
Vesterbrogade 9A, DK-1620
Copenhagen
Tel. 31-31-36-00; fax 31-31-33-50
An excellent modernization of a classic building, with good rooms and restaurant, all close to centre. 146 rooms.

Ibsens Hotel |-||
Vendersgade 23, DK-1363
Copenhagen K
Tel. 33-13-19-13; fax 33-13-19-16
Central, corner site for 18th-century building. One street back from city lakes, close to Rosenborg Slot and several museums. On second-fourth

storeys, no lift. Interesting period furniture and homely breakfast-room. Many restaurants nearby. 49 rooms.

Hotel Kong Arthur ▮▮
Nørregade 11, DK-1270
Copenhagen K
Tel. 33-11-12-12; fax 33-32-61-30
A family-run hotel facing one of the three city lakes, close to Rosenborg Slot. Sunny central courtyard garden. Fine restoration of 1880s building, with good restaurant-café. 107 rooms.

Hotel Kong Frederik ▮▮▮
Vester Voldgade 25, DK-1552
Copenhagen V
Tel. 33-12-59-02; fax 33-93-59-01
No rooms are identical in this old hotel on the site of an ancient inn. Beautifully furnished, with charming atrium, Queen's Restaurant and Pub. 110 Rooms.

71 Nyhavn ▮▮▮
Nyhavn 71, DK-1051 Copenhagen
Tel. 33-12-15-19; fax 33-93-12-82
A high-standard, unusual, atmospheric hotel built into a converted warehouse along Nyhavn canal. Splendid harbour views. 82 rooms.

Radisson SAS Royal Hotel ▮▮▮
Hammerichsgade 1, DK-1611
Copenhagen
Tel. 33-14-14-12; fax 33-14-14-21
A modern tower block, opposite Tivoli Gardens, with the high room standards and facilities expected of Radisson SAS. Fine views from 20th-floor Summit Restaurant, also Café Royal. 265 rooms.

Radisson SAS Scandinavia Hotel ▮▮▮
Amager Boulevard, DK-2300
Copenhagen S
Tel. 32-96-33-20; fax 31-57-01-93
Central, high-quality hotel, overlooking moat and ramparts, with Copenhagen's only casino. Emphasis on business guests with sauna and pool. Good food. 542 rooms.

Savoy Hotel ▮–▮▮
Vesterbrogade 34, DK-1620
Copenhagen V
Tel. 31-31-40-73; fax 31-31-31-37
Quiet bedrooms overlooking green courtyard garden. In 1906 building carefully restored in 1980s with advice from National Museum. Danish restaurant. 66 rooms.

Sheraton Copenhagen Hotel ▮▮▮
Vester Søgade 6, DK-1601
Copenhagen V
Tel. 33-14-35-35; fax 33-32-12-23
Modern building close to business and shopping areas. All high standard facilities. Good international and Danish restaurant, 'English' pub. 471 rooms.

Sophie Amalie ▮▮
Sankt Annæ Plads 21, DK-1250
Copenhagen K
Tel. 33-12-34-40; fax 33-32-55-42
Close to quayside near Nyhavn, with good harbour views, not far from Royal Palace and Kongens Nytorv. A quiet old building, well renovated, with high quality for price. 134 rooms.

Hotel Triton ▮▮
Helgolandsgade 7-11, Copenhagen
Tel. 31-31-32-66; fax 31-31-69-70
A hotel of character in 19th-century building combined with good, modern facilities. Very central. Good personal service. 123 rooms.

Webers Hotel ▮▮
Vesterbrogade 11B, DK-1620
Copenhagen V
Tel. 31-31-14-32; fax 31-31-14-41
It would be hard to be more central than Webers, a well-modernized hotel that has kept its character in corner building. Comfortable rooms, good breakfast restaurant, popular bar. 103 rooms.

Hotels in Odense

Outside Copenhagen, equivalent prices tend to be lower for cities such as Odense and Århus
▮▮▮ above Dkr 1200
▮▮ Dkr900-1200
▮ Below Dkr800

Ansgar: Østre ▮
Stationsvej 32, DK-5100 Odense C
Tel. 66-121-96-93; fax 66-11-96-75
Newly refurbished hotel, centrally situated close to station and pedestrian precinct. 44 rooms.

Blommenslyst Kro and Motel Brasilia ▮
Middelfartvej 420, DK-5491
Blommenslyst
Tel. 65-96-70-12; fax 65-96-79-37
Beautiful motel added to old kro in lovely gardens. Excellent traditional food. Five miles west of Odense.

Frederik IV Kro ▮
Rugårdsvej 590, Slukefter,
DK-5210 Odense NV
Tel. 65-94-13-13; fax 65-94-23-23
Comfortable old inn, with conference hotel added, in northwest of city. 76 rooms in hotel and inn.

Grand Hotel ▮▮–▮▮▮
Jernbanegade 18, DK-5000
Odense C
Tel. 66-11-11-71; fax 66-14-11-71
A fine traditional hotel right in centre, with good service and excellent cuisine. 137 rooms.

Ydes Hotel ▮
Hans Tausengade, DK-5000
Odense C
Tel. 66-12-11-31; fax 66-12-17-82
Small traditional hotel with good service and atmosphere. Handy for rail and bus stations. 28 rooms.

Radisson SAS H.C. Andersen Hotel ▮▮
Claus Bergs Gade, Odense
Tel. 66-14-78-00; fax 66-14-78-90
Good, modern hotel in the old part of Odense, next to museum. 145 rooms.

Hotel Windsor ▮
Vindegade 45, DK-5000 Odense C
Tel. 66-12-06-52; fax 65-91-00-23
Very central hotel with good personal service and excellent facilities, including fine library. 61 rooms.

Hotels in Århus

For prices see Odense.

Ansgar Hotel ▮
Banegaardsplads 14, DK-8100
Århus
Tel. 86-12-41-22; fax 86-20 29-04
Next door to City Hall, and close to concert hall, train and bus stations. A good home from home. 168 rooms.

Hotel Atlantic ▮▮
Europaplads 10-14, DK-8000 Århus
Tel. 86-13-11-11; fax 86-13-23-43
In a fine position close to the harbour. Good restaurant. Rooms all renovated 1994. 102 rooms.

Hotel Kong Christian den X ▮▮
Christian den X vej 70, DK-8260
Viby J
Tel. 86-11-61-11; fax 86-11-74-00
A modern hotel with first-class facilities and good food. Sauna. 80 rooms.

Hotel La Tour
Randersvej 139, DK-8200 Århus N
Tel. 86-16-78-88; fax 86-16-79-95
*Low-priced family hotel, 3km
(2 miles) north of centre. 70 rooms.*

Hotel Marselis
Strandvejen 25, DK-8000 Århus C
Tel. 86-14-44-11; fax 86-11-70-46
*First-class hotel close to sea in
Marselis woods. Marvellous views
over bay. 112 rooms.*

Radisson/SAS
Scandinavia Hotel
Margrethepladsen 1, 8000 Århus
Tel. 86-12-86-65; fax 86-12-86-75
Reservations: Tel. 89-36-28-40
*A magnificent new, interestingly
designed hotel, opened summer
1995 within the Scandinavian
Center. Very comfortable, first-class
food. Close to Musikhuset, very
central. Good facilities for business
and holiday guests.*

Hotel Royal Store Torv
Box 43, 9000 Århus
Tel. 86-12-00-11; fax 86-76-04-00
*A very high standard hotel in
beautifully restored building, some
150 years old. Modernized in
character with a fine conservatory
restaurant, Queen's Garden. 105
rooms.*

Scandic Hotel Århus
Rytoften 3, 8210 Århus V
Tel. 86-15-68-44; fax 86-15-68-77
*Modern six-storey building with
glass atrium, 3km (2 miles) from
centre, close to motorway. Fine for
touring. 148 rooms.*

Tarskov Mill
Tarskovvej 1, 8462 Århus (Harlev)
Tel. 86-94-25-44; fax 86-94-25-66
*Listed 14th-century watermill
with working farm. In lovely area
beside the river with millpond and
ancient woods. Golf, riding, fishing,
cycling.*

Hotel Windsor
Skolebakken 17, 8000 Århus
Tel. 86-12-23-00; fax 86-13-64-20
*Charming old hotel near harbour
and centre, with famous fish
restaurant, Fiskekælderen, for fish
and shellfish specialities. Newly
modernized rooms.*

Hotels in Norway

Norwegian hotels keep up the
Scandinavian tradition of high
standards in all price ranges, and
are clean and comfortable.
Licensed hotels may have a full
licence for alcohol, or for beer
and wine only. Many city hotels
are geared to business use,
which means weekends and
summer holidays may offer bargains. Always ask about discounts and special offers (see
p.12, Accommodation in FACTS
AND FIGURES).

Because Norwegian hotel rates
vary enormously, it is difficult to
be precise but price categories
given below are for two people
sharing a room at full rates, including cold table breakfast, tax
and service charge.

  ▌▌▌ Above Nkr1,500
  ▌▌ Nkr900-1,500
  ▌ Below Nkr900

These are Oslo prices. Hotels in
Bergen and Trondheim will usually be around ten percent or
more cheaper at full rate, and pro-
portionately lower with weekend,
holiday and discount rates.

Hotels in Oslo

Hotell Ambassadeur
Camilla Colletts veien 15, N-0258
Oslo
Tel. (0)22-44-18-35; fax (0)22-44-
47-91
*Known as the 'small, pink hotel
behind the palace'. Ten minutes
from the centre. 42 individualistic
rooms. Full licence.*

Anker Hotell
Storgt 55, N-0182 Oslo
Tel. (0)22-11-40-05; fax (0)22-11-
01-36
*Very central, modern hotel with free
parking. Special corporate rates.
Beer and wine licence. 120 rooms*

Hotell Bondeheimen
Rosenkrantzgt 8, N-0159 Oslo
Tel. (0)22-42-95-30; fax (0)22-41-
94-37

*Typical Norwegian style, with good
home cooking. 76 rooms.
Convenient for city centre.*

Hotell Bristol
Kristian IV's gate 7, N-0164 Oslo
Tel. (0)22-41-58-40; fax (0)22-42-
86-51
*Famous hotel with ornate lobby and
antique furniture. Close to centre.
Renowned for luncheon koldtbord
(cold table). Fully licensed. 220
rooms.*

City Hotel
Skippergt 19, N-0152 Oslo
Tel. (0)22-41-36-10; fax (0)22-42-
24-29
*Very close to main Karl Johansgate.
Small, reasonable prices.
Comfortable lounge with free
evening coffee and newspapers. 55
rooms.*

Hotell Continental
Stortingsgate 24/26, N-0161 Oslo
Tel. (0)22-82-40-00; fax (0)22-42-
96-89
*Opposite National Theatre, near
Storting. Fine hotel with two famous
restaurants. Fully licensed. 102
rooms.*

Hotel Europa
Skt Olavsgate 31, N-0166 Oslo
Tel. (0)22-20-99-90; fax (0)22-11-
27-27
*Central for sights, close to palace
gardens and public transport.
Friendly service. Fully licensed. 160
rooms*

Gabelshus Hotell
Gabelsgt 16, N-0272 Oslo
Tel. (0)22-55-22-60; fax (0)22-44-
27-30
*Central yet with secluded garden.
Good, traditional building. Cosy
'English' interior. Fully licensed. 48
rooms.*

Grand Hotell
Karl Johansgt 31, N-0159 Oslo
Tel. (0)22-42-93-90; fax (0)22-42-
12-25
*Famous as playwright Ibsen's
favourite haunt, with his Grand
Café overlooking Stortinget well
preserved. Luxury hotel with rooftop
indoor swimming pool. 275 rooms.*

Holmenkollen Park
Rica Hotel
Kongeveien 26, N-0390 Oslo
Tel. (0)22-92-20-00; fax (0)22-14-
61-92

Traditional building with modern facilities, looking towards Holmenkollen Ski Jump. Linked to centre by underground. Fully licensed. 90 rooms.

Norum Hotel ▌
Bygdøy Allé 53, N-0265 Oslo
Tel. (0)22-44-79-90; fax (0)22-44-92-39
Fine 19th-century building, west centre close to Vigeland Park. Good small licensed restaurant, popular with non-residents. 59 rooms.

Oslo Plaza ▌▌–▌▌▌
Sonja Henie Plass 3, N-0134 Oslo
Tel. (0)22-17-10-00; fax (0)22-17-73-00
Central, modern tower block. Spectacular views from 37th-floor nightclub. Swimming pool. Business service centre. Fully licensed. 662 rooms.

Radisson SAS Scandinavia Hotel ▌▌▌
Holbergs gt 30, N-0166 Oslo
Tel. (0)-22-11-30-00; fax (0)22-11-30-17
Luxurious comfort, good restaurants and rooftop bar. Swimming pool. Fully licensed. Airport bus.

Royal Christiania Hotel ▌▌
Biskop Gunnerus gt 3, N-0155 Oslo
Tel. (0) 22-42-94-10; fax (0)22-42-64-22
Opposite main station. Airport bus. Attractive modern atrium, swimming pool. Fully licensed. 451 rooms.

Ritz Hotell ▌▌
Frederic Stangs gt 3, N-0272 Oslo
Tel. (0)22-44-39-60; fax (0)22-44-67-13
Attractive, smallish hotel in tree-lined west city street. Fully licensed dining room. 50 rooms.

Inter Nor Savoy Hotel ▌▌
Universitetsgt 11, N-0164 Oslo
Tel. (0)22-20-26-55; fax (0)22-11-24-80
Central, traditional hotel, recently renovated. Original bar is one of city's best. Full licensed. 78 rooms.

Scandic Crown Hotel ▌▌
Parkveien 68, N-0254 Oslo
Tel. (0)22-44-69-70; fax (0)22-44-26-01
Modern, city hotel between Palace and Aker Brygge wharf. Good keep-fit room, sauna. Fully licensed. 185 rooms.

Rainbow Hotel ▌
Stefan Rosenkrantzgt 1, N-0159 Oslo
Tel. (0)22-42-92-50; fax (0)22-33-70-22
Heart of Oslo. Price includes afternoon coffee or tea and vaffler (waffles). Good luncheon cold table. Fully licensed. 130 rooms.

West Hotell ▌▌
Skovveien 15, N-03257 Oslo
Tel. (0)22-55-40-30
Traditional building, with attractive balconies. West, near Royal Palace, handy for trams, buses. À la carte restaurant. Fully licensed. 60 rooms.

Hotels in Bergen

▌▌▌ Above Nkr1200
▌▌ Nkr800–1220
▌ Below Nkr800

Hotell Admiral ▌
C Sundsgt 9, N-5004 Bergen
Tel. (0)55-32-47-30; fax (0)55-23-30-92
Authentic Jugend building close to harbour and Bryggen wharf. Fully licensed. 107 rooms.

Augustin Hotel ▌▌
Sundsgaten 22/24, N5004 Bergen
Tel. (0)55-23-00-25; fax (0)55-23-31-30
On Nordnes peninsula. Fine harbour view. Ornamental windows and balconies on Jugend building. Traditional 'rose-painted' furniture, and old-fashioned tearoom. Fully licensed. 80 rooms.

Bergen Airport Hotel ▌▌
Kokstadveien 3, N -5061 Kokstad
Tel. (0)55-22-92-00
Low, modern buildings close to airport in quiet hilly, pine-wooded area. 15km (11 miles) from Bergen. Good touring centre. Fully licensed. 232 rooms.

Bergen Hotel ▌▌
Håkonsgt 2, N-5015 Bergen
Tel. (0)55-23-39-62; fax (0)55-23-49-20
Busy central hotel, close to theatre, cinema and swimming pool. Fine views. Fully licensed. 113 rooms.

Bryggen Orion ▌▌
Bradbenken 3, N-5023 Bergen
Tel. (0)55-31-80-80; fax (0)55-32-94-14
Close to Rosenkrantårnet, Håkons Halle, Bryggen. Comfortable, good

atmosphere. Fully licensed. 229 rooms.

Grand Hotel Terminus ▌▌
Zander Kaaesgt 6, N-5017 Bergen
Tel. (55)-31-16-55; fax (0)55-31-85-76
A fine 19th-century painted-stone railway hotel, with air of elegant comfort. Close to main station. 135 rooms.

Hotell Hordaheimen ▌▌
C. Sundtsgt 18, N-5004 Bergen
Tel. (0)55-23-23-20; fax (0)55-23-49-50
On Nordnes peninsula, close to shops and harbour. Typical five-storey Jugend house. Modern comforts in traditional Norwegian setting. 60 rooms.

Kloster Pension ▌
Klosteret 12, N-5005 Bergen
Tel. (0)55-90-21-58; fax (0)55-23-30-22
Preserved 1790 building on Nordnes peninsula. Comfortable family home, run as pension. Ideal for groups, young people and families. 18 rooms.

Hotell Neptun ▌▌▌
Valckendorfsgt 8, N-5012 Bergen
Tel. (0)55-90-10-00; fax (0)55-23-32-02
Efficient, modern hotel in shopping area, with distinctive, French-inspired food, wide-ranging wine cellar, and large collection of good modern Norwegian art. Fully licensed.

Hotel Norge ▌▌▌
Ole Bulls Plass 4, N-5012 Bergen
Tel. (0)55-21-01-00; fax (0)55-21-02-99
One of Bergen's best hotels, also popular with locals. The Grill Room is a good gourmet restaurant. Airport bus. 347 rooms.

Romantik Hotel Park Pension ▌
Harald Hårfagresgt 35, N-5007 Bergen
Tel. (0)55-32-09-60; fax (0)55-31-03-34
A romantic, white, 1890 building. Family run, close to university, Grieghallen. Ideal for special occasions. Beer and wine license. 22 rooms, augmented in summer.

Radisson SAS Royal Hotel ▌▌▌
Bryggen, N-5003 Bergen
Tel. (0)55-54-30-00; fax (0)55-32-48-08

*On wharf close to Bryggens
Museum and Skt Maria Kirke.
Upmarket with usual SAS comforts
and good restaurants, yet part of
traditional waterside. Airport bus
terminus. 270 rooms.*

Scandic Hotel Bergen   ▮▮
Kokstadflaten 2, N-5061 Kokstad
Tel. (0)55-22-71-50; fax (0)55-22-
75-10
*Less than 1km (0.5 mile) from
Flesland Airport, on quiet wooded
hillside. 15km from Bergen centre.
Modern hotel, ideal for business
and touring.*

Strand Hotel   ▮–▮▮
Strandkaien 2B, N-5013 Bergen
Tel. (0)55-31-08-15; fax (0)55-31-
00-17
*Simple, friendly hotel in top two-
storeys of six in attractive harbour
building. Bergen's best view of
fishmarket and wharf. Beer and
wine licence. 51 rooms.*

Victoria Hotel   ▮▮
Kong Oscarsgt 29, N-5017 Bergen
Tel. (0)55-31-50-30; fax (0)55-32-
81-78
*Central Jugend building. Homely
atmosphere and interesting art
collection. Pleasant bar-cum-dining
room-cum-lounge. Link to Japanese
restaurant next door.*

Hotels in
Trondheim

▮▮▮   Above Nkr1200
▮▮   Nkr800-1200
▮   Below Nkr800

Ambassadeur Hotel   ▮
Elvegt 18, N-3013 Trondheim
Tel. (0)73-52-70-50; fax (0)73-52-
70-52
*In quiet area, only a few hundred
metres from city centre. High
standard large comfortable rooms
and beautiful roof terrace. Fully
licensed. 34 rooms.*

Britannia Hotel   ▮▮–▮▮▮
Dronningensgt 5, N-7011
Trondheim
Tel. (0)73-53-53-53; fax (0)73-51-
29-00
*An elegant, turn-of-the-century town
hotel, popular with business guests.
Interesting Palmehaven restaurant.
Piano bar, cellar restaurant and
'English' pub. 176 rooms.*

Radisson SAS Hotel   ▮▮▮
Trondheim
Kjøpmansgt 48, N-7001 Trondheim
Tel. (0)73-53-53-10; fax (0)73-53-
57-20
*Part of newish centre which
includes, shops, bars, concert halls.
Close to station and harbour. Fully
licensed. 106 rooms.*

Inter Nor Hotell Prinsen   ▮▮
Kongens gate 30, N-7012
Trondheim
Tel. (0)73-53-06-50; fax (0)73-53-
06-44
*Modern, high standard hotel, with
restaurant, bistro, wine taverna,
beer garden and night club. Near
market. Fully licensed. 85 rooms*

Hotel Residence   ▮▮
Torvet, N-7011 Trondheim
Tel. (0)73-52-83-80; fax (0)73-52-
64-60
*Well-modernized but with original
elegant Jugend style. Restaurant
and Parisian-style pavement café
overlooking busy market place.
Fully licensed. 66 rooms.*

Reso Royal Garden Hotel   ▮▮▮
Kjøpmannsgt 73, N-7011
Trondheim
Tel. (0)73-52-11-00; fax (0)73-52-
11-75
*Beautiful spot byNidelven river, with
much glass to reflect water. Interesting modern design. Fine facilities
with swimming pool. Good restaurants. Fully licensed. 297 rooms.*

Viking Hotel   ▮
Thomas Angellsgt 12B, N-7011
Trondheim
Tel. (0)73-51-21-33; fax (0)73-51-
43-14
*Central hotel, ideal for sights and
shopping. Interesting small library
for guests' use. Odin restaurant in
Norse style, bar-pub, all popular
with locals. Fully licensed. 36 rooms.*

Hotels in
Sweden

Swedish hotels are of a high standard with good service but their
full rates are not cheap. As with
other Scandinavian countries, the
fact that many have special summer and weekend rates can help to

cut the costs quite dramatically
(see p.12, Accommodation in
FACTS AND FIGURES). Ask also
about Stockholm, Gothenburg
and Malmö Packages which also
reduce prices.

Hotels in
Stockholm

Prices given are based on
Stockholm prices. Hotels in the
other two main cities – Gothenburg and Malmö – will usually
be at least ten percent lower. The
prices given are for two people
sharing a double room, and include breakfast.
▮▮▮   Above Skr1,800
▮▮   Skr1,100-1,800
▮   Below Skr1,100

Anglais RESO Hotel   ▮▮
Humlegårdsgatan 23, S-102-20
Stockholm
Tel. (0)8-614-16-00; fax (0)8-611-
09-72
*Good, modern hotel. Central but
quiet, opposite Humlegården with
Royal Library. 212 rooms.*

Aston Hotel   ▮
Mariatorget 3, S-118-91 Stockhom
Tel. (0)8-644-06-90; fax (0)8-714-
97-05
*In Jugend-style square with garden,
on old island of Södermalm, south
of Gamla Stan. Comfortable
breakfast hotel, surrounded by
interesting places to eat. Ideal for
budget travellers. 70 rooms.*

City Conference Hotel   ▮▮
Wallingatan, S-107-24 Stockholm
Tel. (0)8-20-15-20; fax (0)8-791-
50-50
*Modern, comfortable building in
quiet street. Outdoor terrace. Close
to Conference Centre.*

City Hotel Gamla Stan   ▮
Lilla Nygatan 25, S-111-028
Stockholm
Tel. (0)8-624-44-50; fax (0)8-21-
64-83
*Old Gamla Stan building, now com-
fortable hotel. Unlicensed, popular
with budget travellers. 51 rooms.*

Claes på Hornet   ▮▮
Surbrunnsgatan 20, S-112-48
Stockholm

Tel. (0)8-16-51-30; fax (0)8-612-53-15
Once an 18th-century inn, now small hotel with lovely atmosphere. Quiet area, north of centre. 10 rooms only.

Fogg's Hotel   I–II
Vårmdövagen 84, S-120 Stockholm
Tel. (0)8-714-53-00
In oldest industrial area, some 4km (3 miles) from centre but good public transport, also parking. Popular with groups. Outdoor terrace overlooking hillside and Viking and Silja Line harbours. Indoor pool and fitness room. 146 rooms.

Grand Hotel   IIII
S. Blasieholmen 8, S-103-83
Stockholm
Tel. (0)8-679-35-00; fax (0)8-611-86-86
Superb, luxury hotel overlooking the water. Very central. 321 rooms.

Hasselbacken Hotel   II
Hazeliusbacken 20, S-100-55
Stockholm
Tel. (0)8-670-50-50; fax (0)8-663-84-10
New hotel sensitively added to 19th-century timber restaurant, in Djurgården royal park. 112 rooms.

Långholmen   I
Gamla Kronohåktet, S-100-72
Stockholm
Tel. (0)8-668-05-00; fax (0)8-84-10-96
Unusual hotel in what was an old prison, making a feature of unlikely past. On beautiful island but convenient for centre by car or public transport. Also Youth Hostel accommodation. 101 rooms.

Prize Hotel   I
Kungsbron 1, S-111-22 Stockholm
Tel. (0)8-14-94-50; fax (0)8-14-98-48
Close to station and next door to World Trade Centre. Breakfast hotel popular with business travellers. Good summer family budget hotel. 158 rooms.

Stockholm Plaza   II
Birger Jarlsgatan 29, S-103-28
Stockholm
Tel. (0)8-14-51-20; fax (0)8-210-34-92
Unusual 19th-century hotel, lots of character and excellent services. Handy for centre but not noisy. Close to Humlegård Park. 151 rooms.

Victory Hotel   IIII
Lilla Nygatan 5, S-111-28
Stockholm
Tel. (0)8-14-30-90; fax (0)8-20-21-77
17th-century Gamla Stan building on quiet street, close to Mälaren. Famous for its Lord Nelson memorabilia. Remains of medieval city wall under glass in restaurant floor. 48 rooms. Sister hotels Lord Nelson and Lady Hamilton a little less expensive.

Hotels in Gothenburg

Hotell Eggers   II
Drottningtorget, S-401-25 Göteborg
Tel. (0)31-80-60-70; fax (0)31-15-42-43
Fine, classic railway hotel with marble floors. Oldest hotel in Gothenburg. Close to Central Station, airport bus terminus and Nordstan shopping. 88 rooms.

Hotell Liseberg Heden   II
Sten Sturegatan, S-411-38 Göteborg
Tel. (0)31-20-02-80; fax (0)31-16-52-83
Lovely gardens, set in Heden park. A free ticket to nearby Liseberg Park included. Good for families. 159 rooms.

Hotell Onyxen   I
Sten Sturegatan 23, S-412-53
Göteborg
Tel. (0)31-81-08-45; fax (0)31-16-56-72
Attractive, small breakfast hotel with fine, well-furnished rooms. Opposite Scandinavium, handy for Liseberg. 34 rooms.

RESO Hotel Rubinen   IIII
Kungsportavenyn 24, S-400-14
Göteborg
Tel. (0)31-81-08-00; fax (0)31-16-75-86
Good position in pedestrian street, Avenyn. Restaurant Andra Våningen and Bistro are popular. 185 rooms.

Hotell Riverton   IIII
Stora Badhusgatan 26, S-411-21
Göteborg
Tel. (0)31-10-12-00; fax (0)31-13-08-66
Close to north harbour and new Opera House. Wonderful view of estuary from 11th-storey Sky Bar and Restaurant. 190 rooms.

Scandic Crown   IIII
Polhemsplatsen 3, S-411-11
Göteborg
Tel. (0)31-80-09-00; fax (0)31-15-45-88
Modern hotel with beautiful atrium restaurant and bar. Bastu (sauna), gym, solarium and pool bar. Family rooms for two adults, two children. 320 rooms.

Spar Hotel   I
Karl Johansgatan 66-70, S-414-55
Göteborg
Tel. (0)31-42-00-20; fax (0)31-42-63-83
Homely breakfast hotel, west of centre near old Majorna harbour. Renewed and redecorated 1993. 150 rooms.

Hotels in Malmö

City Hotel   I
Stortorget 15, S-211-22 Malmö
Tel. (0)40-714-50; fax (0)40-11-32-74
A fine view of Malmö's oldest square and street markets. Everything on the doorstep. 82 rooms.

Garden Hotel   II
Baltzarsgatan 20, Malmö
Tel. (0)40-10-40-00)
Good, quiet hotel in centre, with beautiful lobby-lounge. Well-furnished rooms. Pleasant bar, restaurant, dancing. 172 rooms.

Hotell Kramer   I
Stortorget 7, S-201-21 Malmö
Tel. (0)40-701-20; fax (0)40-12-69-41
Classic, turreted, white building in Malmö's old main square. Good dining, nightclub and disco. 45 rooms.

SAS Royal   II
Östergatan 10, S-211-25 Malmö
Tel. (0)40-23-92-00; fax (0)40-11-28-40
Comfortable rooms in attractive half-timbered house. Thott's Restaurant claims the best steak in town. 221 rooms.

Scandic Crown Hotel   II
Amiralsgatan 19, S-211-27 Malmö
Tel. (0)40-10-07-30; fax (0)40-11-92-24
Modern hotel with lot of glass in concert hall building. Popular nightclub, also sauna and jacuzzi. 154 rooms.

Eating Out in Scandinavia

Scandinavian restaurants not only offer the best of their own native foods, but in the cities it is also possible to try the cuisine of many different countries from French to Japanese. Many of the best eating places are restaurants within the many well-known hotels. They can be chosen with confidence and, largely, need not be mentioned here. The local tourist information offices will also advise.

Restaurants in Denmark

Danish standards are high, and prices are not cheap, though many lunch restaurants have a daily menu that will help reduce costs. Copenhagen and the other cities have so many restaurants that it is only possible to recommend a handful. Everyone's handful will vary and every visitor will find her or his own favourites, be it eating outside in a small courtyard restaurant, or underground in a cellar restaurant, or in an old inn.

The prices given are for an evening meal, per head and without wine, but including tax and service which is normally included in the bill. Customers usually round up the total to nearest Dkr10.

| Under Dkr100
|| Dkr100-250
||| Over Dkr250 Dkr (which can be *well over* Dkr250)

Restaurants in Copenhagen

Ida Davidsen ||
70 St Kongensgade
Tel. 33-91-36-55
Undoubtedly the queen of Danish smørrebrod at lunchtime. Beautiful
open sandwiches served in generous portions.

Era Ora ||
62 Tovegade, Christianshavn
Tel. 31-54-06-93
Close to the water. A good, well-priced Italian restaurant, with the recommendation that it is also a favourite with Italians.

Gilleleje ||
Nyhavn 10
Tel. 33-12-58-58
One of the best of Nyhavn's many restaurants, decorated with antiques from sailing ship days, and some exotic food to match. Advance booking advised.

Hana Kyoto |||
59 Vimmelskaftet
Tel. 33-32-22-96
Very exclusive sushi restaurant.

Jensens Bøfhus |
Kultorvet 15, 1575 Copenhagen K
Tel. 33-15-09-84
Friendly, excellent value restaurant. Always good special offers. Best to book ahead.

Joanna Restaurant |–||
11 Læderstræde
Tel. 33-93-53-53
Good food, both Danish and French, reasonably priced. Nice atmosphere.

Kong Hans |||
Vingårdstræde 6
Tel. 33-11-68-68
Gourmet food in 14th-century setting. Renowned for its own smoked salmon, and has had a Michelin star for many consecutive years. Pricey but superb quality. Book ahead.

Krogs Fiskerestaurant ||
58 Gammel Strand
Tel. 33-12-20-11
One of Copenhagen's best and oldest fish restaurants.

Leonore Christine ||
Nyhavn 9
Tel. 33-13-50-40
Very popular Danish and French cuisine. It is necessary to book in advance.

Peder Oxe |–||
Gråbrøretorv 11
Tel. 33-11-00-77
In delightful square with some

tables outside. Easy-going atmosphere with superb Danish food. Cellar wine bar below main restaurant. Very popular.

Domhuskælderen |
Nytorv 5
Tel. 33-14-84-55
Excellent lunchtime restaurant with fine, fresh Danish food.

St Getruds Kloster |||
Exclusive gourmet dining in a medieval monastery with candlelit dinners. Fine wines a speciality.

Den Sorte Ravn |||
Nyhavn 14
Tel. 33-13-12-33
Fine French and Danish food in 18th-century building. Very good seafood.

Summit Restaurant |||
Radisson SAS Royal Hotel,
Hammerichsgade
Tel. 33-14-14-12
Right at the top of this tall hotel with a panoramic view of Copenhagen. Very good lunchtime menu.

Restaurants in Odense

Arkaden ||
Vestergade 68, 5000 Odense
Tel. 66-14-90-04
This is a restaurant street with national cuisine from several different countries in a selection of restaurants.

A Hereford Beefstouw ||
Vestergade 13
Tel. 66-12-02-22
Right in the heart of Odense. Grill in the middle of the restaurant for the best steaks in town. Good fish too.

Den Gamle Kro |||
Overgade 23
Tel. 66-12-14-33
One of Denmark's oldest restaurants in a 300-year-old building, full of antiques. There is a sliding glass roof over the courtyard for all-weather dining. Danish specialities.

Mamma's Pizzeria |
Karegade 4
Tel. 66-14-55-40
Traditional Italian restaurant with a

large selection of pizza and pasta, and original Italian meat dishes.

Målet
A restaurant-pub with fine cuisine. Renowned for ten varieties of schnitzel.

Marie Louise ▐▐▐
Lotrups gård, Vestergade 72
Tel. 66-17-92-95
Excellent cuisine in a cosy atmosphere.

Prisak
Ovrestræde
Tel. 66-13-00-06
Charming, 18th-century building.

Sortebro Kro
Fynske Landsby (Funen village)
Tel. 66-13-28-26
The only museum building in Denmark used as a restaurant. Changing daily menu and good home cooking.

Under Lindetræet
Ramsherred 2
Tel. 66-12-92-86
Attractive building in the heart of the Hans Christian Andersen district, serving a variety of menus geared to the seasons.

Restaurants in Århus

A Hereford Beefstouw ▐▐
Skolegade 5, 8000 Århus C
Tel. 86-13-53-25
Another example of this excellent steak-specialist chain to be found in many Danish towns.

Guldhornet ▐▐
Banegårdsplads 10
Tel. 86-12-02-62
A good family restaurant with enclosed verandah looking out on city centre.

Jacob's Bar BQ ▐▐
Vestergade 3, 8000 Århus C
Tel. 86-13-06-06
A very attractive setting in an old merchant house. Good Danish food.

Prins Ferdinandden Gamle ▐▐▐
By's Restaurant
Viborgvej 2
Tel. 86-12-52-05
A very popular restaurant at the entrance to the Old Town. Much

used by groups for its good Danish menu.

Restaurant René ▐▐▐
Frue Kirkeplads 1, 8000 Århus C
Tel. 86-12-12-11
French-inspired à la carte dishes of fresh Danish produce are served after a great welcome. One of the country's best restaurants.

Rådhuskafeen ▐
Sonder Allé 3, 8000 Århus C
Tel. 86-12-37-34
Near the Town Hall, with a comfortable, traditional atmosphere and typical Danish fare.

Teater-Bodega ▐▐
Skolegade 7
Tel. 86-12-19-17
Popular with artists of all sorts, and handy for the theatre across the street. Good, reasonably priced Danish food.

De 4 Årstider (The ▐▐▐
Four Seasons)
Åboulevarden 47, 8000 Århus C
Tel. 86-19-96-96
One of the best-known restaurants in Europe with superb French food in elegant surroundings.

Restaurants in Norway

Food is never cheap in Norway but the portions are usually good and often include a salad and coffee at lunchtime. You may well find two courses, or even one, sufficient. Oslo has restaurants offering the cuisines of many different countries but has also gone full circle with many eating places now featuring Norwegian dishes. *Husmanskost* (roughly translated 'home fare') is very popular outside the cities.

The estimated price ranges given are per head for an evening. On a tight budget, it is a good idea to make lunch *dagens rett* the main meal. Watch out for offers and Sunday-specials, too. The prices given below include tax and service, but not wine and other drinks.

▐▐▐ Over Nkr300
▐▐ Nkr150-300
▐ Under Nkr150
The simple *dagens rett* lunch menu will be well below Nkr100.

Restaurants in Oslo

Eating habits in the capital have changed over the last ten years. At one time, the range of food was relatively limited though French cooking was always available. But now, Oslo offers Italian, Indian, Chinese and other restaurants, Japanese being amongst the most recent. The more expensive hotels have at least one gourmet restaurant and, to widen the range, not all are mentioned here.

Annen Etage ▐▐▐
Stortingsgt 24–26
Tel. 41-90-60
This is one of Noway's best known, exclusive, gourmet restaurants on the first floor of the Hotel Continental.

Atrium Biskop ▐–▐▐▐
Gunnerusgate
Tel. 42-94-10
Very reasonably priced meals in Royal Christiania's superb atrium setting (▐; lunchtime (▐▐); gourmet restaurant (▐▐▐).

Bristol Grill ▐▐▐
Kristian IV's Gate 7
Tel. 41-58-40
Famous for its midday store koldtbord. Excellent evening meals in one of Oslo's best hotels.

Gamle Raadhus ▐▐
Nedre Slottsgt 1
Tel. 42-01-07
Traditional food in one of Oslo's oldest buildings. Particularly good for seafood.

Engebret Café ▐▐–▐▐▐
Bankplassen 2
Tel. 33-66-94
Generous lunchtime cold table and à la carte at night. Pleasant outdoor tables where you can just chose a pudding or gâteau with cream and a coffee.

in Store
itional Norwegian food.
, value.

Grand Café   II
Grand Hotel, Karl Johans Gate 31
Tel. 42-93-90
*A fine traditional restaurant, once
the daily rendezvous of Henrik
Ibsen and his friends, its
appearance preserved much as he
knew it. Note the large mural of the
playwright's arrival.*

Holmenkollen Cafeteria I and II
and Restaurant
Holmenkollen 119
Tel. 14-62-26
*Just below the great Ski Jump
Tower with lovely views and outside
terrace. The restaurant is known for
its lunchtime koldtbord (cold table).*

Lanternen Kro   II
Huk Aveny 2, Bygdøy
Tel. 43-81-25
*Traditional inn and steakhouse at
Dronningen, where the ferry stops.
Indoor and outdoor seating.*

Najaden   I
Bygdøynesvn 37, Bygdøy
Tel. 43-81-80
*Part of the Maritime Museum.
Norwegian specialities and good
cold table.*

Stortorvets Gjæstjeveri   I–II
Grensen 1 (entrance Grubbegt)
Tel. 42-88-63
*Traditional inn with jazz on Friday
evenings, and jazz café at lunchtime.*

Taj Mahal   I
St Olavsgt 10
Tel. 36-21-15
*Indian tandoori restaurant, good-
value three-course meals.*

Theatercaféen   II
Hotel Continental,
Stortingsgate 24-26
Tel. 33-32-20
*A haunt of artists, actors and the
intelligentsia, with busy café
atmosphere. Turn-of-century style
with portraits and pencil sketches of
many famous artistes.*

Vegeta Verthus   I
Munkedamsvn 3
Tel. 83-42-32/33-40-20
*The city's leading vegetarian
restaurant offering very good value.*

Restaurants in Bergen

Bergen has a good selection of
restaurants, inns and cafés, several in hotels but well known in
their own right.

Augustin Bistro   II
Augustin Hotel, Sandsgaate 24
Tel. 23-00-25
*A popular bistro with very good fish
specialities.*

Kafe Augustus   I
Gelleriet, Torgalmenning 6
Tel. 32-35-25
*Also run by Hotel Augustin, this
excellent top-floor café is in a
shopping mall. Open sandwiches
and other Norwegian specialties.*

Banco Rotto   I–III
Vågsalmenningen 16
Tel. 32-75-20
*In 1876 this was the banking hall of
the Bergen Kreditbank with a
magnificent interior. There is a
restaurant, piano bar, konditori and
pub here, priced according to which
you chose. Good eating in all.*

Bellevue   III
Bellevuebakken 9
Tel. 31-02-40
*Classical restaurant on a hillside
with a superb view over the city and
sea. Excellent gourmet cuisine.*

Bryggestuen and Bryggeloftet II
*Both restaurants are part of one of
Bryggen's Hanseatic wharfhouses,
with good atmosphere and food.*

Bryggen Tracteursted   I–II
Bryggen
Tel. 31-40-46
*At the heart of Bryggen's earliest
houses, with outside garden.
Thought to be one of Norway's
oldest taverns.*

Fiskekrogen   II
Zachariasbryggen
Tel. 31-75-66
*At Torget, by the harbour. Outside
tables at lunchtime. Specializes in
fish and game.*

Enhjørningen (The Unicorn)   II
Bryggen
Tel. 32-79-19
*Very good fish and seafood in old
Bryggen wharfhouse.*

The Grill Room   III
Hotel Norge, Ole Bullsplass
Tel. 21-01-00
*A top gourmet restaurant, with
excellent food and good service.*

Ole Bull Restaurant   II
Hotel Norge, Ole Bullsplass
Tel. 21-01-00
*For superb koldtbord (cold table)
from 12 noon–6pm. Also light meals
and à la carte.*

Øl og Vin Stue   I
Ole Bullsplass
Tel. 90-07-70
*Bergen's largest restaurant
building, with six bars, including a
beer and wine bar, disco, casino
and Maxime's nightclub.*

Stadsraaden   III
Radisson SAS Hotel, Bryggen
Tel. 54-30-00
Gourmet restaurant of high quality.

Madam Felle Bergen   I
Radisson SAS Hotel, Bryggen
Tel. 54-30-00
*Old-style tap room with wine, beer
and light meals.*

To Kokker   II
Bryggen
Tel. 32-28-16
*This sister-restaurant to
Enhjørningen offers meat, as well as
fish, in a series of small traditional
rooms in old wharfhouse.*

Restaurants in Trondheim

Many of Trondheim's most elegant
restaurants are to be found in the
best hotels, such as the Britannia,
The Radisson SAS Hotel
Trondheim, and the Reso Royal
Garden, but there are many more to
suit all pockets and tastes.

Dickens
Kjøpmannsgt 57
Tel. 73 51-57-50
*Good traditional meals in a restored
wharfhouse, friendly atmosphere.
Also good pizzas and pub.*

Gamle Trondhjæm   I–II
Brattørget 5
Tel. 52-65-51
*An excellent kitchen serving good
food, always accompanied by a
first-class salad buffet.*

Havfruen ⫶⫶⫶
Kjøpmannsgt 7
Tel. 73-53-26-26
An excellent seafood restaurant.

Hos Magnus ⫶⫶
Kjøpmannsgt 63
Tel. 73-52-41-10
A fine view over the river and real Trøndelag food with seafood a speciality.

Kiegle Kroa ⫶–⫶⫶
Hotell Prinsen, Kongensgt 30
Tel. 73-53-06-50
Traditional Norwegian food in an informal setting.

Pinocchio ⫶–⫶⫶
Hotell Prinsen, Kongensgt 30
Tel. 73-53-06-50
A popular meeting place for after-theatre and concert meals.

Kontoret Bar & Spiseri ⫶⫶
Nordre gt 24
Tel. 73-53-40-40
Good meals in a friendly atmosphere.

Lian ⫶⫶
Bymarka
Tel. 72-55-90-77
Take the tram up to Bymarka, Trondheim's favourite recreation area, for a meal with a beautiful view of the town.

Palmehaven ⫶⫶
Britannia Hotel, Dronningensgt 17
Tel. 73-53-53-53
A first-class gourmet restaurant in a beautiful setting.

Jonathan ⫶⫶
Britannia Hotel, Dronningensgt 17
Tel. 73-53-53-53
Restaurant and wine cellar where you can cook your own steak on a red-hot slab.

Prins Olav Grill ⫶⫶⫶
Reso Royal Garden Hotel,
Kjøpmannsgt 73
Tel. 73-52-11-00
A first-class gourmet restaurant.

Restaurant Cicignon Dancing ⫶⫶
Reso Royal Garden Hotel,
Kjøpmannsgt 73
Tel. 73-52-11-00
An excellent à la carte restaurant.

Trubadur ⫶–⫶⫶
Kongens gt 34
Tel. 73-54-43-21
Good traditional meals.

Vertshuset Tavern ⫶⫶
Sverresborg Folk Museum
Tel. 73-52-09-32
This inn from 1739 makes a speciality of traditional Norwegian food.

Restaurants in Sweden

The three main Swedish cities – Stockholm, Gothenburg and Malmö – all have many restaurants and cafés in a range of prices and these lists are, per-force, limited and personal. They are mostly in areas where visitors are likely to be but it is fun to explore and find your own preferences. Some restaurants, aimed mostly at business customers, may be closed during July, the holiday month. Tourist office information booklets and publications, such as *Stockholm This Week*, give listings and tourist offices give advice.

As with other Scandinavian countries, portions are generous and salad is often included. *Dagens rätt* is again recommended and it is a good idea to look out for special offers. Guide prices listed are for a typical evening meal per head, without wine.

⫶ Below Skr100
⫶⫶ Skr100–250
⫶⫶⫶ Above Skr250 (sometimes *well above*)

Restaurants in Stockholm

Blå Porten Café ⫶⫶
Djurgårdsvägen 60
Tel. (0)8-663-87-59/662-71-62
Attractive restaurant in what was once a Djurgården art gallery, with central garden.

Centralens Restaurang ⫶⫶
Central Station
Tel. (0)8-20-20-9
Above the station hall with good food. Specially popular for breakfast.

Hasselbacken ⫶⫶⫶
Hazeliusbacken 20
Tel. (0)8-670-50-00)
Famous 19th-century restaurant with large outside terrace garden in Djurgården. Good food in beautiful setting.

Hermans, The New Green Kitchen ⫶
Stora Nygatan 11
Tel. (0)8-11-95-00
Very popular international vegetarian cooking in Gamla Stan and five other places.

Leijontornet ⫶⫶⫶
Victory Hotel, Lilla Nygatan 5
Tel. (0)8-14-23-55
Historic setting with glass floor above ruins of Gamla Stan's medieval walls. High-class, traditional Swedish cuisine. Also bistro. Relais and Chateaux member. Closed July.

Mälardrottningen ⫶⫶⫶
Riddarholmen
Tel. (0)8-24-36-00
International and Swedish cuisine on Barbara Hutton's luxury yacht, now a floating hotel.

Operakällaren ⫶⫶⫶
Operahuset
Tel (0)8-676-58-00
One of Sweden's most famous, 200 years old, fine décor. Haute cuisine to husmanskost.

Restaurang Per Olssons ⫶⫶
Grevturegatan 36, 114-38
Stockholm
Tel. (0)8-660-06-14
A central restaurant with a farm-house setting. Good husmanskost.

Stekhuset Falstaff ⫶⫶
Tegelundsvägen 90
Tel. (0)8-63-48-40
Watch your steak being grilled at this excellent steakhouse.

Victoria ⫶⫶
Kungsträdgården
Tel. (0)8-10-10-85
Popular outdoor verandah overlooking square. Good traditional Swedish food. Open late.

Restaurants in Gothenburg

Andra Vånigen ⫶⫶⫶
Hotell Rubinen, Kungsportsavenyn 24
Tel. (0)31-81-08-80

One of Sweden's best known chefs, Christer Svantesson, provides gourmet food in restaurant overlooking Avenyn.

Brassserie Ferdinand II
Drottninggatan 41
Tel. (0)31-10-71-60
In atmospheric cellar with good Swedish country cooking.

Gamle Port II
Östra Larmgatan 18
Tel. (0)31-13-10-70
19th-century atmosphere. Good food on first floor, above pub.

The Place III
Arkivgatan 7
Tel. (0)31-18-15-66
Gourmet restaurant in small street close to Avenyn.

Restaurang Räkan II
Loprensbergsgatan 16
Tel. (0)31-16-98-99
Seafood is the speciality here. Order shrimps and steer them across the pool in a miniature radio-controlled fishing boat.

Restaurang Wärdshuset II
Liseberg
Tel. (0)31-83-62-77
Good food in 19th-century atmosphere. Also café and pub. Liseberg has several other restaurants, open in summer only.

Sjömagasinet II
Klippan 6
Tel. (0)31-24-65-10
Good seafood restaurant in historic harbour warehouse, built 1775 by East India Company. Summer only, from 1st April.

Restaurants in Malmö

Centralens Restaurant I
Central Station
Tel. (0)40-766-8
Good value station restaurant. Sometimes has a 'troubadour' in the evenings.

Fisk och Vin II
Hansacompagniet, Malmborgsgatan 4
Tel. (0)40-12-10-32
Good fish restaurant.

Kockska Krogen III
Stortorget
Tel. (0)40-730-20
High-class Swedish and international cooking in vaulted 16th-century building.

Olgas II
Pildammsparken
Tel. (0)40-12-55-26
Old inn, in beautiful, relaxed setting of Sweden's largest park.

Johan P II
Saluhallen, Lilla Torg
Tel. (0)40-97-18-18
In Malmö's market hall and specializing in delicious, fresh fish.

Rådhuskällaren Wein und Bierkeller II
Kyrkogatan 6
Tel. (0)40-790-20
16th-century cellar restaurant specializing in fish. Popular with young people.

Thott's II
SAS Royal Hotel, Östergatan 10
Tel. (0)40-23-92-00
Very good meat dishes with speciality steaks. Beautiful surroundings.

Översten III
Kronprinsen, Regimentsgatan 52
Tel. (0)40-91-91-00
Fine food, and views from 26th floor across to Denmark.

Index

Where there is more than one reference to text, the main entry is in **bold**. References to illustrations are in *italic*, those to maps are marked by an asterisk.

INDEX

INDEX

INDEX

INDEX

Discover the world
with **BERLITZ**®

Australia
Britain
Brittany
California
Canada
Egypt
Europe
Florida
France
Germany
Greece
Ireland
Israel
Italy
Kenya
Loire Valley
New England
Normandy
Portugal
Prague
Pyrenees
Rome
Scandinavia
Singapore
Spain
Switzerland
Thailand
Turkey
Tuscany

BERLITZ DISCOVER GUIDES do more than just map out the sights – they entice you to travel with lush full-colour photography, vivid descriptions and intelligent advice on how to plan and enjoy your holiday or travel experience. Covering the world's most popular destinations, these full-colour travel guides reveal the spirit and flavour of each country or region. Use *DISCOVER* as a travel planner or as a practical reference guide. You'll find sightseeing information and suggested leisure routes, extensive full-colour maps and town plans, local hotel and restaurant listings plus special essays highlighting interesting local features. Colourful historical and cultural background is complemented by practical details such as what to visit and where to stay, where to eat and how much you should expect to pay.

No matter where you're going, make the most of your trip:

DISCOVER the world with BERLITZ.